# SPECTACULAR POWER IN THE GREEK AND ROMAN CITY

# Spectacular Power in the Greek and Roman City

ANDREW BELL

OXFORD
UNIVERSITY PRESS
Great Clarendon Street, Oxford OX2 6DP

Oxford University Press is a department of the University of Oxford.
It furthers the University's objective of excellence in research, scholarship,
and education by publishing worldwide in

Oxford New York

Auckland Bangkok Buenos Aires Cape Town Chennai
Dar es Salaam Delhi Hong Kong Istanbul Karachi Kolkata
Kuala Lumpur Madrid Melbourne Mexico City Mumbai Nairobi
São Paulo Shanghai Taipei Tokyo Toronto

Oxford is a registered trade mark of Oxford University Press
in the UK and in certain other countries

Published in the United States
by Oxford University Press Inc., New York



First published 2004



British Library Cataloguing in Publication Data
Data available

Library of Congress Cataloging in Publication Data
Data available

ISBN 0–19–924234–8

1 3 5 7 9 10 8 6 4 2

Typeset by Kolam Information Services Pvt. Ltd, Pondicherry, India
Printed in Great Britain
on acid-free paper by
Biddles Ltd, King's Lynn.

# PREFACE

This book is designed so that the chapters can be read independently of one another yet together show the significance of spectacular self-advertisements in Greek and Roman cities over a long period, from early Greece to the end of the Roman Republic. The argument is simply that crowds watching and judging pre-eminent individuals in cities were a vital presence in ancient political history. The importance of the dynamics between spectacular actors and their audiences is set out in the introductory first chapter, which acknowledges some theoretical approaches. The second chapter is also somewhat introductory in nature. Caesar, in gesturing to impress, reveals the fluidity of assumptions governing political life in Rome. His complex styles of self-definition correlate with the mixed nature of the Roman polity, in which elements of both demotic populism and kingliness are to be found in his more spectacular behaviour.

The other chapters provide something of a genealogy of such spectacular styles. Chapter Three, examining the democracy of classical Athens, shows the remarkable power of a citizenry to restrict overweening individuality in its ceremonial life but also lingering potential for infatuation with kingly charisma. This can be seen in abundance in the broader Hellenistic world. Chapter Four thus examines the pomp and circumstance of Hellenistic capitals. And Chapter Five considers the importation of such megalomaniacal majesty into the Roman Republic. Chapter Six (much of which first appeared in the *Journal of Roman Studies* 87) uses the oratory of Cicero to show the intricate dynamics of the late Republic, which Caesarism dooms.

I might also add here that I have drawn upon an array of literary evidence with the assumption that ancient authors, even if they were remote from the events they described, had a familiarity with the habits of life in urban cities. This grants their accounts of traditional political phenomena a basic and considerable value despite any inaccuracies or anachronisms in details.

There are many whose kindness has assisted in the completion of this book and I can only trust that they already know my gratitude. I do wish here, however, to acknowledge in particular the aid and friendship of S. M. Treggiari, M. H. Jameson, and M. J. DeVinne at Stanford; in Nevada, L. E. Klein, J. A. Fry, Mary Wammack, Arthur Kramer, Gene Moehring, K. J. Mays, and some of my pupils. The Editorial Committee of the *Journal of Roman Studies* and the readers and officials of Oxford University Press have been marvellous. I acknowledge permission from the Society for the Promotion of Roman Studies to use much that appears in Chapter Six. The helpfulness of the staff of the Dickinson and Lied Libraries of the University of Nevada, Las Vegas has also been indispensable.

A. B.

*Las Vegas, Nevada*
*2003*

# CONTENTS

# 1

# Looking at the Powerful

In Bucharest on 21 December 1989 President Nicolae Ceauşescu gave a noontime speech.[1] To a large crowd of fellow citizens he declared, 'We will do all we can to defend the sovereignty of Romania and the freedom and life of our people, and the well-being of the whole nation.' After six years of severe shortages of food and fuel this cant did not pacify resentments. Individuals in the crowd started to jeer and howl. 'Down with Ceauşescu!' 'Free elections!' The rally had been staged in order to forestall revolution of the sort that had occurred only the previous month in East Germany and Czechoslovakia. The day before, in the western Romanian city of Timisoara, the security forces had suppressed demonstrations; bodies had been carried from the streets.[2] To show his authority Ceauşescu appeared on television, flanked by his wife and top advisers, in order to read a statement, which was nothing but a great deal of incoherent and not unfamiliar clichés about imperialist reactionary elements. The television appearance was important not for what Ceauşescu said—or rather shouted; it 'was how he said it and how he looked . . . It was if [*sic*] the Romanian viewers saw the dictator as he really was for the first time, a frail, bad-tempered old man, lacking the energy to finish his sentences or think straight. He did not look like a strong man any more.'[3] Nor was he.

[1] Much of the following is based upon the *New York Times* of 12 and 13 December 1989, along with other later reports and, in part, my own recollection of radio and television coverage.

[2] The regime was perhaps doomed after 17 December, when the Securitate's bloody repression of the Timisoara uprising was reported outside the country whence it could be broadcast by radio back into Romania: Calinescu and Tismaneanu 1992: 12.

[3] Sweeney 1991: 206.

In fact the failure to obtain in time-honoured, ritual fashion an impressive phenomenology doomed the tyrant. Since the television appearance failed to show Ceauşescu as authoritatively as he wished, government officials were instructed the next day to produce a crowd of one hundred thousand, and orchestrate the old songs.[4] There would be a direct and emotional presentation of a familiar choreography of platitudes and applause, with the president speaking from a balcony of the Central Committee building; from here he had spoken in August of 1968 in condemnation of the Soviet invasion of Czechoslovakia and won 'his supreme moment of glory' at home and abroad.[5] Ceauşescu, we may presume, expected that, by ritually presenting himself as he had done many times before over the twenty-four years of his rule, he would succeed once again in impressing the crowd with his authority. The people, with very few examples of uprisings in their history to serve as inspiration, would defer both to the power of the ruler and their own prudence in the face of a still apparently loyal army and police force.[6] But the tyrant was to be more than disappointed.

'It came from the back, where the ordinary people stood, who normally only came to these rallies so they could get a couple of days off work or thought it would help them get a better flat. They were murmuring.'[7] The murmur grew. For three minutes the whistles and jeers drowned out the man on the balcony. Ceauşescu had succeeded only in offering himself as a focus for popular anger. He appeared visibly shocked; it was not long before he left his balcony. The crowd continued to chant. That afternoon a United States government analyst remarked: 'I think he has lost it. He has been seen shaken in public.'[8] Failure in self-presentation was loss of power.

[4] Sweeney 1991: 207. The regular system for organizing rallies swung into action—for the salient details of the system, ibid. 156–7.

[5] Treptow 1996: 539.

[6] The army had remained loyal in Timisoara even if weakly so (cf. Cullen 1990: 101) and just two years previously an uprising of workers in Brasov on 15 November 1987 had been swiftly quelled by the Securitate: Treptow 1996: 553. In Bucharest in 1989, the crowd's chants of 'The army is with us!' quite possibly fostered its transfer to new circuits of command.

[7] Sweeney 1991: 207.

[8] Quoted in *New York Times*, 22 Dec. 1989.

Events took the particular course that day and the next, when the Ceauşescus at last disappeared from view amid Securitate minders into powerlessness and death, because Nicolae Ceauşescu, that 'savior of the nation' and 'genius of the Carpathians, the Danube of thought, and the most brilliant revolutionary thinker of all times', had decided to show himself in his ritual role as the powerful leader addressing a deferential populace.[9] There was, however, no longer deference.[10] The coup might not have taken place if the crowd's verdict had not been so powerfully expressed. Ceauşescu's ceremonial display, at a time when he still apparently held some control over the state's apparatus of repression, succeeded only in granting a crucial role to the people in judging his worth and thus also his political power.

He had been used to public receptions that clearly articulated the grandiose claims he made for his own importance. Only a month before his overthrow he had addressed the convention of the Romanian Communist Party. His speech was interrupted by 'the ritual cheers, chanting and applause of the party faithful—a total of 106 times, as recorded by Bucharest radio's domestic service on November 20'.[11] Although the unanimity of exaggerated respect was to a large degree artificial, the ceremony of 'a ruler appearing elevated before adoring public' nevertheless operated as an obvious and symbolic way of articulating an ideal and then habitual form of deferential reception

[9] The terms of praise come from Romanian media coverage of Ceauşescu's seventieth birthday celebrations (in January 1988) quoted at Calinescu and Tismaneanu 1992: 20.

[10] Here is one eyewitness, an architect who seized the freedom to contemn: 'When we saw the party people leaving, some of us started going from office to office, and we began discussing the situation. We decided that we would all attend the rally. Spontaneously, all over Bucharest, office workers and students stopped work and began forming groups. We started walking toward the square behind the party members. They ... expected the original crowd to be a few thousand ... but it swelled to hundreds of thousands of people. ... It was first a ripple, then a huge wave ... We shouted "Death! Death! Death!" ... And then "Down with the dictator!", "Down with the bootmaker!" I had chills up and down my spine. I will never forget this as long as I live!' (quoted by Codrescu 1991: 35).

[11] *New York Times*, 22 Dec. 1989.

on the part of the ruled.[12] For, leaving aside the degree to which Ceauşescu imagined that the 106 interruptions reflected heartfelt reverence, or assumed that it would impress those following the coverage at home or even those abroad, he was unable to escape from a fundamental social expectation that some sort of expression of popular approval is necessary, if a leader's pretensions and assumptions of pre-eminence are to be both valid and fully meaningful. Ceauşescu may have been ill-served by sycophantic aides before stepping onto the balcony and thus might have expected only approval or, at worst, deference, but certainly he expected that rehearsal of the familiar and institutionalized articulation of his power in a rite of isolated, physical prominence would translate into security for that power.[13] Instead, hegemony was broken.[14]

The dramatic events that liberated Romania from the Ceauşescus entailed only further turmoil.[15] There is, moreover, all likelihood that the entire affair was stage-managed by more knowing political figures than Ceauşescu himself.[16] Neverthe-

[12] Ceauşescu's grandiosity seems to have been much concerned with a sense of special physical elevation: for example, addressing the Grand National Assembly (23 Oct. 1986): 'From the high rostrum of the Grand National Assembly, on behalf of the Romanian people, I am appealing once again to all countries and people . . . I would like to assure, from this high rostrum . . . all the peoples of the world . . .' (Ceauşescu 1987: 160).

[13] On both Ceauşescu's and his wife's 'regal isolation' at parades see Cullen 1990: 99.

[14] Cf. J. C. Scott 1990: 204, adducing this specific revolutionary example.

[15] At the Central Committee building, 'power seemingly lay for a moment on the littered floor, available to whoever had the wit and determination to grab it' (Cullen 1990: 104).

[16] It now appears that the leadership of the National Salvation Front, which seemed to emerge spontaneously from the December revolution—Ion Iliescu, Petre Roman, Dumitru Mazilu, Silviu Brucan were soon to be seen addressing the crowd on the balcony Ceauşescu had fled—had had plans to stage a coup dating perhaps as far back as 1981 (Codrescu 1991: 84–5). Much of 'the "glorious" Romanian revolution was, in fact, a staged play, a revolution between quotation marks . . . A mass uprising did take place, but it was skillfully manipulated by the men who run Romania today' (ibid. 205). Codrescu also points out that it is reasonable to suppose that the mastermind of the Romania operation was the KGB, and provides details of the deception carried out by skilful use of television. Power was re-circuited through different channels, always projecting images even if they served purposes less obvious to the eye.

less, the political machinations unfolded through a complex dialogue with a national audience. The crowd in Bucharest saw the spontaneous revolt for which it longed, and the images relayed to a wider audience on television confirmed the most obvious and gratifying reading of events. Even so, it is difficult not to feel admiration for the nerve of those individuals who began chanting before the slogans could be amplified by voices sufficient in number and noise to guarantee the sanctuary of anonymity. The power of a crowd to act with a will that transcended the power of the many individual subjectivities and voices subsumed within it was deployed to claim something better—a precious satisfaction of an agglomeration of basic human needs, to live in truth, with a roof over one's head, food on the table and fuel on the fire. Such a deployment is worth treasuring wherever it occurs in history.

But my curiosity was particularly captured by the televised picture of a tyrant who, notwithstanding all his instruments of power—his police, microphones, and torture-chambers—thought it a good idea to step out upon his balcony.[17] Even in a totalitarian state popular audiences have had a presence that should not be overlooked, whether in the deference of a May Day parade or the passions of those tearing down with their own hands so much oppressive masonry, be it walls or the concrete symbolism of grandiose monuments and statues of heroes not always chosen by expression of popular sentiment. No regime can exist comfortably without providing at least a token semblance of its popularity or at least its entitlement to deference.[18] Relationships that comprise glaring asymmetries in power ever require, it seems, ritual articulation in the presence of an

[17] The internal security apparatus was huge and brutally effective—some indication of its scope can be provided by the claim of Romania's former head of secret police that there had been ten million microphones in a country of twenty-three million people (Codrescu 1991: 21). Furthermore, it is estimated (according to Cullen 1990: 100) that at the end of the 1970s, three million out of twenty-three million worked or informed for the Securitate, which had a collection of handwriting samples from 60 per cent of the population and insisted upon the registration of typewriters.

[18] Cf. Ellul 1966: 129. Deference, involving as it does the legitimacy of a social hierarchy, has traditionally inhabited the mainstream of the sociological tradition: Newby 1975: 145.

audience; and an audience of political subjects always has the potential to confirm, transform, or maybe sometimes actually to reject those relations.[19]

Thus I have begun a study of the dynamics operating between political actors and their audiences in ancient Greco-Roman republics with consideration of a modern political event because it serves well as a vivid illustration of how power—or what is often understood as such—and its phenomenology are closely intertwined. Power is manifestly a complex business, as Bertrand Russell insisted:

> Like energy, power has many forms, such as wealth, armaments, civil authority, influence on opinion. No one of these can be regarded as subordinate to any other, and there is no one form from which the others are derivative . . . [P]ower, like energy, must be regarded as continually passing from any one of its forms into any other, and it should be the business of social science to seek the laws of such transformations.[20]

While it is doubtful that social science has exactly succeeded in identifying universal principles at work in the complex operation of such aspects of power, the business of history can certainly draw upon a variety of analytical perspectives in describing the 'staginess of power', in order to help any citizens recognize the habitual power of the varieties of political spectacle that they consume.[21]

Questions raised by the vignette of Ceauşescu stationed vaingloriously pre-eminent upon a Romanian balcony may also be directed towards the posturing of the prominent in the public spaces of ancient cities: perhaps the visible practices of ancient city-states might even help in a very modest way with diagnoses of some of the intricate forms that power can take in many a political system whose leaders (if only occasionally) take it upon themselves to look upon the face of the crowd. At the least this study contends not only that spectacles of power are symptomatic of the general nature of the relations between rulers and ruled obtaining in ancient polities but also that they played a

[19] Cf. J. C. Scott 1990.

[20] B. Russell 1938: 9–10; cf. Geertz 1977: 152, speaking of how the instruments and articulations of power can, 'a bit like mass and energy', be 'transformed' into each other.

[21] Bartsch 1994: 193.

vital role in determining how over time such relations were to be reproduced, or even transformed.

The central concern of this book, therefore, is to look at the things that were done by prominent figures in classical polities, and consider what spectacular behaviours can reveal about political dynamics in highly complex ideological environments. The political lives of Athens and Rome were predicated upon different dialogues between citizens and the politicians whose rhetorics were often as conspicuous as they were audible. The prominence of elite individuals in ancient cities was readily comprehensible in aesthetic terms—in 'the business of affectations and aversions, of how the world strikes the body on its sensory surfaces, of that which takes root in the gaze and the guts and all that arises from our most banal, biological insertion into the world'.[22]

Political leadership was something directly experienced by a political audience: some individuals were the ones usually to be seen standing apart from and above the rest of the citizens, busy and obvious in ritualized roles that it seemed only natural for them to perform. And decision-making was in large measure shaped by the ability of ambitious political actors to be popular and persuasive in civic spaces before the eyes of popular audiences accustomed to apprehension of the idioms of various practical rhetorics. Much of the political life of ancient polities was the visible business of leading men acting out—and occasionally challenging and redefining—the 'communal scripts' of cultural assumptions.[23] And prominent performances were watched and judged by sovereign audiences of citizens, many of whom perhaps devoted as much time and interest to consumption of spectacle as they did to careful evaluation of the meritoriousness of the issues or the candidacies upon which ultimately they were called to vote.

The most significant political leaders were those who (regardless of their effectiveness in various executive offices)

[22] Eagleton 1990: 13. In general, social theory is increasingly willing to be curious about how 'the capacities and senses, experiences and management of bodies are not only central to the exercise of human agency and constraint, but also to the formation and maintenance of social systems' (Shilling 1993: 22).

[23] Geertz 1980: 13.

were well able to be popularly persuasive by projecting public personalities able effectively to engage habitual and normative expectations about the legitimacy of leadership. While to be perceived as a charismatic leader, who seems vitally significant in his or her centrality to the order of the state, is in fact to be such,[24] charisma generally requires sustained engagement with the sensibilities of consumers of political celebrity.[25] Perception is a behavioural practice conditioned by habit.[26] Habitudes are naturally taken for granted, escaping vivisection by contemporary self-consciousnesses as well as by many narratives of political history. When political subjects routinely gaze upon the prominent actors in their communities, an understanding of respective status and significance has already been expressed—and in a manner liable to determine future practical responses to the powerful. Weber noted that a sociopolitical order will be much more stable if it is 'upheld on a purely customary basis through the fact that the corresponding behavior has become habitual'.[27] So, to return to Romania again for illustration of mundane but crucial questions that history might always try to

[24] Cf. Tucker 1968: 737. Weber 1947: 358 ff.: '"Charisma" shall be understood to refer to an extraordinary quality of a person, regardless of whether this quality is actual, alleged, or presumed. "Charismatic authority," hence, shall refer to a rule over men, whether predominantly external or predominantly internal, to which the governed submit because of their belief in the extraordinary quality of the specific person.' It is not easy to know whether Weber viewed its existence as dependent on a sort of psychodynamic power that occurs in particular individuals; or whether the whole phenomenon is really a sociological one (cf. Geertz 1977: 150). Weber does not differentiate between the different potential 'situations of "surrender" (*Hingabe*), some resulting from a faith in divine favor, some from personality traits, such as rhetorical skill or hypnotic power. That several of these factors might occur in combination does not permit confusing them' (Friedrich 1961: 12–13). Nor does Weber offer explicit guidelines for distinguishing which leaders are actually endowed with charisma and which are not. Shils (1965) has developed Weber's formulations by stressing that the two strands of Weber's analysis are united by a common concern with the capacity of the charismatic to offer an essential connection to some very central feature of man's existence and the cosmos in which he lives.

[25] Cf. Brookhiser 1996: 113: 'even rulers who are intelligent, prudent, or visionary must make a sensual impact if they are to lead.'

[26] As Merleau-Ponty insisted: Crossley 1995: 47.

[27] Weber 1947: 125.

address, wonderful indeed was the revolution in the behaviours of embodied subjects, since those murmuring, shouting, and marching had long been accustomed to practise deference. A few years before the revolution, at an unplanned appearance near the building site for his (grossly absurd) planned House of the Republic, Ceauşescu had been spotted by pedestrians. In a moment of direct aesthetic contact with their ruler, his subjects' reactions, perhaps cravenly, perhaps inevitably, fell into harmony with the mode of response rehearsed in countless more formal, orchestrated public appearances.[28]

> When they realized who it was they gathered into a crowd. There were about a hundred people there. Ceauşescu started to speak and people began to applaud. When he left they clapped him some more. I was surprised. I studied the pedestrians. They were ordinary people. Why were they clapping him? When I started to walk away I heard them start to insult him. It was extremely shocking. No one forced them to applaud. There was no Securitate around. The incident revealed for me a sort of duplicity. Ceauşescu was sort of a monster, but in a way we were his accomplices.[29]

Too often in history has it been prudent to remember the maxim, 'Don't ever be the first to stop applauding!'[30] The reactions of the bystanders in this instance can in no way have been free of the influence of other dimensions of political power, including omnipresent fear of the Securitate. Yet the accusation of complicity on the part of Ceauşescu's audience prompts curiosity about the power that comes from the ability of just one remarkable egomaniac to impose his own preposterous ideas about his own significance routinely upon others—and, moreover, to be able to impose in such a way as to effect a translation of that significance into the habitually deferential comportment of subjects whose presence seemed fully both to confirm and legitimate this power. To peers of a wider world

[28] Ceauşescu's visits to workers and peasants had since 1965 become integral to his political style: Treptow 1996: 534. On control of the media and propagation of the Ceauşescu 'cult' see Fischer 1989: 160–89. For discussion of the potential starkness of the dichotomy between engineers of rituals and their consumers in totalitarian regimes see Lane 1981: 26 and *passim*.

[29] Told by G. Costache, reported by Sweeney 1991: 158.

[30] Solzhenitsyn 1973: 70; cf. Atkinson 1984: 30.

beyond the 'dreary place' where he ruled he seemed quite monstrous.[31]

Moreover, Ceauşescu's own perception of himself appears to have been conditioned by such routines.[32] By the regular domination of the media by news and views of daily doings, or special ceremonial occasions such as party conventions or state visits, Ceauşescu had arranged for the systematic advertisement of his extraordinary status in the state. There was a profound absence of any opportunity to air rational dissent about the desirability of his brand of leadership, and the monopolization of all channels of presenting himself in his own chosen images resulted in a remarkable routinization of the relations between Ceauşescu and those he dominated. The authority of the ruler appeared not only irresistible but, to the tyrant himself, wholly legitimate, since both before his downfall and at his summary trial he would insist upon his popularity: 'I have evidence of it every day. Every time I make a speech, people rise and applaud.'[33]

Vainglory as well as a sense of legitimacy might sometimes, it seems, be a matter of 'the non-organization of an effective counterimage'.[34] Yet it is also likely that everyday occurrences do have the power to structure embodied subjects' relationship to power. Indeed it might be suggested that the 'main mechanism of domination operates through the unconscious manipulation of the body'.[35] It is reasonable to suppose that much that is consequential in 'everyday life is situated somewhere in the rift opened up between the subjective, phenomenological, sensory apparatus of the individual and reified institutions'.[36] The physical—and highly ritualized—appearances of Ceauşescu

[31] Bush 1994: 184; note also (185) how '[a]ll during the dinner Ceauşescu talked and talked and talked . . . We were stunned by his ego'.

[32] Perhaps not infrequently tyrants believe their own myths: e.g. Kershaw 1987: 82.

[33] Cullen 1990: 100; at his trial Ceauşescu protested, 'Have you not seen how the people cheered when I went to the factories?' (ibid. 108). It is interesting to compare Stalin's anger (in 1951) when a crowd gathered and made a spontaneous fuss over him; his daughter found him no longer able to believe people capable of sincerity: Bullock 1992: 963.

[34] Verdery 1991: 10. [35] Bourdieu 1992: 115.

[36] Kaplan and Ross 1987: 3.

before his people, until that fateful day in December, had been institutions of power as efficient as the keenest workers in his security apparatus.[37] Any monopoly of symbolic communication can produce docile citizen bodies full of the 'numb imperatives' of those orchestrating such control.[38] This book, in considering the 'impress' of presentations of power upon the senses, emotions, and memories of all citizens,[39] ponders the role, including the complicitousness, of civic audiences in determining and sustaining the authority of political leadership. While ultimately there are no secure answers, nagging curiosity about the habitual phenomena of ancient politics might not only underscore the persistence of communal scripts but also throw into sharp relief episodes when there were changes in how the prominent popularly presented themselves.

Since in classical Athens and republican Rome a right to pre-eminence was not automatically awarded to particular individuals, innovations in self-presentation were only fruitful if there was a general appreciation of the individual's entitlement to advertise himself in an original fashion, and if prevailing expectations were not too outrageously challenged. There were some individuals active upon the political stages of the ancient world who made their own diagnoses of what would count as an impressive appearance, and so advanced their careers by improvements in self-advertisement. To see Pericles

[37] In using the term 'ritualization' I am referring to the performance of actions 'in a repetitive, formal, precise, highly stylized fashion' which have a physiological effect—'witness their behavioral basis, the use of repetition and the involvement of the entire human sensorium through dramatic presentations involving costumes, masks, colors, textures, odors, foods, beverages, songs, dances, props, settings, and so forth' (Moore and Myerhoff 1977: 199). The concept has also been usefully glossed by C. Bell (1992: 204–5) as describing 'the differentiation and privileging of particular activities' which may use 'a delineated and structured space to which access is restricted; a special periodicity for the occurrence and internal orchestration of the activities; restricted codes of communication to heighten the formality of movement and speech; distinct and specialized personnel; objects, texts, and dress designated for use in these activities alone; verbal and gestural combinations that evoke or purport to be the way things have always been done; preparations that demand particular physical and mental states; and the involvement of a particular constituency not necessarily assembled for any other activities'.

[38] Bourdieu 1990: 69. [39] Handelman 1990: 4.

or Alcibiades, Demetrius or Antiochus, Pompey or Caesar was to bear witness to individuals who were wilfully striving to make of themselves an attractive and memorable aesthetic phenomenon. There may be various discursive formations but there are also men who maintain, develop, and profit from privileged positions within all their inflections. All in a society might share assumptions about what power and the powerful are and should be like, but there probably always will be a few political actors who can see, as though from a loftier, more privileged position, the symbolic furniture for what it is, and who are ambitiously able and willing to embark upon some fresh thinking by way of interior design whether they act by cautious experiment or by triumphantly confident leaps of glorious magnificence. The vicissitudes of political celebrity speak volumes about the dynamics within grand cognitive, epistemic, or discursive formations that hold all subjectivities in place—or even in hapless thrall.

It is a historical appreciation of continuities and changes in the articulations of political prominence that is wanting in the theoretical approaches that have perhaps most stimulated modern analysis of questions of spectacle and power. A cognitivist approach into spectacular rituals was pioneered by the anthropologist Clifford Geertz, whose work has stressed the need to understand the symbolic framework that constructs a community's conception of itself and its prominent leaders. In viewing culture and society as shared structures of events and practices, as a public 'acted document' that has significance and meaning, great emphasis is placed upon the symbols that people use: social activity is only comprehensible in terms of shared cultural matrices, systems 'of public ideas and attitudes embodied in words, things, and conventional behavior'.[40] As Durkheim pioneeringly pronounced, 'without symbols, moreover, social feelings could have only an unstable existence'.[41] This perspective, as in Geertz's work on nineteenth-century Bali, throws a bright spotlight upon an established dramaturgy of power performed by prominent sociopolitical actors before

[40] Geertz 1973: 10 (with C. Lloyd 1986: 272); Geertz 1965: 8.
[41] Durkheim 1995 [1912]: 232.

the eyes of the whole community.[42] Yet while this 'alternate conception of what politics is about and what politics comes to' has encouraged many to look hard at the ritual dramas of political life,[43] the (happily ahistorical) presumption that political leaders, or any ritually prominent individuals, act entirely at the behest of cultural structures cannot really get to grips with the choice of a particular script and any modifications to it. Both symbols and social feelings develop and change historically just as social science has tried to do.

Ancient expectations governing the phenomenology of impressive individuals also have the semblance of a Foucauldian 'regime of truth' serving not so much the interests of a particular socio-economic class as the system of ever circulating power as a whole. But Foucault too declines to ponder the existence of any opportunities for individuals to claw out some subjective space for manoeuvre, innovation, or rebellion beneath the crushing weight of discursive formations. Such a view contains a monolithic (and perhaps paranoid) circularity in its abolition of any possibility of finding a vantage point that is not itself wholly caught up in the discursive formation—and, naturally, if power is all there is (and, indeed, all there possibly can be), then no ethical footing can ever be attained from which to issue judgement on the legitimacy of power exercised and executed. Perhaps unsurprisingly, Foucault showed explicit interest in neither subjects' resistances or dissents nor the operation of power in the totalitarian states contemporary to his theorizing.[44] All inhabitants of ancient polities were subject to habits of thought which exercised a tyranny over perception of true prestige and memorability in an individual. Prestige in many an event may be glossed as 'the public face of domination'.[45] Yet the paradigm had to have evolved somehow and

[42] Geertz 1980. The history of Balinese states is looked at in terms of the *negara* as model of a social order and also as a site for dramaturgy. The court and the capital are seen 'as an ideal material embodiment or paragon of the political order so that it "shapes the world around it into at least a rough approximation of its own excellence"' (Lloyd 1986: 276).

[43] Geertz 1980: 135.

[44] For such critique see further Wolin 1988: 184, 190–1.

[45] J. C. Scott 1989: 146.

I am not loath to credit in some measure both happenstance and the idiosyncratic knowingness of ambitious individuals.

The theorizing of Pierre Bourdieu does provide encouragement to comprehend individuals engaged in highly complex relations with those dominant social norms objectively identified by social scientists. Bourdieu's concept of 'habitus' underscores the fact not only that culture is inscribed in all those who are subject to it, as history is 'turned into nature', but also that *practice* should be figured as a relation between tradition and innovation.[46] Individuals invariably 'misrecognize' the determining power of the system and never doubt their autonomy in social action, even though an objectifying perspective might be tempted to read their actions as determined by normative 'rules' of a society's culture.[47] The splendidly vain personalities that interest me are very much products of their time and place but also personalities determined to exploit a freedom to make the most of themselves. Competition among ambitious individuals helped to shape the idioms of spectacular politics.

While spectacles of tyrants and monarchs commonly tend to command more historical attention than do those of other sorts of government, the frequent absence of monopoly in the dialogue between actors and audience in republican communities makes their histories so instructive.[48] In non-autocratic environments such as Athens and Rome, citizens enjoyed decisive sway over the careers of their leaders, who perforce manoeuvred earnestly to win the supreme prizes of executive office, as well as esteem and approval commensurate with their idiosyncrasies of ambition and colourful vagaries of self-importance. The great men who set forth from Rome to command armies and civilize broken enemies possessed *imperium* which, bestowed by

[46] Biersack 1989: 90; Bourdieu 1977: 78. In a society '[e]ach agent, wittingly or unwittingly, willy nilly, is a producer and reproducer of objective meaning. Because his actions and works are the product of a *modus operandi* of which he is not the producer and has no conscious mastery, they contain an 'objective intention . . . which always outruns his conscious intentions. The schemes of thought and expression he has acquired are the basis for the *intentionless invention* of regulated improvisation' (ibid. 79). On *habitus* note too Elias 1978.

[47] Bourdieu 1977: 171.

[48] Cf. Cannadine (1987*a*: 6–7) on the enduring interest in rituals of royalty.

the *populus*, had to be earned by making the right impression. Since the senatorial aristocracy never really developed into an 'hereditary estate' over the course of the last two centuries of the Republic, there was always the vital element of competition in the deployment and development of the dramatic practices of power.[49] In both democratic Athens and republican Rome there were untold riches of normative habit guiding how citizens viewed their leaders, but competition among the leading actors ensured that no one of them could either readily monopolize the attentions of their humbler fellow citizens or be long deluded about the legitimacy of their singular place in society: it is precisely because in Rome this fundamental aspect of the republican city-state came to an end with the Augustan *Risorgimento* that my account of political spectacle takes the arrival of Caesarism and the demise of the Republic as its terminus, albeit with some reflection upon Caesar Augustus' styles of self-advertisement.

Julius Caesar, scrutiny of whom will be found in the next chapter, stood before Roman crowds as heir to a long and richly various tradition of spectacular practice. Throughout his career he was an adept rhetorician with far more than his persuasive words alone: with his 'unique talent for the public advertisement of himself and his family'[50] in a centrally visible manner, he nevertheless faced grave choices in the last months of his life about how to represent his position in Rome. Was he to be more like a Hellenistic king? Or would he prefer to count his own prestigious triumphs all the more precious by allowing political competition to continue? Could he fashion something both new and lasting from the paradigms of both *polis* and palace? A solution could best emerge through careful exploration of popular sentiment in Rome, the only place that in the final reckoning could determine a glorious place in history.

It is surely not unreasonable to admit deep uncertainty about why some individuals crave political power. But historical ambitions have affected millions:[51] Caesar's aggrandizing defence of his *dignitas* cost (in Pliny the Elder's estimation) over

[49] Hopkins and Burton 1983. [50] Millar 1998: 67.

[51] Cf. B. Russell 1938: 11: 'Love of power . . . is a characteristic of the men who are causally important.'

a million lives.[52] One might bestow a rationality upon the ambitions of individual pretenders to power and entire like-minded cohorts but no rational-choice theory can explain what the point of it all is without taking into account fundamental axioms of cultural habit. Of course, there may be questions of personal security and material enrichment. For a Ceauşescu, power offered security against the encroachments of rivals and indulged a taste in absurd fancies. But surely his ambition did not aim at palaces, hunting lodges, and big automobiles alone.[53] It is not necessary to venture intrepidly into the darkly unpleasant psychological reaches of individual egos to suppose that what was craved and for all too long so cruelly guarded was security of that desire for significance and consequentiality, which has perennially animated countless people (usually men) in history—and in all likelihood in prehistory too.[54] Prestigious self-assertion has been for many the true premium of power.[55] And individuals have commonly wished not merely to occupy positions of power but also to be seen and ritually acknowledged as naturally deserving of such elevation.

Thoughts of immortal glory are really something of 'a spiritual force' which historians ought never to ignore;[56] and 'to the Roman noble the pursuit of power and glory, position and prestige was paramount. It was this that he equated with the Roman Republic.'[57] The realities of a successful

[52] *HN* 7. 91–2. Going to war for his *dignitas*: [Caesar] *BC* 1. 9. 2; well emphasized by Meier (1995: 5).

[53] Cf. B. Russell 1938: 9: 'The desire for commodities, when separated from power and glory, is finite, and can be fully satisfied by a moderate competence.'

[54] On the likely universality of desire for prestige see Pinker 1997: 493. On competition for status as symptomatic of an individual's sense of identity and purpose in general see Hatch 1989. Note too, for sweeping comparative purposes, Greenhalgh's (1980: xii) gratitude for his experience in the City's corridors of financial power for the start of his understanding of the megalomania of Pompey and his peers.

[55] Caesar at the onset of the civil war said, and often, that it would be harder to push him down from pre-eminence to second place than it would from second to last place: Suet. *DJ* 29. 1. On Octavius' desire for universal rule, Nic. Dam. *FGrHist*. 130 F 54–5.

[56] Wistrand 1978: 29.

[57] Earl 1967: 16; cf. especially the effective and concise remarks of Wiseman 1985: 3–13, esp. 4, discussing the epitaphs of the Scipiones: '[t]his

political life in the *res publica* were *always* manifest in practical terms, and *dignitas* was to be registered through such practical manifestations that fundamentally shaped the nature of everybody's assumptions—and from an early age—about what success in the city actually looked like. True glory in Rome was, Cicero asserted, dependent upon how a leading man's inner qualities were received when illumined for crowds gathered at the primary venues of the city.[58] If a political life at the highest levels of dignity is assumed to be aimed at *gloria*, in the winning of which the people's judgement is indispensable, then *gloria* is best comprehensible as the acceptance of an individual's importance and power in the state by a crowd.[59] So, after Caesar had done his life's work, Cicero, frantically determined to do something of his own, badgered Antony with his insistence that the *populus* alone gave genuine glory:

est autem gloria laus recte factorum magnorumque in rem publicam meritorum, quae cum optimi cuiusque, tum etiam multitudinis testimonio comprobatur.[60]

Glory is praise for righteous deeds and for great services to the *res publica*, and it is validated by the testimony both of every man of excellence and of the multitude.

The cheering of a crowd should be understood as an end in itself for those Romans with the grandest ambitions. Imagine,

preoccupation with personal achievement and competition for the greatest glory, which stands out as the most conspicuous characteristic of the Roman ruling class in the third century B.C., can be traced through the history of the middle and late Republic and into the early Empire.'

58 Cic. *Sest.* 106.

59 *Gloria* and *laus* are in many respects complementary terms (*Inv.* 2. 166: 'gloria est frequens de aliquo fama cum laude'); along with *existimatio* and *fama*, 'au sens subjectif, ils expriment l'opinion que l'on a de quelqu'un ou l'estime que l'on éprouve pour lui; au sens objectif, la réputation qui en résulte pour ce dernier' (Hellegouarc'h 1963: 362). Cicero's formulation obviously fits the claims he has made for himself, in the *Fourth Catilinarian* and elsewhere.

60 *Phil.* 1. 29. Cicero can use *multitudo* as a rough equivalent to *populus*, e.g. *Amic.* 41: 'Now I seem to see the *populus* disassociated from the Senate and matters of the greatest importance decided by the judgement of the multitude' ('Videre iam videor populum a senatu disiunctum, multitudinis arbitrio res maximas agi'). *Multitudo* does, of course, retain something of a derogatory force, being 'assez proche de *plebs*' (Hellegouarc'h 1963: 515).

mused Velleius Paterculus, if Pompeius Magnus had died in his theatre when his dedicatory celebrations were taking place! Then he would have had an immortal possession of the heights of *felicitas*. Plutarch thinks much the same of Pompey's position after his third triumph, up to which point he had enjoyed the fortune of Alexander the Great.[61] The acclamation, the approbation of the *populus universus* was a grand prize for which great men steered their course and even sometimes risked their lives. Success in such competition demanded elaborate care in maintaining careers before the public gaze, in the heart of the city. As Paul Veyne has observed, 'everything for which men ruined themselves, over which they fought or of which they boasted, was bounded by the city'.[62]

In the city, the Forum in particular, as Millar has properly insisted, was the place where much of the business of a 'face-to-face' political system was played out. Politicians acted self-consciously as upon a stage. Cicero, our best witness to the political culture of the later Roman Republic, preaches a simple message in one of his missives to M. Caelius Rufus, admittedly a man hardly in need of conversion to faith in the notion that the city of Rome represented the only setting in the world adequate to the task of displaying the activities and prestige of its most splendid inhabitants: 'The city, cherish, my Caelius, the city and live in its light!'[63] The apothegm is heartfelt in expressing the pain Cicero felt at his involuntary service in Cilicia; it also effectively encapsulates the meaning of the space, practices and people he had left behind. To be in Rome was, for Cicero, not merely to be involved in the richest civic life available in the western Mediterranean but actually to have his presence and activities illumined for the attention of one's fellow inhabitants, fortunate outsiders and visitors, and even for the edification of posterity. To live in that light was to be seen as one hoped to be seen, as a truly glorious Roman; and it was impossible for an individual to have such significance without being seen to possess it in the city. Elsewhere Cicero had told the story of his own naivety in assuming, upon his return from service as quaestor in Sicily, that the repute of his scrupulous service would have

[61] *Pomp.* 46. [62] Veyne 1990: 39.
[63] *Fam.* 12. 2 ('Urbem, Urbem, mi Rufe, cole, et in ista luce vive').

gained some general currency. The language with which he details his assumptions is revealing. He remarks that he had thought that 'the eyes of all had been cast upon myself alone' and that 'I and my quaestorship would have a presence in a sort of global theatre'.[64] From Sicily came great wealth into Rome. But Rome alone, not Sicily, was the stage of the world, where political consequence entailed becoming routinely recognized, habitually viewed, and systematically scrutinized as a spectacle by citizens.

In this respect there are obvious similarities to other great city-states of antiquity, not least democratic Athens, even though neither the imperial reach nor the consequent backwash of wealth were as great there as in late republican Rome or magnificent Hellenistic centres. Athenian history can be thought a glorious monument to the ancient invention of democracy, a far from common phenomenon.[65]

Prominent Athenians were, as the evidence of comedy well attests, well-known figures whose notoriety came above all from being seen in civic spaces: 'as soon as they stepped out of doors they exposed themselves to a forest of eyes . . .'[66] Athenians rose to the challenge of projecting an appropriate public celebrity in their quest for the grand prize of their community, *timē* (prestige). One of the principal processes at work in the evolution of Athenian democracy had been the increasing willingness of political leaders to recognize and embrace the *dēmos* as a repository of validity for their claims to possess *timē*. With regard even to the grander and more crowded venues of democratic practice, a small minority of men were ever to be seen 'standing forth', such as in the Agora, the theatre, the courts, and especially the Assembly where, even at the risk of resentful rejection

[64] *Verr.* 2. 5. 35: 'omnium oculos in me unum coniectos esse' and 'me quaesturamque meam quasi in aliquo terrarum orbis theatro versari.' Cf. *Planc.* 66 on Cicero's decision to live in the public eye and in the Forum in particular; cf. Yakobson 1999: 102.

[65] Little is known of other Greek democracies. There is some (sketchy) evidence for functioning democracy before 480 in Achaea, Croton, Acragas, Ambracia, Argos, Chios, Cyrene, Heraclea Pontica, Megara, Naxos, and Syracuse: Robinson 1997: 126. Democracies were established by the fiat of a satrap in Ionia in the 490s: Hdt. 6. 43. 3.

[66] Davidson 1997: 219.

or merely petty humiliation, they ascended the Bema to offer counsel, urge actions, and claim prestige in the judgement of the *dēmos*.[67]

Although democratic Athens, in contrast with the late Roman Republic, granted precious little scope to aristocrats for demonstrations of grandly spectacular selfhood, the functioning of both polities involved intense personal competition for popular recognition of individual merit. The *res publica* was, I am fairly convinced, much more of a mixture of an aristocratic notability's acceptance of popular sovereignty and a persistent popular readiness to accept the natural entitlement of the notability to power and pre-eminence.[68] In all the hustle and blather of Rome's central places and spaces, there was a thriving aesthetic and emotional intimacy between political actors and audience. The routines of urban life in Rome afforded many opportunities for an ambitious man to be seen as he wished, beginning from the moment he rose from his bed for another day of involvement not just with the destiny of his country but with the attentions of a validating audience.[69] The eyes as well as the ears of a crowd were attentive to men gesticulating in the Forum, sacrificing and praying to the gods, presiding at the games, advertising personal, national, and divine might in triumph, and to the commemorations of men through statues, coins, funeral processions, and monuments. Through the blending of various modalities of symbolic expression individuals were able to capture an immortality in the minds of citizens habitually able to believe the men whom they saw to be truly deserving of their attentions and affections. They had little choice but to work hard to cultivate popular sentiment.[70]

[67] Xen. *Mem.* 3. 6 (Glaucon wants προστατεύειν ... τῆϲ πόλεωϲ) and 7 (Charmides).

[68] Yakobson 1999.

[69] Cf. Hölkeskamp 1993: 30: '"Publicity" in all respects, appearance in public, permanent interaction with the people in a variety of ways, a genuinely "public" political life, in the Forum and elsewhere, were absolutely indispensable for this "ruling class" as a whole, because popular participation was part and parcel of the institutional, social and ideological framework which this élite dominated and defined.' Also note Treggiari 1998: 3–4.

[70] Note the remarks of Johnson (1987: 115): '[I]t is perhaps more accurate to say crowds create leaders than to say leaders create or shape or mold crowds. Crowds may be "drawn" by leaders, in a manner of speaking, but

The mass of citizens who perceived the great men remain largely in sociological obscurity. But nevertheless their sentiments, given the assiduity with which their attentions and favours were sought by those interested in amassing prestige, clearly must be integral to any analytical narratives of Roman as well as Greek history. Recently the *populus* has loomed larger in historical significance.[71] Inevitably, however, it remains largely an anonymous and demographically ill-defined entity, with all manner of nuanced statuses compressed into a single mass by elite observers.[72] In the absence of any extensive documentation, specific lives, hopes and fears of 'ordinary' citizens are lost; and when 'thousands of people present themselves on the street, their individual value systems are reduced, condensed, filtered and reinterpreted by those who comment upon them'.[73] It cannot, however, escape notice that crowds in any time or place do often become animated by a dominant emotion; and, while crowds are too easily figured in historiography as dangerous in their irrationality, it is the case that this is often so unfortunately: we only have to think of Nuremburg rallies. Classical civic spaces were filled with bodies, an immense press of beings—that 'motley and excitable rabble'[74]—which reeked and rhythmically moved with the animations wrought by all the rushing neuro-chemicals of excitation. Still in general, whenever possible, attention really ought to be paid to 'definite individuals . . . as they operate, produce materially, and hence as they work under definite material limits, presuppositions and conditions independent of their will'.[75] When the individual

looked at in another way, it is the leaders who are drawn to and by the crowd, who are themselves collected by invisible forces that can be guessed at and "named" but not understood.'

[71] In large measure because of the work of Brunt, Yavetz, and Millar.

[72] Purcell (1994: 676) remarks upon 'the distortion of a long perspective of diminishing plebeian statuses from the viewpoint of the higher aristocracy'; cf. Yakobson 1999: 27.

[73] Harrison 1988: 5. It is the great virtue of Millar's recent study of the Roman crowd (1998) to underscore the calmer routines involved in the exercise of civil, enfranchised dignity but even in such a treatment the *populus* cannot much escape being read as a single actor in the grand epic drama of the late *Res Publica*.

[74] Syme 1939: 100.

[75] Marx, *German Ideology* in Tucker 1978: 154.

subjectivities of a true multitude remain anonymous and invisible, an attempted adumbration of the things they saw as admirable and exciting will have to suffice—along with the necessary recognition that they were there all along. Countless numbers of more humble folk judged for themselves the spectacular histories that their presence caused to unfold before their eyes.

Such a perspective does not suggest that social and economic structures, which made the spectacular habits of urban life possible, are relatively unimportant. It would be nice (but too ambitious by far) to draw some precise correlations between the communal scripts governing civic behaviours and 'the hard surfaces of life—with the political, economic, stratificatory realities within which men are everywhere contained'.[76] Surely consideration of how some individuals were accepted and understood as special can, somewhat indirectly to be sure, help to justify continued interest in a man's clothing or the affectations of his statue, and assuage any frustrations at ignorance about those who spun and laundered or quarried and hewed and hauled and did whatever else was necessary for making the aesthetics of politics, well, wonderful.

To a far greater degree than in the case of Athens success in the intimacies of Roman politics cast its shadow upon 'an incomparably wider area than those that . . . ever had derived from any Greek city-state'.[77] One man's glory in the limelight usually meant many a distant multitude's ruin. The fashions of obtaining popular favour, moreover, were fuelled by money brought to the city from faraway places, ultimately expropriated from the industriousness of peasants, or extracted from the bodies of miners made to scrabble into the entrails of the earth for the riches *dignitas* consumed.[78] Ancient political economies rested upon lands as the main source of wealth—a situation that greatly constrained liquidity. Large sums of money came most easily from imperial theft. All the money from all the nations came to a few.[79] Big-time politics explains the visitations of

[76] Geertz 1980: 135. [77] Millar 1998: 214.

[78] e.g. Pliny *HN* 2. 158: 'quot manus atteruntur ut unus niteat articulis!'

[79] Cic. *Verr.* 2. 5. 126.

armies, when only ruthless plundering could redeem a man from spectacular indebtedness.[80]

Julius Caesar became pre-eminently consequential because he was happy to spend monies he simply did not have. His self-glorification required thefts of the sorts only natural in a world governed by people who preferred that farmwork be done by feet that had been chained, hands that had been punished, and faces that had been branded.[81] The politics of the Forum were altogether a prettier business and it is time to turn there, to the wonderful intricacy of affect aroused by the spectacle of a prince of posturers.

[80] e.g. Suet. *DJ* 54. 1–2 describes Caesar's rapacity in Lusitania and Gaul.
[81] Pliny *HN* 18. 21.

# 2
# Looking at Caesar

en adsum victor terraque marique
Caesar, ubique tuus

Behold, here I am, victorious on land and sea,
Caesar, everywhere yours

Lucan 1. 201–2

On 15 February 44 BC, the hopes and fears of Julius Caesar, wearing a triumphator's cloak and a crown, looking down upon the animated crowds of the Lupercalia from a gilded chair set upon the Rostra, were magnificently inscrutable. This polyvalent figure, whose memory has never ceased to impress, has always elicited different judgements:[1] Hegel saw 'a paragon of Roman adaptation of means to ends', Mommsen the last great man of the ancient world, Meyer a power-hungry realist seeking the legitimation of royal dignity, and Syme a masterly political technician shepherding the talents and ambitions of a partisan ruling elite.[2] Nor could his contemporaries have known quite what to make of him—certainly no more than could Caesar himself fully comprehend how his position in the *res publica* should be defined both to his own satisfaction and that of his audience of sophisticated, civic consumers. The novelty of Caesar's political primacy would be played off against traditional expectations and memories of advertisements of the lives, moral qualities, and actions of pre-eminent men, upon whom the history and destiny of Rome had always and axiomatically rested.[3] In the environment that had created Caesar

[1] Cf. Meier 1995: 25.

[2] Yavetz 1983: 21, 22, 26–7; Syme 1939. Yavetz (1983: 10–57) offers a succinct overview of various interpretations.

[3] Cf. Ennius 156 (Skutsch): 'moribus antiquis res stat Romana virisque'.

and his somewhat fanatical fancies, civic festivities were occasions for aesthetic and affective engagement with 'the conflicting values and traditions shared by the Roman citizens'.[4]

The *res publica*, at the heart of which is Caesar seated in majestic dignity, was animated by intricate cross-currents of political sentiment and spectacular stylization. As Polybius noted of the Roman *politeia* in the second century BC, there was an admirably balanced blend of types of constitution: monarchy was represented by consuls, aristocracy by the Senate, and the source of honour and legal punishment resided in the people. There will be discussion later in this book about both Polybius and the nature of power in the later Republic (Chapter 6). It is enough to say at this point that not only does such a standard constitutional typology have crude hermeneutic utility but Polybius is also a guide attentive to extra-constitutional matters that nevertheless had a bearing upon authority and governance at Rome: funerals and religious ritual in particular impressed him as ways in which the authority of the elite could elicit the deference of the majority of the citizenry. In the later Republic not only did populism grow in power but there was also a steady increase in the routine flamboyance of individual self-advertisement. Humbler citizens expected deference whilst big men emulated kings. Caesar's spectacular, self-aggrandizing behaviours represented in eminently practical terms the remarkable complexities of the political culture in which he operated. He could wrest wonder from a crowd, obtaining complicity for his ambition. And yet, habituated to imperiousness,[5] he could also strike the nerves of republican civility. We shall certainly find in all his behaviour in Rome the complex mixture of basic constitutional styles. Caesar could be charmingly demotic in the Forum, was often excellent in the best of company with his social peers, and yet ultimately all rather kingly. He even attained a divinely spectacular presence in his city and immortality in its history. He was nothing, however, without an audience who shared the same history and habitual values—although he was no more the same man either in everybody's appreciation or upon every occasion—any more than the

[4] Millar 1998: 38. [5] Suet. *DJ* 30. 5 for his *imperii consuetudo*.

*res publica* itself ever represented a unanimity of ideology and sentiment.

At the Lupercalia the *populus Romanus* had as central a part to play in the whole conspicuous drama of Caesar's rejections of the diadem proffered by Antony as it had exercised in the politics that had brought Caesar to this moment of spectacular pre-eminence. Recognition of the crowd's central presence came more readily to Romans reflecting upon their history than it has to many modern historians whose attentions have frequently lingered upon the enigmas of the hero (or anti-hero) to the neglect of the fully communal context which both informed and rewarded even overweening ambition.[6] Ancient writers, whether familiar with republicanism or autocracy, took for granted that the powerful were visible to the populace. A century of Julio-Claudian autocracy after Caesar, the crowd certainly seemed to Lucan to be 'a major character' in the epic of political struggle turned bloody and terms such as *turba*, *vulgus*, *populus*, and *plebs* recur throughout the *Pharsalia*. Characters such as Pompey or Cato are placed before crowds but it is Caesar who is most 'naturally juxtaposed' with them.[7]

Closer sources duly register popular reaction when twice a diadem was offered, twice ostentatiously refused by the majestically enthroned Caesar when no applause encouraged its acceptance.[8] Nicolaus makes much mention of the *dēmos* shouting.[9] Plutarch, who makes his subject's relations with the *dēmos* central to the thematic architecture of this biography,[10] also mentions the noisy reaction to the offer of the exceptional honour (*Caesar* 61): 'And there was unimpressive

[6] The work of Millar (1984, 1986, 1989, 1998) corrects the neglect.

[7] Johnson 1987: 112–13 and n. 10.

[8] Plut. *Caes.* 61; Dio 44. 11. 3; Nic. Dam. F 130, 73.

[9] Nic. Dam. Fr. 130, 72: βοῶντος δὲ τοῦ δήμου . . . τοῦ δήμου βοῶντος; 73: ὁ δῆμος ἐβόησε.

[10] In the *Life of Caesar*, Caesar's rise to tyranny can be charted as an ambition dependent upon his popularity (esp. 5). In particular his activities in his aedileship meet with the approbation of the *dēmos* (which was voiced counter to the protests of a minority). The description of Caesar's boastful speech after his return from Africa and the scale of his munificence as a triumphator are also noticeable (55; cf. 57). Plutarch's theme rises to a climax with the popular reactions to Caesar's 'lust for monarchy' (τῆς βασιλείας ἔρως) (60). Plutarch's overall assessment of Caesar (69) is sorrowfully cynical: the

applause, the little that had been arranged. Yet when Caesar pushed the diadem away, the whole *dēmos* applauded.'[11] Not all ancient writers share such concern for popular participation: in Suetonius, Appian, and Dio the voice of the people is muted. Both Plutarch and Nicolaus apply to Roman politics the implications of the division between the few and the many, the *oligoi* and the *dēmos*. This is a natural analytical categorization for Greek historians which, although it fits Rome crudely, is accurate enough in its appreciation of the basic dynamics operating in scenarios of elite individuals posed before the crowd.[12]

Nicolaus' stress upon the noisy business of constructing charisma finds a highly significant echo in a contemporary observer of Roman political relations who was very much interested in using the Lupercal scenario to gauge the sentiments of the *populus*. Cicero too emphasizes that the sentiments of the crowd were expressed through their cries: 'you placed the diadem upon him to the distress of the *populus*, he rejected it to their applause.'[13] The crowd had already voiced its opinion about the removal of the diadems placed upon statuary. In Nicolaus the shouts come as the culmination to the series of dramatically unfolding events. Caesar protests the removal to the Senate and the offending tribunes are exiled. Then, 'the people shouted that he be king and not delay at all in being crowned, since Fortune had already crowned him'.[14] The diadem had

only profit he reaped was a name and 'glory envied by the citizens'. Plutarch philosophically refuses to grant prestige the importance it had for the ambitious Roman himself. On Plutarch finding the *dēmos* 'always and everywhere a menace' see D. A. Russell 1995: 80, citing *Thes.* 25, *Cam.* 36, *Tim.* 37, *Mar.* 28.

[11] *καὶ γίνεται κρότος οὐ λαμπρός, ἀλλ' ὀλίγος ἐκ παρασκευῆς. ἀπωσαμένου δὲ τοῦ Καίσαρος ἅπας ὁ δῆμος ἀνεκρότησεν.*

[12] See esp. Polyb. 6. 11–18, 43–58; Pelling 1986: 167. There are many aspects of Roman political life to which Plutarch is less than attentive; but he is also willing to read Greek history in many of the same terms that he applies to Roman history. Gomme *HCT* i. 72–4; Pelling 1986: 175.

[13] Cic. *Phil.* 2. 85: 'tu diadema inponebas cum plangore populi, ille cum plausu reiciebat'. Weinstock ignores the 'more colourful narrative' (1971: 331–2) of Nicolaus of Damascus, following the criticisms of Jacoby. The preoccupations which provide the colour are nevertheless revealing.

[14] Nic. Dam. Fr. 130, 70: *ὁ δὲ δῆμος ἐβόα βασιλέα τε αὐτὸν εἶναι καὶ ἀνα δεῖσθαι μηδὲν ἔτι μέλλοντα, ἐπεὶ καὶ ἡ Τύχη αὐτὸν ἀναδέδεκεν.*

been placed in full view upon statues which advertised Caesar's greatness in the most prominent way, placed as they were upon the Rostra at the heart of the civic space of the Republic; the removal of the diadem by L. Caesetius Flavus and C. Epidius Marullus might or might not have been applauded.[15] That coronation was intended to be seen as a symbol once it was *seen*: 'but the Romans regarded it with suspicion, considering it to be a symbol of slavery.'[16] Such episodes are open to various interpretations—Caesar either soliciting consent or approval for his own rejection of kingliness, or a truly exploratory combination of both possibilities[17]—but certainly popular reaction was at the centre of all the symbolic manoeuvring.[18]

A festival was a natural setting for Caesar's dramatic flirtations with new modes of self-presentation. Romans gathered in large numbers beneath the gaze of the gods, the ultimate spectators. And the splendidness of the leading human actors was readily apparent. While the ritual ingredients would have had differing significances for all the various identities to be found thronging the streets of the city on any day,[19] in all eyes the Lupercal choreography could call attention to more powerful men in the city. There was Antony, leading the pack of revellers.[20] And the big man himself looked altogether as no Roman really had ever done before. All aspects of Caesar's person were now dressed with freshly magnificent splendour, entitlement to which had been given by the Senate and citizens of Rome with pointed attempts at flattery or even irony.[21] The honours might have had their prestigious precedents in the *memoria* of the Republic; but never before were so many qualities attributed to one individual.[22]

[15] So e.g. Plut. *Cic.* 61; *Ant.* 12. 7: εὐφημῶν μετὰ κρότου. This is an awkward detail omitted from Nicolaus' reading of Caesar, and of these events.

[16] Nic. Dam. Fr. 130, 69: ὤφθη ... ὑπόπτωϲ δὲ πάνυ πρὸϲ αὐτὸ ἔχουϲι Ῥωμαῖοι δουλείαϲ οἰόμενοι εἶναι ϲύμβολον.

[17] Cf. Meier 1996: 476–7.

[18] Thus in his denunciation of the tribunes who had removed the diadem, Caesar claimed the tribunes had sought to slander him εἰϲ τὸ πλῆθοϲ: Nic. Dam. Fr. 130, 69.

[19] Hopkins 1991.

[20] Nic. Dam. Fr. 130, 71: προῄει διὰ τῆϲ ἀγορᾶϲ.

[21] Dio 44. 4–5.

[22] As Weinstock's usefully exhaustive study of 1971 documents.

Caesar's political pre-eminence systematically had been made aesthetically obvious to all. After news of Munda reached Rome, Senate and citizens had devised all manner of honours, including fifty days of thanksgiving, the addition of the anniversary to the calendar as a festival to be celebrated with races in the Circus, as well as the title of Imperator which was to be a hereditary possession. There was clearly a somewhat manic attempt at improvisation on the part of the Senate in finding new ways to acknowledge and appease by the gift of all the various honours, most of which Caesar accepted.[23] In May it had been further decreed that his ivory statue, together with its special carriage, should be conveyed with the images of the other gods in procession to the Circus. A statue inscribed 'to the unconquerable god' was to be erected in the temple of Quirinus and another joined those of the kings and Lucius Brutus on the Capitol. Dio lists the conglomeration of honours voted to him by the time of the assassination, although not all were necessarily acted upon. Among them, and right at the top of the list, are the rights always to be first in procession, to wear a triumphal cloak in the city, to sit upon a curule seat everywhere except at the festivals, where he had the right to watch from the tribunes' bench.[24] Marks of Caesar's position such as lictors carrying *fasces* decked with laurel, the right to ride after the Feriae Latinae from the Alban Mount into the city on horseback, chairs to be carried into the theatres, and an escort of *equites* and senators all point to a visibility of honour that all could readily appreciate. On all official occasions he could appear in triumphal garb and wear a laurel wreath.[25] All parts of his person, down to his feet clad after 45 in the fancy slippers of an Alban king, were dressed to impress all in the multitude.[26] At the Lupercalia Caesar appeared for the first time in public in the ceremonial garb of ancient Roman kings. Adorned with purple toga and golden wreath he watched from the Rostra,

[23] Cf. Meier 1996: 474.

[24] Dio 43. 42. 2–3: *τὰ μὲν γὰρ πρῶτα φέρεσθαί τε αὐτὸν ἀεὶ καὶ ἐν τῇ πόλει τὴν στολὴν τὴν ἐπινίκιον ἐνδεδυκότα, καὶ καθέζεσθαι ἐπὶ τοῦ ἀρχικοῦ δίφρου πανταχῇ πλὴν ἐν ταῖς πανηγύρεσιν, ἐψηφίσαντο· τότε γὰρ ἐπί τε τοῦ δημαρχικοῦ βάθρου καὶ μετὰ τῶν ἀεὶ δημαρχούντων θεᾶσθαι ἔλαβε.*

[25] Dio 43. 42. 2–3; Gelzer 1968: 307.

[26] Dio 43. 43. 2.

seated upon a gilded chair.[27] Naturally he was elevated above all others.[28] Citizens routinely attended to the sight and sounds of a select few standing upon the Rostra. But now a kingly pre-eminence had settled in as solely a spectacle and a central focus of the communal festivities.

The vast ambition attributed to Caesar, which events made so plausible, had long aimed at such distinct pre-eminence.[29] As manifestly first man in the state he was using communal rites to fuse personal significance with that of the community as a whole. Prior to his own successes Caesar advertised the importance of his family in collective memory. He restored the monuments of Marius and delivered an affecting eulogy for his aunt, Marius' widow, from the Rostra to a crowd in the Forum.[30] In the games he gave for his late father (in 65) he exhibited not just men and animals but their fights also glittered with all the splendour borrowed monies could bestow, giving, one supposes, the *populus* some satisfying glam-pop butchery.[31] These games for his father were combined with those it was his duty as aedile to give with his colleague. His colleague was, of course, Bibulus, who split the cost of the required entertainment but found all the credit taken by Caesar.[32] He also gave feasts in his aedileship.[33] A feast was even given in remem-

[27] Throne and toga: e.g. Cic. *Phil.* 2. 85; Pliny 11. 186; Val. Max. 1. 6. 13; Nic. Dam. Fr. 130, 71; Dio 44. 6. 1; Plut. *Caes.* 61; throne alone: App. *BC* 2. 109; Weinstock 1971: 271, 331–2.

[28] Nicolaus patiently explains (Nic. Dam. Fr. 130, 71) to his Greek readers the most salient fact about the Rostra: it was, he explained, elevated: ἦν γὰρ ὑψηλὸϲ ὁ τόποϲ ἐφ' οὗ Καίϲαρ ἐδημηγόρει.

[29] He preferred to be first in an Alpine village rather than second at Rome: Plut. *Caes.* 11.

[30] Suet. *DJ* 6.

[31] Pliny *HN* 33. 53: *noxii* fought 'feras' and were armed with 'argenteis vasis'.

[32] Dio 37. 8. 2. Suet. *DJ* 10 also describes Caesar's euergetism as aedile in 65, recording that he decorated the Comitium, the Forum, basilicas, and the Capitol itself, building temporary colonnades for exhibition of some of his abundant items; there were animal-hunts (*venationes*) and *ludi*, with his colleague and independently. He gets all the *gratia* and Bibulus compares himself to Pollux. A *lex* limited the number of gladiators he could exhibit; also Plut. *Caes.* 5–6 on his lavishness and innovation. Caesar also restored the Marian monuments (e.g. also Vell. 2. 43. 4).

[33] Plut. *Caes.* 4–5. There was to be another grand feast and distribution of food: *Caes.* 57.

brance of his daughter, a private loss that no one had ever before marked so publicly.[34] The *munera* for long-dead Julia were held in the Forum and coincided with the dedication ceremonies for the temple of Venus Genetrix which he commissioned. These, following hard on the heels of his unprecedentedly grand four-fold triumphing of September 46, surpassed all previous *ludi*.[35] Caesarian significance embraced the whole community.[36]

While, to a remarkable degree, Caesar as dictator set a brisk pace in building realizations of what in practice Roman glory could be, including gestures toward divinization which were perfectly reasonable under the circumstances, there could be no uniformity of response to these developments. Some might bridle at the transgression of boundaries between men and gods and at the obvious vanity it demonstrated. Others might be swept up by the wondrousness of all Caesar's self-display. Nicolaus describes the types of reactions with a telling simplicity: 'He himself, exulting in many fine victories, not unreasonably counting himself now to be something more than human, was an object of wonder to the many, but to the great and the pretenders to power he seemed too much to bear.'[37] Syntax appropriately makes Caesar the subject throughout and casts his audience as passive repositories of powerful if conflicting emotions. The admiration of the many and the resentment of a few were responses not just to Caesar's extraordinary position in the state but also to the ways in which he was insisting upon fresh articulations of this—and wanting them to be popularly accepted.

Nevertheless Caesar, not least in all his visible glory, surely did seem wondrous to many. His gestures towards

[34] Suet. *DJ* 26. 2, noting too that, to raise expectations, he had his own household make preparations for the banquets, even though he had contracted them out to the markets as well. Gladiatorial *munera* were often accompanied by *viscerationes* and *epula*, e.g. Livy 41. 28. 11. Faustus Sulla provided a gladiatorial *munus* in the memory of his father and feasted the *dēmos* splendidly (*τὸν δῆμον λαμπρῶϲ εἰστίαϲε*), along with baths and a supply of olive oil: Dio 37. 51. 4.

[35] Dio 43. 22. 2–23.

[36] Cf. Beacham 1999: 78.

[37] Nic. Dam. Fr. 130, 64: *αὐτόϲ τε ἐκεῖνοϲ ἐπὶ πολλαῖϲ καὶ καλαῖϲ νίκαιϲ ἀγαλλόμενοϲ οὐκ ἀπεικότωϲ πλέον τι ἢ ἄνθρωποϲ ἀξιῶν ἤδη εἶναι τοῖϲ μὲν πολλοῖϲ ἐθαυμάζετο, τοῖϲ δὲ μεγάλοιϲ καὶ δυναστείαϲ μεταποιουμένοιϲ ἐπαχθὴϲ ἐδόκει εἶναι.*

being appreciated as something more than human were in fact more successful than all the fuss about the diadems. Honours—and all highly visible—given to Caesar before his murder certainly 'assimilated him to divine status'.[38] Many other great Roman leaders before Caesar had enjoyed close relations with the gods, including most memorably Scipio Africanus, Marius, Sulla, and of course Pompey. But Caesar 'finally brought to Rome a degree of outright identification with the gods' that Pompey had allowed to be indulged only in the East, 'out of range of the constraining gaze of his peers'.[39] Caesar installed cult of victory to which Sulla, Pompey, and Caesar's familial lineage had all laid claim, in the civic calendar.[40] An ivory image of him travelled in the company of other gods in the Circus procession.[41] In 44 this statue was processing in more impressive style, in a carriage drawn by four horses.[42] Before his death he could boast of the divine honours of *pulvinar* (seat of honour), statue, pediment to his *domus* (house), even a *flamen* ('priest', in the person of Antony).[43] Modern uncertainty about what all this meant exactly was surely shared by all spectators of all the lavishness of display to be seen in the days of Caesar's dictatorship, be they his friends, other not so great pretenders to power, the multitude, or probably in fact Caesar himself.[44]

When all is said and done, the very important and complicated business of religion at Rome directly involved a multitude in practices that certainly could be correlated to the broader sociopolitical structures of the *res publica*.[45] Yet it is true to say that 'society never stops creating new sacred things'.[46] Religion offered valuable opportunities for confirming (truly hierarchical) power relations prevailing in other areas of Roman sociopolitical life not only because it depended upon clearly

[38] Beard, North and Price 1998: 141. Beacham (1999: 81–4) provides a useful and succinct account of divinely spectacular honours, Weinstock has (1971) a full discussion.

[39] Beard, North and Price 1998: 147.

[40] Weinstock 1971: 81. When the *ludi Victoriae Caesaris* were first celebrated, Cicero was pleased to note an absence of applause for both Caesar and Victory: *Att.* 13. 44. 1.

[41] Dio 43. 45. 3.

[42] Suet 76. 1; Dio 44. 6. 3; Weinstock 1971: 284 ff.

[43] Cic. *Phil.* 2. 110.

[44] Cf. Beard, North and Price 1998: 148.

[45] Cf. Polyb. 6. 56.

[46] Durkheim 1995: 215.

differentiated roles between mass and elite but also because such differences seemed all the more natural on occasions often fraught with powerful emotions, whether solemn awe or joyous giddiness or, much more likely, an ever shifting spectrum of moods. Thus no civic occasion was more highly prized by the Roman notability than a triumph, which was a charismatic ceremony which in some sense deified the triumphator. We shall look in more detail at some memorable triumphs later and notice that despite many reversals of the mundane, such as a mortal decorated to resemble a statue of Jupiter, or the very presence of an army within the *pomerium* (sacred boundaries) of the city, the occasion underscored central ideological foundations of the *res publica*. An individual was indisputably and transcendently great, the representations of his patriotic achievements usually quite wondrous as empire came home to the heart of the city and to the gaze of the citizenry in whose name and by whose bestowal of *imperium* he had been sent forth. The crowd could marvel and cheer. The citizens could also smirk and jeer, joining in with the carnivalesque taunts of bawdy songs.[47] There was the solemnity of sacrifice upon the Capitoline. And then good food and nice wine. Everywhere there were things to admire and affective experiences to remember.

Even strangers, if believed to be able to access divine power, could receive a warm reception from the Roman crowd despite hostility from political leaders. The strange but wondrous Battaces Battaces, a priest of the Magna Mater, arrived in Rome from Pessinus in Phrygia (in 102 BC). He claimed to have come by command of the goddess and obtained an audience with the consuls and the Senate before addressing the people from the Rostra. His success in instilling awe (*deisidaemonia*) in his audience was probably helped by a costume that was, in Roman eyes, simply remarkable: an enormous gold crown and a robe shot through with gold. Aulus Pompeius, a tribune, however, forbade him to wear his crown and attacked him verbally on his next appearance on the Rostra. The priest thereupon refused to appear again in public, saying that both he and the goddess had been insulted. After Pompeius had fallen ill and then died three

[47] Suet. *DJ* 49. 4.

days later, Battaces was granted special permission to wear his costume, was presented with notable gifts, and when he set off homewards, was escorted by a large crowd of both men and women.[48] The powers of divinity had confirmed popular sensibility. Protest at such unauthorized charisma was futile. Times were troubled by fear of barbarian invasion, and it is a truism that people are more mindful of divinity in times of misfortune.[49] Caesar's pre-eminence after Munda at least brought a promise of peace for Italy.

Furthermore, especially when their striking emotionality is struck within a religious context, the graces of majestic notables need not *ipso facto* have been resented by humbler citizens. Moreover, it could fairly be claimed that 'the routine deference that men invested with high social positions receive is not qualitatively different from religious respect'.[50] It was useful that the crowd believed great men to be of divine origin.[51] It was inevitable that both audience and actor went forth into the streets carrying the same assumptions of what men of traditional value might be like.

The most illustrious exemplar of glorious individual achievements in Roman history had been Scipio Africanus Maior, in whom it is fair to say that a 'new age' was personified, that of the individual . . .whose civic pre-eminence was universally recognized yet whose 'personality was so outstanding that it caused offence to many and admiration in others'.[52] Such a man would find it difficult to find comfortable accommodation for his exceptional self within the routine constraints of domestic politics. He was remembered for exhibiting *gravitas* and *maiestas* for which Cicero gushed admiration, finding him 'a leader not a comrade of the Roman *populus*'.[53] And he could be well celebrated as a leader who on occasion was happily followed by a crowd who understood his significance to the *res publica* in religious terms. Ceremony presented him as the charismatic embodiment of all that was best about the values and

[48] Diod. 36. 13; cf. Polyb. 21. 37. 5 on this Phrygian priesthood.

[49] e.g. Diod. 23. 13.

[50] Durkheim 1995: 215.

[51] Varro Fr. 1. 24; Galinsky 1996: 291.

[52] Scullard 1970: 234.

[53] Cic. *Am.* 96: 'ut facile ducem populi Romani, non comitem diceres'.

achievements of Rome and its history. Scipio (and there would be others of his *gens* who could do the same) made direct appeals to the citizenry in their streets as effective as those he made to the citizens in his armed camps and battle-ranks. Even before his triumph he was the object of spectacular attention in Rome: when he returned from Africa at elections, he sacrificed one hundred oxen on the Capitoline to Jupiter. There were, of course, crowds watching.[54] Scipio was, moreover, closely linked with gods: with Neptune, Hercules, and with Jupiter.[55] Jupiter is, of course, the most important connection struck by this extraordinary individual in his search for a way to convey his extraordinariness. The allusions to divinity were firmly in the public domain. His *imago* after all dwelt in the *atrium* of Jupiter. It was at the *ludi* that the intervention of Neptune in Spain was kept alive in the popular memory;[56] it was by a dramatic destruction of accounting books in the Senate that he articulated his conscious belief in himself and the rightness of his cause.[57] It was by that procession to sacrifice to Jupiter that the victor of Zama asserted his power before the *populus*, when he was faced with judicial trouble. The legal proceedings of the trial before the *populus* came to an end when Scipio Africanus was escorted to thc Capitol—to give sacrifice—in 187 by 'universa contio'.[58]

Scipio's anniversary procession might easily be taken as an example of the inability of the popular will to express itself in 'any significant sense' through judicial verdicts.[59] Even so we

[54] Livy 28. 38. 8.

[55] Walbank 1967. Scullard 1970: 19–23. Neptune helping to lower the waters protecting New Carthage: Polyb. 10. 11. Scipio is compared to Hercules by Cicero (*Rep.* Fr. 3), Horace (*O.* 4. 8. 15 ff.), and Lactantius (*Inst.* 1. 18). See further Galinsky 1996 for references to Scipio in Plautus. Gruen 1990: 128 and n. 16 (with good bibliography) stresses the difficulty of pinning down Plautus' political inclinations.

[56] Skutsch (1968: 174 f.) argues that Mercury's reference in the prologue of Plautus' *Amphitruo* to Neptune's benefits to the Roman people refers specifically to the events at New Carthage, reminding the audience of events almost two decades earlier.

[57] Scullard 1970: 235.

[58] Livy 38. 51. 12. The cries of the crowd ('universorum voces') urge the reconciliation of the feuding censors in 179: 40. 46. 13.

[59] Gruen 1991: 264–5, who treats the evidence lucidly, arguing for this date and suggesting that only L. Scipio was accused. The messiness in details of the testimony suggests how only the central event of the drama was truly memorable.

should be wary of seeing power solely in terms of its exercise through constitutional channels. Power is certainly a more complicated matter than is implied by any assertion that constitutional arrangements corresponded, 'to a relatively high degree, to the actual distribution of power'.[60] The crowd surely exercised something of a conscious choice in its decision to escort to the Capitol this extraordinary embodiment of all that was best about Rome. They made Africanus powerful, since Scipio's evocation of his greatest moment, the victory of Zama, the anniversary of which fortuitously fell upon that very day, allowed him to become the charismatic centre of the polity. He flexed his presence and the meaning of that presence before the memories and the gaze of his fellow (but individually infinitely less significant) citizens. He led the crowd to trample over its constitutional prerogatives. They marvelled and they followed. This power can conveniently be understood and described as kingly. It perhaps corresponds to practical manifestations of power and thus popular comprehensions of power as much as it does to the unwritten rubrics of constitutional norms.

Scipio's charismatic immunity did not easily endure outside the emotive context of remembrance of triumph and salvation. Not only was the pseudo-divine *felicitas* of a triumphator normally ephemeral but there was also a prevailing expectation of reciprocity in civic deference. And certainly the routines of the later *res publica* were animated by populist insistence upon an ideology of habitual *civilitas*.[61] This ideology was realized in remembrance of the exemplars of a glorious past, as is well remarked in Greek sources. Dionysius of Halicarnassus, for instance, became particularly interested in this 'democratic' feature of the Republic: Coriolanus is warned (in a speech) to make himself like other men—to descend 'to the more demotic';[62] in contrast, Cincinnatus is the antithetical, positive paradigm.[63] The story of his summons from a virtuously simple life on the farm is expressly cited to show to all 'what men were like then, the prominent men of the city of the Romans'.[64] The

[60] Harris 1990: 292, who champions this proposition whilst admitting that constitutional rules do not reveal enough about actual political practice.

[61] Cf. Wallace-Hadrill 1982.

[62] ἐπὶ τὸ δημοτικώτερον.

[63] Dion. Hal. *Ant. Rom.* 7. 45. 4.

[64] Ibid. 10. 17. 6 (οἱ τῆϲ Ῥωμαίων πόλεωϲ προεϲτηκότεϲ).

prominent were neither physically nor pompously prominent. Hence the men of old did not pursue powerful offices (*exousiai*) but rather shunned them when offered—unlike men of Dionysius' own day whose practices he finds to be typically quite opposite, except for a few through whom both the good reputation of the city as well as the preservation of equal treatment of other men still stood firm.[65]

Plutarch too was very much interested in the demotic tendencies of various historical players, and how these found expression in practices besides rhetoric from the Rostra. One notes, for example, how Crassus was able to return the greeting of anyone he met, however obscure or lowly, with knowledge of the man's name.[66] This notable's life was always well arranged for winning the honours that he sought. As had always, of course, been Caesar's too. In his populist performances, such as his orchestration of the funeral for his aunt Julia, Caesar tapped into the remembrances of a man whose pre-eminence had always been girt about with respect for citizenhood. Marius had so shared the travails of his soldiers that Sallust could plausibly portray him proclaiming, 'Hoc est utile, hoc civile imperium.'[67] Marius, seven times elected consul and saviour of Roman civilization from barbarian deluge, had his flirtations with divinity.[68] Marius also posed in triumph with a Bacchic tankard in his hand.[69] Such significance was happily entertained in turn by the populace: when news of victory over the Cimbri reached Rome, he received libations as the gods did.[70] When families celebrated the anniversary of the victory, offerings were made to honour the gods and Marius too.[71] Even felicitous Sulla might have appeared sexily charismatic in some

[65] Note too Dionysius' remark (*Ant. Rom.* 5. 60. 2) about the ἡγεμόνες of his own times who have failed to shun tyrannical stubbornness.

[66] Plut. *Crass.* 3. It is perhaps instructive to contrast Plutarch's sense of Cicero's ambitions as a social climber: he knew who everybody τῶν γνωρίμων was and where their grand houses were (Plut. *Cic.* 7).

[67] Sall. *BJ* 85. 34–5: 'this is helpful command, this is civil leadership.'

[68] Cf. Beard, North and Price 1998: 143–4.

[69] Val. Max. 3. 5. 6; Pliny *HN* 33. 150.

[70] Val. Max. 8. 15. 7: 'nemo fuit qui non illi tamquam dis immortalibus apud sacra mensae suae libaverit'; cf. Plut. *Mar.* 27.

[71] Plut. *Mar.* 27.

popular contexts. And Pompey certainly did, as we shall see. But none of these men had quite Caesar's gifts or opportunities.

Throughout his life, Caesar's comprehension of his place in the nature of things had been founded upon experiences that embraced the whole gamut of emotions proper to a multitude massed in the city on a festive occasion. But he was also civically adept in any situation. People had seen him canvassing, at the centre of an enormous entourage. They had watched a *pontifex maximus* speak solemnly and passionately to gods as well as most charmingly to jurors. They had heard him acknowledge their dignity too, and secured his sincerity upon remembrance of exquisite material offerings, which showed the rightfulness of the subordination of men and beasts to all the treasure and the dignity enjoyed by his sovereign Roman audience, as well as his own control of such instruments of patriotic pride. As we saw at the Lupercalia, the sentiments of audiences required constant heedfulness. No skilled interpreter of the phenomenology of *dignitas*, as Caesar was by instinct and habitual practice, would shirk the challenge of engaging the *iudicium* and *voluntas* of the crowd, even though men with great and impressive *dignitates* perhaps never deferred to their environment and its normative, civil expectations any more completely than did Scipio.

In provision of the stuff of joy Caesar had always worked unrelentingly to show himself to be most generous. He was, of course, only following trends set by others. But he had certainly had a masterful touch in dealing with the 'innermost feelings of the community'.[72] In his earlier career he had spent massively, with eyes set ever more squarely upon a popular *dignitas*. He worked the affective dimension of politics hard, providing the very best of glad times that would dispose his audience to see him in the most favourable light. Those feasts, for example, were fabulous. In the last years of the Republic a great deal of money was spent on feasts by all the 'notability'.[73] At Rome, feasts could be for thousands.[74] Unsurprisingly it was vital for an electoral candidate to be suitably convivial.[75] Although

[72] *Sest.* 119: 'intimi sensus civitatis'. [73] Plut. *Cic.* 10 (*οἱ ἐν δόξῃ*).

[74] e.g. Cic. *Vat.* 31: 'Epulum populi Romani, festum diem...cum tot hominum milia accumberet'.

[75] '[Benignitas] est etiam in conviviis, quae fac ut et abs te et ab amicis tui concelebretur et passim et tributim' (*Com. Pet.* 44).

expensive food had become, for those who could afford it, a more luxurious social practice in the second century,[76] and there was a persistent trend towards display of wealth and taste in more private consumption, the whole city might be welcomed to a great Roman's feast. This was usual after triumphs.[77] Lucullus, the reclusive gourmand later in his life, finished his triumph and feasted the city splendidly, even including outlying villages in his liberality.[78] Ostentatious generosity traditionally had to allow for no suspicion that the people were not given their due respect.[79]

Caesar assuredly had phenomenal mastery in advertising a *dignitas* which invariably advanced his popular advertisement of his own, personal brand of generous civility. His gift-giving was truly a form of political power, as Plutarch notes in speaking of how he gradually increased his 'political power' through dinners and hospitality.[80] When he had Gallic and much other loot besides to spend, he continued in his habits. It was for triumphal celebrations that he was at his most conspicuously and memorably generous: 'he added a feast and a distribution of meat and, after his Spanish triumph, two lunches; for when he

[76] e.g. Livy 39. 6. 8.

[77] Triumphant generals usually gave their public banquets in the temple of Hercules: Athen. 5. 64. Pliny the Elder reports on *triumphales cenae* for the *populus* (*HN* 9. 171): there were 6,000 pounds of lampreys from Gavius Hirrius. Cf. Macrob. *Sat.* 3. 15. 9. Sicilian wines were good for 'publicis epulis' (*HN* 14. 66). The food might be themed with triumphal cinnabar—it was usual, says Pliny (*HN* 33. 112), even in the days of Camillus to add cinnabar 'in unguenta cenae triumphalis'.

[78] Plut. *Luc.* 37. His magnificence retreated to a more private sphere of competition in contrast to Cimon whose *Life* is paired with his own by Plutarch; Lucullus spent his money on food for a few (*Comp. Cim. & Luc.* 1). He kept a slave for the specific purpose of keeping him away from food (Pliny *HN* 28. 56). Crassus, however, was not so private in his spending, choosing to set up thousands of tables to feast the people in his first consulship. Plut. *Crass.* 2. His private entertainments had, Plutarch claims (*Crass.* 3), simple fare and, for the most part, an egalitarian guest-list (δημοτικὴ καὶ λαώδης).

[79] The story (Val. Max. 7. 5. 1) of Q. Aelius Tubero is telling. When asked to fit out a dining-room by Q. Fabius Maximus, who was giving a feast in the name of his uncle Scipio Aemilianus, he chose shabby furnishings. Voters took offence and revenge at the praetorian elections. They liked private frugality but public splendour.

[80] *Caes.* 55: δύναμις εἰς τὴν πολιτείαν.

considered that the first was stingy and did not represent his liberality, he gave another very ample lunch five days later.'[81] In 46, for his Spanish triumph, Caesar dispensed Chian and Falernian wine ('vini Falerni amphoras Chii cados in convivia distribuit'); in his third consulship, Falernian, Chian, Lesbian, and Mamertine—the very first occasion (and goodness knows that Pliny liked to check and remark upon precedents) when the four types had been served together.[82] This ought to be understood to be in and of itself an important political event. After his fourfold triumph Caesar needed thousands of tables for his festive hospitality.[83] Such behaviour surely succeeded in reconciling pre-eminence with the necessities of showing his respect for the *populus*, as Cicero (*Phil.* 2. 116) was well aware:

> multos annos regnare meditatus magno labore, magnis periculis, quod cogitarat, effecerat; muneribus, monumentis, congiariis, epulis multitudinem imperitam delenierat.

> having contemplated kingship for many years, he accomplished his plan by great effort and by great dangers; by public shows, buildings, gratuities, and by feasts he seduced the naive multitude.[84]

Of course, the *multitudo* was not so pathetically inexperienced as Cicero might care to imply. Caesar was only exhibiting himself and his resources in a spectacular fashion that had evolved over centuries. Humbler Romans had seen all sorts of splendours and had had all sorts of wonderful experiences at others' expense before Caesar's festivities. For many, politics had everything to do with money and memories, food and all manner of wondrousnesses that confirmed a dignity not allotted

[81] Suet. *DJ* 38. 2: 'adiecit epulum ac viscerationem et post Hispaniensem victoriam duo prandia; nam cum prius parce neque pro liberalitate sua praebitum iudicaret, quinto post die aliud largissimum.' Caesar also staged big banquets in the provinces (Suet. *DJ* 48).

[82] Pliny *HN* 14. 97. For Pliny's diligence in documenting 'feasting-firsts' note too that P. Servilius Rullus, father of the tribune of 63, was the first man to serve whole boar at a feast (*HN* 8. 210).

[83] Plut. *Caes.* 55; cf. Livy *Ep.* 115.

[84] There is thus a particular point (and pointed cruelty) to Cicero's description of the Ides of March as an *epulae* (*Fam.* 10. 28. 1, or as *cena*—*Fam.* 12. 4. 1). The *munus* organized by Faustus Sulla in 60 in memory of his father the dictator attracted a lot of attention. It was accompanied by an *epulum* (Cic. *Vat.* 32, cf. *Sull.* 54–5; Dio 37. 51. 4).

all the hapless people not born or freed into membership of the Roman nation as citizens. In the protocols of a generous deference to the multitude there operated a dimension of politics in tandem with a constitution predicated upon sovereign entitlement to exercise of the franchise, but not confined to it: there were crowds, with all their attendant emotions and needinesses, perambulating, gawking, and feasting even on days when no voting nor legislating was to be done.

Yet nobody perhaps had seen anything quite so impressive as Caesar's kingly escort of elephants. He was escorted home (or, in Suetonius' account, to the Capitol) from his triumph by forty elephants, arrayed to his right and his left, each carrying a torch with its trunk.[85] There will be more to say later about the phenomenon of elephants in the spectacles of ancient Mediterranean cities—and above all about the connotations of magnificently monarchic power. Caesar's generous indulgence of popular dignity was always matched by insistence upon his own singularity. And if the essence of Caesar was constructed upon what he could be seen doing, then in the latter days of his life audiences might have witnessed a man whose civil solicitudes, sometimes so appealing to popular favour, could now be overwhelmed by the world-weariness of an autocrat. The hauteur evident in his behaviour had likely been nurtured by all the years imperiously spent in provinces, camps, and alien cities where he could shun the rituals and disingenuities of earlier self-advertisements. In the public spaces of Rome it was quite manifest. His attitude towards magisterial dignity, in regarding the consulate as a prize to bestow rather than as a merited gift of the *populus*, was certainly shocking to some. They yelled in the theatre at Fabius Maximus, whom Caesar had made suffect consul and who now entered for the first time and called the *populus* to order, to the effect that he was no legitimate consul.[86] Caesar paid little heed. His appointment of a suffect consul to serve the *res publica* for a mere matter of hours at the end of 45 was surely outrageous to many citizens besides Cicero, who obviously retained his own heavy personal investment in the value of consular dignity. This was unacceptable to a citizenry used to a dialogue of mutual respect between an

[85] Dio 43. 22. 1; Suet. *DJ* 37.

[86] Suet. *DJ* 80. 2.

official and the sovereign source of his power and authority.[87] Moreover, the time Caesar was able or willing to devote to a presence in Rome itself was simply not long enough for people to grow better used to his more recent conception of his *dignitas*.

His treatment in particular of the most visible symbols of the state jeopardized his popularity in a society in which 'all order' did indeed depend upon 'deference and acceptance of the symbols of office'.[88] In July 45, when his image was first carried in procession, there had indeed been no applause.[89] Although his exceptionality was undisputed he indulged it by refusal to defer manifestly to the mundanities that bespoke historical continuity, behaving wantonly in his belittlement of Roman civic dignity, in respect of not just the persons of Romans but also those familiarities of officialdom symbolic of popular sovereignty. He ordered, for example, a soldier, who was grumbling about money squandered on entertaining the people, executed; and two others were supposedly sacrificed to Mars on the Campus Martius and their heads displayed outside his official residence as *pontifex maximus*.[90]

Such despotism could, however, be forgotten in occasions of high emotion. Caesar's ability to summon forth all the frenzied excitement of a crowd was never more striking than after his death, when funeral ritual, carefully and elaborately orchestrated to provide spectacular affect, definitively marked his significance and also animated further rounds of civil war and misery for millions in his world. The *populus* was out in force in the Forum to remember the *dignitas* of Caesar and found the pathetic traces of its martyrdom recollected in the sight of a pillar hung with the cloak he was wearing when struck down. Piso brought the body into the Forum: 'a countless crowd rushed together with weapons to guard it; and with cheering and an abundant escort placed it on the Rostra.'[91] Amid wailing, lamentation, and the clashing of shields, the crowd repented of its decision to grant amnesty to the assassins. It succeeded in producing further affecting displays in the outpouring of grief. The musicians and actors present at Caesar's funeral threw their robes upon the flames, veterans their arms,

[87] See Ch. 6. [88] Millar 1998: 83. [89] Cf. Meier 1996: 459.
[90] Dio 43. 24. 3–4. [91] App. *BC* 2. 143.

matrons the *bullae* and *togae praetextae* of their children.[92] However hysterical, such sentiment bespeaks a love complicit with Caesar's own fondest ambitions. Of course, this emotional outpouring was prompted by stage-management of the sort customary for the funeral of any great grandee of that *res publica*,[93] but on this occasion it was directed specifically towards emblems of a majesty that transcended traditional protocols. There was a gilded shrine high upon the Rostra made to look like the temple of Venus Genetrix. Inside was an ivory couch with coverlets of purple and gold. In this powerfully harmonious brew of aesthetics and emotion, there was inevitably a striking egalitarianism: nameless people brought gifts without there being any protocols of *dignitas*—'omisso ordine'.[94] This is an historical spectacle of kingly power—there being one charismatic (indeed divine) star, with whom nobody could compete, and then simply everybody else—which is surely indicative of how the kingly element in the *res publica* had found practical harmony with the demotic. This was the end of a republic.

All of Caesar's singular successes in the aesthetic, affective, extra-constitutional dimensions of politics had long brought intense fear and envy among his fellow *principes* in the *res publica*. He destroyed for good the cohesion of their oligarchy. The shifting complicities between pre-eminence and populism manifest in Caesar's career had often neglected solidarity with his fellow members of a rarified peer group. All notables had been bred into intensive awareness of how their comportment was watched by others and how they should police themselves accordingly.[95] So some behaviours were simply inappropriate in public, such as pulling faces,[96] singing in the street,[97] or dancing in the Forum.[98] Caesar had remarkable self-discipline.

[92] Suet. *DJ* 84. 3–4.

[93] Flower 1996: 126.

[94] Suet. *DJ* 84. 1. When things became more emotionally heated there was an attempt, stopped by priests, to carry off the bier to the Capitol. For Antony's involvement see Plut. *Ant.* 14 (with Pelling 1988: 151–4) and *Brut.* 20. Cicero (*Phil.* 2. 91; cf. *Att.* 14. 10. 1) suggests an emotional performance was given; but in Suetonius (84. 20) Antony speaks only a few words. The funeral instead took place in the Forum (e.g. Nic. Dam. Fr. 130. 48 ff.; App. *BC* 2. 148).

[95] Cic. *Off.* 1. 146; Lendon 1996: 39.

[96] Plut. *de Vit. Pud.* 535 A.

[97] Cic. *Off.* 1. 145.

[98] Cic. *Off.* 3. 75 and 93.

When the captive of the pirates, Caesar did not remove either by day or night the shoes or toga that indicated his Roman-ness and his social rank.[99] In Rome, he adjusted his style and behaviour so as to stand in some sharp relief against normative expectations. He did not dress, for instance, as was expected of a senator—as Suetonius mentions, 'they say that he was remarkable in his dress'.[100] There was a loose edge to his toga and he walked in an effeminate manner.[101] Sulla in particular called attention to the famously ill-girt fellow: 'a detail of Caesar's dress was the most apt sign his enemy could invoke to sum up the nature of the threat he posed to political, social and cultural order.'[102]

Our sources do not really give enough encouragement fully to envisage Caesar's self-presentational skills and inclinations at work amid the more exclusive, aristocratic camaraderie of Senate-house and opulent, countryside villas. We can see him as Cicero's guest at a villa in the Bay of Naples at the end of 45, when the food, drink, and conversation were excellent but the talk was of books not of politics, in which ambience 'homines visi sumus'; but Caesar brought a small army with him.[103] We must merely imagine the skills of his youth, when assuredly he must well have been able to know just how, in the company of his peers among the possessing classes, whom to greet in what order of precedence, how to kiss, flatter, and when to listen—all the things that a humane sociology would recognize as 'face-work'.[104] Surely his glance noticed the gold rings or senatorial slippers as they padded suavely across marbled reception rooms, all stuffed with choice fancies of arts and treasures. And he could surely well read and register the smiles of curiosity, disinterest, or distrust.[105] As dictator he perhaps sought to make himself much harder for others to read and certainly his elevated pre-eminence cannot have helped interpretation.

[99] He carried himself to be 'pariter iis terrori venerationique' (Vell. 2. 41. 3).

[100] 'etiam cultu notabilem ferunt' (*DJ* 45. 3; cf. with embellishment Dio 43. 43. 1–4).

[101] Macr. *Sat*. 2. 3. 9.

[102] C. Edwards 1993: 90.

[103] Cic. *Att*. 13. 52. 2.

[104] Goffman e.g. 1959 and 1963.

[105] For the dignities of (semi-) private palaces see Wallace-Hadrill 1988*a*.

The inscrutability of ambitious men complicates oligarchy, and sometimes fatally. The difficulty of reading Pompey's true inclinations was particularly vexing for Cicero, who complains to Atticus about the 'mixed signals' he transmitted, including the *vultus* which in most human interactions is used as evidence to support the veracity of what was being said.[106] In addition, it was always difficult to know whether he wanted something or not.[107] There were normative but vulnerable standards of personal appearance and demeanour as in any society.[108] Cicero also discusses the difficulty of masking his own feelings in order to make his facial expression and general demeanour conform to the demands of particular times and troubles.[109] Oligarchic cohesion can too easily be overestimated. Although a caste of 'two thousand men of property' readily understood itself to be distinct from the humble,[110] there was quite a lot of in-fighting, some of it often quite unpleasant. Clearly, though, there was an escalation of violence in the post-Gracchan *res publica*. When every generation of the notability had known men to murder other members, awkwardness in conforming to the codes of private sincerity made matters fearsomely complicated.

Upon routine and intimate hermeneutics ultimately depended the cohesion of an oligarchy, whose members in their more secluded walks and talks long maintained the 'delicate but necessary balance that would both preserve the exhilaration of personal glory and entrench the dominance of the collective'.[111] Analysis of such coherence requires perhaps

[106] *Att.* 8. 9. 2: 'signa conturbantur quibus voluntas a simulatione distingui posset'. Note how Cicero narrates to Atticus the marital relations between his brother and Atticus' sister (*Att.* 5. 1. 3). Quintus is being sincerely sweet to Pomponia 'idque cum verbis tum etiam animo ac vultu'. Pomponia's feelings are made plain with word and look (ibid. 4): 'sic absurde et aspere verbis vultuque responderat'.

[107] *Q Fr.* 3. 8. 4; Stockton 1971: 152. Cicero even scolds brother Quintus for failure to use successfully, as it were, the semiotics of his mien: *Q Fr.* 3. 1. 23.

[108] e.g. *Off.* 1. 128: 'status incessus, sessio accubitio, vultus oculi manuum motus teneat illud decorum'.

[109] *Att.* 11. 24. 4–5: 'Quod me mones de vultu et oratione ad tempus accommodanda, etsi difficile est, tamen imperarem mihi, si mea quicquam interesse putarem.'

[110] Cic. *Off.* 2. 73.

[111] Gruen 1996: 217.

more emphasis upon 'how the elite were perceived by others' and not so much 'how they perceived themselves' if one wishes to understand 'that deliberate balance between individual ambition and common values' which served 'for four centuries to sustain aristocratic ascendancy'.[112] In dealing with Caesar, Cicero was obviously an anxious student of the signs of his inner dispositions, whether claiming to find hope for Q. Ligarius' restoration,[113] or finding no clear clues about Caesar's thoughts of Mamurra when the big man came in all his imperial power to dinner.[114]

Pompey, and then in turn Caesar, faced the difficulty, in following the protocols of appearance demanded by all the elements of the idiosyncratic republican political system, of acting in a manner appropriate to both popular and elite audiences, as well as to their own sense of exceptional *dignitas*. With regard to Pompey, Cicero could stress (to a *contio*) his accessibility to private citizens ('faciles aditus ad eum privatorum').[115] But habitual pride in *dignitas* befitting the Roman Alexander could not be effaced by *civilitas*. It could also be lodged against Pompey as a fault that 'in a free polity which also ruled the world, while he regarded all citizens equal before the law, he resented to behold anyone his equal in dignity'.[116]

Pompey was not the only one of the later republican *principes* who made much advertisement of what was in effect the kingliness of his position in the world and history. Caesar himself had obviously found much that was attractive about kings (such as Nicomedes IV of Bithynia). Cicero thought both Pompey and Caesar wanted to reign as king.[117] Ancient writers also understood the wish to be the first man in the state and to conquer mightily in far-flung places as essentially individualistic enterprises. And there was all manner of good reason why the motif of Caesar musing sadly upon the precocity of Alexander's deeds should be so prevalent: history, most intuitively and so popu-

[112] Thus *contra* Gruen 1996: 225.

[113] *Fam.* 6. 14. 2. 7.

[114] *Att.* 13. 52. 1: 'tum audivit de Mamurra, vultum non mutavit'.

[115] Cic. *Man.* 41.

[116] Vell. 2. 29. 4: 'in civitate libera dominaque gentium indignari, cum omnes cives iure haberet pares, quemquam aequalem dignitate conspicere'.

[117] *Att.* 8. 11. 2.

larly, has been concerned (as Posidonius influentially urged for a readership that included Pompey and Caesar, Cato and Cicero) with the moral characteristics of great men.

That is not to say that Alexander provided some sort of blueprint for Roman ambitions. There is no evidence to suggest that Caesar might have done anything more than hold Alexander in his consciousness as a model of supreme fame and glory;[118] and, to be sure, Alexander was not a completely happy model for emulation in all respects—Pompey after all attracted derision for his 'sedulous aping' of Alexander.[119] But the singularity of Alexander's memory did forever establish the potential of an individual agent to bring change throughout a wide world. This power forever had become definitively associated, if ever it was not, with a glamorous kingliness. All of Caesar's flirtations with the trimmings and appurtenances of kingliness, including his likeness to gods and his dismissal of diadems, bespoke not only the suspicion of ambition specific to his position in the state after 45 but also a greater readiness on the part of the grand and the glorious to refer to a broader frame of reference for describing their impressive agency. Analogies for individual dignity might best be found in Hellenistic monarchy.

The superiority of Rome was clear in the second century BC but there was no eagerness to adopt the manners of monarchy. The vignette of Popillius Laenas drawing a line in the sand around Antiochus IV of Syria spoke volumes about the significance of Rome's representatives in an ever widening world: 'generals and governors not only administer areas the size of kingdoms, but insist on precedence over the grandest monarchs.'[120] Increasingly, Roman grandees and Hellenistic monarchs, abroad on battlefields or diplomatic parley, in opulent tents and urban palaces, came to seem equivalent, and as much was said in political theory.[121] But although the number of Roman provinces grew steadily and the imperial capital became increasingly preoccupied with all the spectacles of

[118] Green 1978. [119] Plut. *Pomp.* 2. Green 1978: 5.

[120] Polyb. 29. 27; Justin. 34. 3. 2; Rawson 1975: 152.

[121] Kings and Roman nobles were equated by Philodemus (Murray 1965: 178).

ever more expensive ambitions styled in more cosmopolitan fashions, the physical persons of Roman grandees were still projected in much the same guises as of old: 'Roman dynasts were the heirs of the power and resources of the kings but they did not, in fact, adopt their image.'[122] Hellenistic monarchs were much more ready to find a place for themselves—in a scheme of things increasingly overshadowed by Rome—by borrowing from Roman civic and military spectacle.[123] Romans' need to articulate their national distinctiveness which was so superior demanded conspicuous allegiance to the routines and comportments held proper in Rome, and to present images faithful to both *mos maiorum* and the men that necessarily moved among them in civic intimacy. There was particular need to give soldiers money that represented him with uncompromising faithfulness to the man they actually knew: Caesar's coinage at Rome in 44 portrayed him as short, thin-necked, and with the baldness that bothered him badly (and to hide which he was supposedly so keen on honorific wreaths).[124]

Yet clearly Caesar did aim at spectacular appurtenances that could bespeak a truly spectacular presence in history, if only to emulate and surpass a Scipio or a Pompey the Great. And Pompey in particular, in his allusions to Alexander, exemplified how the matrices for rendering and remembering achievement had widened onto a more universal plane of perspective with the incorporation of a Greek cultural tradition receding far into a mythic past. In their willingness to endow their own lives with grand significance and memorability great Romans of the late Republic readily turned to epic allusions: both the solipsistic self-importance of the Homeric models and the value placed upon *kleos* were quite comprehensible and attractive to members of the Roman elite. Thus Cicero, in expressing his disappointment in his political career with a quotation from Homer, offers a revealing notion of what had been the keystone

[122] Smith 1988: 136.

[123] See Ch. 4. Weakness greatly increased adoption of Roman styles of presentation—the portrait on the coinage of Ariobarzanes I Philoromaios is older, true to life and far from divine: Smith 1988: 130.

[124] Smith 1988: 128; the decrepitude is toned down a little on portraits struck at Nicaea and Corinth. Baldness: Suet. *DJ* 45. 2.

upon which his ambition was figured: 'that passion which I had had from boyhood—"to be best by far and to be distinguished above others"—has completely died.'[125] There are numerous references to the *Iliad* in Cicero, and the epic was probably so present in his mind that he did not need to bother to keep a text to hand as he cited.[126] The figures alluded to might have been more obscure to less bookish citizens but there was a general comprehension of prestigious pre-eminence at large in Roman as well as Greek culture, imparted by the theatricalities of both dramatic poetry and the poetics of spectacular politics.[127]

Grand, epic notions of personal prowess, moreover, were universal in ancient history. They were not necessarily unwelcome to an audience of consuming subjects. Homeric heroism had an afterlife in the vainglories of kingly warriors such as Alexander and the Diadochoi as well as Roman *principes*.[128] Big-time pretenders to immortality infiltrated too the consciousnesses of humbler folk, living anonymous lives of work and worry, urbanity and festivity, and so able to imagine glamorous kingliness the most natural way of ordering worldly affairs.[129]

A tendency to privilege individual agency is further to be found in historiography's focus upon the deeds (and sometimes too the morality) of singular men in some global theatre. Ancient writers of history, including Plutarch, easily thought

[125] *Q. Fr.* 3. 6. 4: 'illud vero, quod a puero adamaram, "*πολλὸν ἀριστεύειν καὶ ὑπείροχον ἔμμεναι ἄλλων*" totum occidisse'. The line is an approximation of *Il.* 6. 208 or 11. 784. Now in disillusionment, Cicero claims 'nec honores sitio nec desidero gloriam' (ibid. 3).

[126] Gell. 15. 6. The lines are *Il.* 7. 89–90. Cicero's (now lost) *De Gloria* in particular contained many examples from Homer. Elsewhere, by allusion, he imparts the heroism of Hector preparing to fight Achilles to his plans to resist the alliance of Pompey, Crassus, and Caesar in 60; he is again a Hector in April 59, choosing the glory of rejecting Caesar's offer of legateship to Alexandria, but an Achilles reflecting on Patroclus when contemplating his allegiance to Pompeius in March of 49: *Att.* 2. 3. 3–4 and *Il.* 12. 243; *Att.* 2. 5. 1 and *Il.* 22. 105, 12. 100; *Att.* 9. 5. 3 and *Il.* 18. 94 and 96–7; Wiseman 1985: 10–12.

[127] Cf. Bell 1999.

[128] Even an impressive Carthaginian such as Hamilcar Barca could be represented in Homeric terms (Diod. 24. 5, quoting *Il.* 3. 179).

[129] For example peasants in late antiquity might well have thought the emperor to be Agamemnon: Syn. *Ep.* 148 (Gorzyra).

of great conquerors as athletes. In his comparison of Lucullus and Cimon, Plutarch describes Lucullus throwing kings to the ground—three kings indeed, in succession.[130] Both Pompey and Caesar are also subjected by Plutarch to the athletic comparison.[131] This way of conceiving of military victory of course effaces almost everything else in history—and not least the instruments of the victories, the armies that did all the fighting and dying and killing.[132] Furthermore, besides its emphasis upon individual agency, this sort of trope also reminds us of the pervasive ancient familiarity with competition undertaken before an audience, whether of posterity or contemporaneous, for whom conquests were painstakingly described and represented in triumphal parades and all the assorted richnesses of Roman civic monumentality. History is rendered comprehensible as a competition for popular attention in order to attain charismatic dignity and epic memorability. Thus again the *multitudo*, or for that matter the *dēmos*, becomes for us largely constructed by the discourse of ancient observers and writers as a mass entity whose political business it was to be present to bestow value upon the competition of the chief actors.

Certainly, 'any valid assessment of the Roman Republic' upon which Caesar cast his increasingly grumpy gaze 'must take account of the power of the crowd'. The 'democratic' nature of life in the public spaces of the city was founded upon the 'vital necessity of visibility'.[133] But it is difficult precisely to diagnose both subtleties of popular sentiment and its power over its would-be orchestrators and reciprocal specta-

[130] Plut. *Comp. Luc. & Cim.* 2; *Luc.* 30. Soldiers are compared by Appian to athletes: *BC* 5. 37. Polybius provides an image of war as an athletic event: Polyb. 1. 57. 1, 27. 9. 2, 39. 1. 8 (*pancration*).

[131] *Pomp.* 8 and 53. The application of this metaphor to Pompey is not confined to Plutarch: Diodorus, for instance (38/39. 9), also draws it in discussing his self-discipline: *διὰ δὲ τῆϲ ϲυνήθουϲ τῶν ἀπίϲτων μελέτηϲ ἀθλητὴϲ ἐγένετο τῶν κατὰ πόλεμον ἀγώνων.*

[132] Plutarch was not blind, however, to the bloodier business of war. Witness his Homeric description of the death of the Caesarian centurion Crassianus (*Pomp.* 71) who predicted victory at Pharsalus: he forced his way through the front rank of the Pompeian legions until a soldier stood up to him 'and drove his sword into his mouth with such force that its point came out at the back of his neck'.

[133] Millar 1998: 224–5.

tors. Neither political actors nor their spectators can have been wholly certain of the relationship themselves. Such uncertainty constantly encouraged experimentation. When rivals are ready and able to pounce with public rebuke, individual actors are less likely to depart from remembered precedents of visible comportment and ceremony of self. Surrounded by friends and flunkies, notable enemies dead or silent, Caesar would no longer suffer severe constraint. His determined exploration of an acceptable charisma could become bizarrely bold, constituting a truly exciting *poiēsis* of power in familiar spaces in unusual times.

Fundamentally unclear, however, is how coherently admiration and approbation founded upon the more intense emotional complicities uniting protagonist and audience at festive occasions could be translated into lasting legitimacy for his position. Response to spectacular individuals is nothing if not situational. The big man whose charisma seemed both attractive and quite natural in the eyes of many on occasions when the gods were assumed to be looking down upon the whole communal affair might seem to loom threateningly large in more mundane circumstances. This consideration is borne out by the long and epic history of vigorous competition for pre-eminence, and not least in the *polis* of the Athenians, where the presence of other ambitious men and frequently suspicious citizens made sure that really heroic effort was necessary in the competition to become an accepted object of wonderment. Victories, however, were all the more valuable since democracy gave to citizens the power of sovereign judgement, the likes of which Romans after Caesar would cease to enjoy, if ever they really had. But even in the ideological and affective environment of democratic, civilly egalitarian, classical Athens individuals of 'extreme self-regard' were sometimes able to exploit the 'monarchical dreams' of more circumspect political consumers.[134]

[134] Gribble 1999: 2; Wohl 1996: 32.

# 3
# The Affections of the Athenians

ὥσπερ σκοπὴν τῆς οἰκουμένης, ταχὺ τῇ δόξῃ διαπυρσεύειν εἰς ἅπαντας ἀνθρώπους τὰς πράξεις.

Athens, as a beacon of the world, would quickly blaze their actions out to all men with distinction.

Plutarch, *Demetrius* 8

Pericles the Athenian has enjoyed an immortal reputation as the emblematic personification of the most glorious age of his *polis*. Given the authority which he is reported to have exercised in a democracy and which he reinforced by cultivation of his political celebrity, this is only fair. So the man nicknamed 'the Olympian' by his peers can be remembered walking in public only along the street that took him directly to the Agora and to the Boule. He avoided the belittlements of mundanity. He declined invitations to dinner-parties. He spoke in the Assembly but only on great issues.[1] The aloofness of his public image also threw into sharper relief his perennial significance in the Assembly, the democracy's central institution of evaluation of a man's persuasive authority. He is a grand example of a man 'first in wealth and breeding' who, finding his own style of articulating his civic standing, became a 'champion (*prostatēs*) of the people (*dēmos*)'.[2] Other Athenians of ambition (*philotimia*) who also had treasure, notable forefathers, and 'extreme

[1] Ar. *Ach.* 530. Plut. *Per.* 7: he resembled, thought Critolaus, the Salaminian trireme, reserved by the *polis* for great missions and emergencies.

[2] Eupolis Fr. 103; cf. Fr. 205; Connor 1971: 76. 'It is money that creates friends and honors for men . . . and makes an ugly man handsome and an ill-spoken one a good speaker . . .' (Sophocles Fr. 88). The *Ath. Pol.* cites these as 5th-cent. *prostatai*: Solon (2. 3), Cleisthenes (20. 4), Hipparchus in 488/7 (22. 4), Aristeides (23. 3), Themistocles (23. 3), Ephialtes (25. 1), Cimon (26.

self-regard'[3] aplenty found all manner of ways to satisfy their desire to make themselves 'well thought of and . . . admired' in the democratic *polis*.[4] The ability to impress fellow citizens favourably conferred prestige (*timē*); and prestige was a necessary condition for possession of power (*dynamis*).[5] The conspicuous behaviours of prestigious individuals speak volumes about the complexity of political sentiments and dynamics in democratic Athens.

The business of the Athenian Assembly itself can fairly be said to have 'reproduced and ritualised an image of the Athenian polis'.[6] A few were watched and heard and evaluated by many; aristocrats could there become intimately scrutinized celebrities. The Assembly, therefore, effectively realized a chasm of sociopolitical significance separating a majority of Athenians, probably too shy to heed the herald's invitation to step forward and speak to a crowd, from a minority who stepped up to the Bema before the crowd of notional peers.[7] Athens did not exactly provide the 'face-to-face' communications of the preindustrial villages that intrigued Finley;[8] Thucydides remarked (8. 66. 3) that many members of the Athenian *dēmos* were unknown to one another. But the faces of a few 'famous rich men who appeared in public' were readily recognizable.[9]

1), Pericles (28. 1), Theramenes (34. 3, 36. 1). Undoubtedly, famous faces (such as Myronides or Tolmides, the big men before Pericles' ascendancy) have effectively been lost from history.

3 Gribble 1999: 2.

4 Xen. *Mem.* 3. 6 re Glaucon who risks ridicule (according to Socrates) in wanting προστατεύειν . . . τῆς πόλεως.

5 Cf. Plato *Alc. I* 105b. Wealth was most valuable politically in its expenditure rather than its accumulation: e.g. Gorgias 82 B 20 (Diels) re Cimon; Sinclair 1988: 186.

6 Strauss 1985: 73; for an illuminating theoretical examination of effects of ritualized practices see C. Bell 1992: 197–223.

7 The term *prostatēs* (etymologically, 'he who stands forth') readily denoted a physical distinctiveness: cf. Pope 1988: 284.

8 Finley 1973: 17–18; Shaw 1991: n. 24.

9 Ober 1989*a*: 206. The most useful political revelation of the texts of late 5th-cent. Attic comedy is the obvious one that comedic cartoonish lampooning, such as emphasis upon the shape of Pericles' big head, was readily comprehensible to the audience: cf. Dover 1972: 33–4. With great determination and ingenuity Vickers (e.g. 1989*a* and 1989*b*) finds massive and systematic allusion to contemporary figures in Aristophanes' characters.

Rhetors were seen as well as heard and thus judged through keen attention to the aesthetics of voice, gesture, delivery, and other aspects of their comportment.[10] Curiosity about the dynamics of democracy, therefore, requires consideration of practical situations eliciting mutual engagement, aesthetically and emotionally, between politicians and their audiences. But occasions for self-presentation remote from the Assembly should also be considered.

There sometimes is voiced a sincere (and somewhat valiant) desire on the part of modern analysts of Athenian democracy to use it as 'an important tool for rethinking contemporary political dilemmas'.[11] It may well then be useful to consider how politicians acquire the significance which also affects the persuasiveness of the policies they espouse.[12] Wherever the sentiments of humbler citizens are acknowledged by those of greater consequence to bestow legitimate authority, 'every successful politician knows intuitively' that 'political experience, skill, and result often involve conventions of persuasive composition that depend on aesthetic reactions'.[13] Some Athenians, like Pericles, were particularly crafty about how they exposed themselves to the 'forest of eyes' as soon as they went out of their houses.[14] Contemporary experience can confirm for us the sense that

[10] Cleon, most conspicuously, 'was the first man upon the *bēma* to shout and be abusive and make speeches with his clothes hitched up, while everybody else spoke in an orderly fashion' (*Ath. Pol.* 28. 3). There is a whole range of testimony to men remembered in antiquity for loud voices and cloaks girt up: Theopompus *FGrHist* 115 F 92; Plut. *Nic.* 8, *Tib. Grac.* 2; Cic. *Brut.* 28. Other Athenians perhaps made vivid impressions for different reasons, even if not upon the historical record, except for the nicknames bestowed by comedians which often became proverbial; recollection of Hyperbolus, Peisander, or Paches provided a matrix of humorous connotations in defining and describing later men and their idiosyncrasies; 4th-cent. litigants after all were apparently 'celebrities' (Ober 1996: 95). Generally 'spectatorship provides an affective education' attuning individuals 'to a collective dramatization of status relationships' (Gleason 1995: xxiii).

[11] Ober and Hedrick 1996: 3.

[12] Bourdieu (1975: esp. 185) describes the general phenomenon of the persuasiveness of the speaker behind the words; this I hold to be largely a truism.

[13] Hariman 1995: 3. 'To be in an audience was . . . a fundamental political act' (Goldhill 1999: 5).

[14] Davidson 1997: 219.

politics are meaningful to participants in concrete ways dependent upon subjective experiences.[15] Whether or not we shall actually solve any dilemmas, we need to imagine Athenian citizens consuming much more than the stodgy diet of political discourse that too often feeds contemporary political analysis. Nobody would deny that it is important to pay heed to democracy's institutional infrastructure.[16] But even in the functioning of any institution of governance (and not just those of non-bureaucratic societies) there will invariably be a whole micro-politics of ritualized roles. Power relations at Athens played out in other social interactions besides the histrionics of Assembly, or courtroom, or council-chamber.[17] Athenians 'did much better' than historians who have 'painstakingly described the achievement' of democracy, for 'they lived it'.[18] Citizens devoted more of their lives to hanging out in places beyond the Assembly, socializing happily rather than cherishing the canting of political speeches.[19]

Ambitious Athenian aristocrats found or manufactured situations in which their personal advertisements could solicit admiring approval from the sovereign *dēmos*. Although the impressions made at other ritualized social occasions could not have been excluded from the institutional processes of democratic decision-making, even the best analyses of the ideological environment of Athens have a tendency to ignore practices such as those that fall into the (ever so tricky) category of 'religion'.[20]

[15] Modern American political campaigns apparently still operate upon the assumption 'that it is virtually impossible for an ordinary citizen (as opposed to an activist) to vote against a candidate whom he or she has talked to in person' (Hart 1987: 45); most ordinary citizens, of course, primarily watch television.

[16] Hansen has remarked (1989: 109) that 'never before or since in world history has such an elaborate network of political institutions been created and developed in order to run a very small and fairly simple society'. There has never been, however, a society which was simple for its members.

[17] Cf. Goldhill 1998.

[18] Shaw 1991: 194.

[19] Cf. Lane Fox 1996: 120–1 on the general importance of social pleasures.

[20] There is scant attention in Ober 1989*a*, which (with regard to the 4th cent.) emphasizes the texts of political oratory as bespeaking a basic hegemony of democratic assumptions; but, some attention (152–5) to theatre notwithstanding, ignores other forms of discursive practice that also articulated and

Athenians were notorious for the number of their festivals;[21] and festivities centred upon sacrifice were fundamental to Greek notions of sociability.[22] To preside over such a happy occasion was to stand charismatically between a community and its gods, and in a long tradition of ritualized pre-eminence. The Athenians, however, did their best to deprive political leaders of the sacrificial knife. Democrats were suspicious of such ritualized importance.

It was potentially dangerous to appear to put oneself either above the ordinary or above the collective identity of the *polis*. Ostracism for instance threatened those who seemed to loom too large; and accusations of pretension to tyranny might readily fly—unsurprisingly Pericles was himself compared to a tyrant.[23] Tyrants generally, in standing in an exceptional relationship to their *polis*, were liable to accusations of *hybris*, obvious disrespect of citizen dignity.[24] Great individual pre-eminence encouraged the sentiment that 'the rich were much too powerful and that their power was both an affront to egalitarian ideals and a very real threat' to the Athenians' democracy in any period.[25] Ambitious Athenians for the most

established relations of power (cf. the succinct scepticism of C. Patterson (1992: 110)). While I am not so confident that a court is a synecdoche for a city, Ober's diagnosis of egalitarianism is obviously right.

[21] [Xen.] *Ath. Pol.* 3. 8; Thuc. 2. 38. 1; Parker 1996: 127–9; Connor (1996: 217) shows a keen awareness of political priorities. More splendid festivity tops Xenophon's list (*Por.* 6. 1) of the benefits better revenues would bring to the Athenians.

[22] Greek children, opined Plato (*Leg.* 803c), were to be shaped at an early age by playing games of sacrifice, song, and dance, although one expects they played so anyway.

[23] Cratinus Fr. 258 (Kaiber and Austin); Plut. *Per.* 3 and 16. He looked like Peisistratus, to whom he was related: Plut. *Per.* 7 (which might, interestingly enough, suggest that Peisistratid statues were still present in Athens somewhere).

[24] Thuc. 6. 57. 3; Dem. 21. 170; Arist. *Pol.* 1312$^{b}$ 30; Seager 1967: 7. The outrageousness could of course be quickly apprehended in aesthetic terms, as satirized by Aristophanes' image of 'tyrannic' consumption in the fish-market: *V.* 493–5, with Davidson 1993: 53–4.

[25] Ober 1989*a*: 220. Aristotle (*Pol.* 1284$^{a}$17 f.) says that democracies seem to seek equality (ἰσότης) and so ostracize those who seem to be 'exceptionally powerful because of wealth or abundance of friends or some other political strength' (ὑπερέχειν δυνάμει διὰ πλοῦτον ἢ πολυφιλίαν ἤ τινα ἄλλην πολιτικὴν ἰσχὺν . . .).

part deferred to the circumspect sensibilities of their fellow citizens, most of whose lives were of greater obscurity and scant glamour but all of whose votes counted just as much as the rich man's. The accommodation of aristocracy to democratic protocols of prestige is one of the most salient features of the history of Athenian politics.

Democratic ideology, however, did not always correlate neatly with some of the most enjoyable and meaningful of habitual social practices. Given the 'undeniably daunting' quantity of scholarship which the democracy continues to generate and the 'querulous urgency' with which its principal characteristics are debated, the essential diversity of Athenians' ideas and sensibilities speaks for itself.[26] Aristocratic notions never disappeared from democracy and never could be completely subjugated by its ideology.[27] And even though to live large was not without its dangers, fondness for a stylish pre-eminence, redolent of all the graces of mythic kingliness, encouraged ambitious evocations of epic charisma. In looking for 'champions of the demos', Athenians of more modest means and pretensions might be excited to behold embodiments and dramatizations of a 'sense of beauty or a dazzling perception of power'.[28] Although demographic details of this politics, at once phenomenological and ideological, are lost to the ugly obscurity in which more humble Athenians will always dwell, suffice it to say that a few were able to engineer wonderment—it was perhaps always axiomatic that aristocrats, the 'good and beautiful' (*kaloi k'agathoi*) held sway (*kratos*) in this *polis*.[29] As reward for successful negotiation of demotic longings as well as loathings big men earned power over the sensible affections of free citizens, who were proudly conscious of their prestigious power to choose their own heroes.

[26] Kallet-Marx 1994: 307; Shaw 1991: 194.

[27] Cf. Griffith 1995: 109. Loraux 1986 finds fields of aristocratic hegemony persisting in democratic discourse.

[28] Geertz 1973: 90 and 109.

[29] Plato *Alc.* 1. 104a. Alcibiades considers his personal beauty to be impressive; cf. 1. 119c and 123e. *Kratos*: e.g. Xen. *Mem.* 2. 6. 26.

## HOMERIC POWER

Homeric epic had consequence in Greek history. It presented monumental images and timeless truths to all Greeks. And, like any great work whose canonization needs little epistemological or pedagogical conspiracy, Homer speaks to many aspects of humanity, both engaging subjective sensibility and informing cultural attitudes. Not all in a society will have the same responses but at least they will all potentially be thinking about the same questions. Fundamentally both the *Iliad* and the *Odyssey* demand critical reflection upon the relationship of self-assertive individuals to a community. More specifically, kingship is put under massive scrutiny: Homeric epic is packed with reference to big-men, to *basileis*.[30] And Homer long continued to provide paradigmatic representation of entitlement to pre-eminent prestige and authority.[31] The superiority of his heroes fascinates because it is both spectacular and invariably aware of how it will be viewed by an audience.[32] *Timē* cannot properly exist without collective bestowal and confirmation.

Within the text, heroes face from time to time a formal body of collective judgement. The epics are 'filled with assemblies and discussions'.[33] *Basileis* were expected to stand forth and show themselves to be fine speakers of words as well as fearsome doers of big deeds.[34] Achilles makes his case (in the first book of the *Iliad*) to an assembly of Greeks, many of whom must suffer and die when his logic of selfhood requires practical demonstration in his sulking withdrawal from battle. The assembly consists of all the Greeks camped at Troy but lowly types do not usually speak. Thersites receives a right royal thrashing from

[30] Cairns (1989: 3) counts 'literal' references to kingship in Homer: the *Iliad* has 15,693 lines and 287 kingship references, the *Odyssey* 12,110 and 194. Quiller (1981) discusses the application of Sahlins's concept of 'big-man' to Homeric society.

[31] A Socratic discussion of kingship refers explicitly to the Homeric model, quoting the description of Agamemnon as shepherd of the host (Xen. *Mem*. 3. 2). Socrates is, unsurprisingly, concerned too with arguing that kings should have knowledge: ibid. 3. 9. 10. On Homer as the basis for reflection upon the nature of Hellenistic kingship see Murray 1965; cf. Cairns 1989: *passim*.

[32] Redfield 1984: 13. [33] Finley 1978: 82.

[34] Deeds: *Il*. 9. 443; cf. 2. 273, 18. 105–6, 252. Glory: 1. 490; cf. M. Edwards 1987: 165.

Odysseus for his attempt to make points very much like those received quite differently when voiced by Achilles.[35] If baser men have a voice in the *Iliad* it is not as individuals formally voting but as a collective entity roaring together.[36]

Historical audiences prized Homeric epic so highly that they made it not only prestigious narrative but also authoritatively true and useful knowledge. In the fifth century in Athens' diplomatic arguments from precedent, Homer was the authority used in settling crucial diplomatic negotiations over pan-Hellenic leadership.[37] Plato poured scorn upon acceptance of Homer as true knowledge—and felt that he needed to, seeing rhapsodes in his *polis* and probably knowing all too personally the centrality of the poems in elite pedagogy. Yet, centuries later, the geographical writer Strabo still felt more than justified in mounting a dogged defence of the validity of Homer's information about his wider Mediterranean world.[38]

Homeric representations were fully accessible and legible to all Athenians regardless of literacy. Greeks were healthily preoccupied with the singing of their favourite stories, and so familiarity with epic poems was by no means confined to a privileged elite.[39] They were appreciated by anybody with the time and patience to hearken to the rhapsodes and state-sponsored recitations.[40] Alcibiades is described as knowing the texts precisely because he had heard them, although he and other boys who had fathers and families able to pay for schooling thereby also had access to the epics in textual form. They were expected to know the poetry by heart.[41] While it is

[35] Thersites might in fact be a nobleman: Edwards 1987: 165. It is nonetheless important that he is represented as ugly of bodily appearance: both the poet and Odysseus uphold the persistent ideological equation between *aretē* and beauty.

[36] 19. 42–5.

[37] Hdt. 7. 161. On Homer's pan-Hellenic authority see esp. Hdt. 2. 53 and 116–17; cf. Nagy 1990: *passim*. Even into the Hellenistic period *poleis* used Homer in support of their claims: Harding 1994: 47.

[38] Plato *Ion* 540d and *passim*; see in particular the first book of Strabo.

[39] As conveniently documented now by Buxton 1994: 21–31.

[40] Recitations were thought to have been established in the 6th cent.: Diog. Laert. 1. 57; [Plato] *Hipparch*. 228c; Davison 1958: 23–4.

[41] Plato *Alc*. 1. 112b. Xenophon presents (*Symp*. 3. 5) Niceratus claiming to be able, at his father's insistence, to know the whole of the *Iliad* and the

difficult to imagine exactly the impression such education made upon plastic male consciousnesses, Plato's/Socrates' worries about the effects of soulful miming of epic characterizations were probably not narrowly or arcanely academic.[42] Plato might easily have been in a very small minority in finding poetry politically dangerous (and essentially a matter of democratic aesthetics) but, since the metaphysical underpinnings of his objections fall away at the end of his ruminations, his attitude is probably symptomatic of a broader realization of the pedagogical effects of close acquaintance with Homeric representations. Homeric heroes were, simply, the most compelling available model of spectacular masculine action. And they seemed real.[43]

At Athens, tragedy (and particularly that of Sophocles) had continued to present characters who did big things by virtue of their unrelenting egoism: much Athenian drama was rightly fixated upon the difficulties of accommodating the heroic individual to the co-operative values of the *polis*.[44] Indeed, Plato depicts Socrates at his trial casting himself in heroic guise, making comparison to Heracles and to Achilles.[45] It is interesting that Xenophon glosses (*Mem.* 1. 2. 14) the ambitions of two (youngish) Athenian aristocrats of the later fifth century, Alcibiades and Critias, by pointedly using an archaizing dual inflection: 'these two men were by nature the most ambitious of all the Athenians, wanting everything to be done through themselves as well as becoming the best known names of all.'[46] Many

*Odyssey*; likewise Euthydemus is reputed ἔπη πάντα κεκτῆσθαι (*Mem.* 4. 2. 10). Alcibiades castigated teachers who did not treat the texts with due respect: Plut. *Alc.* 7. One of them possessed no copy of Homer and another presumed to be competent to edit the texts himself. Cf. Plut. *Mor.* 186e and Ael. *VH* 13. 38. The numbers of Homeric papyri suggest that 'if any Greek owned any books—that is, papyrus rolls—he was almost as likely to own the *Iliad* and *Odyssey* as anything from the rest of Greek literature' (Finley 1978: 21).

[42] Esp. Plato *Rep.* 395–8.

[43] (Provocatively) Nagy 1996: 61: 'a Homeric narration or a Homeric quotation of a god or hero speaking within a narration are not at all representations: they are the real thing.'

[44] Knox 1964.

[45] Plato *Apol.* 22a and 28b–d.

[46] Of Alcibiades it was said (by a Spartan at Plut. *Alc.* 23), 'no son of Achilles he, but Achilles himself'.

fifth-century Athenians seem to have 'cherished elitist, heroizing symbolism'.[47] A few believed they embodied it.

Homer disseminated a ready set of associations for understanding powerful (and thus problematic) individuals and their struggles to obtain prestigious accommodation within even a democratic *polis*. Heroically headstrong in their desire for *timē* Xenophon's pair may have been but such vaunting ambition nevertheless had also 'to be filtered through the explicitly coded egalitarianism' of Athenian democracy.[48] Yet on occasion, in some measure because the imagery of epic was so capable in infiltrating Greek sensibilities and fancies, crowds did stare in wonder at those 'first in wealth and breeding' who represented a pre-eminence that was fleeting but practically heroic. At the least, Homeric epic's authoritative demonstration of the clashing valuations placed upon civic health and upon an individual's obsession with his honour must have helped (if humanity has ever actually needed such help) to perpetuate critical appreciation for the dramas of rich and pedigreed celebrities.

Any audience for Homer in the classical period would have no difficulty, moreover, in assuming the existence of cultural continuity extending from Achilles to Alcibiades (and far beyond). Neither the communal habits of the Greeks gathered in the *Iliad* nor the competitive concerns of big-men had changed any more radically than had the landscape itself and the rhythms and aches of its farming. The humble verities of humanity acknowledged in poetic simile did not become anachronistic with the passing of generations. The figures of gods and heroes coined by Homer surely inhabited the physical and intellectual landscape of the ancient Greek world: they lurked in shrines; and Homeric gods and ghosts were to be seen in dreams.[49] Nor for that matter did warfare in the mythic

[47] Morris 1994: 79 who also properly uses Homer as paradigmatic for rich Athenians, arguing (unconvincingly from funerary fashions) that Athens was more egalitarian in the 5th than in the 4th cent. Morris too observes (1996: 32) that 'lavish display [had] made the aristocracy something more than human'.

[48] Whitehead 1983: 60, describing 4th-cent. Athens.

[49] On the continuity of cultural presence of the Homeric representations of the gods right through into later antiquity, see conveniently Lane Fox 1989: ch. 4.

past seem much different from later realities of equal grimness.[50] And, of course, everything was watched over by the same gods who lived on and on, all the while expecting and receiving their dues of *timē* in traditional fashion.[51] The practices, described in Homer, for properly managing the community's relations with the gods were substantially the same as those of later generations of Greek consumers of Homeric representations.

Sacrifice, the principal business of acknowledging and involving divinity in the drama of social significance, had hardly changed in respect of specific procedure nor, presumably, the various pleasures and affects of participation.[52] The whole of sacrificial procedure, with the exception of rites of purification or soliciting signs of divine favour, 'was highly visual and dramatic' and performed before an audience whose spectatorship of ritual 'was a prime component in participation'.[53] The main elements in sacrifice in historical times were a procession, in which the victims were brought before the altar and before the presence of the gathered community; subsequent were the prayers, libations, the offering of grain or cakes, the slaughter, and then the barbecuing of specific entrails, and the division of the carcass. Sacrifices in Homer contain all these features.[54]

In Homer, moreover, truly kingly men are charismatically centre-stage in such ceremony. It was the 'whole nexus of a man's powers and prerogatives that marked him as the communal priest'.[55] Audiences can, their imaginations fed by Homer's description, readily envision Agamemnon standing preeminently before the congregation, taking obvious charge of all the praying and killing and cosmic gift-giving, since they

[50] Polybius, for example, easily understood Homeric battle in terms of the hoplite phalanx: 18. 29. 6 (referring to *Il.* 13. 131–3), astutely noted by Raaflaub 1996: 151.

[51] Lane Fox (1989: 103–10) well describes the persistence of the Homeric representations of the gods even into late antiquity.

[52] Burkert 1983: 3.

[53] Jameson 1999: 322–3.

[54] The fullest descriptions of sacrifice occur in the *Iliad* at 1. 447–68 (Chryses' invocation of Apollo), in the *Odyssey* at 3. 430–63 (Nestor's elaborate sacrifice on the sea-shore near Pylos).

[55] Thomas 1965: 98 albeit extrapolating from Homer.

are offered formulaic glimpses of what the king wears as the tools and tokens of his powers and prerogatives. Next to the scabbard of his sword is an ever-present knife with which he performs the rites of sacrifice:

> *῾Ατρείδης δὲ ἐρυσσάμενος χείρεσσι μάχαιραν.*
> *ἥοί πὰρ ξίφεος μέγα κουλεὸν αἰὲν ἄωρτο,*
> *ἀρνῶν ἐκ κεφαλέων τάμνε τρίχας αὐτὰρ ἔΠειτα*
> *κήρυκες Τρῴων καὶ ῾Αχαιῶν νεῖμαν ἀρίστοις.*
> *τοῖσιν δ῾ ᾿Ατρείδης μεγάλ῾εὔχετοχεῖρας ἀνασχών·*
>
> Atreus' son drew forth the dagger always slung
> at his battle-sword's big sheath, cut some tufts
> from lambs' heads, and heralds passed them around
> to Achaean and Trojan captains. Then Atreus' son
> Agamemnon stood in behalf of all, lifted his arms
> and prayed in his deep resounding voice, 'Father Zeus!'[56]

The presence of the knife iconographically marks Agamemnon as the figure in charge of the sacrifice, just as a knife normally indicates that its bearer is a priest, or keys (to a temple) indicate a priestess in painting or sculpture.[57] He also wields a god-given sceptre.[58]

Agamemnon's authority in religious matters is never challenged. Obviously 'the workings of the authority-system' are so much disputed in the *Iliad* that the whole plot of the epic is driven by Achilles' raging challenge to Agamemnon's prestige.[59] Ceremonial charisma reinforces Agamemnon's other claims to superiority. When he sacrifices and prays to Zeus, 'the armies held fast to their seats in silence, | all by rank and file, listening to their king'.[60]

[56] *Il.* 3. 271–5 trans. R. Fagles. Cf. 19. 249–54.

[57] Marinatos 1988.

[58] Thalmann (1988) elegantly over-analyses the ideological complexity of the Thersites episode, where Agamemnon's position is challenged by a base man (2. 211–77) whom ultimately Odysseus strikes down with a godly (2. 103) sceptre; comparison with such Near Eastern symbols of divinely ordained authority (Griffin 1980: 10 and n. 25) perhaps militates against Thalmann's perspective.

[59] Donlan 1979: 51.

[60] *Il.* 19. 255–6 trans. R. Fagles (*εὔχετο· τοὶ δ῾ ἄρα πάντες ἐπ῾αὐτόφιν ἥατο σιγῇ|῾Αργεῖοι κατὰ μοῖραν, ἀκούοντες βασιλῆος|εὐξάμενος δ῾ ἄρα εἶπεν ἰδν εἰς οὐρανὸν εὐρύν·*)

The number of ships and the allegiance of serried ranks of warriors,[61] stores of well-wrought treasure, personnel aplenty in palaces, and guest-friends all over their world amounted to a power to which it was difficult or even simply unthinkable to deny deference. These resources generate *timē*, whereas Achilles' claims rest ultimately upon his athletic efficacy in battle. Achilles' challenge reveals that Agamemnon's power does not reside inherently in his person but rather in the things that he does, and is seen to do; thus, sacrificing is an activity that defines and contributes to his power whilst being undertaken precisely because of his powerful position. There can be an attractive, affectively swirling, circularity to power—which operated not only on the subordinates within the narrative of the story but also on audiences given concrete detail with which to flesh out their own imaginative portraitures. Like all Greeks, Athenians could presume Agamemnon and all his qualifications for leadership worthy of prestige and respect, and yet also find Achilles and all his murderous and efficacious and glamorous manliness wholly impressive. And Achilles too will have his authoritative moments in the ceremonial spotlight, when he presides over the community at the funeral games in honour of Patroclus in Book 23, and when there he takes careful charge of the sacrificing. Ritualizations both connote and construct prestige.

Indeed, before we consider the complexity of the refraction of this image into the history of Athenian political life, it is worth dwelling upon how in other classical Greek polities the happier and more affecting ceremonies of spectacular pre-eminence continued to be performed by kingly men as appurtenances and reinforcement of other instrumentalities of their power. Monarchs and tyrants alike exercised heroic authority in ritual congregations.

The comportment and the prestige of Spartan kings was truly kingly in epic style, obvious to both Spartans and other Greeks who witnessed them.[62] After all, Menelaus himself lived on in

[61] Cf. Thuc. 1. 9. On Homeric 'status warriors' in general see Van Wees 1992.

[62] Xen. *Lac. Pol.* 15. 9. Cartledge 1987: 339 remarks that 'it is tempting to . . . find the immediate inspiration for the heroic conception of Spartan kingship in Homer'. The applicability and relevance of Homer extended to

heroic immortality in Spartan cult.[63] Spartan citizens, moreover, were above all else warriors who keenly used Homer as a guiding paradigm for their sense of identity: while Hesiod might be the poet of the helots, Homer was very certainly the poet of the Lacedaemonians.[64] Their two kings were to be seen doing all sorts of authoritative things.[65] Herodotus (6. 56–7) recounts their prerogatives, detailing priesthoods, the right to wage war, an official entourage, and sacrificial perquisites. At all public sacrifices, they were the first to take their seats, pour libations, and be served their double portions. Upon the battlefield—and in matters concerning the gods too—their instructions traditionally were final.[66] It is not surprising that ephors, always seeking to gain in power at the expense of the kings, sought to encroach upon religious prerogatives, successfully arrogating to themselves responsibilities such as the rite of star-gazing.[67]

Much of a Macedonian king's authority also rested upon the pre-eminence he was seen to perform.[68] Unsurprisingly, Macedonian kings too were conspicuously and practically comprehensible in Homeric terms.[69] This is particularly evident in

the perceived persistence of connections to other characters in the *Iliad*: thus Spartan heralds were Talthybiadai, and their eponymous heroic ancestor possessed a shrine at Sparta: Hdt. 7. 134. 1; Paus. 3. 12. 7.

[63] In the (8th-cent.?) lifetimes of Theopompus and Polydoros a shrine was erected for him: Cartledge 1987: 339.

[64] According to Cleomenes I: Plut. *Mor.* 223a.

[65] Spartans were sophisticated in their use of visual effect: Powell 1989: 179–89.

[66] Arist. *Pol.* $1285^{a-b}$ and $1258^{a}6$: *τὰ πρὸς τοὺς θεοὺς ἀποδέδοται τοῖς βασιλεῦσιν*. One of the ordinances attributed to Lycurgus specifically concerned the religious role of a king, that he should sacrifice on behalf of the *polis* (Xen. *Lac. Pol.* 15. 2: *ἔθηκε γὰρ θύειν μὲν βασιλέαπρὸ τῆς πόλεως* . . .).

[67] A. Toynbee 1969: 242.

[68] Cf. esp. Samuel 1988.

[69] To such an extent that references to the epics were explicitly used for describing the king: for Philip as Agamemnon, see e.g. Diod. 5. 87. 2, where Philip, drunk at a *κῶμος*, is jeering at Greek captives; a certain Demades (but in Philostratus *Vit. Ap. Ty.* 7. 2 a Diogenes of Sinope) rebukes the king for playing the part of Thersites, not Agamemnon. Isocrates in his *Philip* urges Philip to lead a pan-Hellenic expedition against Persia in the manner of an Agamemnon or Agesilaos but avoids mention of the Homeric king, which is hardly surprising as Agamemnon's characteristics preclude easy

the way in which they routinely took charge of sacrifice.[70] In the subsequent feasting, moreover, they distributed portions of meat as tokens of *timē* to their friends and companions by whose side they fought. It is unwise to construct some supposed rubrics governing the powers of Macedonian monarchs, whose authority was restricted only situationally: 'the king could do

translation to panegyric compared with Heracles (109–12) or Jason (119–20). The mention in the *Panathenaicus* (72 and 74) of Agamemnon might seem to suggest a comparison to Philip (see e.g. Blass 1962: 331 and 334) but it is not explicit. Famously, Alexander the Great actually slept with a copy of the *Iliad* beneath his pillow (next to his dagger), and seems to have thought of himself as an Achilles: Lane Fox 1974: 59–67.

[70] The parallel emerges most clearly in a passage of Diodorus (5. 86. 6): after a successful battle Philip 'celebrated the victory with sacrifices and duly honoured the brave'. But unlike the case of the Homeric *basileus* who was far from home, the sacrifices offered by Spartan or Macedonian monarchs were regular and prescribed by custom: e.g. Arr. *Anals*. 7. 24. 4; 7. 25. 6. Campaigning, however, entailed inability to perform the sacrifices at home, for which deputies had to be appointed. Philip II left the 16-year-old Alexander in charge to carry out the royal duties in Macedonia: Plut. *Alex*. 9. There was a range of festivals to organize and conduct, including that in honour of Heracles Patroüs, the ancestor of the royal house, at Aegeae and at Pella, and a nine-day festival for Olympian Zeus and the Muses at Dium: Hammond 1989: 23. Not surprisingly such delegated superintendence was a mark of honour, for these sacrificial occasions were held before a wide audience, and the delegator seems to have been careful to avoid leaving one man in charge of the full range of kingly activities and, thereby, in a position from which he could attain to full kingly power: Hammond 1985: 156–60 details how first Olympias and then Craterus were left in charge by Alexander of civil duties in Macedonia 'of which the most important were the religious duties'. Antipater controlled only military matters. Both Alexander and Spartan kings began each day with a sacrifice: Plut. *Alex*. 23. 3; Xen. *Lac. Pol*. 13. 3. When abroad a king assiduously offered sacrifice before every undertaking such as crossing a river or launching a campaign and determined, in consultation with the appropriate experts, the necessary sacrifices, as is particularly clear during Alexander's conquests (Hammond 1989: 22–3; examples at n. 33). This responsibility is especially striking when Alexander even quit his sickbed in order to discharge his responsibility for maintaining relations with the gods: Plut. *Alex*. 75; Arr. *Anals*. 7. 24. 4 ff.; Ael. *VH* 3. 23. Often the recipient was a foreign deity—e.g. in Egypt, Apis and other gods; or in Babylon Alexander carries out the sacrifices suggested by the Chaldaeans, especially to Bel: Arr. *Anals*. 3. 1. 4, 3. 16. 4. For a convenient (if not exhaustive) list of Alexander's sacrifices see Samuel 1983: 77 n. 36; cf. Agamemnon deciding (*Il*. 2. 308 ff.) upon the appropriate sacrifices to appease Apollo.

exactly what he could get away with.'[71] Ceremonial performance together with its legitimation by an epic paradigm was of value to even homicidally self-aggrandizing Macedonian kings. In time we shall see the ways in which Macedonian kingliness was articulated, once they had conquered and needed to impress a much wider world.

It might also be noted that tyrants (on a less cosmopolitan Greek stage), including Pindar's fifth-century tyrant patrons, the Deinomenid tyrants of Sicily, were *basileis* who aggressively aspired to the Homeric style of visibility living out familiar dreams of heroically aristocratic pre-eminence.[72] These warlords might be expected to know what they were doing, for Deinomenids had good pedigrees and had long held hereditary priesthoods.[73] Their qualities were enough to overawe the populace: there is no evidence to suggest that they bothered to pose as champions of the *dēmos*. To the contrary, Gelon was remembered as considering the people 'a thing most unpleasant to dwell with' and he enslaved the *dēmos* of Megara.[74] Much of the audience to which they directed their expensive and very visible articulations of status were the aristocrats to be found gathered from all over Greece, at the Olympic or Isthmian festivals where they dedicated grand shrines.[75] Wherever they turned their loot (earned from graft, plunder, and enslavements) into stone and space, their huge altars 'must have functioned as large smoke and smell machines, whose operations were to be seen, sensed and marvelled at even from afar'.[76] Along with the festive business of the altars, there were songs of victory to capitalize upon their prestigious achievements. The citizenry may not have been particularly esteemed but a crowd's adulatory presence was surely welcome. Thus, as

[71] Borza 1990: 237–8.

[72] Kurke 1999: 132; cf. McGlew 1993: 53 and Bassi 1998: 146. Frost (1981) remarks that in the 6th and early 5th cent. *lamprotēs* was an end in itself.

[73] Kurke 1999: 131: Gelon and Hieron traced their ancestry back to the original colonists of Gela; they were priests of the cult of infernal gods.

[74] Hdt. 7. 156. 2–3; Kurke 1999: 132.

[75] Kurke 1999: 133. They exceeded even Polycrates in *megaloprepeia*: Hdt. 3. 125. 2.

[76] Jameson 1999: 325–6.

Kurke has well emphasized, in epinician odes for tyrants, in contrast to those for mere citizens, the rhetoric is not concerned to 'allay envy from a peer-group'.[77] And in a song of Bacchylides we see a thrice-fortunate man indeed, who does not hide his towering wealth in blackness and darkness, but brings forth ox-sacrificing festivals. And there is shouting. This poem does 'allow us to hear its entire length as the admiring shout of a Greek crowd, thereby enacting the Hellenic approval it works to forge for Hieron'.[78] It is helpful to remember that the eloquence of epinician was translating into some sort of textual record a ritual performance which had great power to infiltrate the consciousnesses of contemporary spectators. As would be the case in reception of Homer's descriptions of the ritual performances of big-men, an archaic or classical audience could easily draw upon its own memories of celebration in order to flesh out the imagery of text and song.

## ATHENIAN CHARISMA

Athenians in pre-classical times had opportunities to witness and evaluate men who stood to the ceremonial fore of their community. Although not much is known about them, kingly individuals on a modest scale, *phylobasileis*, presided over the tribes' sacrifices, as they would even in classical times when the political organization and institutions of Athens had attained much greater and more centralized authority.[79] One can also try to envision at the centre of Athenian public cult at the start of the seventh century a 'king', whether a king 'of very attenuated powers, or in fact a magistrate', who presided at sacrifices and led processions to sacred sites.[80] Presumably such men were well-born, Eupatrids, whose religious authority and dignity reinforced their control of judicial matters and leadership in battle. Most residents of Attica, however, lived more than a stroll or lengthy mule-ride away from the political centre. The organization and membership of infra-political cultic and social

[77] Kurke 1999: 131. [78] Bacch. 3. 9–16; Kurke 1999: 136.

[79] Parker 1996: 45.

[80] Parker 1996: 27, noting too that the public rites at such a period might well resemble Nestor's sacrifice in Book 3 of the *Odyssey*.

communities, especially tribes and phratries, will always be opaque but such associations clearly inserted individuals into patterns of sociability that in turn became woven into the structures of political citizenship. The system of *genē* provided, moreover, for the allocation of priesthoods and there can be no doubt that the well-born gained both prestige and authority from presiding over many Athenians' happier times of social belonging on feast days.

Powerful Eupatrid status, however, would not exactly have represented pre-eminence at the centre of the *polis* as a whole, for until the sixth century there was not much of a *polis* to serve as either an administrative or aesthetic focus for any sort of national identity, although presumably the 'men of this primitive Athens came together occasionally to sacrifice a cow to Athena'.[81] For most of the seventh century the Athenians were still inhabiting a backwater—there was not physically much of a *polis*; and there is no testimony to involvement in the habits prevailing in other parts of Greece, such as competition in pan-hellenic games, hoplite warfare, or colonization schemes.[82] Athens perhaps caught up with more politically developed places in about 630, when a powerful and overweeningly ambitious aristocrat tried to make himself tyrant and occupied the Acropolis. There was insufficient popular support and his followers were killed.[83] Following the Delphic oracle but judging wrongly what was the greatest festival of Zeus, Cylon attempted his coup at the time of the Olympics when he might have fared better at the Diasia.[84] But he was an Olympic victor, and so perhaps emboldened to think of putting himself at the head of the *polis* at a time of communal festivity. Clearly this violent political drama might bespeak the existence of some sort of a political community, although one in which collective Athenian emotions inclined more towards war against Megarians than towards installation of a Megarian tyrant's daughter and son-in-law at the heart and hearth of Athens.

If Athens had become vulnerable to tyrants, it had become a more developed *polis* and a more tempting prize for aristocrats

[81] Parker 1996: 22. [82] Morris 1993: 35.

[83] Hdt. 5. 71; Thuc. 1. 126. 1996 3–12.

[84] Jameson (1965: 167–72) sorts out the various versions of this episode.

hitherto content with pre-eminence in regional and sub-political communities. Even so, the reforms enacted by Solon addressed chronic problems that had prevented Athens from becoming a cohesive civic entity, let alone one with 'uniform, fair, centralized governance and resolution of disputes'.[85] Most fundamentally, Solon insisted that no Athenian could be a slave to another Athenian in their shared homeland. Solon, moreover, changed the ways in which Athenians associated with one another to make them harmonize with an ideology that proclaimed political inclusivity over heroic or aristocratic exclusivity: *eunomia* is contrasted with the *adikia* of the previous leaders of the *dēmos*, which could be cast in terms of the private, exclusive feasting.[86] Sons of the black earth of Attica also would feel less and less obligation to provide rich men with the pre-eminent responsibility of mediating communal dealings with the gods.[87] The *polis* was set upon a trajectory of egalitarianism that will lead us to contemplate all the remarkable sociopolitics of the democratic and imperial collectivity of the fifth and fourth centuries.

Self-aggrandisement did not disappear but even its new styling continued to be comprehensible in the traditional terms of epic individuality. Among the Athenians Solon took his stand (Fr. 34), defiantly proclaiming, 'I had my reasons; I brought into assembly | the people.' His songs of self-justification had an unmistakable heroic flavour, as he described himself whirling

[85] Manville 1990: 212.

[86] Solon Fr. 4 (West) 9–10 and 31–3; cf. Schmitt-Pantel 1990 and esp. 200–3 for consideration of the sociopolitical significance of more inclusive participation. But in truth generalizations are dangerous (more than Schmitt-Pantel implies) because it is so little known which *polis*-cults existed prior to Solon and how exclusive the *genē*-gatherings were. Jacoby's assessment of the effects of Solon's changes (1944*b*: 69–71) is rather bold.

[87] Thus, whereas in earlier times Athenians looked to aristocratic *basileis* to swear on their behalf oaths that the laws of the community would be obeyed, now citizens swore for themselves: *Ath. Pol.* 7 and 55. This oath persisted until at least the end of the 5th cent.: And. 1. 90 and 97. The inalienable value of simply being an Athenian citizen was articulated, since the enslavement of any one of them would now be held to be a communal outrage; a wrong done one man was to be regarded as the business of another (Solon Fr. 36 (West) 8–15; *Ath. Pol.* 9). Access to the law was widened by the codification and public display of the laws: *Ath. Pol.* 7; ἔγραψα Solon. Fr. 36 (West) 20.

like a heroically isolated hound in a pack of wolves, to ward off, with his weapons of wisdom, *stasis* and tyranny. Homer specifically continued to provide much of the repertoire of vivid imagery for political discourse at Athens,[88] even though both the aggressive self-assertion and routinely charismatic pre-eminence of a kingly man would clash with the preferred ceremonial practices of a well-ordered community. Yet the prize of success in becoming the principal figure in Athens had increased in value. The approbation of free citizens conscious of an inalienable and shared dignity could begin to count for more than had done the deference of slaves, share-croppers, and everybody else who did not have the best lineages. In the sixth century, therefore, Athenians in many respects constituted a more intimate peer-group in a city that had become a more valuable stage upon which the well-born could posture. Peisistratus and his sons exercised pre-eminence before the Athenians for lengthy periods whilst doing little to make the mass of citizenry resentful.[89] They did not subvert the Solonian order.

They did explain themselves in imaginative fashion, combining the verities of mythic symbolism with their situational surprises. Citizens were welcomed and valued as spectators and interpreters of their dramas. Peisistratus and his family were believed to have been responsible for introducing recitative performances of Homer at the Panathenaea.[90] That would be all the more significant to a family that claimed a splendid pedigree descending from Nestor, that well-intentioned Homeric *basileus* as comfortable at a charioteering competition as in superintending a sacrifice.[91] Peisistratus also famously entered Athens in a chariot in his second attempt at tyranny.[92] This was impressive in its own right, since chariots physically elevated their passengers, for visibility and also prestigious dignity;

[88] Thus, for example, a guest at Athenaeus' banquet naturally ascribes (4. 137e) an Homeric precedent for Solon's prescriptions of foods for feasts provided by the *polis*.

[89] Thuc. 6. 54. 5.

[90] [Plato] Hipp. 228b–c; Nagy 1990: 21–4 and 1996: 69–71. The tyrants acted as patron to other poets, particularly Anacreon, Simonides, and Lasus of Hermione (Andrewes 1956: 114).

[91] Hdt. 5. 65.

[92] Hdt. 1. 60.

athletic victors also re-entered their cities in such style, and gods naturally rode chariots.[93] Peisistratus' odd vignette thus can be viewed against a 'busy background of phenomena in ancient Greece attesting the entry of gods and heroes in the mortal realm'.[94] Peisistratus also embellished his drama in a way that called further upon his spectators' interpretative involvement. He was accompanied in his chariot by Phye, a tall and beautiful woman, clad in armour and posing in arresting style as Athena bringing Peisistratus back to her acropolis. Herodotus took the episode seriously, but finds that it bespoke an astonishing Athenian naivety. Connor has urged that the Athenians not be thought to have been fooled but rather imagined as having been actively involved in a piece of symbolic communication.[95] Their ability to make sense of the symbolism of the drama was facilitated by heralds who explained the presence of Peisistratus' patroness, presumably for the benefit of those who were not too familiar with mythic dramatizations acted out before their eyes. Before too long, of course, democracy would bring forth 'upstart . . . vulgarly spectacular art forms'[96] of drama complete with heroic actors consorting with gods. For now it is enough that Peisistratus had presumed to want Athenians complicit in a stirring *poiēsis* of his own epic significance.

Once established in power, Peisistratus' regime quite probably fostered the development of more demotic, spectacular, and generous festivals of the *polis*, at which the big man could be seen to stand at the charismatic centre-stage.[97] Rather fittingly it was at the grandest of festivals that the regime of the Peisistratids started to unravel. When (in 514) Hipparchus was

[93] At least in the pictures on black-figured pottery: Sinos 1993: 75–7.

[94] Sinos 1993: 79.

[95] Connor 1987: esp. 44. Sinos, in the best discussion of both this event and Connor's important discussion, stresses (1993: 86–8) that Herodotus has programmatic interest in Athenian self-infatuation which explains his insistence upon their foolishness.

[96] Davies 1992: 32.

[97] Parker 1996: 76–9, stressing uncertainty over the exact Peisistratid contribution to the development of Attic festivals (including provision of large numbers of sacrificial victims for feasting) but also stressing spectacular festive entertainment. Also Georges 1993: 96–7.

assassinated at the Great Panathenaea, his brother, Hippias, was busy marshalling the *pompē*.[98] Later collective memory and its narrators might have mistaken the identity of the murder victim (so irritating Thucydides), but the assassins had acted in full civic view—and would immortally remain there as heroes of the democracy their deed was believed to have helped bring into being. Harmodius and Aristogeiton were cast in Homeric terms. In song they were to be envisaged joining heroes of the *Iliad*, Achilles and Diomedes, in the Isles of the Blessed.[99] In the fabric of the *polis* the tyrannicides also received lasting reward after statues of them in their moment of homicidal glory had taken their stand in the Agora.[100] The powerful eroticism of sculptural art had now become politicized.[101] Athenian citizens, who had initiated and fought for their own revolutionary freedom,[102] now looked upon only the idols they desired.

## SPECTACULAR ATHENIANS

Unlike Homeric leaders, fifth-century Athenian aristocrats could not customarily aggrandize themselves as sacrificants at the centre of festivity. Characteristically, democratic Athens did retain the office of a king archon (*archōn basileus*) exercising religious responsibilities but he was appointed by lot, as were all the archons after 487. Most Athenian priests were merely appointees of the state, often selected by lot, and so any honour they derived from their offices was understood to adhere to their function rather than their persons.[103] Their

[98] Thuc. 1. 20 and 6. 56–7; *Ath. Pol.* 18. 3. Parker has observed (1996: 89), 'the opportunity of organizing the Panathenaic procession, of presiding authoritatively over the city's display of its own munificence, was itself one of the sweetest fruits of power.' Processions are attested for many Attic festivals: references conveniently at Mikalson 1982: 217.

[99] Skolion 894 (Page). Particularly for a time when upper-class lyric was being amalgamated 'with the significantly out-of-town bucolic Dionysiac ritual of the *komos* and the *tragos*' (Davies 1992: 32), I see no reason to presume that such songs were sung exclusively by aristocrats.

[100] Taylor 1981: 26.

[101] Stewart 1997: 70–5.

[102] Cf. Ober 1996: 32–52.

[103] Cf. Seaford 1994: 217 (duly acknowledging Bourdieu 1977: 187–8): 'the polis depends on the distinction between the (permanent, abstract) office

principal duty seems to have been restricted to the administration of sacred property, which entailed submission to the apparatus of democratic control, including its financial scrutiny.[104] Priests even had to curse (and retract their words, however ritually powerful) upon command.[105] Such subordination of individual authority, beyond being an instructive symptom of how democratic ideology was put into practice, also meant that aristocrats who were priests were unable to use that status to gain any especial influence in other areas of political life, particularly the courts, since Athenians prided themselves upon their equality before the law.[106] Thus Callias, a rather splendid and beautiful figure who wore an equally enviable hat as an Eleusinian priest, found that his excellences counted for little when he was embroiled in judicial dispute, even though Socrates thought that Callias' qualifications, including his splendid physical appearance, were such that the *polis* should entrust itself to him.[107] The Athenians did no such thing.

Furthermore, the number of sacrifices attractive in their provision of meat increased in democratic Athens, further reducing the importance of individual sacrificants. The conceit of Cleisthenes' admission of the *dēmos* to the hitherto exclusivity of aristocratic sociability (*hetaireia*) was programmatic for

and the succession of specific individuals who fill it, in sharp contrast to Homeric society.' Allotment is evident for those cults for which we have decrees dealing with their establishment: e.g. Meiggs and Lewis no. 44, which deals with the establishment of the priesthood of Athene Nike; cf. the cults of Bendis and Asclepius (Sokolowski 1962 nos. 6 and 11).

[104] Plato *Laws* 738e–759d; Feaver 1957: 148–9. Scrutiny: esp. Aeschin. 3. 18.

[105] Plut. *Alc.* 22 and 33; Garland 1984: 120.

[106] e.g. Thuc. 2. 37. 1; Eur. *Supp.* 404–8; Dem. 21. 67, 24. 59.

[107] Xen. *Symp.* 8. 40: 'and nowadays at the festival you seem to excel over your predecessors in your distinction as a priest (*ἱεροπρεπέστατος*) and you have a body that is the most becoming in the city (*σῶμα ἀξιοπρεπέστατον*) and yet able also to withstand tribulations.' Callias was of course a descendant of the torchbearer who was such a spectacular figure at Marathon (Plut. *Aristid.* 5). He was trying to use his priestly authority in accusing Andocides of placing a bough in the Eleusinium during the Mysteries: And. 1. 115 ff. Cf. in general Clinton 1974: 114: 'in the pre-Roman period there is no sign that the Eleusinian priests possessed political clout in any significant or consistent way.'

the developments that would continue to shape the politics of communal festivity in Athens. Within the *polis* there was established a more intricate web of overlapping sub-communities in which tribes and demes had their own communal practices—centred upon companionship, food, and general good cheer—to supplement the pan-political occasions such as the Dionysia and Panathenaea.[108] And the smaller events provided parochial ties of allegiance.[109] Citizens thus knew both their neighbours and also men from other demes; fellow councilmen may be imagined as having already sat with their colleagues in the smoke of a huge barbecue or shared emotions over hours spent in the same row at the theatre. Sacrificial festivities were parties at which wine ideally was plentiful;[110] and to which people went both to be seen and to see.[111] They also made, therefore, memorable appeal to appetites other than those for charismatic spectacle.[112] Gratification of appetites for food and

[108] On the interlocking communities cf. Kearns 1985: 199; ibid. 193 for the Cleisthenic tribes as religious groups. The demes were very much involved in the maintenance of religious observances, with appointments of *hieropoioi*, *hieromnēmones*, or *epimelētai* as well as retaining duties for the demarch (Whitehead 1986: 127; 128 for the demarch as sacrificant). The sacrificial calendars from demes provide a wealth of information, though largely concerned with the costs of the sacrifices rather than with details of ritual: see e.g. Jameson 1965: esp. 155–6; Whitehead 1986: ch. 7 gives a helpful overview of the deme as a religious community.

[109] Plato, in the *Laws* (738c–e), recommends that at the founding of the state sacrifices should be established for groups (τοῖϲ δὲ μέρεσιν ἑκάστοιϲ θεὸν ἢ δαίμονα ἢ καὶ τινα ἥρωα ἀποδοτέον), so that people come to know one another.

[110] A fragment of Epicharmus (p. 271 L, preserved at Athen. 2. 3) provides a happy emphasis on the contribution of drinking to the festivities: 'feasting followed sacrifice, and drinking followed feasting' (ἐκ μὲν θυσίαϲ θοίνα ... ἐκ δὲ θοίναϲ πόσιϲ ἐγένετο). A fragment of Aristotle (89 R = Athen. 2. 11) offers an etymology of the word for alcoholic intoxication, associating it with the words for 'after the sacrifice' (τὸ δὲ μεθύειν φησὶν Ἀριστοτέληϲ τὸ μετὰ τὸ θύειν αὐτῷ χρῆσθαι). On holiday the Greeks did not sit quaking in awe but chatted, drank, waited for the meat to cook, ate with gusto, drank some more, and engaged in all manner of activities that could bring both pleasure and indigestion (see e.g. Ar. *Nu.* 385–91—flatulence after the Panatheneaea).

[111] Cf. Mikalson 1982: 216–17 and 221.

[112] Arguably there is 'absolute coincidence' of meat-eating and sacrificial practice: Detienne 1989: 3. Discussion of sacrifice, especially in the work of Burkert (e.g. 1985: 255), has a tendency to over-state the 'horror of bloodshed and the renunciation' in the presence of the *tremendum*, the shivers up the

drink potentially might be directly associated with a patron both wealthy and charismatically present among them. In providing the good things in life such as these, a wealthy aristocrat stood every chance of enjoying a fine reputation and visible primacy in his community.[113]

But meat had become something less of a treat after the Cleisthenic *Risorgimento*. This had established fresh patterns of association within the *polis*, instituting a dense 'web' of overlapping communities in which tribes and demes had their own religious practices, revolving around *philia*, food, and festivity, which supplemented *genos*, phratry, and *polis* celebrations.[114] The disconsolate carping of the 'Old Oligarch' reminds us that the state and its subdivisions paid for many victims[115] which otherwise would have had to have been obtained directly through individuals' resources or at least by private arrangements. The increased provision of food and drink would make a patron's generosity less ingratiating.[116] Much of the meat at sub-political sacrifices, moreover, was

spine as the violence within the human condition is directed away from the species. Smith 1987 argues that sacrifice is not such a fraught emotional occasion, its ritual no 'big deal'. This view is a salutary corrective but may easily be challenged by evidence of Greek sacrifices that explicitly require victims to be of outstanding physical form and beauty, e.g. Herzog 1928: no. 1 line 10.

[113] Cf. Theopompus' summary (*FGrHist* 115 F 89) of the effects of Cimon's hospitality, that he 'possessed a good reputation and was first among the citizens' (εὐδοκίμει καὶ πρῶτος ἦν τῶν πολιτῶν); cf. Plut. *Cim.* 10. Athenians spent their money on food rather than possessions such as furniture: Davidson 1997: 310–11.

[114] Greek gatherings centred upon sacrifice likely did foster group-identities and allegiances: Plato *Leg.* 738d; Xen. *Hell.* 2. 4. 20–1. Besides new affective relationships of Athenians to each other and the *polis*, Cleisthenes' changes also provided so many invitations to feasts that the influence of wealthy men who were prepared to act as gift-givers was surely eroded.

[115] [Xen.] *Ath. Pol.* 2. 9.

[116] Conspicuous generosity was obviously expensive: especially informative is Xen. *Oec.* 2. 5–6; note too Arist. *EE* 233[b]. On private patronage generally: Millett 1989.

taken home by citizens and not consumed in collective celebration.[117]

Little room in the ceremonial life of the *polis* in fact was readily ceded to those who wished to be seen in positions of individual distinction. Revealing illustrations of this tendency are to be found in Plutarch's *Life of Cimon* (7–8). At the festival of the Dionysia, the board of generals (*stratēgoi*) offered libations collectively; few opportunities were available for the *stratēgoi* to enjoy prominence before the *dēmos* as individuals. Cimon's chance to act as a judge at the theatrical contest at the Dionysia offered an unexpected ceremonial importance—but of course it was shared with his fellow *stratēgoi*.[118] Likewise, Athenians 'reasserted the public sphere's primacy over the individual by forbidding the generals who had expelled the Persians from northern Greece to erect portraits of themselves in the Agora, restricting them to inscribed herms instead'.[119] Plutarch quotes (*Cim.* 7–8) the inscriptions to reassure his readers, who were familiar with a plethora of decrees commemorating all manner of euergete or honoree, that, although Cimon's name was nowhere actually inscribed, fifth-century Athenians nonetheless regarded this memorial as a supreme mark of honour, which neither Miltiades nor Themistocles had received. Only in exile could Themistocles take centre-stage in the ceremonial of religious ritual. If (the obscure) Possis is to be believed, Themistocles instituted a whole festival to afford him charismatic pre-eminence:

τὴν στεφανηφόρον ἀρχὴν ἀναλαβόντα θῦσαι Ἀθηνᾷ καὶ τὴν ἑορτὴν Παναθήναια ὀνομάσαι καὶ Διονύσῳ χοοπότῃ θυσιάσαντα καὶ τὴν χοῶν ἑορτὴν αὐτόθι καταδεῖξαι.

Assuming the office that brought the right to wear a wreath he sacrificed to Athena and named the festival Panathenaea; and in sacrificing to Dionysus Choopotes ['who drinks whole measures'] he thereupon established the festival of Choes.[120]

117 Jameson 1999.

118 The anecdote may be dubious (for its date see Sommerstein 1997: 69 n. 5) but surely says something about the politics of honour at Athens.

119 Stewart 1997: 141.

120 Athen. 12. 533e. Even if scurrilous, the story is still telling.

More than just the ache of nostalgia, this is the stuff of ambition's dream. In Athens, if ambitious men settled for less of the civic limelight, it had at least counted for more—and before a more valuable audience of choosy citizens.

Entering the period of the greatest collective Athenian cultural and imperial achievement, Athenians preferred as far as possible to associate prestige with national qualities. Henceforward there would be little rapture for heroic individuals either orchestrating massive festivals or wielding daggers in the city. For ambitious aristocrats life would on the whole be less turbulent and certainly less violent—it was in large part an emotional quarrel among well-born families over the allocation of *timē* through ritual ceremonies that had led to the killing of Hipparchus.[121] Disputes among competitors for primacy could instead be settled by the verdicts of the sovereign *dēmos*. More value was put upon the approbation of the mass of the citizenry and not least because it had become much harder to stand out routinely as indisputably the big-man among the Athenians. Of course, the habitual handicaps put upon pre-eminence made its attainment, even in attenuated form upon the terms of suspicious democrats, all the more desirable to the ambitious. Through persistence, considerable ingenuity, and indisputable heroic persistence a well-born few did manage to impress themselves upon the attentions and affections of peer-groups of fellow citizens, translating prestige into power even amid the circumspections of egalitarian democracy.[122]

Themistocles had already provided the best example in the post-Cleisthenic democracy of a man crafting celebrity. In his youth, he arranged for a celebrated harp-player to play at his house; and when he went to the Olympics, he rivalled Cimon in ostentation, although it could be claimed that his expensive furniture and big tent only made him appear pretentious.[123] Cimon improvised in another spectacular fashion when he led a

[121] According to Thucydides (6. 56. 1) the dispute concerned whose sister was to have the honour of being a basket-bearer, an explanation that need not be true to be telling.

[122] Cimon was elected as a general of his tribe ten times, Pericles between fourteen and sixteen, Nicias thirteen or fourteen, and Alcibiades seven or eight times (figures conveniently at Hamel 1995: 32–3).

[123] Plut. *Them.* 5.

procession and delivered a bridle to Athena at the time of Salamis, and when he returned to Athens amid great fanfare proudly escorting the bones of Theseus.[124] Cimon too, who was as rich as a tyrant, was assiduous in using generosity to make himself first man in the *polis*, sharing the produce of his estates, making gifts of money to the needy, and even giving away the clothes of his own friends' backs.[125]

Grand festivals directly sponsored by the democratic *polis* also brought new opportunities for individuals to shine, provided they were wealthy, generous, and ambitious for sociopolitical prestige. The institution and development of the *chorēgia*, that is the financing of choruses for festivals, might have been encouraged by the chance it afforded for 'ostentation, power, and self-representation for its performers'.[126] While more is known of this liturgy in the fourth century than in the fifth, we do hear of some well-known champions of the *dēmos* winning with their choruses quite early in the century: in 476 Themistocles was the victorious tragic *chorēgos*;[127] in 472 Pericles.[128] Later in the fifth century Nicias achieved some fame for spending heavily upon dramatic as well as gymnastic liturgies, and also upon a statue, a shrine, and elaborate ceremonial spectacles at Delos (in 427), hoping that pre-eminence bought in one political context of competition could be translated into others.[129] The basic criterion for selection of *chorēgoi* was wealth and selection was not guided by membership of any particular tribe or other sociopolitical sub-grouping.[130]

[124] Plut. *Cim.* 5 and 8. He also built a splendid shrine, engaging Mikon to paint frescoes: Stewart 1997: 141.

[125] *Ath. Pol.* 27. 3; Theopompus *FGrHist* 115 F 89; Connor 1971: 20.

[126] Wilson 1997: 86.

[127] Plut. *Them.* 5.

[128] Sommerstein 1997: 69.

[129] Plut. *Nic.* 2–3. The visibility of *chorēgoi* surely made them more attractive than other liturgies (Wilson 1997: 101 n. 96). Alcibiades in the *pompē* at the Great Dionysia, whenever he was *chorēgos*, entered the theatre in a purple robe and attracted the wonder of both men and women: Athen. 12. 534c; cf. Wilson 1997: 102.

[130] Wilson 1997: 96–7. The selection process was taken very seriously by Athenian officials: the 'first practical task of the leading civic officer was to appoint the three wealthiest Athenians liable for the duty as impresarios for the tragic dramas which were still a full eleven months away' (Wilson 1997: 96, adducing *Ath. Pol.* 56. 2–3).

*Chorēgoi*, especially those whose productions were successful, were able in ancestral fashion to be at the centre of attention surrounded by merriment, the streets filled 'with the savour of sacrifice, with all wearing garlands'.[131] Such festive merriment represented an age-old chasm of status between rich celebrities and their happy consumers. As Wilson has powerfully observed, 'the rich lead in khoroi, the demos is led'.[132]

The dramatic productions inside the theatre might themselves have further reinforced the ritualization of statuses and roles found in the streets and city at large. Mythic plots were not remote from contemporary concerns, as so much excellent interpretation of tragedy demonstrates. Moreover, there are obvious correlations between the activities of acting and watching inside and outside the theatre.[133] On the dramatic stage powerful individuals are not scarce. Royal personages are characters in all the best and the most popular tragedies, and are to be seen praying, sacrificing, dedicating offerings and spoils 'very much (so far as we can judge) in accord with fifth-century formulas and protocols'.[134] Their authority on stage quite plausibly affected the attitudes of the spectators, even if the impact of such representations upon sensibilities and ideologies cannot adequately be registered for any society, projecting unquestionable legitimacy 'as leaders and guarantors of prosperity and order' in a geography most Athenians could only imagine.[135] Certainly there was a well-born elite at Athens which continued to steer the state's fortunes and whose expertise and entitlement met with some deference.[136] In drama,

[131] Dem. 21. 51; Wilson 1997: 87–8. [132] Wilson 1997: 94.

[133] Cf. Bassi 1998: 13. The demographic composition of theatrical audiences is not, however, wholly clear: Sommerstein in particular (1997: 67) cautions against simple equation of audience at theatre and Assembly.

[134] Parker 1997: 146.

[135] Griffith 1995: 82, discussing dynastic families in the *Oresteia*. Sennett observes (1994: 58) that the 'theatre indeed is a kind of ambassadorial activity, bringing a story from another time or place to the eyes and ears of the spectators'.

[136] Griffith has cogently described (1995: 66) how 'each and every one' of the 'middling or poor male citizens of Aeschylus' Athens . . . looked to this elite for commands, direction, protection, and examples of deportment and style, in virtually all important dealings with the world beyond his own domestic affairs'.

however, the peculiar pleasure of watching grand lives take terrible and piteous turns complicates the hegemonic affect; and so too does the wide array of individuals and families portrayed in the full programme of competing sets of plays. Comedic presentations, moreover, allowed the *dēmos* to express its reservations about the politically prominent.[137]

There was one ritual of democratic Athens that did make it possible for the gaze of congregated citizens to be focused exclusively, if only fleetingly, upon a single pre-eminent leader. At the ceremony of the public funeral the audience was more representative of the whole *polis*, with women and foreigners in attendance, than upon any other occasion. There was a procession but no sacrifice. The central action was the Epitaphios, the speech delivered by a leader of the *polis*.[138] Thucydides (2. 35) presents the speech delivered by Pericles, and in the preamble to this (2. 34) illustrates how political firsthood, grounded in a phenomenology we have found to be highly traditional, might still be enjoyed.[139]

Pericles' action of stepping forth to the *bēma* is denoted by a single humble participle that speaks volumes about both the special nature of this ritualized rhetorical event and its importance in defining the authority of Pericles' speech. The participle used is not the *parelthōn* routinely used of a speaker taking his turn to speak symbouleutically in the Assembly but instead *proelthōn*.[140] This latter participle signals a man already visibly stationed as leader of his community and authorized to speak with unchallenged, truly epideictic authority. For Thucydides, this was perhaps the way that a pre-eminent ruler such as

137 Carey 1994.

138 The final choice of the deliverer of the Epitaphios rested with the Assembly who decided upon a recommendation made by the Boule: Plato *Men.* 234b; Dem. *De Cor.* 285; Loraux 1986: 349 n. 22.

139 Thucydides, like most ancient historians, placed a high value upon the visibility of historical events: cf. Connor 1984: 10; Macleod 1983: 144; Walker 1993: 356.

140 e.g. describing Pericles at 1. 139. 4. *LSJ* too readily ignores the distinction. Thucydides also provides details of the physical setting of the speech: 'and when it was the proper moment, moving out front (προελθών) from the tomb to the *bēma* that had been built high so that he could be heard from as far as possible in the throng, he spoke as follows.'

Pericles should always be contemplated. As we saw in his aloof comportment at the start of this chapter, Pericles worked hard to put himself above the fray and Thucydides' text has also presented him as a politician of a different stamp, one who did not need 'to strain after' primacy in the *polis*.[141]

But Pericles never did escape completely the trammels and travails of the democratic environment he helped to construct.[142] All demagogues lived in intimacy of scrutiny by fellow citizens, and certainly in competition for persuasiveness in the Assembly. It cannot have been easy to identify the *prostatēs* of the *dēmos* at any given moment.[143] A perfect image of pre-eminent authority would look very different from the practice of Periclean Athens. A description of Timoleon's ritualized visibility in Corinth, for example, indicates his routine preeminence.[144] He is summoned for more important deliberations and he travels through the agora in a mule-carriage to the theatre, to be greeted by the people with one voice. Listening to the matter under debate, he gives his opinion which is adopted. The citizens send him on his way with shouting and clapping before turning to other, less significant items of business. At Athens, even the most important men ascended the speaker's platform only to have to face down a sometimes vociferously hostile audience.[145] Indeed, 'he who thrust himself forward to the bema, abandoning his place in

[141] Thuc. 2. 65. 10. In Pericles' first speech to the Assembly (1. 139. 4) he is the 'first of the Athenians' that he is in the 'obituary notice' of 2. 65.

[142] Thuc. 2. 64. 4.

[143] Ironically because of his desire to belittle the big men of the past, Theopompus drew up the roster of successive leaders which has been bequeathed to posterity: Connor 1968: 123.

[144] Plut. *Tim.* 38.

[145] Thucydides presents Nicias challenged by a supporter of Alcibiades (6. 25. 1) and Pisander posing questions to individual speakers (8. 53. 2). Cleon is pressured to accept the command at Pylos at least in part because of the noisy comments of the ὄχλοc: Thuc. 4. 28. 1 and 3. In Aristophanes (*Ach.* 37–9), Dicaeopolis comes to the Assembly ready to shout, interrupt, and jeer; cf. *Ecc.* 399; note too: Xen. *Hell.* 1. 4. 20, 1. 7. 12–13, 2. 3. 50. In another era we hear the jeering of Aeschines and Philocrates at Demosthenes as they stand by the *bēma* (Dem. 19. 23); cf. [Dem.] 10. 11; Dem. 8. 38, 25. 64; [Dem.] 26. 19, 59. 43. There might be claques ready to cheer or jeer in the service of their hero, a phenomenon well and succinctly discussed by Calhoun 1913: 121–3; cf.

the mass, had, by that act, declared an individuality that was potentially suspect'.[146] Hence it was difficult for rhetors to generate any secure sense of political primacy, unless perhaps the impressions they made upon the *dēmos* in other settings conditioned how they were viewed in the Assembly.

Thucydides makes the speeches of Pericles delivered in deliberative debate in the Assembly approximate as much as possible to the more stately condition of epideixis that ideally suits Pericles' standing in the *polis*.[147] Although in most political practice Pericles was as much a champion (or even corruptor) of the *dēmos* as was Cleon,[148] Cleon's authority most notably is not depicted in such terms.[149] Indeed, Thucydides' treatment of Cleon cleverly alludes to Homer,[150] the paideutic resource that his own useful and enduring rhetorical history was designed to supplant.[151] Cleon identifies himself in Periclean terms.[152] But there is only the illegitimacy of an ugly Thersites, who recycles Achilles' words but cannot invest them with any authority deriving from his own person. Unlike Pericles' speeches (*logoi*), those of other rhetors in Thucydides are paired with ones urging an opposite course of action upon the *dēmos*. Thus Alcibiades speaks (6. 16–18) in favour of making a great naval and military expedition to Sicily but he is countering a speech by Nicias (6. 9–14).

All the same, the cogency of Alcibiades' *logos*, Thucydides makes clear, is improved by the authority his reputation brings. Alcibiades did not enjoy epideictic pre-eminence in giving a political eulogy but he had already found ways to make himself the centre of attention, fashioning an heroic charisma which, translated into the most important democratic arena of the

Connor 1971: 36. In 415, however, the supporters of Alcibiades appear in Thucydides (6. 13. 1) to be scattered and stationed (though perhaps artfully) next to supporters of Nicias. In general cf. Bers (1985: 4) which is primarily concerned with dicastic din.

146 Ober 1989*a*: 296.

147 Cf. Dion. Hal. *Comp.* 9; *pace* Westlake 1968: 34. Plutarch speaks (*Mem.* 347a) of 'spectatorship' with regard to the Epitaphios.

148 Plato *Gorgias* 515e; *Ath. Pol.* 27. 3–4 and 28. 2–3; Finley 1962.

149 Cf. Ober 1998*a*: 97.

150 Cairns 1982.

151 Cf. Fornara 1983: 106.

152 3. 38. 1 with 2. 61. 2; 3. 37. 2 and 40. 4 with 2. 63. 2.

Assembly, won him both persuasive *dynamis* and the opportunity to win honour in military command.[153] When he spoke in the Assembly, Alcibiades could not necessarily boast a proven competence in public policy: what did he know about Sicily—or even Carthage or Libya for that matter—that was not better known by others at Athens, all busy drawing their lines and maps in the sand?[154] Some politicians might have devoted countless hours to 'matters of detail, personal privilege, amendments and surrejoinders'.[155] Charismatic celebrity, however, was important for getting to the position where such things mattered.[156] Alcibiades first enters Thucydides' narrative already presuming entitlement to political consequentiality: Thucydides remarks upon both the selfish quality of his motives in opposing the Peace of Nicias and the prestige in which he was held—by virtue of the worth of his ancestry.[157]

[153] Nicias feared that the proposed expedition to Sicily would be undertaken only to glorify Alcibiades further: Thuc. 6. 12. 2 (*τῷ τῆϲ πόλεωϲ κινδύνῳ ἰδίᾳ ἐλλαμπρύνεσθαι*). The fame of Alcibiades and his victory did become immortal: a century later Demosthenes (21. 145) praised Alcibiades' victory as an example of the benefits brought to Athens by the Alcmaeonids.

[154] Plutarch (*Alc.* 17) claims these were the destinations about which Alcibiades dreamt of moving the military campaign after the subjection of Italy and the Peloponnese. Thucydides intends to show that he for one had substantive knowledge of the more westerly Mediterranean world by prefacing Book 6 with geographical and historical description of Sicily. There must, however, have been many Athenians directly acquainted with the island (Kagan 1981: 165).

[155] Connor 1971: 23. Arist. *Rhet.* 1359$^a$ 30 ff. gives a list of the topics and problems confronting a public speaker; cf. Andrewes' stress (1962: 83) on the bulk of business needing to be dealt with by 'the indispensable expert' or Brunt's confidence (1961: 144) that, by the late 5th cent., political activists needed 'a comprehensive grasp of the resources and interests of their own and other cities' and 'a constant readiness to advise on all manner of questions'.

[156] W. E. Thompson (1981) emphasizes the importance of charisma in Athenian leadership over administrative competence. Kagan (1981: 153) observes that the rivalry between Nicias and Alcibiades 'brings to mind more recent political campaigns in which issues are subordinate to personalities and each politician tries to project a favorable "image" by means of some spectacular activity'.

[157] 5. 43. 2: *ἀξιώματι δὲ προγόνων τιμώμενοϲ*. It is difficult to capture exactly the connotations of *ἀξίωμα*: cf. Hornblower 1991: 301. Alcibiades is described as a young man, although he was probably about 30 years old—it is possible he

## ALCIBIADES

Alcibiades, of Alcmaeonid descent, had invested much money and effort into making the wisdom of his *logos* apparent through the quality of the person espousing it, namely a self-consciously well-born man of heroic style and temper. He impressed Thucydides.[158] He also impressed humbler Athenians with his entitlement to primacy in the years after Pericles' death. When we look at Alcibiades' spectacular career, we realize further the opportunities for prestigious self-fashioning that complicate the character of the democratic polity. Many succumbed to a man who found eminently practical and happy ways to translate *timē*, which he amassed outside the central discursive institutions of the democracy, into *dynamis* in the egalitarian arena of the Assembly. This conversion ensured that his *timē* was as precious and memorable as possible, awarded as it was there by the sovereign power of men with a freedom they would risk their lives to defend and extend.[159] Alcibiades had been highly visible in his advertisements to Athenians outside the Assembly, particularly as a beautiful young man about town and as a charismatic victor known throughout Greece for providing all the beautiful and good things in life.

Since boyhood Alcibiades had, much like Themistocles, assiduously made a spectacle of himself. He was a busy celebrity out and about in town, at large amid all the hustle and bustle of Athenian civic life, including that of the Agora, where Athenians thronged on public or private business.[160] Bystanders there

is one of the μειράκια whom Eupolis (Fr. 118) satirizes, as Connor (1971: 147) remarks. He is first barbed in comedy in Ar. *Banqueters* (Fr. 198).

[158] Alcibiades conspicuously escapes Thucydides' censure for the Sicilian debacle: Brunt (1952) stresses that Thucydides exaggerates Alcibiades' strategic talents and is willing.

[160] Dem. 25. 51–2; stressed by Lewis 1996: 14. An immense range of activities was conducted there, as has been succinctly underscored by Millett (1998: 215): 'the classical Agora was the setting for administration, publicity, justice, ostracism, imprisonment, religion, processions, dancing, athletics and equestrian displays. In addition to persons passing through, individuals might gather to get information (official or otherwise), gather a crowd, gamble, torture a slave, get hired as labourers, bid for contracts, accost a prostitute, seek asylum, have a haircut, beg for money or food, fetch water, watch a cockfight and find out the time. This list is hardly exhaustive.'

saw Alcibiades doing all sorts of precociously interesting things. There was his posting of surety for an unlikely lover, the punching of Hipponicus, the man-handling of his long-suffering wife, the splendid dog whose equally splendid tail he docked ('I want the Athenians to chatter about this, so they will not have worse to say about me'), and the quail hunted in the crowd.[161] He also defined himself by his dress, in a society of great uniformity in male clothing,[162] promenading in the Agora in long purple robes.[163] Some in his audience might have been shocked but others might have been susceptible to his glamour, especially those with sensibilities impressed by his generosity in *chorēgiai*.[164]

Alcibiades' beauty apparently was also well worth beholding. He made for a convincing embodiment of the traditional connotations of aristocratic excellence. After all, Homeric heroes were beautiful.[165] The cliché *kalos k'agathos* denoted a man of a certain social standing and associated style of life, a man deemed 'both good to look at and manifesting goodness in action'.[166] Such a valuation might be further upheld by negative contrast with humbler members of the *dēmos* and by the explicit philosophic claim that the beauty of a few was truly symptomatic of those invisible, inner qualities that justified privilege.[167] Men working in banausic occupations—artisans—had, according to such hermeneutics, a body unnaturally distorted.[168] Naturally, wealthy men were able to invest time and money in education

[161] Plut. *Alc.* 2, 5, 8, 7, 9; there were also lavish *epidoseis*, *philotimēmata*, and escorts home from the Assembly.

[162] Geddes (1987) describes the politicized rhetoric of Athenian dress, noting the slow evolution of restrained, egalitarian fashion as well as the flamboyant dynamism of Alcibiades (esp. 312–13 and 323).

[163] Plut. *Alc.* 16.

[164] Ibid.

[165] Segal 1995: 185; Thalmann 1988: 15 n. 37. Achilles of course was the glamorous protagonist, 'the ideal figure of the Greek aristocratic tradition' (Knox 1964: 121, adducing Pi. *N.* 3. 70 ff.).

[166] Dover 1974: 41.

[167] [Xen.] *Ath. Pol.* 10 on the uniformity of humble Athenians' looks, e.g. Plato *Leg.* 655; Socrates (Xen. *Mem.* 3. 10. 5) was also interested in the visual arts' representation of *ēthos*.

[168] Xen. *Oec.* 4. 2–3: souls too are damaged, and such men are not good defenders of the *polis*; farmers who work their own land, however, are regarded as far more valuable and attractive citizens. Toil is, however, presumed

and ability to do other things that paid handsome dividends in maintaining aesthetic distinctions of body and tasteful life-style;[169] specific practices were needed to support the ideological categorizations of the body politic, making notions of *kalos* and *kakos* aesthetically comprehensible regardless of the contingency of their ideological artifice.[170] Thus 'the poor Athenian was normally willing to apply the expression *kalos k'agathos* to any man who had what he himself would have liked to have (wealth, a great name, distinguished ancestors) and was what he himself would have liked to be (educated, cultured, well-dressed and well-groomed, with the physique and poise of a man trained in fighting, wrestling and dancing)'.[171] Apart from intimate engagement with Homer, Alcibiades' education as a *kalos k'agathos* had also taught him to write, wrestle, and play musical instruments.[172] Although he probably preferred to orchestrate chorus-lines, one likes to assume he was also a rather graceful dancer.

The currency of such admiring perceptions among those who were not *kaloi k'agathoi* points further to how Alcibiades acted with great knowingness to advance the privileges afforded a well-born man like himself. The 'class label' was neither historically stable nor free of contestation, especially in the later fifth century when the scions of families rich in financial capital—but not necessarily the symbolic capital that came with noble pedigree—were educated to compete for political primacy.[173] After the Persian wars the 'high urbane' aristocratic subculture

deserving of respect in courtroom speeches: Andoc. 1. 144; Dem. 42. 20 and 32; Dein. 1. 70. Isocrates also consistently values the production and trade of handicrafts as the basis of civilization: W. E. Thompson 1987: 29.

169 e.g. Xen. *Symp*. 4. 13; cf. Johnstone's (1994) recognition of the theoretical insight of Bourdieu 1984.

170 Even Xenophon's idealized Cyrus (*Cyr*. 8. 1. 40–2) adopts Median robes for himself (and the fashion for his courtiers) in order to hide his bodily defects; he also wears high shoes and uses cosmetics.

171 Dover 1974: 45—a historian fully, frankly (cf. esp. 1994: 20), and admirably sensitive to all the phenomena, stigmatic or otherwise, that inform people's sense of self.

172 Plato *Alc*. 1. 106e.

173 Theopompus admits (*FGrHist* 115 F 325) that the elder Demosthenes was a *kalos k'agathos*; Davies (1981: 71) cites this as evidence of 'growing tolerance' of the newly rich in 4th-cent. Athens.

which had emerged in the archaic age 'was now subject to erosion—or rather was so attractive as to generate pressure to extend it down the social scale'.[174] It is not surprising that there was 'a rather unstable sense of elite identity' in classical Athens.[175] The imperial success of the Athenians, moreover, had imported commercial profit and adventuresome luxury.[176] The democratic city had become a central stage in an ever widening Mediterranean world. Aristocrats ventured abroad from the *polis* more than humbler citizens, especially as ambassadors.[177] Consequently there was more flexible scope in what treasure could buy as prestigious glamour, and men could fuss with new fashions in slippers and poultry and things of that sort.[178] Alcibiades we have already seen properly dressed as a keen student of the seductions of fashion but he also appears early in life to have insisted that his visible beauty be understood to reflect personal nobility and not merely membership of a class increasingly hard to define except by conspicuous wealth.

The class of rhetorically assertive Athenians should not be imagined as obviously constituting a single class, not least because distinct personalities would be perceived to assert various persuasivenesses in different settings. Competition further generated innovation in habits of consumption. Some bodies, some precious few, always (it may be hoped) will possess the freedom and show the desire to choose to do things that suit themselves. Not all men of wealth were equal in their ability to elicit admiration. Some did not have ancestors alive in stories told all across the Greek world, whose acquisition of wealth happened picaresquely and in mythic time:[179] the fortunes of

[174] Davies 1992: 32. [175] Davidson 1997: 235.

[176] Cf. Miller 1997: 41.

[177] Perhaps most famously that of Callias to Susa (449?): Hdt. 7. 151. Miller (1997: 114) remarks upon embassies as 'the prerogative of the politically conspicuous—that is, the moneyed, often aristocratic—Athenians'.

[178] Miller 1997: *passim*. Banquets with kingly connotations, for instance, were even held: Persian banqueting at Ar. *Ach.* 65 ff.

[179] e.g. Hdt. 6. 125. 2–5. Kurke (1999: 146) suggests that this anecdote about Alcmaeon's wallow in Croesus' gold has an anti-aristocratic tenor, using 'the grotesque body and effeminate Eastern garb to stigmatize extra-polis aristocratic gift-giving *tout court*'. But still, good for Alcmaeon!

Cleon and Nicias were associated with all the nasty smells of earnest commercialism.[180] If some rich men seemed to enjoy a greater sense of entitlement to their privileges than others, it is unclear just how useful it is to speak of 'the unity of an elite class', or why indeed Athenian power relations should merit only 'structural not personal' analyses.[181] Admittedly the distinction between rich and poor should continue to remain as central to political analysis as it has been since before the time of Aristotle.[182] But, although usually the dynamism in socio-political self-identification and the agency behind its transformations too easily escapes grasping schemas of synchronic analysis, it is clear that neither the membership nor the connotative ideas and practices of a class of *kaloi k'agathoi* were stable generation after generation.

One example of Alcibiades' insistence on a distinctive personal excellence illustrates both the capacity for new fashions to spread in Athens and also his awareness of the power of more traditional habits of thoughts favourable to the well-born like himself. In his aristocratic education, Alcibiades refused to play the pipes. Like Athena herself, he realized that this activity actually distorted his features and did not make him look beautiful at all.[183] Significantly, this disdain supposedly set a

[180] Connection to 'trade' is charged of various 5th-cent. men: Sophocles (*Vita* 1); Cephalos (Schol. ad Ar. *Ec.* 253); Cleon (e.g. Ar. *Eq.* 129 ff.); Cleophon (And. 1. 46); Anytos (Plato *Meno* 90a); Hyperbolos (Ar. *Eq.* 1315). Comedy and 4th-cent. political invective are quick to bring charges of foreign and/or servile birth and unsuitable occupation, thus denying men the possibility of being counted among the *kaloi k'agathoi* (Dover 1974: 32–3, with examples).

[181] Johnstone 1994: 224 and 225 n. 39—who seems to assume (e.g. 240 n. 94) that the identification of a 'specific class' is self-evident. Davidson (1997: 233) urges that 'the difficulty involved in getting a fix on class in Athens should not be seen as a problem; it is an important feature of Athenian culture'.

[182] Ste. Croix 1981: 71–4. Of course, I should prefer not to dress 'rich' and 'poor' with any specific socio-economic detail here.

[183] Plut. *Alc.* 2. Aristotle thought (*Pol.* $1341^{b}4$–8) the point about Athena's physical features to be 'fair' enough but thought her disdain was due to the goddess of knowledge and skill recognizing that flute-playing had an effect upon intelligence.

precedent.[184] If so, it is possible to see how Athenian education was adjusted by the agency of one boy, who had perhaps ingenuously realized the power of his naturally charming assets. Plato's epistemic wistfulness notwithstanding, the ontology of aesthetic ideals really does reside only in specific, sensible particulars, and in the eyes of all their beholders. Subjective choices have always had the potential to tweak or to transform normative expectations of what constituted a great man. Alcibiades, it might therefore be fancied, actually clarified and confirmed assumptions about *kalogathia* simply because people actually did find him attractive in his stylized habits of comportment. In awarding Alcibiades' beauty its appropriate prize of the admiration and political deference to which handsome heroes had always been entitled, the *dēmos* was merely exercising the usual sovereignty that was its prerogative in adjudicating performance in other agonistic arenas in the *polis*.[185] And, if the *dynamis* of highly aristocratic privilege depended upon success in pandering to the theoretic inclinations of the *dēmos*, it should simply be admitted that there was (and is, to judge by any contemporary chit-chat of political punditry) as much sovereignty in the acknowledgement of celebrity as there was in the casting of *ostraka* and the clatter of dicastic pebbles.

Alcibiades' habits of self-aggrandisement in the public eye of Athenians further depended upon systematic exploitation of an age-old and practically archaic style which amounted to being a 'retro-fashion' of aristocratic advertisement. Nowhere is this better evident than in his athleticism. For no prominent political career at Athens could be more aptly compared to athletic competition than that of Alcibiades who excelled in winning the prize of political primacy before an audience—whose spectatorship, applause, and affectionate memories alone made his

[184] Aristotle also notes (*Pol.* 1339$^b$10) that it was not manly to perform music, except when drunk or just fooling around. Fluting in particular had an exciting rather than moral influence according to Aristotle (1341$^a$); see further Wilson 1999. Alcibiades is, however, also said to have been as particular about his fluting instructor as his teacher of Homer: Duris *FGrHist.* F 29.

[185] Judgement of male beauty, moreover, was not a characteristic unique to Athens since many a Greek *polis* was just as likely to articulate its criteria of beauty in agonistic formalities (Crowther 1985 provides details of male beauty pageants throughout Greece).

success meaningful.[186] Although some of the well-born found the honour of victory in political competition a poor substitute for that of athletics, chiefly because there was potential for grave humiliation in the requirement that *philotimoi* submit to the judgement of the *dēmos* and its values,[187] Alcibiades' whole career was like that of a heroically sporting man: according to Xenophon's Socrates, his easy success ultimately makes him overweening and neglectful of himself (and the true Socratic programme of self-improvement).[188] The culturally specific meaning of the prized fruits of his ambition can be glimpsed in his celebration of athletic achievement. Here too Alcibiades' agency in the history of Athenian politics of spectacular prominence is highly revealing of the possibilities for articulating status through ritualizations of personal primacy in occasions of festivity and merriment.

Alcibiades not only revived charioteering on a heroic scale but also matched his successes with celebrations that enabled the phenomenon of his 'firsthood' to be fully appreciated by fellow citizens. In the first half of the fifth century, as Kurke has observed, 'epinikion, victor statues, and the heroization of athletic victories proliferated', all of which were 'symptoms of an active negotiation between the aristocracy and the community at large over the forms of charismatic power'.[189] Epinician ceremony, moreover, was 'a genuine occasion of prestige for

[186] For the comparison see esp. Xen. *Mem.* 3. 7; Carter 1986: 59.

[187] Carter 1986: 55–9. Plato frequently uses the imagery of athletics to describe politics: esp. *Gorg.* 515e and, emphatically, *Alc.* 1. 120a. Euripides' Hippolytus (*Hip.* 986 ff.) would prefer to hold first place at the games and be second in the city.

[188] Xen. *Mem.* 1. 2. 24—a long sentence moves from mention of the man hunted erotically by many women to *dynamis* both in Athens and with the allies (which was spoilt by many men who themselves had *dynamis*) before culminating in the portrait of sorry self-neglect. Although women and foreigners are here significant audiences for Alcibiades, political prestige and primacy before the *dēmos* seems the sufficient premise for this athletic career of political self-indulgence: 'honoured by the demos and easily being first, as competitive athletes who easily come in first neglect their training, so he neglected himself' (*ὑπὸ δὲ τοῦ δήμου τιμώμενος καὶ ῥᾳδίως πρωτεύων, ὥσπερ οἱ τῶν γυμνικῶν ἀγώνων ἀθληταὶ ῥᾳδίως πρωτεύοντες ἀμελοῦσι τῆς ἀσκήσεως, οὕτω κἀκεῖνος ἠμέλησεν αὑτοῦ*).

[189] Kurke 1993: 155.

the contemporary figure who is being glorified, and this poetic glorification [was] correlated with the realities of wealth, power, and prestige in the here and now'.[190] Charioteering may well have fallen out of fashion: there were no longer Deinomenids nor Spartans to raise the stakes of the competition.[191] It was, moreover, the most exciting but inegalitarian of sports—Alcibiades supposedly withdrew exclusively into horsey sport, complaining that in other contests there were athletes of low birth.[192] But charioteering had traditionally brought especially potent political glory because the stakes were high and the wealth necessary to compete was also serviceable for lavish *megaloprepeia* in celebration.[193] It is to this celebration that Alcibiades alluded when (in the Sicilian Debate) he replied to Nicias' personal attacks with a defiant assertion of his Olympic achievements: 'I won and came second and fourth and arranged everything else in a style worthy of my victory. By custom such things are *timē* and yet at the same time too an impression of power is made by the performance.'[194] Politics is competitive like athletics.[195] But Alcibiades can also find persuasiveness in affecting memories. Thucydides does not specify the 'everything else' of the previous year, supposing the ingredients of such an occasion to be quite familiar.[196] Certainly a sacrifice

[190] Nagy 1990: 12. Admittedly there were 5th-cent. victors of whom we know little, but it cannot be argued from their historical obscurity that their victories made no impression in the *polis*, even though it is doubtful that they had either the ambition or the flair for self-promotion of Alcibiades. A list of victors is at Davies 1981: 167–8 and Kyle 1993: 195–228.

[191] Davies 1981: 102–3 on chariot-racing's decline.

[192] Isoc. 16. 33.

[193] Although Alcibiades was physically strong he did not compete in gymnastic contests, since those athletes were badly-born, from small *poleis*, and of base *paideia* (Isoc. 16. 33; cf. Rhodes 1986: 137–8). On attention explicitly drawn to the wealth of the competitors note Xen. *Ages*. 9. 6; cf. Plut. *Ages*. 20. On Alcibiades' *megaloprepeia* see Kurke 1991: 171–82, stressing it as the mark of the 'incipient tyrant'.

[194] Thuc. 6. 16. 2: . . . *τἆλλα ἀξίως τῆς νίκης παρεσκευασάμην. νόμῳ μὲν γὰρ τιμὴ τὰ τοιαῦτα, ἐκ δὲ τοῦ δρωμένου καὶ δύναμις ἅμα ὑπονοεῖται.*

[195] Ober 1998: 110.

[196] *Ἀλκιβιάδης . . . θύσας Ὀλυμπίῳ Διὶ τὴν πανήγυριν πᾶσαν εἱστίασε* . . . . 416 must be the date, for Lichas won first prize in 420 (Thuc. 5. 50. 4) and 424 is too early for such stress upon the event: Gomme, Andrewes, and Dover, *HCT* 1970 ad Thuc. 6. 16. 2, with discussion of inconsistencies in reports of the event.

and a feast should be assumed to have been held. The Epitomator of the lost first book of Athenaeus (1. 5) confirms that this was certainly the case at Olympia: 'With the gaze of the Greek world upon him, he was keenly aware of what it was impossible to do at home.'[197] Alcibiades must have been delighted to be an object of wonder, processing at the head of the *pompē* to the altar.[198]

Greek athletic victors had always been generally understood to be exceptional men, who not only might be buried in public ceremony but might, even in the fifth century, receive hero-cult.[199] Such glorification was tolerated at Athens, where victors had always been accommodated within the more egalitarian constraints of the post-Solonian state.[200] But even if victors continued to loom stylishly large in the life of the fifth-century *polis*, there was, however, an ambivalence about their exceptionality, since such successful men not only evoked envy

[197] Cf. Gribble 1999: 65. Themistocles (Plut. *Them.* 17) had also succeeded in drawing the gaze of Greece upon himself at the first Olympic games after the Persian Wars: when he entered the stadium, the audience switched their attentions away from the athletes and spent the whole day looking at him, pointing him out to others, admiring, and applauding. This was the reward for saving Greece; and, while Themistocles surely enjoyed himself, he did not win a race.

[198] The parade might have been all the more impressive if he had borrowed, as it could be claimed, the Athenian ceremonial utensils for his own celebration, so that those who saw them in the Athenian parade the next day either supposed that Alcibiades had loaned his vessels to his *polis* or, realizing what he had done, laughed at the Athenians when 'they saw one man more powerful than his entire *polis*'; Athenian allies too perhaps contributed generously, enabling Alcibiades to invert the relationship between individual and *polis*: [And.] 4. 29–30. Supposedly, the Ephesians generously erected a Persian marquee twice as large as that for the official Athenian deputation, the Chians contributed sacrificial victims and fodder for his horses, and the Lesbians chipped in with wine and other sundries: [And.] 4. 30. This speech is fictitious, inasmuch as it was not actually delivered to the Assembly (on the occasion of a vote on ostracism) and is probably a literary exercise, but the details can still suggest Alcibiades' attitude toward his *polis*.

[199] Ael. *VH* 8. 16. Heroes (but not at Athens): Fontenrose 1968. Victors at the most important festivals figure prominently in battle: Kurke 1993: 133–7.

[200] Solon was thought to have fixed the rewards to be paid by the *polis* to victors of the Isthmian and Olympic games: Plut. *Sol.* 23; Diog. Laert. 1. 55–6. In classical times the victors at major festivals dined in the *prytaneion* upon their return: *IG* I³ 131. 11 ff. and Plato *Apol.* 36d 5–9.

(of men and gods) but also precisely possessed power. Epinician celebration carefully effected a ritualized 'reintegration' of a victor, in which the glory of victory became a lasting possession for both the athlete and his *polis*.[201] Upon his return to Athens, Alcibiades' firelit festivities of singing and also feasting were able to effect Athenian pride as well as adumbrate personal heroism.

Thc bricf surviving fragments of the ode by Euripides reveal the familiar epinician link made between the victor and his community, mentioning the city of high repute (*τὰν Πόλιν εὐδόκιμον*).[202] Sadly, the grievous loss of the complete ode makes it impossible to know how exactly the balancing act between spectacular individuality and communal sensibilities was effected in the allocation of praise between the victor and the *polis*: was the victor as much the principal focus as seems to be the case in Pindar, or did Athens loom gloriously great throughout the song?[203] The only other extant fragment purportedly from this ode lays unsurprising stress upon the exceptional nature of the achievement—it was a victory unprecedented in Hellas.

*σὲ δ' ἄγαμαι,*
*ὦ Κλεινίου Παῖ. καλὸν ἁ νίκα,*
*κάλλιστον δ', ὃ μηδεὶc ἄλλοc Ἑλλάνων,*
*ἅρματι Πρῶτα δραμεῖν καὶ δεύτερα καὶ τρίτα⟨τα⟩,*
*βῆναί τ' ἀΠονητὶ Διὸc στεφθέντ' ἐλαί*
*κάρυκι βοὰν Παραδοῦναι.*[204]

But of you, son of Cleinias, I stand in awe. Victory is a beautiful thing, but most beautiful is to do what no other Greek has done—run first, second, and third with the chariot, and arrive without toil, wreathed

[201] Crotty 1982: esp. 104–38 and Kurke 1991: *passim*.

[202] Plut. *Dem*. 1.

[203] Loraux 1986: 52: 'the eulogy of the city is grafted onto that of the individual.'

[204] The text is that of Campbell 1992 no. 755 from Plut. *Alc*. 11, with emendations well discussed by Bowra 1960. Even this short passage does, however, show that the conventions in Pindar's praise-poetry possessed no normative force for Euripides: Pindar would never have said that the victory was won without toil (cf. Bowra 1964: 172). Euripides is not known to have composed any other epinicia.

with the olive of Zeus, to supply the herald with something to shout about.

The poem also seems to have acknowledged the heroic stature of Alcibiades, in making reference to Zeus, as would be appropriate not only to the Olympic context but also to Alcibiades' own purported heroic lineage.[205] Thus the individuality of this victor at least was not wholly subsumed in his reintegration into a *polis*.

An ode, furthermore, is only a partial script for a victor's moment at the centre of an admiring *polis*.[206] Alcibiades' epinician celebrations would be moments of merriment in which he could easily be seen at his charismatically beautiful best.[207] I do not know whether Alcibiades should be imagined as having actually wielded a sacrificial knife at his epinician celebration but, in filling the air of Athens with smoke and song, he surely seemed as close to being godlike as any very rich slave-owner could dream in a democracy. The rituals of victory located prestigious agency simply in the person of the victor and no distinction was drawn between driving and merely financing a fast chariot.[208] Moreover, memory of this sublime moment was made enduring. The collective felicity lived on, since lyrics by Euripides could become part of the popular repertoire of song that provided a great deal of domestic entertainment.[209]

[205] The emendation of Διὸϲ, first made by Hermann, seems right. The crown was taken from an olive tree that stood near the temple of Zeus: Paus. 5. 15. 2, Bowra 1960: 75. Yet, as Bowra points out, neither Pindar nor Bacchylides 'goes out of his way to give this degree of holiness to the olive-crown'. Alcibiades, however, claimed descent from Eurysaces and thus Zeus himself (Plato *Alc.* 1. 121a).

[206] Cf. McGlew 1993: 37 n. 48.

[207] In epinician song, beauty was celebrated as an integral aspect of aristocratic excellence in the fifth century: e.g. *O.* 8. 19–20, 9. 94, 10. 100; *I.* 2. 4, 7. 22; *N.* 3. 19–20, 11. 13; Donlan 1980: 107; Crowther 1985: 1.

[208] Soph. *Elect.* 680–763 describes both Orestes and the ultimately victorious Athenian driving themselves. Agesilaus prompted his sister's competition precisely to show that money alone was victorious: Xen. *Ages.* 9. Most statues of the victories of Demetrius of Phalerum showed him actually in the chariot: Diog. Laert. 5. 75.

[209] Euripidean verses were sung at informal household meals: Ar. *Nu.* 1353–75. There is, I admit, little evidence to prove that epinician odes became songs familiar to a community wider than the *philoi* of the *laudandus* but I see

Ambitious Alcibiades also employed other traditional tactics of commemoration. The physical fabric of the *polis* bore permanent testimony to his contribution to its visible beauty after he commissioned works of art depicting his victory.[210] All in all, Alcibiades had chronic, charismatic *kudos*.[211]

It is not, therefore, surprising that a most powerful perception of him was of a certain desirability, which was best (if imprecisely) understood through reference to *erōs*. This affect is recorded as central to the political *dynamis* of Alcibiades—and not just in the Platonic tradition.[212] Thucydides first interpreted Alcibiades' persuasiveness in the Sicilian Debate by reference to eroticism,[213] in accord with his systematic diagnosis of the 'pathology' of a heroically irrational commitment to *dynamis*.[214] Aristophanes' audience in the theatre can regard him as they would a tragic hero, his significance embraced by the whole *polis*: 'it craves him but hates him yet still wants him.'[215]

Quite predictably then, Alcibiades' final appearances in Athens (in 407) stirred both *erōs* and fearfulness for his potential to be a tyrant. He made a grand arrival at the Peiraeus, although this was made inauspicious by its coincidence with the

no reason why they should not have been. The ithyphallic hymn in praise of Demetrius Poliorcetes (preserved in Athenaeus' quotation of Duris *FGrHist* F 13) was apparently performed both privately and publicly: 'the warriors of Marathon sang this not only collectively but also in their homes' (ταῦτ' ἦιδον οἱ Μαραθωνομάχαι οὐ δημοσίαι μόνον, ἀλλὰ καὶ κατ' οἰκίαν).

[210] Pausanias (1. 22. 6) describes a picture in the library of the Propylaea representing Alcibiades and his victorious horses. Paintings were done by Aglaophon according to Satyrus (Athen. 12. 534d), by Aristophon according to Plutarch (*Alc.* 16); Bowra 1960: 72. A statue by Pyromachus is attested at Pliny *HN* 34. 80; his *virtus* lived on at Rome in a statue in the Comitia: ibid., 34. 26. The names of several Athenian charioteering victors, including Alcmaeonid ancestors, are preserved in inscriptions: Kyle 1993 nos. A3, A6, A57, P108.

[211] Kurke 1993. [212] Strauss 1993: 152.

[213] 6. 24. 3: 'and a passionate desire to sail seized them all alike' (καὶ ἔρως ἐνέπεσε τοῖς πᾶσιν ὁμοίως ἐκπλεῦσαι); cf. Plutarch (*Alc.* 17) describing Alcibiades' persuasion as fanning an erotic passion into life.

[214] Immerwahr 1973.

[215] *Ra.* 1425: ποθεῖ μέν, ἐχθαίρει δέ, βούλεται δ' ἔχειν.

Plynteria;[216] and spoke in self-justification to the Boule and the Assembly—and in the latter venue his audience was unusually reverent, allowing nobody to speak in opposition.[217] The next pre-eminence he enjoyed was traditional, ceremonial charisma that he himself fashioned: Athenian morale was raised and amends made for past misbehaviour when he marched at the head of the *pompē* to Eleusis.[218] This performance elicited a potent response, according to Plutarch (*Alc.* 34): 'he so demagogued the vulgar and the poor that they lusted with a wondrous lust to be tyrannized by him.'[219]

This formulation might serve well to encapsulate the intricacy of the dynamic between distinct classes of citizens, in which powerful emotions—all the greater of course at this time of grave crisis in the fortunes of the Athenians—could be provoked by an impressive visibility. Those emotions aimed, Plutarch avers (ibid. 35), at removing a hero from political contention, putting him above envy and the general ugliness of politics, so that he could save his *polis*.

Not only do notions about leaders and governance often have powerful affective significance for people but, as Plutarch's syntax itself suggests, the agency involved in such political arousal is not easy to pin down exactly: on this occasion, a leader impressed his significance upon his audience of citizens, which then in turn had an emotional response—and one so remarkable as to defy precise understanding—comprising specifically a longing to become the subjects of a tyrant. While it is impossible, as Plutarch noted (*Alc.* 35), to know quite what

[216] His enemies possibly manipulated the calendar to forestall a glorious return for the exile: B. Nagy 1994. Plutarch describes (*Alc.* 32) the return as a magnificent spectacle—a purple sail and the oarsmen rowing to the piping of Chrysogonus and the call of the actor Callipides; he takes his information from Duris, who claimed to be a descendant of Alcibiades, but notes that Theopompus, Ephorus, and Xenophon did not mention such details.

[217] Xen. *Hell.* 1. 4. 20.

[218] Plut. *Alc.* 34: 'showing off that generalship as a solemn and devout spectacle' (*θέαμα σεμνὸν καὶ θεοπρεπὲϲ τὴν στρατηγίαν ἐκείνην ἐπιδεικν ύμενοϲ*...). The *parodos* of Aristophanes' *Frogs* vividly recalls the procession and the impression it left in the collective memory: Dover 1993: 371; cf. Hatzfeld 1940: 329–30.

[219] *τοὺϲ δὲ φορτικοὺϲ καὶ πένηταϲ οὕτωϲ ἐδημαγώγησεν ὥστ' ἐρᾶν ἔρωτα θαυμα στὸν ὑπ' ἐκείνου τυραννεῖσθαι*....

Alcibiades thought of all this willingness, his entire career of ambitious self-advertisement which was so memorably capped by this splendid march to Eleusis had systematically exploited traditional perceptions of what was deserving of *timē*. Plutarch's biographical analysis is extremely acute.[220]

But while he undoubtedly so effected *dynamis*, Alcibiades' subjectivity was as much shaped by the traditional representations of manly success as were those of the humbler Athenians who came unbidden but gladly to some of a kingly citizen's parties. Throughout his life Alcibiades performed heroically and yet also quite dutifully the roles he had first mimed in the schoolroom, so that always he is to be remembered as more than merely a tyrant manqué; because he improvised upon occasion to perform so brilliantly an idiosyncratic *poiēsis* of power, his dialogic interactions with the appetites and habitual expectations of democratic society ensured that, highly adaptable though he was, it was still Alcibiades' most poignant tragedy to die without a *polis*, far from the Athenians whom he had loved to embrace as really the jurors best worthy to pronounce a sovereign verdict upon his epic significance in the history of his times.[221]

Alcibiades had generated the power to project such value from the reciprocity of needinesses that lay at the heart of the *polis*. Glamorously grandiose figures prior to him had found their own ways to infiltrate the affections of the community, and by whose standards Alcibiades obviously was greatly influenced. Those who came after him found his memory, including his pathetic end, of a quite problematic nature and less commanding of emulation. Codes limiting individual ritual prominence remained in place. But by the time Demosthenes and Aeschines were squabbling over the allocation of honour in the civic arenas of the Athenians, the judgement carried a diminished significance in the wider Greek world: Greeks were not

[220] Cf. Pelling 1992: 24: Plutarch, in developing Thucydidean analysis, 'traces the popular reaction to Alcibiades with more subtlety than Thucydides, and this renders his analysis both more historically interesting and more artistically arresting'.

[221] His bones did not return to a hero's grave (unlike perhaps Themistocles': Plut. *Them.* 32, citing Diodorus the Periegete and Plato Comicus; Kearns 1989: 41).

watching in the way they might once have.[222] Circumstances generally, even after the Athenians revived their city's hegemony in the Aegean and beyond after 377/8, were materially more constrained and there were not the same resources available to aristocrats with impeccable lineages, although that is not to say that there were not those minded in generations to come to try and capture something of that glamorous past.[223] Alcibiades' own descendants, of course, mimicked something of the precocity of the big man but were hindered by lack of resources. The political arena in the fourth century also became more crowded with men who had not held military authority.[224]

Pretensions to pan-hellenic significance continued to be articulated in epic and kingly terms by those commanding the latest imperial materiel. In the spring of 396, King Agesilaus of Sparta, preparing to carry Greek arms to Asia, conducted a sacrifice at Aulis.[225] And before long powerful Macedonians will invade the histories of the city-states, acting beautifully big and sleeping happily with Homer still lodged beneath their pillows. Such kingly warriors could wilfully command demotic feelings of excitement and wonderment,[226] capable of overwhelming any *ressentiment*.

## KINGLY SPECTACLE

In 307 a Macedonian warlord and a host of ships arrived unexpectedly at the undefended Athenian port of Peiraeus, where there was only a disquieted and hastily armed crowd, bringing his pretensions to a truly kingly position in the world.[227] From

[222] Aeschin. 3. 31–4; Dem. *De Cor.* 120.

[223] Thus, for example, Chares who 'gave a feast for Athenians in the Agora, giving epinician sacrifices for the victory against those hospitable to Philip' (Theopompus *FGrHist* F 249; for Chares' lavishness towards the Athenians cf. F 213).

[224] There were more prominent men who had never held a generalship than was the case in the 5th cent.: Hamel 1995: 31.

[225] The fullest account is that of Plutarch (*Ages.* 6); Xenophon plays down the incident (*Hell.* 3. 4. 3). Note also another echo of Agamemnon at Plut. *Mor.* 209b (where the reference is to *Il.* 23. 296 ff.).

[226] At Xen. *Hell.* 1. 4. 13, when Alcibiades sailed home, the crowd gathers 'wondering at and wanting to see Alcibiades'.

[227] The description is at Plut. *Demetr.* 8–10.

his ship a herald proclaimed that Demetrius Poliorcetes was bringing freedom to the Athenians. Thereupon Poliorcetes was hailed, amid much clapping and shouting, as saviour and benefactor of the Athenians. The effective ruler of Athens for the last decade (with the backing of Cassander), Demetrius of Phalerum, disappeared. After settling ashore, Poliorcetes did proceed to restore the Athenians' ancestral constitution. He also pledged 150,000 *medimnoi* of grain, and timber enough for the construction of one hundred triremes. In gratitude for such generosity, the epigraphic record suggests that the Athenian Assembly was between 307 and 301 'almost frenetically active' in honouring Demetrius (and his supporters too)—and earning a reputation for extravagant flattery.[228] The Athenians were the first, avers a disdainful Plutarch, to call Demetrius Poliorcetes (and his father Antigonus Monophthalmus) *basileus*.[229]

Athens had as much political as strategic significance. No other *polis* could bestow quite such valuable prestige. To be sure, this king possessed the power to command satisfaction of his desires. Athenians soon knew what Demetrius could do to a *polis* that was not so favoured a destination for a new and headstrong king, when he made a pillaging foray into the territory of the Megara. He could be cruel.[230] Should need or caprice strike him, he was capable of destroying Athens and condemning all its inhabitants to death or enslavement. Fortunately at this time the Athenians had a rich tradition of discerning familiarity with men of uncommon desire for prestigious repute. They had *timē* to give. Happily enough Demetrius and his father were interested in this.

It was prudent on the part of the Athenians to recognize the kingly power realistically and to offer honours precisely. By entering into a relationship of reciprocity, the Athenians traded for freedom from all their worst fears.[231] Such mutuality of regard brought forth a ruler-cult predicated upon the actual

[228] Habicht 1997: 71, noting too that the Assembly was also eager 'to exhibit the results of its work in a highly visible manner' in the traditional style.

[229] Plut. *Demetr.* 10; Billows 1990: 156.

[230] He crucified over eighty opponents in front of the city of Orchomenos (in Arcadia): Diod. 20. 103. 6.

[231] Cf. Price 1984 and Koenen 1993: 44.

presence of a king. Demetrius and his father received cultic honours as 'savior gods' complete with a priesthood and full package of festivity.[232] There were athletic contests. There were statues—of gold—installed alongside those of the tribal heroes and the tyrant-slayers, Harmodius and Aristogeiton, in the Agora, the heart of the *polis*, when two tribes were named after the kings; two new state triremes were also named for them. The statues of Demetrius of Phalerum were destroyed.[233] After the Athenians rebelled for a second time in 287, most of the honours for Antigonus and Demetrius were abolished but not the religious cult and the names of the two tribes.[234] Demetrius, after all, was a powerful presence in Athenian history.[235]

Many Athenians may well have voted in their Assembly for the lavish honours, proposed by politicians of the likes of Stratocles, in order to conciliate Demetrius and allay their fears for what he might do to them, their livelihoods, their liberties, their kin, and their *polis* itself. At the same time his species of kingliness possessed a style they had habitually respected and often loved. In all likelihood Athenians found much to admire in Demetrius Poliorcetes. He was not (apart perhaps from sleeping with Athene) doing much that was wholly unprecedented, although certainly no single man had hitherto shaped his behaviour to allude to so many grand models simultaneously. The pragmatic generosity of the Athenians was perhaps tinged with an ingenuous willingness to indulge a man whose person as well as his power were able to afford moments and memories of pure wonderment, theatrically projecting himself as a beautiful celebrity. As a spectacular figure much observed and talked (and sung) about, Demetrius was intimately associated with sex and wine, with traditions of kingliness and religious charisma.

Athenians at the end of the third century had become accustomed to regal graces in the form of Demetrius of Phalerum.

232 Details of honours at Habicht 1970: 46–7 and n. 15 and 1997: 68–9; Diod. 20. 46. 1–2; Plut. *Demetr.* 11. A convenient list of Demetrius' honours is also supplied by Scott 1928: 238–9.

233 Diog. Laert. 5. 77. Reputedly there were 360 statues of him in Athens: R. Smith 1985: 211.

234 Habicht 1997: 88.

235 The Rhodian democracy accepted the past—as well as looked prudently into an uncertain future—and retained statues of Demetrius (and his father) after withstanding his siege: Diod. 20. 93. 6–7.

Although he ruled with the support of Cassander of Macedon, there is nothing in the historical tradition to associate him with any particularly repressive actions. Nor is there evidence that there was any serious resistance to his power. He carefully cultivated his image and his pre-eminence in the *polis*. Like many memorable Athenians before him, Demetrius of Phalerum possessed eloquence.[236] It is also telling that he invested heavily in chariot-racing.[237] Furthermore, he placed, as Ferguson rather cuttingly observed, 'so much stress upon an effective appearance that he blondined his hair, and cultivated an extreme elegance of manner'.[238] While much of his domestic legislative activity seems to have been directed at curtailing extravagances, where the reception of his own significance was concerned, he had scant scruple: it may fairly be suspected that a decrease in the level of other aristocrats' ostentation would gratifyingly throw into a sharper relief his own magnificence.[239] This 'dandified intellectual' lived in a style 'at startling variance with the rules he imposed' upon other prominent, wealthy Athenians:[240]

> He entertained in regal fashion . . . His love for magnificence was displayed in the wonderful Dionysiac procession which he arranged while archon in 308; and his passion for public distinctions—his pleasure in the numerous crowns and statues offered to him by the Athenians—was so notorious, that a comic poet affirmed that he had accepted a statue for every day of the year.[241]

[236] Cic. *Off.* 1.3; Quint. *Inst.* 10. 1. 80.

[237] Charioteering: Ferguson 1911: 50 and 59.

[238] Ferguson 1911: 40; Duris *FGrHist* F 10: 'he cultivated his appearance'; he even used rouge. His seductions were apparently a frequent source of censure (Carystius in Athen. 12. 542).

[239] Details of legislative reforms of liturgies and sumptuary legislation: Ferguson 1911: 55–8. He protested Periclean lavishness: Cic. *Off.* 2. 60.

[240] Green 1990: 46. Duris at Athen. 12. 542*b–e*; Carystius of Pergamum, ibid. 542*e*–543*a*. Interestingly his grandson, according to Hegesander, also lived large, his arrogant actions including the building of a massive viewing stand at the Panathenaea and a throne for his *hetaira* Aristagora at Eleusis: Athen. 4. 167*e–f*; Habicht 1997: 153.

[241] Ferguson 1911: 59, based on Pliny *HN* 34. 27; Diog. Laert. 5. 75.

There was the same capturing of the limelight at the festivities of the Dionysia that the next Demetrius would also find so congenial. Demetrius of Phalerum heard poems sung in his honour as the *pompē* moved along, in which he was celebrated extravagantly as *heliomorphos*.[242] His procession was even remembered for including a mechanical snail, which appeared to move of its own energy and left a trail of slimy mucus along its route through the city.[243]

Demetrius Poliorcetes clearly lived even larger in the world but he also made certain to position his beautiful self at the centre of communal wonderment. A Hellenistic king needed to have 'personal qualities of physical attractiveness, dignity and culture'.[244] He was tall, if not as tall as his father, and wondrously good-looking; no painter or sculptor succeeded in capturing his likeness.[245] He was in fact something of a pioneer in putting himself upon coins—and he had at many times in his life, of course, rather a lot of bullion from which to coin.[246] In other respects as well Demetrius was constructing a grand presence. Duris notes his dramatically innovative costume: his feet were clad in the most expensive purple felt; he wore fancy cloaks embroidered with depictions of the heavenly firmament and the signs of the Zodiac, as was fitting for a divinity; his hat too was of purple, fastened by a band shot through with gold and finished with fringes that hung down his back.[247] With this finery Demetrius surpassed, Duris was prepared to believe, all his kingly predecessors, including

[242] Duris *FGrHist* 76 F 10.

[243] Polyb. 12. 13. 11. Demochares interpreted this marvel as a symptom of the degradation of the Athenians. Still, surely well worth seeing, one would have thought.

[244] Sherwin-White and Kuhrt 1993: 199.

[245] *Demetr.* 2. The overall aesthetic impression of his features is described by Plutarch in a manner programmatic of his thematic interest in the man's significance: 'he had at once grace and strength, dignity and beauty, and there was blended with youthful eagerness a certain heroic look and a kingly majesty that were hard to imitate' (trans. Perrin) (*τὸ γὰρ αὐτὸ χάριν καὶ βάρος καὶ φόβον καὶ ὥραν εἶχε, καὶ συνεκέκρατο τῷ νεαρῷ καὶ ἰταμῷ δυσμίμητος ἡρωική τις ἐπιφάνεια καὶ βασιλικὴ σεμνότης*).

[246] Green 1990: 126.

[247] Duris at Athen. 12. 535 f.; cf. Plut. *Demetr.* 41. Such a striking cloak has Persian antecedents (L'Orange 1953: 65 and 80–7).

Pausanias of Sparta, Dionysius of Syracuse, or even Alexander the Great himself. He also made his presence felt pan-hellenically. He presided over the games at Argos, holding festivities for all Greeks, making a marriage to Pyrrhus' sister, and at Sicyon—well, apparently he actually moved Sicyon and renamed it after himself. The new *polis* of Demetrias was founded with the appropriate ceremonies, including sacrifices.[248] At the Isthmus there was an assembly, and crowds gathered: he was proclaimed *hēgemōn* of Greece, as Philip and Alexander had been proclaimed before him. His stylish life demanded exceptional housing in which to show himself and his relative proximity to immortality to proper advantage, so he set up quarters, apparently at the invitation of the fawning Athenians, in the rear chamber of the Parthenon.[249] As has been well remarked, there was generally 'a staginess, a theatrical panache about all Demetrius' actions, which has been recognised as a highly characteristic feature of the whole Hellenistic age'.[250]

All the wondrousness of such visibility nevertheless points to timeless conceptions of heroic, autocratic power.[251] People travelled to view with wonder the big, beautiful, and heroically impressive man of war.[252] There was specifically Homeric allusion in Demetrius' visit to Argos—and also in the stories that circulated about all his activities and especially his notorious devotion to concubines.[253] The dalliances with the most beautiful and the most sophisticated *hetairai* must have made for endlessly satisfying fame through gossip and titillation, and so too his marriages were fascinating in their combination of erotics and grand diplomacy.[254] Thus his dealings with women could in epic fashion be understood to shape the narrative of history. His life also contained numerous episodes that begged

[248] Diod. 20. 102. 2–3.

[249] *Demetr.* 23.

[250] Green 1990: 126; cf. Pollitt 1986: 6–7.

[251] K. Scott 1928: 224; Hornblower 1981: 195.

[252] Diod. 20. 92. 3.

[253] When Demetrius demands of Mania her *πυγή*, she demands a present of him too; when he obliges, she remarks 'son of Agamemnon, now that is permitted you' (*Ἀγαμέμνονος παῖ, νῦν ἐκεῖν' ἔξεστί σοι*) (Athen. 13.579a).

[254] Demetrius was the most of all kings inclined to marry: Plut. *Pyrr.* 10, cf. 9. Plentiful information about Demetrius' *hetairae* is in Athenaeus (Books 3, 4, 6, 13, and 14).

for tragic dramatization (and perhaps too with some scope for a rambunctious, if maybe somewhat dark, comedy).[255]

It is no surprise to hear that the presence of Demetrius Poliorcetes among the Athenians was celebrated in popular song. The ithyphallic hymn (performed in 291 or 290) was an ever necessary token of devotion, whilst at the same time it also articulated expectations for concrete benevolence in return, since at the heart of this surviving song was an appeal to the king for help against the Aetolians.[256] The lyrical acknowledgement of Poliorcetes' power took the form of stressing not only his associations with other divinities but also expressing his entitlement to such apprehension in virtue of his actual presence among the Athenians: he was there as other powerful gods obviously were not. This lavish if honest conceit attracted the scorn of Duris of Samos, indignant at how the proud history of the Athenians had so been degraded. It is advisable, if all the realities of political life are to be properly comprehended, to note that songs such as this one were in fact quite popular. This ithyphallic performance lived on beyond the occasion and the circumstances for which it was composed. For Duris, seeking to reveal the extent of the Athenian degradation, mentions that the song caught the popular fancy: the people who fought at Marathon sang it in their own homes.[257] Music, of course, would be an important feature in the cult of the new saviour gods, just as it had always, of course, been a delight for almost all gatherings of ancient socio-religious life.[258] Dancing too is mentioned in Demochares' description of Athenians enjoying this festivity of flattery:

> When Demetrius returned from Leucas and Corinth to Athens, not only did the Athenians welcome him with offerings of incense and crowns and libations, but processional choruses also, and mummers with the elevated phallus met him with dancing and song; and as they

[255] In Plutarch's *Demetrius* the imagery of dramatic tragedy recurs so persistently 'that the whole structure of the biography appears to be conceived in terms of a tragedy': De Lacy 1952: 168.

[256] Habicht 1997: 93.

[257] *FGrHist* F 13: *supra* n. 208.

[258] K. Scott: 1928: 144. Philochorus reports that the Athenians sang paeans in honour of Antigonus and Demetrius which were composed by Hermippus of Cyzicus: Athen. 6. 253b.

took their places in the crowds they sang and danced, repeating the refrain that he was the only god, while all the others were asleep, or on a journey, or did not exist; he, however, was sprung from Poseidon and Aphrodite, pre-eminent in his beauty and embracing all in his benevolence. (Loeb translation)

Poliorcetes was all gladness, as is fitting for a king and a god. Ruler-cult was 'in the last resort the result of the impression made by personality'.[259] He was, as the song says, a god actually present amidst the Athenians.

If the phenomenon of ruler-cult, moreover, is 'part of a larger, complex process which involves both the distancing and the mystification of politics and the appropriation of ritual to represent tradition',[260] the process involved happy feeding of Athenian appetites. 'One link between Demetrius and the divine is his beauty, his grace and his love of mirth and pleasure.'[261] New festivities were unlikely to be exactly unwelcome to many in Athens. Libations were poured to Dionysus but wine surely was poured down citizens' throats as well.[262] In fact, given the disposition of Demetrius for merriment (as well as for other moods associated with dipsomania), it was pleasing to think of him as a Dionysus and this drinker consciously acted out the mythology of that god.[263] Skilled Dionysiac artists also spread the association.[264] They had plenty to work with.

The Athenians' accommodation of Demetrius to their (enlarged) communal scripts may have had its delights but it still also had its pragmatic advantages. Rulers can be called upon to live up to their own idealized presentations.[265] Demetrius was good at reciprocation. Even when he could have used simple force to maintain the obedience and submission of the Athenians he employed his stagy panache. When he had overthrown by armed force (in 295) a demagogue, Lachares, who had in some sense taken control in Athens (probably in the spring of 300, and probably too at a time of severe food crisis),[266] the king made a

[259] Nock 1972: i. 152. [260] Humphreys 1993: xix.

[261] K. Scott 1928: 226.

[262] Libations: Phylarchus apud Athen. 6. 261b–c. Such toasts for kings were particularly associated with Alexander: K. Scott 1928: 153–5.

[263] Diod. 20. 92. 4. [264] K. Scott 1928: 234.

[265] J. C. Scott 1989: 161. [266] Habicht 1997: 82–5.

dramatic appearance before the *dēmos* in the theatre, where he had told them to assemble. Guards were posted and then, 'in a melodramatic gesture', he entered from the rear and made his way in stately silence the entire way to the stage. His tone was chiding but mild. He promised grain. And of course he received in return fresh honours, including a day and a month in the calendar; and a festival commemorating his majesty was added to that of Dionysus.[267] But better such deference and festivity of accommodation than a king's civic exercise of military power.

Other fourth-century Greek *poleis* where perhaps the value accorded citizen spectators and the habits of pre-eminence were not as durably continuous as at Athens witnessed violence. In Sicily, for example, tyrants could not be qualitatively recognized as entirely distinct from other competing big-men and yet, some periods of democracy notwithstanding, power determined more in battles than in assemblies. At Syracuse, the oscillating styles of self-presentation appear to have reflected idiosyncratic relations to the mass of citizenry rather than any durability of civic habit, with some rulers seeking charismatic pre-eminence whilst others were willing on occasion to descend to demotic familiarities.[268] Dionysius I maintained his power but was not loved at home or abroad. In search of pan-hellenic prestige he went to compete at the Olympics in 388. But his chariots not only failed to win but either broke down or collided with others. He had his own compositions performed but the audience jeered.[269] Dionysius II sent a chariot to meet Plato from his ship and gave a sacrifice in thanksgiving for his arrival

[267] Habicht 1997: 87. For the honours themselves see Plut. *Demetr.* 12. 1–2, where the honours of both 295 and 307 are bundled together; cf. Habicht 1970: 50–5. The games were annual: Diod. 20. 46. 2. His associates were also generously treated: Herodorus, who had helped the Athenians to gain a pact of friendship and the continuation of democratic government, became entitled to free meals in *prytaneis* for life and a bronze statue in the Agora next to those of the tyrant-slayers and the saviours themselves, Demetrios and Antigonus: Habicht 1997: 88.

[268] Other Sicilian cities had tastes for elaborate political display. The Acragantines, for example, were famous for this: e.g. Diod. 13. 82. 7–8 and 84. 3 and 5.

[269] Diod. 14. 19.

but his banquets and his entourages were not excessive.[270] When in exile in Corinth, Dionysius was a pleasingly humble and intriguing sight, at the fishmonger's or the perfumer's shop, drinking in the taverns, fooling around in plain view with prostitutes, earnestly teaching song-girls, and so generally prompting speculation about his motives. Was he naturally affable or did he desire to be held in contempt rather than fear?[271]

Dion's authority was initially represented by grandly heroic pre-eminence. He commenced the liberation of Syracuse by mustering his mercenaries on Zacynthus, leading a march to the temple of Apollo, and presiding over a magnificent sacrifice to Apollo. After the sacrifice, there was a feast in the stadium, with gold and silver beakers.[272] Once victory had been achieved, Dion proceeded through the Achradina district where the Syracusans had set out tables and sacrificial meats and mixing-bowls on both sides of the street. He was pelted with flowers and hailed as though he were a god. Finally Dion ascended a conspicuous and tall sundial (set up by Dionysius) as his *bēma* from which to delight the citizens with his proclamation of their freedom.[273] But in contrast to Dionysius II, Dion did not slacken the gravity of his demeanour in dealing with the common people.[274]

Agathocles, on the other hand, thought it prudent to avoid the overweening attitude of a tyrant or monarch. He tore off his military cloak and put on a regular *himation*, to show he was one of the many. This was mere acting but effective nonetheless.[275] He did not start to wear a diadem, which by (newly developed Hellenistic) convention would have indicated kingliness, but habitually wore a wreath instead. This marked the priesthood he had held before becoming tyrant (and did a better job of covering his thinning hair).[276] He could regard the crowd as his bodyguard and he used to enter the Assembly alone, unlike the

270 Plut. *Dion* 13. 271 Plut. *Tim.* 14. 272 Plut. *Dion* 23.

273 Plut. *Dion* 29. Dion would be hailed as saviour and *theos* by the Syracusans: ibid. 46.

274 Plut. *Dion* 52. An opponent, Heracleides, refuses to meet with Dion in the Council and insisted upon dialogue in the Assembly before the other citizens (ibid. 53).

275 Diod. 19. 9. 2. 276 Diod. 20. 54. 1; cf. Ael. *VH* 11. 4.

famously paranoid Dionysius.[277] In meetings of the assembly he jeered and mimicked individuals so that often the crowd would laugh as though they were watching performers of mimes or marvels.[278] And in drinking sessions he showed himself as more humble than the men who happened by, in order again to solicit the goodwill of the many.[279] Yet despite such ingratiating behaviour, there could be no doubt of the instrumentalities of power he possessed. Apparently Agathocles' bronze bed, which roasted his victims alive, was superior to that of Phalaris, the sixth-century, archetypical Sicilian tyrant, simply because those dying in agony were visible.[280]

Spectacles of physical suffering have their own power and Sicily had its share of them. Mamercus surrendered to Timoleon and was brought to Syracuse for trial. The people shouted him and his carefully prepared speech down, so he flung away his *himation* and ran across the theatre and tried to kill himself by bashing his head against one of the stone steps. Failing in this, he was taken away to suffer the punishment of a pirate.[281] Such things must have had a profound effect upon the sensibilities of children and youngsters. Timaeus told (in great detail) of Philistus stripped and insulted and beheaded. His body was given to boys to drag through the city.[282] In the Sicilian town of Messana, schoolchildren were brought into the theatre to watch the torture of the tyrant Hippo—a 'very fine spectacle'.[283] All in all it is not surprising that Pyrrhus (a king convinced of his own descent from Achilles) became less a demagogue and more a tyrant when in Sicily.[284]

The Athenians escaped the need of becoming accustomed to habitual violence in their civic arenas but rather remained a notably valuable source of prestige in the Greek world, even

[277] Diod. 20. 63. 3. [278] Diod. 20. 63. 2.

[279] Diod. 20. 63. 1. The frankness of intoxication also kept him well informed.

[280] Diod. 20. 71. 3. Such visible inducements to submission were obviously effective in war: Agathocles hung Utican prisoners upon his siege engine (Diod. 20. 54. 2).

[281] Plut. *Tim.* 34.

[282] Plut. *Dion* 35.

[283] Plut. *Tim.* 34; cf. Clearchus ap. Athen. 12.541d–e; Green 1990: 217.

[284] Hornblower 1981: 195. Plut. *Pyrrh.* 23 (between 278 and 276).

with its widening Hellenistic horizons.[285] The whole world never exactly did look exclusively upon men such as Dion.[286] But prestige among the more peaceable Athenians was counted as valuable as the harbour of Peiraeus, in large part because of their complex traditions of discrimination, in which assertive self-aggrandisement had in all sorts of intricate ways been reconciled to the sensibilities of commonality, both inescapable and inalienable. Democracy had valued the votes and the approbations of the humbler, and such significance of judgement persisted into a period more favourable to the posturing of kings and prosperous aristocrats.[287] There were fresh wonders through which to proclaim a new age of possibilities for spectacular civic life yet there were also echoes of aristocratic prominence from within the narrower confines of Athens' days of glory.[288] Never would all have the same reactions. One man's wonderment can be another's contempt. But even flagrant innovation in spectacular selfhood could reinforce awareness, on the part of both actor and audience, of precisely what durable norms and values were being transgressed. Popular appetites, moreover, did not fundamentally change from the days of Alcmaeonids to those of later but still pretty men, their bigger fortunes, and all their expensive snail-slime. Tastes changed, but memorable wonder and merriment and the men who dispensed them were always worth treasuring, whatever the schemes and techniques by which they had been wrought.

Athens offered, therefore, a stable but flexible critical environment to serve as a favoured destination for big-men determined to cut a fine figure for themselves. Of course, the city was

[285] εὐδοξία and τιμή (Plut. *Demetr.* 8). Ferguson remarks (1911: 69) that 'to be praised and known there was the highest ambition of generals, artists, and literary men'.

[286] [Plato] *Ep.* 4. Dion keeps his gaze exclusively upon the Academy: Plut. *Dion* 52.

[287] Athenians in Hellenistic times would have a constitution that favoured the interests of the wealthier citizens: Habicht 1997: 57.

[288] Lineage, for example, helped Ptolemy's governor of Cyrenaica, who had a wife who claimed descent from the family of Miltiades, the victor of Marathon, to recruit many Athenians (particularly from the group which lost political rights in 317) as mercenaries for a war against Carthage: Habicht 1997: 65.

also a pleasant place for the great and the glamorous to spend lengthy sojourns as celebrities. It boasted, from a fifth-century heyday of democracy and imperial wealth, fine buildings, monuments, statues and paintings, and an interesting collection of talented inhabitants. As an important *emporion* it could provide a wealthy man with many of the good things of a life of luxury. But, above all, the Athenians' sophistication as political consumers provided the gratifying power of prestige that would continue to attract kingly grandees long into the future, ambitious to test themselves upon the touchstone of demotic affection, just as it had brought out the best in well-born Athenians. Julius Caesar would show great mercy to the Athenians whilst unable to resist noting that they were indebted for their deliverance to the fame of their forefathers.[289] Other cities did not have quite such a legacy.[290]

Sulla had been crueller, sacking Peiraeus and much of the city itself in 86, but he also desired festive celebrity and immortal prestige of the sort enjoyed by Demetrius Poliorcetes. In 84/3 there was a festival for him, he cavorted with Dionysiac artists, received a statue, and chose as a symbol for his coinage a depiction of Harmodius and Aristogeiton, the tyrant-slayers, commemorating and validating the execution of Aristion, the pro-Mithradates Athenian leader.[291] He never regretted his mercy.[292] After Caesar, Antony came to stay for a while at Athens and his progress eastwards away from Rome was, at least in the shrewd schematics of Plutarch's biographical narrative, reflected in his civic comportment. At large in Greece he interested himself in literary discussions and making judgements at law; he was generous; and he was to be seen too at the centre of games and religious ceremonies: 'Greece sees him at his best.'[293]

[289] App. *BC* 2. 368.

[290] Augustus Caesar mounted a bema to make a proclamation to the citizens of Alexandria after his capture of it: he would spare it because of its size and beauty, Alexander, and a friend: Plut. *Mor.* 207a–b.

[291] Raubitschek 1951; Habicht 1997: 311.

[292] Sulla counted it one of the two most significant pieces of fortune in his career: Plut. *Mor.* 202e; cf. *Sull.* 6 and 14, *Comp. Lys and Sull.* 5.

[293] Pelling 1988: 175.

Antony had a fondness for Greek cities in general but he found presence among the Athenians to be most satisfying.[294] He erected a scaffold in full view above the theatre. It was roofed with green boughs like caves for Dionysian revels, from which hung tambourines, fawnskins and other Dionysian objects. Here Antony, starting in the early morning, reclined with his friends, drinking. Artists brought from Italy entertained the party, while Greeks from all over came to see the spectacle. Sometimes, Socrates of Rhodes claimed, Antony moved his revels to the top of the Acropolis, to look down upon the city illuminated by lights hanging from the roofs. Antony ordered that he should be proclaimed as Dionysus throughout all the cities.[295] Indulgence of his especial affection for Athens was most manifest in his prominent involvement in civic life during the winter of 39/8, when his behaviour was nicely calibrated to the environment of his hosts. Plutarch in particular is happy to emphasize the simplicity of Antony in his philhellenism, in contrast to the excesses to which he will be tempted by the grandiosities of Alexandrine courtly ways.[296] He has no mention of Antony and Octavia being hailed as euergetic gods nor of his general encouragement of his identification with Dionysus.[297] In performing, for example, the office of gymnasiarch, Antony was happy to dress the part, exchanging his Roman insignia for the rods of the local office. Wearing Greek dress and white shoes, he refereed the sporting contests, actually separating the combatants in the ring.[298] The Athenians, of course, were connoisseurs of such management of a dignity which, while resting upon an *imperator*'s military might that could easily have made all suffer thoroughly at his coming, was happy to defer instead to vernacular traditions; and the more liberal the Athenians could appear in their hospitality, the more admirable became the celebrity of their guest, especially if with studied casualness he modulated his autocracy to a

[294] Plut. *Ant.* 23. [295] Athen. 4. 148b–c.

[296] Cf. Pelling 1988: 208–9.

[297] He made his wishes clear to Greeks: Dio 48. 39. 2.

[298] Plut. *Ant.* 33. An inscription (of 37/6) refers to an Antonian Panathenaic festival honouring a new Dionysus: Habicht 1997: 361–2.

dignity founded upon attentiveness to the interests and pride and dignity of all.

Undoubtedly the greatest potential for a most memorable and happy celebrity was to be found in festivities, whether those providing the community with Dionysiac merriments or more simple and mundane occasions for association with friends, neighbours, and strangers. Happy socializing also offered the greatest potency to those who appeared prominently. The affections aroused by collective merriments were remembered. As we have already seen in the case of Caesar's Rome, prominence as historical celebrities was best established through the practical vehicles of popular culture. Success in self-presentation fixed standards and fashions of pre-eminence. Communal scripts evolved over time but were unfailingly predicated upon fascination with the image of the supreme, heroic individualist. Gone, of course, was the circumspection of democracy. Robbed too of geopolitical autonomy by imperial powers, the *polis* would nevertheless endure as a stage upon which audiences enjoyed spectacular poetics of power. A Hellenistic king's 'glory and pre-eminence would also be such that all he rules think and talk of his actions: like an actor he must attune his behaviour to his station in life'.[299] This has always been true of men ambitious for prestigious distinction.

[299] Aristeas (2A) as cited and translated at Murray 1967: 356; cf. Seneca's suggestion (*Ep*. 76. 31) that dramatic mimesis effectively called into question the business of real life: there was little difference between those who held real power and those who played the part of rulers only upon the stage. Even Demetrius Poliorcetes, ever sensitive to both circumstance and audience, went about town (Thebes) in the garb of an ordinary citizen, after being driven out of Macedon by Pyrrhus and Lysimachus: Plut. *Demetr*. 45, noting how he made apt a quotation from Euripides' *Bacchae*.

# 4
# Kings and Elephants

277 bakers, 29 pot-tenders, 13 milk-dish-makers, 17 drink-mixers, 70 wine-strainers, 329 musical concubines, 46 chaplet-weavers, and 40 perfumiers.[1]

Hellenistic monarchies were predicated upon loot. Homer had sketched a world in which habits of expropriation accompanied heroic prowess. Once Alexander the Great had shown himself so determined to make eastern resources available for Greeks to take and enjoy, the Diadochoi—the Successors to Alexander who sought to fill the imperial vacuum his death left—plundered upon an extraordinary, systematic scale.[2] The spears of Macedonian kings conquered all sorts of places and peoples.[3] Victoriousness in war fundamentally served as demonstrable proof of personal merit and thus entitlement to autocracy: 'it is neither descent nor legitimacy that gives monarchies to men, but the ability to command an army and to handle affairs competently.'[4] By 300, personal monarchy had shown itself the only way to control large territory and great revenue.[5] And when Hellenistic kings were not busy making war or superintending their streams of revenue, they also devoted a

[1] These were among Alexander's spoils after the battle of Issos: Athen. 13. 608a, highlighted by Miller 1997: 37.

[2] Green 1990: 362 and 367; Aristotle regarded warfare as a natural mode of income (*Pol.* 1256[b] 23 ff.).

[3] 'Spear-won': Diod. 18. 43. 1, 19. 105. 4, 20. 76. 7, 21. 1. 5, 21. 2. 2, 22. 1. 3, after Davies 1984: 296 n. 238.

[4] Suda s.v. *basileia* (tr. Austin); Walbank 1984*a*: 66. Green 1990: 32 stresses the persistence of this tradition throughout Hellenistic times. On the kings as driven primarily by militarism, Austin 1986 is fundamental; on the importance of war to ancient political commentators, note Sherwin-White and Kuhrt 1993: 129.

[5] So Davies 1984: 291.

great deal of energy and resources to managing affairs that concern 'what may perhaps be called self-validation'.[6] Kings of self-made dynasties were probably little responsible themselves for introducing all the fiscal improvements which often produced 'wonderful results'.[7] Rather, one might suspect, they were primarily immersed in the business of wonderment.

Personal stylings had always drawn upon traditional assumptions of kingly wondrousness. Alexander himself had wanted and had won the immortal significance of a Homeric, heroic warrior-leader. Of the Diadochoi the most successful in establishing a royal dynasty was Ptolemy son of Lagus, about whom it could be supposed in suitably eulogistic fashion that 'by ancestry' he was a man 'to accomplish some big deed'. Pedigree notwithstanding, massive resources were put to work to generate new wonders. But with all the soldiers, the slaves and livestock, the treasure and technicians, just what might the power of those who came after Alexander look like when it had mighty and, in Greek eyes, exotic resources with which to explain itself?

Possessing the resources to produce fabulously new stagings of personal significance and prestige, Hellenistic kings continued to define and validate themselves through their spectacular gestures in their cities. Spectacular parades, such as those of Ptolemy Philadelphus or Antiochus IV of Syria which are particularly telling, constituted a simultaneous demonstration of both the instruments and the naturalness of a power that increasingly could be understood best through the rubrics and emotions germane to widely shared notions of divinity. In large measure power was the very ability to generate explanation and justification. The intertwining of the representations of power with its instrumental foundations, moreover, acted to establish the images of a kingliness that would impress immediate observers as well as instil in future generations of Mediterranean warlords and their subjects comprehension of a definitive style of legitimate historical consequence. In aesthetic complicity actor and proudly knowing audience had felt their way together towards mutually satisfying conceptions of

[6] Walbank 1996: 119.

[7] Rostovtzeff 1941: i. 407.

kingliness. As we have already seen, Demetrius Poliorcetes played his part very well, adapting his appearance to fit expectations of what a king ought to look like.[8] No one invented entirely afresh the genres of ritual advertisement by which he intended himself to be understood. But there was also plenty of scope—and all manner of encouragement—to propagate enriched assumptions of what a king could both do and therefore be.

The absolute Macedonian monarchy was the model for all the Diadochoi.[9] It had always been articulated by the king's obvious distinction. On military campaign, kings cut distinctively splendid figures and were able to be readily recognized by their troops.[10] At home in Macedonia, there was not a great deal of elaborate pomp and circumstance.[11] But Macedonian monarchs were always conspicuous, as they maintained close contact with their subjects.[12] They toured the countryside and spoke with their people.[13] They also, of course, presided at sacrifices and other public ceremonies. Kings, however heroic, may have had their own existential issues to confront but they still had to be solicitous of national admirations and those of many other peoples besides, if they were to be properly construed as legitimately powerful, prestigious, and memorable. But Hellenistic kings did not restrict themselves to the traditional stuff of spectacle, the sacrifices, the stolen prominences, the mundane advertisements of their singularity.

Once victorious armies had won new territories to exploit, much of the self-advertisement of Hellenistic kings would be performed in great cities, from which would be issued demands across enormous territories for taxes and obedience, and would

[8] As Plutarch 'shrewdly' (Habicht 1997: 77) observed (*Demetr.* 18), kingship changed the men's behaviour, stirring the men's pride and made them arrogant in their behaviour, just as tragic actors adjust their comportment to their roles.

[9] Sherwin-White and Kuhrt 1993: 119.

[10] Ibid. 126.

[11] Suspicion befell Demetrius Poliorcetes for his ostentatious clothing in the homeland: Plut. *Demetr.* 41–2.

[12] Errington 1990: 219.

[13] e.g. Diod. 16. 3. 1 (Philip II); Polyb. 5. 27. 6 (Philip V); Errington 1990: 219.

employ magnificence to an inflationary degree. Mainland Greek cities, as we have observed, had already become stages for demonstrating the power of the rulers. Alexandria, Alexander's new city on the coast of Egypt, would be a shimmering memorial to the dynasty of the Ptolemies that established itself in the country, a city praised by poets 'almost exclusively in terms of its size and affluence'.[14] In such an environment popular participation in civic institutions was largely a matter of spectatorial consumption. The Hellenistic *polis* usually was more permeable than that of earlier eras, attracting immigrants from diverse lands.[15] Many, whether highly literate or humble, gained a sense of belonging to a civic community through shared experiences. When the crowd thronged the streets to see much, much more promenading before their eyes and into their memories than merely a goddess's garb or even a mechanical snail, all could share in the dramatic semiosis of a king.

There developed ever more lavish theatricality in Hellenistic power-politics.[16] Hellenistic culture can fairly be characterized as having been obsessed with all things theatrical, including masks, actors, and scenes from plays.[17] Some rulers even dabbled with writing as well as producing drama:[18] after being sent westwards for some education, it was perhaps 'symptomatic' that what Ariarathes V of Cappadocia or Nicomedes IV of Bithynia most obviously took back home with them was 'a superficial taste for Greek theatricals'.[19] On the whole, Diogenes the Cynic's radical disdain for the normal habits of his times is evident in his opining that Dionysiac competitions were great spectacles for fools.[20] But some productions took kingliness out before the crowds in the streets.

As might be expected, there is little information with which to gauge the reactions of the crowds in Hellenistic cities to

[14] Cf. esp. Green 1990: 156–7. [15] Davies 1984: 309.

[16] Walbank 1996: 120: 'the hellenistic procession differed from that of the polis . . . in its direction from above and its conscious incorporation of theatrical elements.'

[17] Pollitt 1986: 5–7; Green 1990: 92.

[18] Ptolemy IV Philopator wrote a tragedy, Adonis, and 'presumably played the lead' (Green 1990: 355; Schol. ad Ar. *Thesm.* 1059). This king also founded a *homereion* in Alexandria.

[19] Green 1990: 320. [20] Diog. Laert. 6. 63.

spectacle, even though we can be sure that it worked its effects powerfully upon people, whether or not they were exactly as foolish as a cynic might care to fancy. Our extant sources for great set-pieces of Hellenistic spectacle speak little of audience reactions and appreciations, being more interested simply in cataloguing the sorts of stuff that most happily memorialized the significance of its displayers. In contrast, there will be more to say about the role of the crowd in late republican Rome—precisely because of the competition of grandees for the favour of the *populus*. Roman impresarios naturally were keenly interested in registering responses both favourable and otherwise. The dynamics of a competitive republic can be thrown into sharper relief through contrast with the habits of more regal regimes.

But even expatriate Macedonians manifested a sense of competition with the memorable records of other famous and powerful kings. So, for instance, the name of Ptolemy Philadelphus succeeded in living on as a monumental example of power and also as an adjective for historic grandeur: 'nowadays, in the manner of a proverb, magnificent acts of munificence and mighty buildings are called "Philadelphians" after him.'[21] The resonances of such an exemplary reputation were originally founded upon the impressions made upon urban spectators. Through spectacle the benchmarks by which posterity could judge the classical significance and success of kings first became established. The indirect testimony to the quantities of resources and their investment in festive wonders for urban consumption is implicitly making comparison with the memories of past figures and shaping the ambitions of those to come.

Through one spectacular episode after another, then, new meanings were put upon both ideas and objects in the world. Accordingly this chapter suggests how monarchy freshened its phenomenology in the Greek city and then in a wider world. It deployed the most impressive things it could muster or plunder. Thus, among other wonderfully significant instruments of power, elephants were to be seen in centres of cities. Yet no more were the fortunes of elephants the same in Alexandria, Antioch, and Rome as were other idioms of advertisement

[21] Philo *Vit. Mos.* 2. 29–30, quoted by Coleman 1996: 64.

stable. Habits were once experiments. And so we can see Antiochus IV borrowing Roman—and demotic—presentational styles. In turn, the grandiosities of the later Roman Republic, for all its insistencies upon aristocratic solidarity and democratic deferences, bespoke a kingly element at the heart of its civic life, vigorously animated by the examples and opportunities of the wider Mediterranean world.

## PTOLEMAIC POMP

New conventions of connotation were established in public practice. Hellenistic royalty's audiences had neither the power nor the inclination to insist upon restraint of pre-eminence. But naturally enough they were capable of readily recognizing the most obvious trappings of grandeur. Many things, which in time would come to seem automatically emblematic of monarchy, had been made so by repeated articulation before popular attentions. Kings in Egypt or Syria wore garb that communicated the desirable glamour of royalty, such as boots, cloak, and broad-brimmed hat (or a helmet for war). But these items, modest in comparison with other Near Eastern appurtenances of kingship, were only the traditional dress of Macedonian kings who now enjoyed a vastly different quality of power.[22] Thus too the diadem, which became the key symbol of kingship at issue in Caesar's careful pantomiming before the Roman *populus*, was simply a flat white cloth worn around the head.[23] This article of dress originally took on royal meaning, becoming the 'main exclusive symbol of Hellenistic kingship' even though it had long been worn by many Greek mortals and immortals,[24] through explication of an aetiology which described it as worn by Dionysus victorious.[25] Alexander compared his eastern campaigns of victory to those of Dionysus and the headband highlighted the allusion. After Alexander's death the diadem suggested Alexander-like kingship 'predicated on personal charisma and victory'.[26] Thus when, many generations later,

[22] Walbank 1984*a*: 67. [23] Symbol: Polyb. 30. 2. 4.

[24] R. Smith 1988: 34 and 36.

[25] R. Smith 1993: 207; Diod. 4. 4. 4; Pliny *HN* 7. 191.

[26] R. Smith 1988: 37.

Athenion, the leader of a slave revolt, was chosen by his comrades as king, he naturally assumed a diadem.[27] But, of course, such habitual symbolism could only have been fostered by the diadem being seen worn by kings, in person or represented as statues and faces upon coins.

Even the image of Alexander, to which his successors would appeal for their own dynastic legitimacy, was not firmly established until after his death. Through remembrances of Alexander an allusive repertoire came to inform definitively a whole grandiloquently commemorative tradition. This constituted the prevailing measure of worldly success in the Hellenistic world. After his death Alexander was everywhere. His image had become, as Stewart has splendidly argued and documented, a technique for expressing 'overwhelming charismatic power'.[28] This was obviously and especially the case in Alexandria, where his image was perennially deployed so that it enhanced the Ptolemies' 'position as the legitimate heirs of Alexander in Egypt and endowed them with a convenient legitimization of the divine status of their dynasty'.[29] Alexander's tomb was located in Alexandria, for it was there, not Siwa nor Macedon, that his cortege reached its final destination. All the Diadochoi were busy employing reference to Alexander and so much did the kings jostle in this respect for pre-eminence in their conquered worlds that any outstanding success in appropriating the resonance of Alexander's memory was a cause for alarm.[30] Alexandria in Egypt would continue to make its claims to be the new capital of the Greek world.[31] In its grand, brand-new Alexandrine quarters, the kingship of the early Ptolemies was devoted to money.[32] And in their new city a discourse of spectacle had allowed Alexander to become specifically conceptualized in the terms of divinity.[33]

Thus between December 275 and February 274, Ptolemy Philadelphus showed his power in a Grand Procession staged in

[27] Diod. 36. 5. 2. [28] Stewart 1993: 60. [29] Rice 1983: 192.

[30] Apparently Lysimachos' emphasis upon his own intimacy with Alexander encouraged Demetrius' perception of him as a potent rival for the throne of Macedon: Lund 1992: 155–6.

[31] Rice 1983: 190. [32] Adcock 1953: 171: 'a vast business concern'.

[33] Theoc. *Id.* 17. 13–14.

Alexandria.[34] At the heart of the spectacle were the twinned themes of Dionysus and Alexander. It all still seems an 'astonishing display of ostentation'.[35] So lavish was the spectacle that it would be wearisome to recount or to hear absolutely all the ingredients of this spectacle, as described in the lengthy quotation of Callixeinos incorporated into Athenaeus (197c–203b).[36] Suffice it to say it was impressive and memorable. But let us at least appreciate some of its key ingredients.

In expatiating extravagantly upon the themes of Alexander and divine conquest, the Grand Procession established firmly in historical memory a comparison of Alexander to Dionysus which had been encouraged by Alexander's visit to Nysa.[37] Writers such as Megasthenes discussed this visit; and doubtless readily recalled too was Alexander's detour to the oracle of Ammon at Siwa (perhaps just because it was there, perhaps to confirm his belief in his descent from Zeus).[38] At Athens the proud citizens debated whether to honour Alexander as a god. The question of belief in some existential quality of the Macedonian conqueror was not at issue in the debate.[39] Arguments

[34] Foertmeyer 1988 for this date, arguing in addition that it was part of the second celebration of the Ptolemaia established in 279/8. This remains controversial: see now Walbank 1996: 121 n. 16.

[35] Fraser 1972: i. 202.

[36] = *FGrHist* 627 F 2. Text and translation most conveniently in Rice 1983, together with a commentary that obviates any need for any more systematic description here.

[37] The visit was perhaps commemorated by his companions: 'some have recorded, if anyone believes it, that many of Alexander's companions of repute wreathed themselves with ivy, and when they invoked Dionysos were possessed by him and they invoked him with Bacchic cries' (Arr. *Anab*. 5. 2. 7, translated by Nock 1972: i. 138). Clitarchos' panegyric history of Alexander also described Dionysus' conquest of the Indians: *FGrHist* 137 F 17.

[38] Taeger 1957: i. 192; a vast bibliography on the visit is conveniently sketched at Fishwick 1987: 8.

[39] Use of the imagery and associations of divinity to represent the powerful may involve attribution of the iconography of a deity or even several deities to an individual; or a ruler might actually be identified as a god, although it is prudent to insist 'that identification . . . is still a form of comparison' (Fishwick 1987: 30, following Nock 1972: i. 235). The evidence encourages suspicion that Alexander felt himself to be, of all the available connotative personae, the successor of Dionysus. But how such an allusive sensibility expressed itself in the mind or habitus of the great man remains inscrutable, however

were made and decisions made on the basis of pragmatism and diplomatic utility.[40] And it was not in fact through the suggestions of diarists travelling in baggage-trains advancing ever eastwards, nor on account of the debates upon the Pnyx that the significance of Alexander was immortalized. It happened through spectacle.

Thus while the great procession (*pompē*) perhaps seems to presuppose its 'audience's familiarity with the god's Indian campaign as a model for Alexander's',[41] this familiarity still needed to be engineered through a wholescale deployment of the imagery of Alexander. Thus in Philadelphus' parade Dionysus rides upon an elephant and his retinue includes chariots drawn by four elephants (200d–f). Elephants came to be a big part of the commemorative package of Alexander: a statue of him, together with Athene and Nike, was pulled by elephants in a chariot (202a). But there is absolutely no evidence to suggest that the animals were ever associated at Alexandria with Dionysus before this great display.[42] 'Animals are a predictable feature of a Dionysiac procession, given Dionysus' legendary command over savage beasts attested in vase-painting as early as the sixth century BC.'[43] But such animals were not specifically elephants, which seem to have remained unknown to Greeks. The imagery of divinity was not determined by tradition. The traditional elements of mythic retailing in fact offered little determinative stability of connotation, being drawn from repertoires of ever increasing riches. Thus, as Nock acutely remarked, Dionysus 'is given some of the characteristics and achievements of Alexander, then Alexander is represented as following Dionysus'.[44]

We would do well to think that a representation is something that 'addresses itself to a mind. It is only in so far as it does this

determinedly the accretions of later historiographical fancy are stripped away. Cf. Nock 1972: i. 136, 138 ('But that Alexander felt himself to be Dionysus-like (even as much as he felt himself to be Perseus-like or Heracles-like or Achilles-like or possibly Zeus-like) is very doubtful').

[40] Demades told the unwilling citizens 'I fear, men, for you, lest in begrudging Alexander heaven you lose your land to him' (*Gnomol. Vatic.* 236 (Sternbach); Val. Max. 7. 2. ext. 13).

[41] Stewart 1993: 238. [42] Ibid. 234–5. [43] Coleman 1996: 58.

[44] Nock 1972: i. 139.

that it is a representation.'[45] Conceptions of divinity have always been a dynamic product of history—and a history of representative phenomenologies which were activated by wilful actors but still necessarily found pleasing by successive generations of audiences and their ever mobile memories, sensibilities, and affections. Both Dionysus and Alexander were always actively constructed—and consumed. We can see such a process occurring under Ptolemy's orchestration in the streets of Alexandria.[46] Such an operation works best, moreover, upon occasions of pleasure and wonder. The Dionysiac aspects to Alexander's phenomenology would be most happily welcomed by crowds of anonymous individuals of doubtless diverse temperaments but most of whom shared in all likelihood some essential and universal appetites: Tondriau pointed out that Hellenistic rulers, in identifying with deities in Egypt, showed marked preferences for Dionysus and Aphrodite.[47] One hopes that it is a revelation to nobody that proper acknowledgement of the divine provinces of booze and sex tends to be popular at all levels of society. Both these divinities were in conspicuous evidence throughout all the festivities associated with the grand parade.

Prior to the description of the *pompē* proper, there is a splendid spectacle which not only establishes the central Dionysiac theme of the entire proceedings but also rehearses, as an exquisite microcosm saturated with sensuous affectations, a wondrous conception of the nature of power which is to be both enjoyed and advertised. Callixeinos tells of a magnificent hospitality tent for an exclusive few. They were admitted to recline and feast within a 'Dionysiac bower, a luxuriant arbour' redolent with all the happiest associations of the god.[48] Callixeinos lists the features of Philadelphus' big, beautiful tent. It held 130 couches, arranged in a circle. There were columns, a square epistyle, and a scarlet canopy for a roof framing, sheltering the privileged few who would join the king's symposion. Inside were marvels, drawn from the big, wide world whose conquest

[45] C. S. Peirce as quoted at Asad 1993: 30 n. 3.

[46] The Ptolemies could also claim descent from Dionysus through Soter's mother: Gow 1965: ii. 331; Rice 1983: 84.

[47] Tondriau 1948: 35.

[48] Rice 1983: 32.

became meaningful and valuable in the fine products it made available for consumption: Phoenician curtains, the pelts of animals ('incredibly variegated and large'), a roof of myrtle and laurel, and a floor strewn with fresh flowers (particularly astounding, since only in Egypt were such flowers available in the middle of winter). There were Delphic tripods, and eagles in the pelmets; more couches, of gold, along two sides, with exquisite embroidered purple rugs; Persian carpets, gold tripod-tables; one couch was filled with goblets and other utensils of idleness. There were, furthermore, statues and paintings by famous artists, tunics of cloth of gold, and military cloaks with the portraits of kings and mythological figures woven into them, shields of silver and of gold, and in recesses there seems to have been symposia of figures from tragedy, comedy, and satyr plays, wearing real cloaks. Against such a background the magnificence of the Ptolemies could all the better bespeak their own divinity.[49]

The tent also derived its conception of delectation from a varied repertoire of traditions besides those concerning Dionysus. This was the wondrous work of a catholic aesthetic of grandeur and kingliness worthy of an internationally significant pot-latcher. There are allusions to the aesthetics of Egypt, Alexander's behaviour, and indeed also to the Persian kingliness which had never failed to impress Greeks. The main parade too would offer themes to which Egyptians, even if they are not explicitly mentioned in the narrative, could attach their own traditional significations.[50] Yet although the tent had Egyptian and other elements in its design, it would still appear readily familiar to Greeks.

Big marquees were present at every grand pan-Hellenic gathering—indeed we have already noticed them at Olympia, sheltering the honour and glory of Themistocles and Alcibiades. The Egyptian features of Ptolemy's tent may have added merely 'novelty and curiosity' but of course all in Egypt already had some familiarity with Egyptian decoration.[51] Big tents were also typically Persian, but they had long been imitated by Greeks, ever since they had peered—after victory in the battle

[49] Cf. R. Smith 1988: 25.

[50] Cf. Walbank 1996: 123.

[51] Rice 1983: 149 n. 33.

of Plataea (479)—into Xerxes' tent left behind for the Persian commander Mardonios. This impressive artefact was adorned with gold and silver and hung with tapestries of many colours.[52] It was also large enough to accommodate a dining area, stables, and perhaps too a harem.[53] Some of its grandeur of design may have been echoed in Greek tents. Interestingly enough, the tent that had been provided for Alcibiades by the Ephesians was remembered as being Persian.[54] The one described in Euripides' *Ion* (1128–66) also has barbarian textiles. This interest in 'luxurious transient architecture' perhaps shows Greek imitation of Persian ways of doing things—specifically, living in surroundings appropriate to individuals of exceptional importance.[55] As might be expected, Alexander, always transient, took to Persian tents in a big way. At Issus he captured and then inhabited Darius' tent, indulging a new scale of oriental, luxurious living, which could conveniently be encapsulated as a catalogue of service personnel.[56] The tent travelled with the army and was used to host festivities celebrating a variety of occasions, from the king's recovery from wounds in India or the mass marriage ceremony held at Susa in 324.[57]

In general, ever since Greeks from the fifth century onwards had started to fashion luxuriousness in terms of consumption of Persian splendours (with Athenian aristocrats of course conspicuously pioneering the fashion which, like so many others, became 'democratized' over the course of the fifth century),[58]

[52] Hdt. 9. 80. 1 and 9. 82. 1. The following remarks are especially indebted to the important work of Miller (1997: 49–53).

[53] Hdt. 9. 82. 2 and 70. 3; Miller 1997: 50.

[54] Plut. *Alc.* 12; Athen. 12. 534d. Dionysius I of Syracuse sent a tent decorated with gold and fancy textiles to Olympia in 388: Diod. 14. 109. 1; Polyb. 12. 24. 3. Also, as Miller has observed (1997: 52), Attic red-figured pots from about 480 that depict the mourning Achilles show him sitting in some sort of a tent.

[55] Miller 1997: 52.

[56] Diod. 17. 36. 5, Curt. 3. 13. 1–3; Borza 1983: 46–7. The personnel are cited at the head of this chapter.

[57] Curt. 9. 7. 15; Athen. 12. 537d–40a—Phylarchus is naturally vivid here. The 'Tent of a Thousand Couches' is also mentioned at Diodorus 17. 16. 4 (at the great Dium festival in 334; Tomlinson 1970. Aelian (*VH* 9. 3) describes Alexander's tent at Susa as having no less than fifty golden columns.

[58] Miller 1997: 243–58.

the very conception of what a king was, along with material manifestations of kingly living, had been informed by eastern models. Socrates had directed (in the *Alcibiades 1*) the young, ignorant Alcibiades' attentions towards monarchy: if he plans to be the leader, the *hēgēmon* of the Athenian *polis* (1. 120a–b), then perhaps he must place himself in competition with the enemies of his *polis*, the kings of Sparta and Persia. Socrates, moreover, remarks not only upon the kings' possession of the appropriate knowledge but also upon their personal qualities (1. 120e and ff.). Hence he describes how the power of the kings is evident both in wealth and also in their corporal aesthetics—and even specifically in the way that royal children's bodies were physically manipulated by eunuchs so that they would have the attractiveness expected in the body of a ruler (1. 121d). Accordingly a glance at the fine sight of Persians ought to make Alcibiades ashamed of his inferior self (1. 122c): they have wealth, luxury, trailing robes, anointments of myrrh, and a large retinue of attendants. The king's mother would not be impressed by either the apparel or landholding of Alcibiades. Thus Alcibiades would be expected to be able to compete only in *epimeleia* and *sophia* (1.123d). Xenophon too would dilate at great length upon such themes in the *Cyropaedia*. Alcibiades, of course, was not steered very far along this ideal Socratic trajectory. But such argument remains revealing of how Greek aristocrats had always engaged an ever richer and more international matrix of aesthetic associations surrounding kingship, in order both to conceptualize their place in the political cosmos and articulate such understanding before audiences of equally increasing worldliness and sophistication.

The Ptolemies showed themselves to be worthy inheritors of such a generous and truly worldly tradition. In his orchestration of big-tent-politics in Alexandrine festival, Ptolemy Philadelphus would be at the centre of the world's attentions, manifestly able to command materials that gratified and astonished and presumably deserving of this power. The luxuriousness in itself bespoke something more than just another rich and ambitious Greek: the flowers alone, for instance, made an impression appropriate to a divine man, they were scattered in profusion on the floor of the pavilion, 'truly bringing about the look of some heavenly meadow'.[59] Presumably too the meadow smelled as pleasantly as it looked. Luxurious extravagance had been thoroughly approved by the example of Alexander himself who was entertained by his friends at feasts in which desserts were wrapped in gold. This was thrown away, so that their friends might be spectators of their extravagance.[60]

Such delights were for the enjoyment of an exclusive few. It is regrettable that Callixeinos either did not know or did not see fit to tell posterity about the details of the guest list for such a lovely party. In a royal politics of personality and friendship, as opposed to the inclusivity of citizen sociability, it must be understood that the king invites only whom he chooses. Here was suitable material of luxury to delight the intimate guests invited from overseas to participate in a 'large-scale system of international gift-exchange'.[61] And there would be the courtiers too, since no king could rule alone without some functioning oligarchic infrastructure.[62]

But if his aesthetic delights were meant to impress intimates and foreign dignitaries besides, it was also obviously meant to impress future rememberers. In the context of Athenaeus' feast of know-alls, the citation of Callixeinos certainly affords a certain satisfaction to connoisseurs of exclusive delectation. Callixeinos' fetishization of the cataloguing of extravagant consumption is a product of age-old tendencies of seeking to leave one's mark as a man of magnificence, and he is continuing the connoisseurship of the terms and lineages by which historical memorability could be properly reckoned. This is big-time (new) money doing what it was supposed to do, letting its expropriations be immodestly reduced to cruder measurements of value. Indulgently our recorder simplifies his task by finding it tedious to describe all the details about the materials and workmanship that went into the contents of Ptolemy's bower; it suffices to say that their total weight was ten thousand silver talents. Such bald quantification is appropriate for a regime both proud of its pre-eminence among kings both present and future and obviously also possessing the moneys which could

[59] *Alc.* 1. 196e: θείου τινὸϲ ὡϲ ἀληθῶϲ ἀποτελοῦντα λειμῶνοϲ πρόσοψιν.

[60] Athen. 4.155c–d.

[61] D. J. Thompson 1997.

[62] On which Fraser 1972: i. 101–5 and ii. 183–93.

buy the armaments necessary for maintenance of such a position. Which other kings would indeed be able to match such a man?[63]

Besides these exclusive audiences assessing such significance, there were also the people outside the tent in the city without whose presence the privilege of admittance to the tent would have had drastically less significance, and perhaps less delectation besides. Outside the columns, in a portico with a peristyle (complete with vaulted roof), there stood conspicuously the retinues of those invited inside.[64] And then there was everybody else. Ptolemy's *skēnē*, and thus too a view of who was invited in, was 'established inside the enclosure of the citadel away from the quarters of the soldiers, artisans, and foreign visitors'.[65] Lesser folk could not see inside yet they too would surely come to hear all about it: 'it turned out to be extraordinarily beautiful and well worth hearing about.'[66] It would be imprudent to assert that a king would be ready 'to proclaim his own glory even if nobody is listening': to be sure, the 'ruling power obtained additional prestige from the very irrationality of its expressions, which spoke for themselves' but they would not be 'proudly indifferent to their audience' unless they were fully conscious of an audience that was being so proudly marked off as merely spectatorial subjects of the king and all his fancies.[67] Statuses were being firmly articulated through ritualized expressions of the unbreachable divide between a precious few and those who were being made to experience and thus understand an 'increasing verticality in their relationship' to both their gods and their absolute rulers.[68]

If spectacular staging represented a king—elevated and remote and comfortable and so very gracious in his Dionysian surroundings—as something divine in his power to amass, to

[63] Athen. 5.203c: 'Philadelphus surpassed many kings in wealth and has been ambitiously zealous in all his establishments' (*πολλῶν δὲ ὁ Φιλάδελφος βασιλέων πλούτῳ διέφερε καὶ περὶ πάντα ἐσπουδάκει τὰ κατασκευάσματα φιλοτίμως . . .*). Knowledge of his libraries and books are in all men's memories: 203e.

[64] 5. 196c: *τὴν τῶν κατακειμένων ἀκολουθίαν ἑστάναι συνέβαινεν.*

[65] Athen. 5.196a: *κατασκευασθεῖσαν . . . ἐν τῷ τῆς ἄκρας περιβόλῳ χωρὶς τῆς τῶν στρατιωτῶν καὶ τεχνιτῶν καὶ παρεπιδήμων ὑποδοχῆς.*

[66] Ibid. *καλὴ γὰρ εἰς ὑπερβολὴν ἀξία τε ἀκοῆς.*

[67] Veyne 1990: 381 and 380.

[68] Van Straten 1993: 263.

possess, and to display, then the prestige of such an impresario was further confirmed by the scale of the procession proper. This was seen by anyone who happened to find himself in the city, either living there or having travelled some distance to be a spectator. Urban festivals were normally accessible.[69] Quite clearly, this Grand Procession was 'obviously calculated to have the maximum effect upon spectators'.[70] Spectacle indeed 'is what it all was' and with its enormous scale it certainly would carry 'a straightforward message'.[71]

Nevertheless, it remains a rather disquieting truth of ancient history that so little can be known about the precise impressions all this made upon spectators in a city. But certainly there was at work an astonishingly wilful determination on the part of a royal regime to impose a meaning upon all sorts of worldly objects, and especially those things which could be marched, led, wheeled and hauled through streets and stadia. Our reports, through Callixeinos and Athenaeus, are third- or fourth-hand and offer a bald summary that poorly conveys the affective riches of the actual spectacle. Speculation about these alone is possible; a variety of reactions can be reasonably presumed. The crowd, which did have the power at Alexandria, at least in its later history, to send kings scurrying off for refuge to their friends,[72] is largely ignored in Callixeinos' account.

Yet what, inevitably, must be stressed is that all this gigantically pompous power rendered its viewers the subjects of a power that rested on much more than military might. To be sure, Philadelphus' display of military resources alone made clear the foundation of the regime: and it is indeed worthwhile to consider 'what the numbers involved must have meant to the spectators' if the spectacle of infantry marching six abreast took, on reasonable estimate, a solid three hours or so, affording 'an impressive if somewhat tedious spectacle'.[73] But unlike other Hellenistic parades, such as that of Antiochus IV which we shall

[69] Walbank 1996: 123. [70] Rice 1983: 35.

[71] D. J. Thompson 1997.

[72] e.g. Paus. 1. 9. 2–3 (Ptolemy X Alexander I); see the exemplary treatment of the collective action in Alexandria in 203 (Polyb. 15. 25–33) by Barry 1993, who also provides references to other unruly demonstrations.

[73] Walbank 1984*b*: 54.

consider later, the soldiers did not precede the main body of the *pompē*. It was enough that in spectating, people were ritually confirmed in a respective position of passive subjecthood at once both physical and symbolic. Although our text is not concerned with the full context of performance, we *can* see how the procession displayed the king's power, insofar as the memoir envisages Ptolemy's display as the effortless articulation of his power and consequent historical stature. Thus the *pompē* simply 'came to take place' (γεγενημένης ὑπὸ . . .) as a result of the effortless agency of Ptolemy (Athen. 196a). The verb is not one of executive arrangement. With the absence of interest in any tedious details of logistics and administration, executive power is appropriately commemorated as something utterly effortless.

One does not have to be a Situationist, or a doggedly modern and cynical student of television, to suspect that subjectivities are in large measure informed, nay even interpellated by spectacle: people learn from what they see and come to take as naturally admirable whatever stirs an affective response. Hence this historical event served actively, it could be said, to define 'symbolically the political order of the universe, from the heavenly bodies and Olympian deities to the lowly Alexandrian who sat in the stadium or stood in the street to watch the procession'.[74] Any power on the part of the viewer probably lay in the degree of consciousness that, were they not there to see, nobody of significance would be quite so eager to enter Ptolemy's big tent. The spectators were, of course, there and 'participating' in their own way, watching and thronging the public spaces of the city—*silēnoi* were stationed to hold them back.

One can also note that the Grand Procession 'was carefully structured and the groups taking part were clearly defined categories within the population of Alexandria, based on age and occupation'.[75] The procession further reinforced such categories, especially because the proceedings may well have taken days. Importantly too, children participated by marching along dressed in fancy costumes as well as by watching from the sidelines. For the most impressionable, such performances must have entailed a prescriptive power, regarding perception

[74] Barry 1993: 425. [75] Walbank 1996: 122.

of the naturalness and scale of the power of a Ptolemy and also their own position and role in the grandiose, political scheme of things in the world. Of course, they came to such realizations through beholding for the first time things impressive in their own right but also stamped firmly with the spectacular rhetoric of the pompous impresario. If the sentiment of the crowd does not much figure in the account of Ptolemy Philadelphus' extraordinary procession through Alexandria, then curiosity must fall upon the values that came to be understood as embodied through the things seen.

Thus, unless we are careful, the sight or thought of a man deploying other men as mere instruments more easily controlled than actual beasts of burden, the men pulling the main part of Ptolemy's Dionysiac procession, towing large carts carrying statues and tableaux, might seem just another natural feature of the ancient environment. But the sight of the men, the 180 men drawing along a four-wheeled cart, twenty-one feet long by twelve wide, surely fixed a great socio-political distinction between inhabitants who watched the spectacle and the uninteresting men who hauled the carriages.[76] These anonymous labourers are certainly not the same sorts of objects for attention in and of themselves as were the Silenoi, the Satyrs, the Nikai, the boys in purple tunics, more Silenoi, more Satyrs, the beautiful woman representing the Penteris, Philiscos the priest of Dionysus, the *technitai* of Dionysus, the priests and priestesses of Dionysus, the Macedonian bacchants, more Satyrs and Silenoi, those carrying a variety of mixing bowls and utensils, the 1,600 boys in white tunics wearing crowns, the boys carrying jars, the girls in purple tunics with

[76] Athen. 5.198c. Rice 1983: 59: 'Manpower may have been considered more aesthetic than groups of draught animals controlled by shouting drivers with whips, or perhaps it was thought that draught animals would detract from the effect of the other animals who were bona fide participants in the procession.' Elsewhere: 60 men pulling the cart in which was the *agalma* of Nysa (198f), 300 men pulling the cart containing 60 singing satyrs treading grapes (199a), 600 men for the cart that carried the wineskin that dispensed libations along the route (199b), 600 again for the cart with a 6,000-gallon mixing bowl (199b), 500 men for the cart that carried a grotto from which pigeons and doves fluttered free with nooses tied to their feet so that they could easily be caught by the spectators (200c).

gold girdles, more Satyrs, more Silenoi and Satyrs on asses; the little boys and girls riding in chariots pulled by elephants, billy-goats, gazelles, hartebeests, ostriches, antelopes, wild asses, and by horses; the camels, and their cargoes of Indian women cast as captives, the Aethiopian tribute-bearers, the hunters, the 2,400 dogs, the 150 men carrying trees containing animals and birds, the sheep, oxen, the albino bear, the leopards, the panthers, the lynxes, the panther-cubs, the giraffe, the rhinoceros, the choral band of 600, the elephant-chariot carrying the golden effigy of Alexander the Great, and the tens of thousands of infantry and cavalry. The men without costumes or ornamentation are lost amid the finery, their numbers only the crass quantification of grandeur and their significance in the world wholly subordinated to treasure.

They are also subordinate to machines of wonder. The *pompē* represented Alexander's memory and meaning through extraordinary and ingenious devices: after the priests, priestesses, and bacchants, there 'came a four-wheeled cart twelve feet wide and drawn by sixty men, in which was seated an *agalma* of Nysa, twelve feet high; she wore a yellow tunic, spangled with gold; she was wrapped in a Laconian shawl. This *agalma* rose up mechanically with nobody applying their hands to it, and after libating milk from a gold *phiale*, it sat again.'[77] While in any political economy a new mechanical technology can generate new dimensions of power, in antiquity such existed exclusively in service of the all-important businesses of war-making and spectacle. Early kings of Macedonia might have pottered about in simple herb-gardens or workshops but later kings took a keen interest in devices such as siege-engines.[78] They also had spectacular automata to amaze any urban audience. Alexandria was where the inventive technician Ctesibios was to be found experimenting with pumps and water devices.[79] But 'even the Ptolemies (for all their interest in bigger and better war machines) never thought of harnessing the inventiveness of a Ctesibios to practical application'.[80] What was produced was

[77] Athen. 5.198f. [78] Plut. *Demetr.* 20; Hornblower 1981: 200.

[79] Fraser 1972: i. 426.

[80] Grant 1982: 158; on ancient automata in general, see further Rehm 1937.

but 'a collection of elaborate mechanical toys, curiosities, the subsidized exotica of an authoritarian regime'.[81] Making a mechanical representation of a personification of a symbol of conquest is an eminently practical thing for an autocrat to do. The modern categories of religion and political power—both consequent upon an ability to hold wandering attention, even awe, quiet and rapt—intersect in the power of a man to order a thing made (and pay for it handsomely), and then offer it as an unprecedented spectacle. All could admire the craftsmanship put to such an end.[82] This is truly the fetishism of a cunning and ingenious power.

Among the objects brought from other parts of the world by the reach of the ruler's power were the ultimate mechanisms of wonder, the animals. In Ptolemy's Grand Procession 'the great multitude of animals . . . outweighs any practical or ritual purpose, and the triumphal procession is partly an excuse for the exhaustive parade of beasts'.[83] There were beasts of burden. There were also animals that by their very presence indicated the lands to which the displayer had imperial access. Military conquest brought rarities and oddities to the cities.[84] Alexander and his armies had ranged widely—and this reach of Greekness translated into a richness of knowledge.[85] This knowledge was not just that of the scholars of the libraries, but was the more common and more potent knowledge of all who saw strange

[81] Green 1990: 478.

[82] As Hornblower (1981: 201) notes, 'Hellenistic descriptions of *thaumasia* dwell on features of workmanship as much as on beauty.'

[83] Rice 1983: 86.

[84] It is interesting to compare how animals 'figured prominently even in the experience of city dwellers' in 19th-cent. London. They were, moreover, 'uniquely suitable subjects for a rhetoric that both celebrated human power and extended its sway' (Ritvo 1987: 5–6). Ptolemy Philadelphus had an interest in rare animals (Ptolemy VIII *FGrH* 234 F 2; Diod. 3. 36. 3; Hubbell 1935; Fraser 1972: ii. 466 n. 39; Rice 1983: 87). Ptolemy probably obtained Forest African elephants from the herds in Eritrea: Scullard 1974: 61–2. The presence of the elephants may well have been an advertisement that Ptolemy had his own supply, of African elephants: Rice 1983: 92.

[85] Thus many of the snippets of information about animals found in Pliny the Elder are associated with Alexander: *HN* 8. 44, 119, 149, 154; 9. 27; 10. 155; Beagon 1992: 128.

beasts in their streets, and learned what they were from how they were exhibited.

One thing all the many spectators in Alexandria of all ages might well be viewing for the first time was the biggest animal in the world. This animal quite obviously is a naturally impressive thing—and better even by far perhaps than a mechanical snail or statue.[86] The elephant not only carried remembrance of divine Alexander but was also a perfect vehicle for a somewhat fraught, emotional apprehension of kingly power. Thus the anecdote about the Roman emperor Augustus, comparing the intimidating effect of his own presence upon someone humbler to an elephant offered a coin, speaks volumes about both kings and elephants.[87] Knowledge of the elephant had first come upon Greeks with Alexander's battle against Poros (or Chandragupta), the Indian king who was reported to have 200 elephants.[88] The scalp of an elephant appeared on the coins of the Diadochoi to allude to the memory of Alexander himself and consequently become 'a symbol of unassailable universal hegemony'.[89] As Smith has observed, elephants' scalps became associated with the iconography of Dionysus because of Alexander's campaigns. For later kings the reference of the elephant could be to either or both Alexander and Dionysus merged in eastern divine triumph.[90] Elephants duly appeared on Ptolemy's gold staters of 305/4 pulling a chariot in which rides an Alexander wearing an aegis and wielding a thunderbolt.[91] The meaning of an elephant in a city had to a large degree been determined by a discourse of spectacle.

The elephant was so powerfully meaningful ever since initial encounters with the big beasts had prompted one clear emotional reaction, fear. The Greeks who fought against Poros and

[86] Aristotle for one (esp. *HA*, *passim*) cannot say enough about every aspect of these natural objects.

[87] Suet. *DA* 53. 2.

[88] Alexander could have deployed some one hundred and fifty elephants that had fallen as booty or come as gifts so far on his conquest, but did not use them (Scullard 1974: 66 *contra* Polyaenus 4. 3. 22).

[89] So Stewart 1993: 236.

[90] R. Smith 1988: 41.

[91] Stewart 1993: 236. Other Diadochs put elephants on their coins, e.g. Seleucus in commemoration of his Indian campaign: Hadley 1964: 40.

his elephants mutinied, unwilling to continue Alexander's advance further eastwards despite his hortations minimizing the military effectiveness of the animals.[92] Elephants were remembered by Greeks for the effect of their charges in battle.[93] But these animals also could be tamed. Elephants were standing sentry outside Alexander's big tent as he lay dying at Babylon. The power realized in the control and orchestration of their bulky might—the reason they were in the battle arrays of Poros and subsequently of Diadochoi in the first place[94]—made them ideal objects of kingly phenomenology. Elephants, as the most powerful animals in the whole wide world, served very well as brute instruments of power in civic rituals, where political meaning burdened their bodies, as well as on battlefields far away from the clamour of carnival. The spectacle of elephants lumbering through Ptolemy's streets was as much an asset of royal power as their charge in battle.[95]

Elephants often were presumed to possess an extraordinary repertoire of human qualities, virtues, and excellences.[96] They never did any harm unless sorely provoked; they acted rationally—and even in the wild they supposedly organized their own

[92] Curt. 9. 2. 15 ff.

[93] The silver decadrachms issued during Alexander's last spell at Babylon show Alexander and Bucephalos charging Poros (and his mahout) mounted upon an elephant; and one of the paintings on Alexander's funeral carriage (which ended up in Egypt) showed elephants ready for battle: Scullard 1974: 75–6.

[94] Seleucus acquired elephants from his invasion of Chandragupta's kingdom (Strabo 15. 724, 16. 752; Plut. *Alex.* 62) which were deployed at Ipsus (Plut. *Demetr.* 28; Diod. 20. 113).

[95] Around the time of Ptolemy's parade, bases for the hunting and capture of African elephants were established on the Red Sea coast (Strabo 16. 14–15; for papyrological and epigraphical evidence, see conveniently Hubbell 1935: 71); but African elephants are not so good as Asian for warfare and there is no mention of Ptolemaic elephants until Raphia (217), when they proved ineffective (Polyb. 5. 84. 1–6).

[96] On the humanity of elephants: Ael. *NA* 3. 46 and the story at Plut. *De Soll. Anim.* 970d. Modesty and matrimonial fidelity: Pliny *HN* 8. 13. Sense of shame: Pliny *HN* 8. 12. Sociability and piety: Plut. *De Soll. Anim.* 971b–c; Pliny *HN* 8. 1–2. Ability as surgeons, removing spears and javelins: Plut. *Alex.* 60, *De Soll. Anim.* 970d, 977b; Juba *FGrHist* F 52; Ael. *NA* 7. 45.

ranks (*agmen*) for battle 'as though by command or method'.[97] They took care of their riders in battle and even when injured.[98] They had a marked sense of honour and shame—their greatest delight, it might be thought, was in medals (*phalerae argenteae*).[99] But all such aspects of the nature of the beast could not be apprehended by those who saw or described it except through the influence of the agency that deployed them upon battlefields, stadia, and streets. An elephant was never just a large and fascinating mammal adapted to its environment, but was an anthropomorphized instrument obviously subjected to the service of someone.

And in cities elephants could also exhibit an ideal of docility towards those who commanded them. Properly managed, one could think of them even in battle as perfect instruments of another's agency—when their brute force destroys fortifications it can be remembered as the doing of 'the men on the elephants' and not the animals who actually do the shoving and so forth.[100] In general, they exhibited a clear respect for the social hierarchy.[101] Thus it is not surprising that demonstrations of tamed animals were wonderful spectacles long before any Greek saw an elephant, or so at any rate attests Isocrates.[102] How splendid it would be to be able easily to tame an animal who instead might have been seen to have trampled men (oh, so easily) beneath its so indistinctly articulated toes![103] The tameness of the exotic animals in Ptolemy Philadelphus' parade is indeed remarkable.[104] The same would hold for the future. As Plutarch remarked, 'let others be astonished that elephants learn, or are taught, to exhibit in the theatre all the many postures and

[97] Pliny *HN* 8. 23: 'velut imperio aut ratione'.

[98] Megasthenes *FGrHist* F 20 = Arr. *Ind.* 13; Curt. 8. 14. 39–40.

[99] Pliny *HN* 8. 12. Furthermore, the one who was disgraced preferred death by starvation to the shame ('ille qui notabatur inedia mortem ignominiae praetulit').

[100] Diod. 18. 33–6.

[101] e.g. Ael. *NA* 6. 61, 7. 15.

[102] *Antidosis* 213–14.

[103] Tamability: Arist. *HA* 488$^{a}$28–9. Perdiccas had rebellious infantry commanders thrown to the feet of elephants: Curt. 10. 9. 18. Elephants' toes: Arist. *HA* 497$^{b}$. In fact Aristotle is interested in almost every part of an elephant's anatomy.

[104] Coleman 1996: 59.

variations of movement that they do, these being so varied and so complicated to memorize and retain that they are not at all easy even for human artists.'[105]

The docility of elephants, much stressed in the ancient literature upon them, thus makes them morally excellent as the servants and subjects of those that command them, although obviously their symbolic significance varied for different observers at different times.[106] Elephants, which entered the Greek world as utterly foreign and came to stand in for foreignness and even foreigners, were ideal subjects which could be tamed.[107] It was a matter of pride that an elephant was able to take its command in Greek rather than the language in which it had been trained and instructed: Ptolemy Philadelphus had an elephant that understood Greek.[108] Their natural deference and obedience might well be contrasted with the refusal of the sacred crocodiles to heed the command of a Ptolemy; it did not look good for a king's command to be disregarded.[109] In return, crocodiles were best respected.[110] Their disobedience indeed seemed like an omen of his death to the priests.

[105] Plut. *De Soll. Anim.* 968b–c; cf. Pliny *HN* 8. 6—the slowest elephant, the one most often scolded and chastised was to be seen rehearsing on its own at night; cf. *Mor.* 98c. Cf. Plut. *Brut. Anim.* 992b; cf. Philo (27, pp. 113 f.), also describing performing elephants. Arrian himself has seen elephants dancing and clashing cymbals: *Ind.* 14.

[106] Cf. Scullard 1974: 258. There is stress, in Pliny and Aelian in particular, upon how easily elephants were tamed (Pliny *HN* 8. 24: when being tamed they are given 'large loaves of bread, barley, dried figs, raisins, onions, garlic, much honey, and bundles of mastic, palm, and ivy leaves'). Ael. *NA* 10. 10. Music might also help to charm them into docility: Ael. *NA* 12. 44.

[107] Comparison with the 19th-cent. display of elephants is suggestive. The best animals 'were those that displayed the qualities of an industrious, docile, and willing human servant; the worst not only declined to serve, but dared to challenge human supremacy'. There was great fondness in Great Britain for the elephant which offered utility as a beast of burden, and displayed both a magnanimous temper and love for its masters. Ritvo 1987: 17 and 23–5.

[108] Ael. *NA* 11. 25.

[109] Plut. *De Soll. Anim.* 976b. It is unclear which Ptolemy this was.

[110] Ptolemy Philopator sacrificed four elephants after his victory over Antiochus. He was tormented at night by dreams of divine anger for the strangeness of the sacrifice. He found relief by setting up a votive offering of four bronze elephants (Plut. *De Soll. Anim.* 972c; Ael. *NA* 7. 44, 9. 1—the sacrifice is to the Sun).

Elephants were, however, generally able to know just how to behave before a king: 'for as concerns docility, they revere a king, kneel down, and offer garlands.'[111] An elephant (after fighting a bull in the arena) even offered adoration to an emperor, Domitian.[112] A Roman prince, far from being scared, could reasonably expect to make them dance for him.

Times would come when the military might of Hellenistic kings was not what it had been in the pompous Ptolemaic heyday of greater awe and glory. Another slave leader, Salvius who took the name Tryphon, proclaimed himself a king for his comrades. He built a palace and an agora but, when he held audiences with his subjects, his trappings of dignity were Roman. He put on a purple-bordered toga and was attended by lictors.[113] In the second century, Hellenistic kingliness met more than its match in the power commanded by Roman magistrates.

## SELEUCID CIVILITIES

After the defeat of Carthage in the second Punic war, Roman attentions immediately turned eastwards, and armies proceeded accordingly. Great kings suffered defeat at Cynoscephalae and Magnesia, and in 168 the legions and auxiliaries commanded by the Roman pro-consul L. Aemilius Paullus defeated Perseus, king of Macedon, at the battle of Pydna, effectively eliminating that state as an international power. Hellenistic kings had already been firmly belittled by Roman magistrates in face-to-face encounters. Perseus had been pointedly made to cross a river in order to meet with Marcius Philippus.[114] Others

[111] Pliny *HN* 8. 3: 'nam quod ad docilitatem attinet regem adorant, genua submittunt, coronas porrigunt.'

[112] Mart. *De Spect.* 17: 'The loyal and suppliant elephant reveres you, Caesar, which here just now was so to be feared by the bull. This it does without command or its teacher's guidance. Believe me, it too feels the presence of our god' ('quod pius et supplex elephas te, Caesar, adorat | hic modo qui tauro tam metuendus erat, | non facit hoc iussus, nulloque docente magistro; | crede mihi, nostrum sentit et ille deum').

[113] Diod. 36. 7. 1 and 3.

[114] Livy 43. 39. 1–6. Perseus and King Genthius would be led in triumph: Rawson 1975: 152.

would experience similarly dramatic demonstrations of the imperial superiority of Romans. The greeting of King Antiochus IV of Syria at a parley was rebuffed by Popillius Laenas, who drew instead a line in the sand around him and insisted that the king give his reply before stepping outside it.[115] Long before their kingdoms typically became little more than Roman protectorates, eastern kings unsurprisingly had found it pragmatic to take the initiative in adopting postures of humility. Thus, for example, Prusias of Bithynia (in 167) greeted a Roman embassy with shaved head, in white cap, toga and Roman shoes, and declared he was a freedman of the Romans—a 'more ignoble remark it would be hard to imagine'.[116] Clearly, however, it was prudent for a king to do whatever he could to ensure that Roman might was not directed against him. Kings, such as Perseus and Genthius, had by then been seen at Rome long ago, led through the streets in chains. Roman success was most conspicuous in the ceremonies of triumph. The news of no triumph can have made more of an impression upon eastern kings than that of L. Aemilius Paullus for his victory over Perseus.

This was a big event in Rome. Paullus had his detractors in the ranks of his army, who grumbled at his high-handedness. Despite the disgruntlement, the Senate voted a triumph and Paullus celebrated it with magnificent memorability. Plutarch's own theatrical sensibilities allow contemplation of how the principal features of the festivity must have impressed its spectators. So much treasure and so much degraded royalty, in chains and with tears streaming, effected a concrete apprehension of Paullus' achievements. All could understand the radical transformations of the world at large. All could share national pride.

Paullus' festivities lasted for all of three days, with each day themed for exhibition of particular centrepieces of boastfulness. On the first day, citizens wondered at the statues, paintings, and colossal figures carried on 250 chariots; on the second, freshly polished Macedonian arms, artfully arranged to appear casually heaped and jangling horribly so as to remind the crowd of the terrors of the conquered enemy; on the third, after the populace

[115] Polyb. 29. 27; Justin. 34. 3. 2. [116] Diod. 31. 15. 2.

was roused by battle-trumpeting, there was the procession of sacrificial personnel and all their expensive equipment, the chariot, weapons, and diadem of Perseus, and his children along with their nurses and pedagogues. All offered supplication to the crowd. Next came Perseus himself and his entourage; then Aemilius himself in his chariot. Plutarch imagines that, as he was gazed upon intently by the crowd, he was admired but not envied by any good person. So wondrous was this attainment of supreme felicity that Plutarch is prompted immediately to mention the personal misfortunes that befell Aemilius later in his life.[117] But this triumphal event had set a benchmark of accomplishment for others to try to match.

Contemporary kings in the world at large surely envied such great personal glory. One at least also sought very soon after to advertise his own consequentiality in those idioms of a strong and stable Republic. Upon hearing of Aemilius Paullus' games, Antiochus IV of Syria summoned (probably in 166/5) the world to a festival and games at Daphne, not far from the city of Antioch itself, where there was a sanctuary of Apollo.[118] Previous Seleucids, including above all Antiochus the Great, had also held brilliant festivals.[119] Yet clearly our Antiochus also wanted to compete with Paullus in great achievement (*megaloergia*). Before the festivities there was a wonderful parade, reported by Diodorus, who is eager to emphasize what had become a canonical portrait of Antiochus as something of a lunatic or at least just plain daft:

*Ὅτι ἔνιαι τῶν ἐπιβολῶν τοῦ Ἀντιόχου καὶ τῶν πράξεων βασιλικαὶ καὶ θαυμάσιαι τελέως ἦσαν, τινὲς δὲ πάλιν οὕτως εὐτελεῖς καὶ ληρώδεις ὥσθ' ὁλοσχερῶς ὑπὸ πάντων καταφρονεῖσθαι. συντελῶν γὰρ τοὺς ἀγῶνας πρῶτον μὲν ἐναντίαν τοῖς ἄλλοις βασιλεῦσι ἔσχε προαίρεσιν.*

Some of the enterprises and actions of Antiochus were kingly and wholly wondrous but some were so tawdry and foolish that he was utterly despised by everyone. In celebrating games he adopted a policy contrary to that of other kings.[120]

117 Plut. *Aem.* 33–5; cf. Livy 45. 33. 1–7, 35. 1–4, 40 *passim*. Diod. 31. 13.

118 Date: Sherwin-White and Kuhrt 1993: 220. Daphne: Walbank 1957–79: iii. 449.

119 Diod. 29. 2.

120 Diod. 31. 16. 1. The parade itself is also described by Polybius (30. 25. 1–26. 9).

As ever in ancient historiography, Hellenistic kings are to be described and assessed through comparison with their peers. And to be sure, as we have suspected in the case of Ptolemy Philadelphus, there was a good deal of cunning as well as pure braggadocio in their determination to be seen (and remembered) outdoing other kingly men. Antiochus IV was, however, leaving his mark in a period when other monarchs, 'while strengthening their personal kingdoms with resources and wealth, as far as possible concealed their intention because of the superiority of the Romans'. As in many respects, as Diodorus continues in this passage, Antiochus was remarkably idiosyncratic:

*οὗτοϲ δὲ τὴν ἐναντίαν λαβὼν διάθεσιν συνήγαγεν σχεδὸν ἀπὸ πάσηϲ τῆϲ οἰκουμένηϲ τοὺϲ ἐπιφανεατάτουϲ ἄνδραϲ εἰϲ τὴν πανήγυριν, καὶ πάντα τὰ τοῦ βασιλείου μέρη διαφερόντωϲ ἐκόσμησεν, εἰϲ ὤνα δὲ τόπον ἀθροίσαϲ καὶ καθάπερ ἐπὶ σκηνὴν ἀναβιβάσαϲ τὴν βασιλείαν ἅπασαν ἐποίησε μηδὲν ἀγνοεῖν τῶν περὶ αὐτόν.*

This man, taking the opposite approach, gathered to the festival the greatest celebrities from almost the whole world. He decorated all the parts of his palace in distinguished fashion and, having assembled his entire kingdom into one place and having put it up as though upon a stage, he dispelled all ignorance of his affairs.

His festival thus gathered everybody who was anybody in his world to see him advertising, in a fashion both elaborate and time-honoured, a truly kingly status of power, putting his entire kingdom upon a stage. There would certainly be men and beasts aplenty, and there would be riches just begging for a cataloguer. All certainly was 'quintessentially hellenistic: it made a vast impression at the time, cost a great deal, and substantially altered nothing.'[121] But Antiochus did show recognition of the mighty military resources. Now the world increasingly ran in accord with the sentiments of the Senate and *populus* of Rome, which certainly could dispose armies to match the 50,000 soldiers that Antiochus was sending through his streets.

In telling contrast to Ptolemy Philadelphus' parade in which soldiers were not particularly prominent, Antiochus' procession opened with a march-past by 5,000 troops. There then followed

[121] Green 1990: 432.

5,000 Mysians; 3,000 Cilicians wearing gold crowns; 20,000 Macedonians, 10,000 with gold shields, 5,000 with bronze, the rest with silver; then 240 pairs of gladiators; 1,000 Nisaean cavalry and 3,000 citizen soldiers, most of whom had folded cheek-guards and gold crowns; then the 'companion knights' and a division of his friends, with matching equipment; then 1,000 picked men and the pick of the cavalry, the *Agēma*. Last was the armoured cavalry, 1,500 of them. All wore purple cloaks, and many of these were woven with gold and elaborately embroidered. After the soldiers, a hundred chariots processed, each pulled by four horses. And then, as perhaps we might now be expecting, there were the elephants. A chariot was pulled by four of them, another pulled by a pair;[122] and thirty-six more decked out and marching in single file.[123] The rest of the procession, given the emphasis upon simple quantity and expensiveness, can be described more cursorily.[124] The impact of all this spectacle will again have to be left to the imagination, since the reactions of the crowd have not been securely adumbrated: one can hesitate to believe that Antiochus' subjects found it all as tasteless as did Polybius, Diodorus, and their sources. The whole production must have stirred many hearts, with all the spectacle suffused by other affective and sensory stimuli, such as the sprinkling of perfumes.[125]

This parade was organized with Rome very much in mind and recognition of the power of the Romans would be the principal animating concern of much else in Antiochus' spectacular monarchy. There was defiance of Roman orders in the exhibition of a long line of elephants. Possession of elephants,

[122] The text is uncertain. This seems a likely reading (Walbank 1957–79: iii. 452).

[123] Athen. 5.194c–f.

[124] Eight hundred ephebes wearing gold crowns; 1,000 oxen; almost 300 sacred tables (Casaubon's *θυωρίδεϲ* is adopted for MS *θεωρια*; Walbank (ad loc.) prefers *θεωρίαι*); 800 elephant tusks; statues aplenty of gods, demigods, and heroes, each with a myth laid alongside; representations of Night and Day, Earth and Heaven, and Dawn and Noon; loads of gold and silver vessels; 1,000 slaves of Antiochus' friend and secretary carrying silver vessels; 200 women scattering scented oil; 80 women in litters with gold supports, and 500 with silver supports.

[125] Polyb. 30. 25. 17; Walbank 1996: 128.

that perennial staple of Hellenistic pomp, had been expressly forbidden to Antiochus' father by the Romans.[126] Seleucid elephants had once been formidable and renowned instruments of war—two Seleucid elephants in fact seem to have become particular ancient celebrities.[127] There was also positive adoption of specifically Roman features. It is a signal fact that the initial troop of 5,000 soldiers were actually clad in Roman armour and carrying Roman weapons; and that there were also gladiators marching in the parade. Soldiers armoured with treasure are as good a way as any to express kingly power. Provision of Roman armour, however, acknowledges the success of the Roman instruments of conquest. Exhibitions of men fighting were not perhaps to Polybius' taste but gladiators were perennial items on the calendar of public gatherings and political entertainments in Rome.

Antiochus was demonstrating his power to his people, to other kings, and to the world at large in what was now an international hegemonic currency of emblems of Roman power and military success. Of course, there were many other vernacular elements reflected and represented in the Seleucid monarchy: terribly ancient Mesopotamian and Babylonian conceptions of conquering omnipotence were blended with the staple traditions of the Macedonian monarchy.[128] The king naturally had to be many things to many varied audiences. But in the second century and for more westerly audiences, worldly or even cosmic success had more and more come to be associated with a Roman style of doing things.

[126] Elephants were indeed important instruments of war for Antiochus IV—his invasion forces for Egypt included some elephants (*1 Maccabees* 1:17).

[127] Pliny *HN* 8. 11: 'Antipater is responsible for the story that two elephants used by King Antiochus in his wars were famous and even known by name; and in fact they knew their names too' ('Antipater auctor est duos Antiocho regi in bellicis usibus celebres etiam cognominibus fuisse; etenim novere ea').

[128] Of Antiochus I a cuneiform inscription (from Borsippa) proclaimed, 'I am Antiochus, the Great King, the legitimate king, the king of the world, king of Babylon, king of all countries . . . May I personally conquer [all] the countries from sunrise to sunset, gather their tribute, and bring it [home]' (Pritchard 1955: 317).

What is most intriguing about the visible comportment of Antiochus IV upon other occasions, about which we hear some interesting details albeit through the unrelentingly scornful Polybius, is that he took systematically (if still somewhat idiosyncratically) to importing aspects of Roman-ness for himself. He had learned from what he had seen for himself of Roman ways of doing things. As a young man he had spent some time, perhaps not unpleasantly, as a hostage at Rome (between 188 and 176/5).[129] And he was nothing if not a king acutely conscious of the power of his visible self.

His epithet, Epiphanes, which he used regularly, is a reminder of the power of visibility: the adjective certainly implied 'the making of sudden *ἐπιφάνειαι*, appearances in person or manifestations of power'.[130] This epithet and another favourite, Nikephoros ('Bringer of Victory'), seem to have been unprecedented.[131] Appian, in relating how the name came to him, puts weight upon his visibility: 'he was called Epiphanes by the Syrians because, when his rule was being snatched away by outsiders, he was seen to be a proper king.'[132] It was, however, no simple business to translate the power of visibility which was so efficacious upon a battlefield into some coherent mode of self-presentation in a city, even if one had the means to build a whole new quarter of Antioch and name it Epiphania after oneself.[133] The things he had learnt at Rome were appropriate to a republic but not to an autocracy, for which a 'plurality of appreciations' is surely ever 'worrisome'.[134] He was, however, quite popular among the Athenians, receiving honorific decrees and statues.[135] A king, we know, must attune his behaviour to the role in life he is playing, as understood in terms of his audience's expectations. Antiochus had his stage but, in the mixture of the familiar and the foreign, he was a pioneer of a somewhat radical but perhaps necessary conceptualization of a more republican kingliness.

[129] Livy 43. 6. 9; Walbank 1957–79: iii. 284. He had also spent time in Athens while his brother was king: Habicht 1997: 223.

[130] Nock 1972: i. 154–5. [131] Habicht 1989: 341.

[132] App. *Syr.* 45: *παρὰ τῶν Σύρων ἐπώνυμον ἦν' Ἐπιφανής, ὅτι τῆς ἀρχῆς ἁρπαζομένης ὑπὸ ἀλλοτρίων βασιλεὺς οἰκεῖος ὤφθη.*

[133] Strabo 16. 2. 4.

[134] Chartier 1997: 101. [135] Habicht 1989: 343.

However, whether because he was an innovative borrower of republican ways of doing things, or a genuine naïf, or bungling buffoon, he did not exactly act as a Seleucid king was traditionally expected to act. As part of his festivities at Daphne, there was a great deal of lavish hospitality—one feast consisted of 3,000 couches, another 4,500. Antiochus took personal charge of the arrangements for these. Consequently Diodorus, elaborating upon Polybius, can declare (31. 16. 2) that the effect was spoiled by this personal supervision (*cheirismos*) of the proceedings: 'consequently, if someone removed his diadem, nobody who did not know him would believe that he was the king, lord of absolutely everything, when they saw him resembling not even a middling servant.' Furthermore, Athenaeus, into whose collage of conspicuous consumption Antiochus enters precisely because the hospitality which he gave violated the norms of exclusivity presumed by the *Deipnosophistae*, tells how the man was labelled (193c and ff.): a passage of Polybius (26. 1–2) is quoted to reveal what was so remarkable about this monarch who 'though called Epiphanes, because of his actions was named Epimanes'—the lunatic.[136] One can wonder quite who initiated such naming. But since the reading of the events at Daphne is programmed by this notion of the strangeness of his behaviour and so the scale of the expenditure involved is not treated with that lavish thoroughness of quotation which Athenaeus accorded Ptolemy Philadelphus' show, it certainly might readily seem more absurd than awesome.

Other civic exploits of Antiochus, as noted by Polybius (26), show him to be adopting practices of Roman *civilitas* rather than following the lifestyle customary for kings. He would slip out from the royal palaces, eluding his attendants, and go wandering about his *polis* with just two or three friends. He was to be found at the workshops of goldsmiths and silversmiths discussing their business. He descended to the company of ordinary men of the people and drank with undistinguished foreign visitors. There was other unlikely rambunctiousness.

[136] The same passage has also been incorporated into the text of Diodorus (29. 32) and may be a more scrupulous transcription of Polybius (Walbank 1957–79: iii. 286).

He crashed the parties of young men, accompanied by horn-blower and musicians, to the shock of the assembled company. The normal order of things would have been for the men to come to his parties, and only with a sure invitation to the big tent or fabulous palace. But this is the partying of a different sort of celebrity and one inspired by a clear comprehension of a different model of engagement with a civic audience, even if that risked baffling the audience with the confusedness of his demeanour.

In his time as a hostage at Rome, Antiochus had certainly identified the key visible symbols and rituals idiomatic to the *res publica*. Thus, Athenaeus further recounts, sometimes he would doff the clothing of a king and actually wear a toga in order to canvass for votes. Sometimes he was canvassing for a tribunate, sometimes an aedileship. The marks of magisterial dignity had also been duly noticed: once elected, Antiochus sat on an ivory curule chair to hear legal disputes. All this was rather bewildering.

Such actions are indeed most curious: just how serious was he?[137] Antiochus was not exactly unique in this sort of dressing-down. Other kings mimed *civilitas*. It was, for example, the habit of Philip V to assume the ordinary clothes of a man of the people (if not to rein in his monarchic licence), just as Demetrius had done in Thebes when his fortunes were temporarily at a low ebb.[138] And Ptolemy VI Philometor, when in October of 164 he was driven by the machinations of his brother to exile in Rome, famously took up residence ostentatiously in a poor neighbourhood, from which the authorities eventually redeemed him.[139] We just do not know what the crowd, as opposed to Polybius, really made of his adoption of the techniques appropriate to the political environment and ideology of Rome.[140] In other respects too Antiochus attempted

[137] Bikerman 1939: 157–8 assumed that these posts had been introduced by Antiochus into the administrative structure; others have thought it pure tomfoolery.

[138] Polyb. 10. 26. 1–2.

[139] Diod. 31. 18; Livy *Per.* 46; Porph. *FGrHist* 260 F 2; Val. Max. 5. 1. 1–2.

[140] Polybius 'did not love kings in practice' and disliked those who flattered them. But he does praise some kings, such as Philip V, and believes it is a king's part to do good and to rule willing subjects (5. 11. 6; Rawson 1975: 152 and n. 136).

to represent himself as a man of the people. He bathed in the crowded public baths, where expensive unguents were brought in for him. When someone remarked upon the happy fortune of kings who used precious unguents and smelled sweetly, the next day he arranged for a very large jar of the most expensive unguent to be poured over the man's head. Everybody, including the king himself, slipped and sprawled on the oil, affording jollity.[141] It was not dignified kingliness. But Antiochus had certainly succeeded in setting himself apart from other kings in historical memory. Even if his actions seem to have careened out of control, they nevertheless were part of a comedy of civility that was not yet familiar to his audiences of subjects.

Subsequent Seleucids adopted the civil style set by Antiochus Epiphanes, albeit without his idiosyncratic boisterousness. Antiochus Sidetes also, as reported by Poseidonius, held receptions daily for great crowds. He provided masses of food and allowed every feaster to take home very substantial portions of uncarved meat and poultry and whole fish, and also honey-cakes and wreaths of myrrh and frankincense with huge long fillets of gold.[142] Antiochus Grypus was also a devotee of great dinners. Poseidonius also reports huge distributions of plenty, at the games at Daphne. Uncarved meat to start; later there followed live geese, hares, and gazelles. Diners also received gold wreaths and silver vessels, slaves, horses, and camels. The living was supposedly good in those days: relieved of anxiety about the necessities of life, all the people of Syria feasted continually and anointed themselves expensively as they lazed in the gymnasia. The towns rang with merriment.[143] Antiochus Cyzicenus also engaged in pursuits unsuitable for kings but which made him the centre of admiring attention. He delighted in mimes and in all kinds of theatrical shows and took to performance himself. He was something of a puppeteer and was able to keep large gold- and silver-plated animals in motion.[144]

Our Antiochus IV Epiphanes does appear, however, to have tried to make his subjects used to the habits of Rome's central arena for the ritualized demonstration of both a civic and a national identity. He introduced *ludi* at his festival at Daphne.

[141] Athen. 5.194b. [142] Athen. 5.210d. [143] Athen. 5.210d–f.
[144] Diod. 34/35. 34.

There were presented, we are told, thirty days of gladiatorial games and animal-killing displays (*venationes*).[145] The practice of staging a hunt is something new in the history of the Greek city. Although Alexander's royal hunts in the countryside were famous and his successors followed the practice that was internationally the habit of kings, be it at Nineveh or in the territory of Persian kings, there is no evidence for *venationes* in cities.[146] Romans might have adopted hunting as an element of lifestyle from Hellenistic monarchs and Greek nobles (including Polybius)—Scipio Aemilianus thought himself as happy as a king hunting in Macedonia[147]—but the hunting shows in the city appear peculiarly their own practice and their own disquieting contribution to civilized dignity. Antiochus' adoption of this means of causing wonderment in his subjects surely bespoke his own comprehension of Roman definitions of what being powerful involved, and perhaps too his recognition of the significance of giving his audience spectacles of violence and death.[148]

*Ludi* were not accepted by their audience with ready ease, however. Indeed, the great interest in Antiochus' innovative importation of this Roman style of entertainment lies in the fact that a king had to show great determination in order to introduce new customs. Livy comments interestingly (41. 20. 10–13) upon the wilful innovation:

Spectaculorum quoque omnis generis magnificentia superiores reges vicit, reliquorum sui moris et copia Graecorum artificum; gladiatorum munus, Romanae consuetudinis, primo maiore cum terrore hominum, insuetorum ad tale spectaculum, quam voluptate dedit; deinde saepius dando et modo volneribus tenus, modo sine missione, etiam familiare oculis gratumque id spectaculum fecit, et armorum studium plerisque iuvenum accendit.

In the magnificence of his spectacles of every kind he defeated previous kings. The rest were of their own proper style and had an abundance of Greek artists. Yet he also gave an exhibition of gladiators

[145] Athen. 5.195a–c.

[146] e.g. Plut. *Alex.* 40; Curt. 8. 1. 11–19; Anderson 1985: 76–80, with illustrations of the late fourth-century Alexander Sarcophagus; Hammond and Griffith 1979: ii. 155–6.

[147] Polyb. 31. 29.

[148] For a convenient bibliography of recent studies of Roman civic spectacles, particularly gladiatorial: Edmondson 1996: n. 8.

in the Roman fashion. At first people felt greater fear than pleasure because they were unused to such a spectacle. But then through more frequent giving of such exhibitions—sometimes only as far as woundings but sometimes without appeal—he actually made the spectacle familiar to the eyes and pleasing, and aroused a zeal for arms in very many of the young men.

Livy has preserved the same emphasis Polybius placed upon the competition of kings to transcend the benchmarks of achievement associated with their predecessors. Victory in spectacle was a prestigious goal in itself.

Yet more is suggested by Livy's account. As a man raised amid republican sensibilities he automatically pays attention to the audience in ways that Polybius does not, recognizing the innovative spectacle as the (initially at least) strikingly repellent violence that gladiatorial combats are to modern sensibilities. The audience, which remains invisible in the account of Polybius who does not seem to care a whit for any audience except the Realpolitikers learning their lessons from Rome's rise and his text, is described as needing to be teased into appreciation of the new pleasure. And it was the younger generation, the *iuvenes*, who were most receptive to the new spectacles—of course.

Livy's account serves, therefore, to remind us that rituals have agency both in their genealogy and their operation as powerful rhetorical messages. A society's habits can be changed in order to make them be more like those of a state truly prosperous in its power. The borrowing of such a distinctive element of Roman culture reveals, furthermore, the power of an autocrat to show what he wants to be seen showing, regardless of the prevailing expectations of the pleasures of political festivity—and showing what he feels he must show if he is to make his power clear and comprehensible to all his audiences. Of course Antiochus' motives ultimately remain rather inscrutable. They might simply have been 'une fantaisie royale, toute personnelle, et sans lendemain'.[149] The psychology of the autocrat may be left to imaginative pondering; and it is not after all deserving of any great curiosity. Yet if these spectacles were a more cunning appropriation of the techniques of display exercised by some of the other most powerful men in the world, they

[149] Robert 1940: 264.

perhaps had the effect of instilling in the audiences, and especially future generations, some burning desire either to be brave on the battlefield or at least to understand something of what a battlefield was. Above all, in a city they wrapped the king with a phenomenology connoting as much control of an awful instrumentality of bloodshed as awesome merriment and wonder. We return to Rome.

# 5
# Elephants and Citizens

and in order to annoy them all the more Pompey is said to have planned to make his triumphal entry in a chariot drawn by four elephants . . . However, the city gate was too narrow . . .

Plutarch, *Life of Pompey*, 14

From the early second century onwards, the power of Roman officials commanding victorious armies had come to be understood as tantamount to that of kings: hence the method in the madness of Antiochus IV who, when the model of what power and success looked like had shifted, borrowed from the rituals of a republican phenomenology of prominence. Yet at the same time the repertoire of imagery by which kingly dignity had been represented in the East was not unattractive to Romans, who had been able to humble kings but who also had every desire to articulate their own stature, in the world, in history, and so in their city, through the idioms of kingliness. In the complicated responses of Romans to Hellenistic kings, there was room for respect and attraction as well as the sense of distaste and superiority which only increased as eastern kings' power yielded militarily and diplomatically to Roman imperial presumption over them in the second century.[1]

Over time, kingly conceit became more conspicuous in Rome, and particularly at times of communal festivity such as triumphs. In contrast to the manner in which the behaviour of kings such as Philadelphus or Epiphanes was remembered, there is rather more information in Roman sources about the sentiments of the urban audience, as will be seen in reports about the employment of animals in order to advertise personal

[1] Rawson 1975.

greatness. Concern for popularity is certainly indicative of the nature of a republic in which the principal political actors conducted their competition for everlasting name with due regard for the sensibilities of citizens who were in some sense sovereign, whereas Hellenistic kings had perhaps usually been chiefly concerned with how their power and prestige would be compared to that of other kings. Ultimately in republican history, whatever the majestic impressions such men made upon the crowd, neither a Pompey nor Caesar could ever rise with complete majesty clear of the protocols of a civil environment, even if (see Chapter 6) the constraining protocols and reciprocities of *civilitas* did not in practice necessarily amount to much that seems intuitively to proclaim the existence of democracy.

Although kings from the Greek East would, in the wake of confrontations with Macedonian and Syrian armies, become despised, there was at Rome early in the second century some admiration elicited by the novelty of exotic autocracy. So when Flamininus sent Amynander of Athamania to Rome to negotiate a settlement in person, the monarch made quite an impression simply because he was a king.[2] There was also a tremendous welcome for King Eumenes in 190/89, and later his brothers as well.[3] But later kings, such as Prusias of Bithynia or that notorious Antiochus IV Epiphanes, had to wrestle with Roman military superiority established abroad and concomitant sensibilities of republican scorn. To their humiliations, calculated to express changes in geopolitical realities, can be added others more petty and perhaps more likely to be gossiped about by populaces at large. The son of the great triumphator Aemilius Paullus, Scipio Aemilianus, compelled Ptolemy VIII Physcon to behave more like a Roman of conspicuous civic dignity even amid the splendours of Alexandria. Scipio made the king, who was a figure of infamously extravagant corpulence, accompany him on foot through the city from the harbour to his palace.[4] In the next century, another Ptolemy

[2] Polyb. 18. 10. 7; Rawson 1975: 152, finding him 'a semi-barbarian petty kinglet'.

[3] Polyb. 21. 18, 24. 5.

[4] Diod. 33. 283. 1–3; Athen. 12.549b–e; Just. 38. 8. 8–10; Plut. *Mor.* 200f–201a.

(XII Auletes) would be received by a Roman pro-magistrate (Cato Minor), who was not even of praetorial dignity, remaining proudly sitting on the privy.[5]

Predictably, Romans became more like kings. The great age of the pre-eminent Roman individual was most memorably launched with the figure of Scipio Africanus, the saviour of his nation in the generally grim war with Hannibal. After the battle of Zama (202), Scipio processed magnificently through Italy back to Rome: 'not only cities poured forth to do him honour but even the throng of country folk blocked the roads. He reached Rome and rode into the city in the most illustrious triumph of all.'[6] This great national hero could have created a kingdom for himself in the Mediterranean world, Polybius thought.[7] His daughter, others furthermore believed, rejected marriage with a king of Egypt, Ptolemy VI.[8] But of course Scipio did not become a king but chose instead to return to the routines (and occasional tribulations) of the city whence he had begun, and to try to insist upon a pre-eminence fraught with challenge from jealousy and political hostility. On the whole this ambitious man succeeded in acquiring goodwill among the crowds and trust in the Senate.[9] And upon one glorious occasion, that anniversary of the battle of Zama, charisma was confirmed and renewed. Scipio's escort to the Capitol should be perceived as a verdict upon the legitimacy of individual pre-eminence. Ambitious Roman notables of later generations could remember such spectacle as a supreme model of the distinction they too might hope to attain in the history of the Republic.

The attempts of individuals to receive the blessing of the crowd was usually a more mundane business. Few of the

[5] Plut. *Cat. Min.* 35.

[6] Livy 30. 45. 2: 'effusis non urbibus modo ad habendos honores, sed agrestium etiam turba obsidente vias, Romam pervenit triumphoque omnium clarissimo urbem est invectus'; cf. App. *Pun.* 66; Sil. Ital. 17. 625–54.

[7] Polyb. 10. 38 and 40; Rawson 1975: 154. Hannibal himself also remained a celebrity of massive, international fame. Even after defeat at Zama and exile from Carthage (195) his reputation was such that, in whatever city he found himself, everybody was eager to look upon him: Diod. 28. 10.

[8] Plut. *TG* 1 and *CG* 19.

[9] Polyb. 23. 14. 1.

Roman elite were saviours of their fatherland. But many Roman generals, because increasingly they had proved themselves the masters of kings, sought ritual demonstrations of the significance of their achievements. The triumph of Aemilius Paullus had come to set a fresh standard for others to try to emulate. It was held not without protest on the part of his soldiers, who felt slighted in distribution of the spoils of the Macedonian war after having been subjected to tough military discipline, and agitation by a tribune.[10] Not least by reminding the assembly of the glorious attractions of a triumph for victory over such a great king as Perseus, M. Servilius turned the tide of the voting.[11] The soldiers did want to be seen as victors; the splendid loot would not be hidden away; the 'greatest spectacle' of a captive king would be seen; all eyes would look upon the tamer of Greece processing in his chariot.[12] The sacrificial victims would meet their proper fate and the great banquet would be held upon the Capitol.[13] Aemilius Paullus knew well how to be a glorious, triumphal host. In Greece, he had given a demonstration of his mastery of the nicety of politic hospitality: 'among the common people was reported his saying that he who knows how to conquer in war can also arrange a feast and organize games.'[14] The festivities he staged there attracted admiration not only for his *magnificentia* but also his *prudentia* in provision of spectacles in which the Romans were then inexperienced.[15] Times had changed and Romans were increasingly the masters of the arts of both war and peace. Paullus' triumph set a fresh standard for spectacular achievement. According to

[10] Livy 45. 35. 5–9.

[11] Livy 45. 37–9.

[12] Livy 45. 38. 14: 'victores conspici velle'; 39. 6; ibid.: 'spectaculum maximum'; 39. 8: 'omnium oculi conspicere urbem curru ingredientem avent'.

[13] Livy 45. 39. 13.

[14] Livy 45. 32. 11: 'vulgo dictum ipsius ferebant et convivium instruere et ludos parare eiusdem esse, qui vincere bello sciret'; cf. Polyb. 30. 14; Plut. *Aem.* 28.

[15] Livy 45. 32. 10: 'ita factum est ut non magnificentiam tantum sed prudentiam in dandis spectaculis ad quae rudes tum Romani erant admirarentur'.

Livy, it stayed fresh not only in people's minds but almost in their eyes.[16]

Paullus' immediate contemporary, fellow commander in the Balkans, and rival, L. Anicius Gallus who was a praetor in 168, had the misfortune of winning a victory over a king neither as famous nor as frightening as Perseus of Macedonia.[17] Gallus had defeated King Genthius in Apollonia in a campaign which had lasted only a month. A record survives of the remarkable triumphal *ludi* he produced upon his return to Rome in order to celebrate the victory in fitting style.[18]

L. Anicius Gallus was able to choreograph something extraordinary—and not least in the very incongruity brought about by its subjection of Greek performers to Roman expectations. This attracted the contempt of Polybius, whose account has been indirectly transmitted for posterity to enjoy the show.[19] Gallus had summoned the most distinguished *technitai* from Greece and erected a large stage in the Circus. Famous flute-players were put on stage, and he ordered them to pipe in accompaniment to the chorus. When they did not satisfy, he sent somebody to give them his instructions: they were not playing finely and he ordered them to make it more of a contest. This puzzled them, but a lictor 'explained that they should turn and go at each other and make a fight as it were'. The artists quickly understood and obediently provided a total (and atonal) confusion. The chorus clashed against them, so strenuously that full-blown argy-bargy ensued. One member of the chorus girded himself, stepped out of the chorus line and put up his fists as though to box the piper who had crashed into him. 'Then the spectators clapped violently and cheered.'[20]

[16] Livy 45. 43. 1: 'haerente adhuc non in animis modo sed paene in oculis memoria Macedonici triumphi'.

[17] Livy (45. 43) points to the inevitability of such comparison; cf. Goldberg 1995: 40.

[18] *RE* 'Anicius (15)'. Triumph: Livy 45. 43; Vell. 1. 9. 5; App. *Ill.* 9. The games may have been the result of a *votum* (Walbank 1957–79: iii. 446).

[19] Polyb. 30. 22 (= Athen. 14.615).

[20] Ibid.: *τότ' ἤδη κρότος ἐξαίσιος ἐγένετο καὶ κραυγὴ τῶν θεωμένων.* There then came upon the stage two dancers with castanets and four boxers, accompanied by trumpeters and horn-players. The situation was indescribable (*ἄλεκτον ἦν τὸ συμβαῖνον*).

Despite Polybius' supercilious diagnosis of grotesquerie, it is possible to suspect that 'Anicius' show was no random display, and it was not entirely devoid of rationale'.[21] Not only did the basic structure conform to Roman tastes but so too did the emphasis upon the entitlement of a great Roman to exert his will upon the Greek performers. The crowd was presumably looking forward to some dancing and something gladiatorial.[22] What is quite certain is that the *triumphator* gave them instructions, and could be seen to do so, through the conspicuous intermediary instrument of his lictor. Gallus did not appear in person upon the stage: the focus of power in the spectacle lies with a removed, but certainly not invisible, orchestrator of his exotic instruments. As Gruen's analysis of this event has well put it, the objective of Anicius' *ludi* was 'not to mount a sterling performance but to demonstrate that Hellas' frontline performers now worked at the behest of the Roman commanders—and he could manipulate them at will'.[23] Gallus is miming in microcosm the relationship of the Republic to the ever widening world before the people that had sent him forth. He uses the instruments more typically available to kings in distant cities. He shows that all sorts of wonders available to empire were coming home to Rome, and that men who are serious competitors for prestige will adopt fresh techniques for fixing new meanings upon their selves in the ritual scripts of civic life. Republican political habits necessarily placed a substantial premium upon popular response to the impresarios of their own glory. This phenomenon lies at the heart of what constituted both political success and power in the late Roman Republic and, as the envious hostility towards Scipio or the rather desperate struggle of L. Anicius Gallus for some of the limelight suggests, put increasing strain upon the cohesiveness of the senatorial aristocracy.

Triumphs more and more became competitions for primacy measured against both the performances of the past and the achievements of contemporary rivals. Individuals

[21] Goldberg 1995: 39.

[22] Cf. Walbank 1957–79: iii. 447, calling attention to the dances described at Livy 7. 2. 4.

[23] Gruen 1992: 217.

adopted a more traditionally Hellenistic and kingly style of self-advertisement in order to impress popular audiences and insert themselves in national memory. Nicolet has well emphasized this trend.

> There is something very Hellenistic about the way in which a purely military and religious ceremony was gradually turned into an enormous show with elements of clowning, a pretext for festivities of all kinds and a means of whipping up excitement among crowds who, by that time, had no idea what a real battlefield was like.[24]

It was by a gradual process of evolution, starting back in the third century, that the Roman triumph became 'the demonstrative and increasingly lavish celebration of an individual commander, his *virtus*, *gloria* and almost divine charisma of victory, under whose *imperium* Rome and her greatness had scored yet another brilliant success'.[25] While the affective grandeur of triumphs was stimulated by Hellenistic influence, there were distinctively Roman features, such as gladiators and the *venationes*, which Antiochus IV had been determined to introduce to his public, which articulated the success of specifically Roman might. The glory of Roman aristocrats would always need a sovereign audience.

## POMPEY'S ELEPHANTS

Pompey the Great was for most of his adult life a celebrity. His face was probably readily recognizable to many Romans, in large part because of his triumphant presence in the capital.[26] Yet Pompey, the Roman Alexander, conqueror of the East, never fully succeeded in securing his pre-eminence within the Republic. Whereas in the East he could be said to have been stared at as somebody not sent from Rome but descended from heaven,[27] it was the Republic that not only had given him the opportunity to perform his great deeds but had also made his significance valuable. A kingly value could not be enjoyed

[24] Nicolet 1980: 354. [25] Hölkeskamp 1993: 29.

[26] One wonders, for instance, exactly where and when Peticius, the ship-captain who rescues Pompey after Pharsalus, had seen the great man so as to be able to recognize him by sight: Plut. *Pomp.* 73.

[27] Cic. *Leg. Man.* 41.

without destroying the currency of its historic worth. Again and again, Pompey acted big but the crowd looms just as large. Furthermore, Pompey, particularly with his third triumph in 61 which was a very big deal indeed in the history of the late Republic, set a new standard for spectacle with which his own subsequent productions and those of his rivals would have to compete. Only at remarkable financial cost did they succeed. Wealth originally grubbed from the earth by slaves and provincial peasants would be lavished upon all manner of exoticism. And citizens more and more would judge the worth of their leading men by their liberality as ludic impresarios.

The whole of Pompey's triumphal festivity of 61 imparted a remarkable visibility to the returning proconsul and his achievements, and so too a sense of his centrality in both the Republic and the world. Magistrates and senators led a procession from the Campus Martius, round the Circus Maximus, through the Velabrum, and up the Sacred Way to the Capitol.[28] Then spoils and captives from the nations Pompey had conquered. All the treasure of Mithridates was to be seen; later there would be an opportunity for further charismatic ceremony when it was dedicated to Jupiter on the Capitol.

Pompey, skilled orchestrator of his own consequence that he was, also imported Hellenistic elements and fitted them into his native environment. Tableaux were commissioned to represent his major battles. Paraded were bejewelled eastern royal personages, and a gigantic statue of Mithridates himself, along with throne, sceptre, and the couch of King Darius I. The climax was a giant float that was labelled 'the inhabited world'; and (perhaps) the sight of Pompey wearing the cloak

[28] For a full description with an eye sympathetic to the triumph's importance see Greenhalgh 1980: 168–77; full references conveniently at Seager 1979: 77–8. Pompey's second triumph, over Gaul and Spain, lacks any elaborate description and was possibly a little overshadowed by the resources Crassus was able to spend upon his own *ovatio*, or the relief coupled with a general, powerful impression of the sight of slaves nailed to crosses and the thought of 6,000 such sights stretching all the way to Capua. Crassus was able to wear a laurel crown, the decoration of a triumphant head, rather than the myrtle one customary for an *ovatio*. Cic. *Pis.* 58; Pliny *HN* 15. 125; Plut. *Crass.* 11; Gell. 5. 6. 23; B. A. Marshall 1972. The survivors of Spartacus' army: App. *BC* 1. 14. 120.

of Alexander.[29] Behind him marched his officers and his legions. He had indeed brought an empire to the streets of the city. He had also showed himself the conqueror of conquerors, the man who made empire, by presenting each conquered nation in miniature, prefaced by placards with explanations and military and financial statistics.[30] Trees were carried to show the lands upon which battles had been fought.[31] Such representation of geography was emulated: in Caesar's triumphs likewise there was not only the desire to provide a magnificent spectacle, but, with the exception of his Gallic triumph, 'there was a very direct relation between the material used and the land over which the triumph was being celebrated'.[32] The use of placards to provide written information is also highly revealing. Achievements are made most meaningful through their representation to those who had authorized the imperial mission and who also possessed a sovereignty over enjoyment of the glory of its success.

Upon this occasion the *populus Romanus* is accorded much greater symbolic significance than in, say, the Grand Procession of Ptolemy Philadelphus. Naturally Pompey displayed a great deal of treasure: excluding the distribution of 6,000 sesterces to each legionary, 20,000 talents of coin and bullion were on view. But this was not merely a quantification of an individual's excellence but was treasure that belonged to the whole community—and it was duly (and conspicuously) paid into the state treasury;[33] the disposal of spoils of war was governed by the laws of the Republic and we are reminded that, for all the kingly connotations generated by Pompey, this triumphal pomp praised the individual by acknowledging the nation. Moreover, despite the general's elevation, the people did things other than merely watch (and one supposes shout). It was not only the kingly man who perfumed the city or drizzled it with wine: before the triumph the triumphant commander had been honoured by the people with honeyed wine, a garland, and his route perfumed with frankincense.[34] Such dynamics of

[29] App. *Mith.* 577. Appian expresses scepticism.

[30] Plut. *Pomp.* 45; App. *Mith.* 116–17.

[31] Pliny *HN* 12. 111.

[32] Deutsch 1924: 266.

[33] Plut. *Pomp.* 45; cf. App. *Mith.* 568.

[34] Dion. *Ant. Rom.* 4. 35. 5.

reciprocity exemplify the complexity of both the changing habits of spectacular consumption and the relations of power specific to a highly intriguing republic.

Nothing perhaps better brought home either the geographical reach of Rome or the power of a notable to command a good show than the exhibition of exotic animals.[35] If Roman citizens did not want to watch merely a parade of armed men in fancy costumes but expected to see them made to do the things of a Roman ludic script, likewise it was not enough just to exhibit exotic animals from around the world. Realization of the capability of obtaining and transporting exotic creatures (usually from places visited by Roman armies) was important.[36] But wonderful was also the power to let a crowd really get to know an animal as fully as possible.[37] Thus animals were choreographed to the extremities of their natures by violence. As Anicius Gallus showed that he could make pipers look lively, then so too did Roman grandees show how animals behaved in fear, anger, and pain. Revelation of the extremities of their natures made for most satisfactory spectacle.[38] The killing of animals in arenas had become a civic ritual at Rome. And entertainment effected collective pride in imperial mastery.[39]

Although there was an Oscan tomb painting of the fourth century of men fighting lions, staged hunts (*venationes*) began at Rome in earnest when foreign animals arrived as spoils of

[35] Cf. Hopkins 1983: 11: 'As for animals, their sheer variety symbolized the extent of Roman power . . . '

[36] Bertrandy (1987) describes the scale of the logistic operations needed to transport animals from North Africa to Italy.

[37] Cf. Beagon 1992: 151: 'animal games catered for a love of *mirabilia* in the form of the size, number, exotic provenance, and fighting qualities of the beasts.'

[38] Plutarch is, as so very often, able to focus precisely upon affecting aesthetics (*Brut. Anim.* 987d: 'The prowess of many animals, when they are dying, retreats somewhere with their courage and is gathered together around one piece. It resists the killer and leaps and bridles until, like fire, it is completely extinguished and dies'; *πολλῶν δὲ θνῃσκόντων ἡ ἀλκὴ μετὰ τοῦ θυμοειδοῦϲ ἀποχωρήσασά ποι καὶ συναθροισθεῖσα περὶ ἕν τι τοῦ σώματοϲ μόριον ἀνθίσταται τῷ κτείνοντι καὶ πηδᾷ καὶ ἀγανακτεῖ, μέχριϲ ἄν ὥσπερ πῦρ ἐγκατασβεσθῇ παντάπασι καὶ ἀπόληται*).

[39] Cf. Wiedemann 1992: 63.

war.[40] The animals were, at least in the early days of such exhibition, in the arena because they had been upon a battlefield.[41] *Venationes*, moreover, articulated in practice central themes of the power of nature and wild animals to be found in Greek art and literature.[42] To stage a killing was to make mythology and mythological constructions of human power come alive before the eyes of the city. And at the same time the crowd could marvel at the animals' spirits and bodies pushed to the limit. Wealthy Romans in the late Republic might be eager to hunt with an ostentation directed chiefly at an exclusive peer group in private preserves.[43]

But, for those with ambitions for high office and glory in general as well as those who strained at the limits of both mortality and citizenhood, hunting became political performance-art, with the virtuosity of marvellous animals redounding to the credit of the impresario of the spectacle. Consequently the names of who first put what on show have still survived, largely thanks to the industry of Pliny the Elder. When a giraffe, for instance, was first seen at Rome during the dictatorship of Caesar—in circus games given by Caesar[44]—the event was

[40] I follow Ville (1981: 51) in using the term *venatio* to cover the category of spectacle including 'des combats d'animaux, des numéros de dressage, des présentations d'animaux rares et l'exécution des *damnati ad bestias*'.

[41] The most famous description of the actual use of animals in war is in Lucretius, who describes the employment of horses and elephants; and also bulls and lions. While this passage has seemed to some indicative of the poet's madness, Plutarch at least appears to have believed that lions might be employed as instruments of war (*De Iside* 19; West 1975: 150). This passage of Lucretius should be read as inspired by the practice of *venationes*.

[42] Animals had taken part in theomachy and gigantomachy in sculpture friezes, such as the lion and chariot of the Magna Mater on the Siphnian treasury at Delphi, and later (lions) on the Pergamum altar frieze (MacKay 1964: 125).

[43] Varro describes (*RR* 3. 13. 1–3) the pretensions of the well-to-do out in the hunting park, such as the one that Varro bought from M. Pupius Piso near Tusculum or Q. Hortensius' place near Laurentum. At the latter park there was a picnic: Orpheus was bidden and duly came complete with *stola*, *cithara*, and *bucina* 'so that I found it no less attractive a spectacle than when the venationes of the aediles take place in the Circus Maximus without the African animals'. A game park for wild boar and other animals was first established by Fulvius Lippinus; L. Lucullus and Q. Hortensius soon had their own: Pliny *HN* 7. 211. (On the subject see further Aymard 1951: 68–73.)

[44] Pliny *HN* 8. 69.

only the continuation of a long and notorious tradition. M. Fulvius Nobilior in 186 staged lion and leopard hunts at Rome, so perhaps making such hunting a spectator sport for the first time since Ashurbanipal's hunt at Nineveh.[45] Cn. Aufidius repealed as tribune the prohibition on the import of African *bestiae*: in 169 the aediles exhibited sixty-three leopards, forty bears, and some elephants.[46] In 169 the curule aediles Scipio Nasica and Cornelius Lentulus provided animals aplenty, including bears and elephants.[47] The meaning or significance of most animals is determined by what they provide humans, and that is certainly the case in Pliny the Elder's natural discourse: 'aesthetic appreciation is rarely of the animal in and of itself.'[48] Rather the animal is thought of in terms of its purpose, its use by man and also a nation. The principal meaning of many animals from abroad, particularly large ones with the ability to kill, was fixed by their appearance in the arena.[49]

Of all animals elephants had obviously the biggest significance in this regard. That unmistakably heroic and kingly man, Pyrrhus, the descendant of Achilles and Alexander both, had first brought elephants to Italy as part of his army, although only two out of twenty of his animals made it ashore with him at Tarentum after a shipwreck;[50] most of the rest, however, did arrive but to little ultimate avail in battle against Roman legions.[51] Eight elephants were captured from the campaign:

[45] Livy 39. 22. 1–2 (the games had been vowed in the Aetolian war); Anderson 1985: 81.

[46] Livy 44. 18. 8.

[47] Livy 44. 18. 8: 'elephantos lusisse'—perhaps the verb means they did not die; Pliny *HN* 8. 64. For a full survey of *venationes* of the period see Ville 1981: 51–6.

[48] Beagon 1992: 125.

[49] Roman attitudes toward animals were certainly complicated (cf. Beagon 1992: 126–7). Barton has well remarked (1993: 67) how 'toward animals . . . the Romans are both indifferent and empathetic'. Cf. the British 19th-cent. exhibition of foreign animals: large and powerful animals were threatening and read as wicked, although the lion, king of the beasts in medieval bestiaries and the iconography of the British Empire, was a prestigious exception (Ritvo 1987: 26).

[50] An elephant motif was put upon Tarentine coins (Scullard 1974: 103).

[51] At Heraclea the elephants did not prove effective (Zon. 8. 3). Pyrrhus famously tried (unsuccessfully) to frighten Fabricius at a parley with a surprise view of an elephant. The animals were more effective at the battle of

elephants were displayed at Curius' triumph in 275.[52] The pleasure felt at Rome upon seeing these elephants led in triumph can be readily imagined.[53] There could be no better emblem of Rome's deliverance from an invading alien (and royal) power.

Elephants were later also associated with L. Caecilius Metellus, who captured many elephants from the Carthaginians in Sicily in 250 and went to no little trouble to transport them from Africa and display them in his triumph.[54] It is not clear, Pliny reports, what happened to these elephants after their exhibition. Lucius Piso said they were merely led into the Circus and, to increase the contempt for them, were driven by *operarii* with spears that had their tips blunted; he does not say what happened to them next.[55] Verrius, Pliny states, asserted that they fought in the Circus and were there killed: no other decision about what to do with them had been reached.[56] He also notes (rather snippily) that those who think their lives were spared just do not say what did happen to them. It cannot ever be easy to know what to do with elephants.

Apart from difficulties in finding accommodation and fodder for them, it must have been hard to decide whether to privilege their nobility or their fearsomeness—it would be some time yet

Ausculum. At Beneventum the elephants were turned back upon their own lines. Florus summed up the three campaigns so (1. 13. 13): 'and thus the same wild animals which robbed the Romans of their first victory and made the second equal gave them their third without dispute' ('ac sic eaedem ferae, quae primam victoriam abstulerunt, secundam parem fecerunt, tertiam sine controversia tradiderunt').

[52] Pliny *HN* 8. 16. Eutropius (2. 14. 3) mentions four in the triumph.

[53] e.g. Florus 1. 13. 28.

[54] Pliny *HN* 7. 139, stating that this was the first triumphal display of the animal. Elephants did feature prominently on the coinage when Metelli were moneyers: Scullard 1974: 152 and n. 90. Quite possibly Pliny failed to reconcile the information he diversely gathered. On elephant transport ships, see Diod. 3. 40. 4–9.

[55] *HN* 8. 17: 'L. Piso inductos dumtaxat in circum atque, ut contemptus eorum incresceret, ab operariis hastas praepilatas habentibus per circum totum actos. nec quid deinde iis factum sit auctores explicant qui non putant interfectos.'

[56] Ibid.: 'eos pugnasse in circo interfectosque iaculis tradit, paenuria consilii, quoniam neque ali placuisset neque donari regibus.'

before their dancing abilities were made apparent. Best probably then to privilege their provenance and to kill the Carthaginian elephants. But it should be emphasized that such a ritual always has to take place for the very first time, when it was no ritual but merely the choice of an historical agent, who, as Pliny has noted (*HN* 8. 17), seeks to inculcate scorn for the mighty weaponry of an enemy but who is also pioneering new tastes in the Roman public. In any event, the triumphal celebrations of the early third century would seem as likely a place for the establishment of expectations that foreign and dangerous animals ought to be seen to be dispatched. Gradually from such a tradition there evolved the habits of the late Republic and Pompey's spectacular associations with elephants.

Romans employed the power of elephants as symbolic rather than military instruments. They were never much used in Roman battle-formations, although in campaigns eastwards in the second century (less than ideal) African elephants could have been supplied by Masinissa.[57] Cn. Domitius Ahenobarbus took elephants on campaign against the Allobroges in 121. Undoubtedly their presence would have been shocking to Gallic foes and their value was also immense in making the proper statement in victory. Domitius supposedly rode through the province in triumph upon an elephant.[58] Other victorious commanders set elephants' strangely massive and foreign might to work against captured enemies, including deserters from their own legions.[59] These animals were in fact becoming Roman. Thus Julius Caesar made generous use of the elephant in advertising his and his nation's glorious achievements.[60] And

[57] Scullard 1974: 178–85. Ten elephants from Masinissa were used in Spain by Q. Fulvius Nobilior at Numantia, where they were not a success: App. *Hisp*. 46.

[58] Florus 1. 37; Oros. 5. 13. Riding: Suet. *Nero* 2, discounted by Münzer, *RE* 5. 1323, accepted by Stevens 1959 and Weinstock 1971: 78 n. 1 and 290 n. 1.

[59] Scipio Aemilianus Africanus threw enemy deserters to beasts in the shows he gave for the people (Val. Max. 2. 7. 13; Livy *Ep*. 51; App. *Bell. Afr*. 135). Aemilius Paullus too had men trampled by elephants (Val. Max. 2. 7. 14). Cf. Lintott 1968: 43.

[60] Associations of elephants with victory: Suet. *Caes*. 37; Dio 43. 22. 1. Note the elephant on the denarius produced in 49/48 by a mint travelling with Caesar: Crawford *RRC* no. 443 although Scullard (1974: 194) rejects

in fact he found that African elephants, when he wanted some to accustom his troops to the sight of the elephants his adversaries had in Africa, were easier to come by in Rome than in Africa itself.[61] The fearsomeness of elephants had been harnessed by Romans; and their regal associations, which had long before been deployed in Egypt and Syria, had been incorporated into a specifically Roman style. Triumphs rather than diadems were the mark of kingly prestige nowadays.[62]

Pompey the Great triumphantly deployed elephants. In 71, after defeating (another) Cn. Domitius Ahenobarbus and the king Iarbas in Libya, he had found himself in possession of some elephants, which he arranged to be delivered to Rome.[63] While their presence could help to stress that the war had been fought against Africans rather than, as it mostly was, against Romans, these spoils could also articulate a young man's exceptional position of prestige in Rome. Pompey had not been a consul nor praetor and his intentions to celebrate a triumph had come in for criticism. Pompey never did have much patience with the demands of aristocratic cohesion. Defiantly irritating his critics but finding the approval of Sulla, he made his plans to claim his due glory, which included entering the city in a chariot drawn by four elephants. The gate was, however, too narrow for the ensemble to pass.[64]

Such a grand gesture, the appearance of logistical incompetence in this case notwithstanding, dramatized well the kingly conceits of Pompey. Elephants connoted much in a Roman

the anecdote. Likewise *contra* Stevens (who adduces Caesar's armoured elephant of Polyaenus 8. 23. 5), Crawford believes it symbolized victory over evil. Caesar's Fifth legion had an elephant on its standard: App. *BC* 2. 96.

[61] *Bell. Afr.* 72; Dio 43. 3. 4. Thapsus was the last Roman battle involving elephants, although the emperor Claudius took some elephants with him on his invasion into Britannia: Dio 40. 21. 2. 'Imperial ceremonial and public spectacle were the spheres in which elephants were seen during the Roman Empire' (Scullard 1974: 198). An *armentum Caesaris* of elephants was maintained at Laurentum, near Rome, in the Empire. Juv. 12. 102 ff.; Ael. *NA* 2. 11; Dessau *ILS* 1578.

[62] By fairly early in the 2nd cent. kings were presented with the trappings of a triumphator: Rawson 1975: 155.

[63] Plut. *Pomp.* 11–12.

[64] Plut. *Pomp.* 14. cf. Pliny *HN* 7. 96 and 8. 4; Weinstock 1971: 37.

history of national achievement—victory over Pyrrhus, Carthaginians, and more recent Greek kings—and also the self-mythologizing history most famously developed by Alexander the Great. The triumph of Pompey in 71 surely also alluded to the exciting and precocious figures of Dionysus and Alexander, who centuries before had first been conjoined for public consumption in Ptolemy Philadelphus' Alexandria. Pliny remarks explicitly that at Rome elephants were first yoked to a chariot at the African triumph of Pompey the Great 'as is recorded earlier of father Liber's triumph for his conquest of India'.[65] Elephants would a generation later feature prominently at the triumphal games of Julius Caesar.[66] And this phenomenon would also stretch into the imperial future. Supposedly L. Cornificius, who had served successfully as Octavius' legate in the war with Sextus Pompeius and prided himself on saving the life of his troops, rode one even at Rome 'whenever he went out to dinner'.[67] Augustus had elephants yoked to his own chariot and thereafter the animals were much more exclusively associated with emperors.[68]

Pompey the Great, however, still had to struggle to realize a more kingly pre-eminence in an environment still characterized by not only sentimental volatility but also the republican, competitive routines that had marked even Scipio Africanus' life and times at Rome. But, with his bulky elephants and all, Pompey did struggle determinedly. His model was none other than the imperial virtuoso, Alexander the Great. 'Pompey from his early manhood, being influenced by the flattery of his admirers, believed that he would be the equal of King Alexander;

[65] *HN* 8. 4: 'Romae [elephantes] iuncti primum subiere currum Pompei Magni Africano triumpho, quod prius India victa triumphante Libero patre memoratur.'

[66] Suet. *DJ* 79; Dio 43. 23. 3.

[67] Dio 49. 7. 6: *καὶ ἐν Ῥώμῃ ἐπὶ ἐλέφαντος, ὁσάκις ἔξω τῆς οἰκίας ἐδείπνει, ἀνακομίζεσθαι.*

[68] The chariot of Divus Augustus on a coin of Tiberius has elephants pulling the chariot (J. M. C. Toynbee 1973: n. 163). The honour of an elephant-biga in the *pompa circensis* is commemorated by Philip of Thessalonica (*Anth. Pal.* 9. 285). Caracalla went about with many elephants, imitating Alexander, or rather Dionysus (Dio 77. 7. 4). I owe some of these and other references concerning elephants to the both useful and humane Scullard 1974.

what is more, he sought to rival his deeds and his plans.'[69] After his Mithridatic triumph, Pompey had displayed a triumphal chariot studded with gems and the cloak of Alexander.[70] That king, whose face and achievements were advertised all round the world, was the obvious model for glossing Pompey, his glory, and, it must have been hoped, his historical consequence. He even looked a bit like Alexander—or, more properly we should say, like statues or paintings of Alexander—and was actually called Alexander in jest.[71] He could, moreover, sport an Alexandrine hairstyle. But from his eyes down his portrait bust remained necessarily that of a bluff man of the people, who made the grain ships run on time but still had to brave the jeers of an excited assembly of fellow citizens, whether gathered in a *contio* or a theatre.[72]

Pompey's games of 55 were also a key moment in his career of remarkable pre-eminence. Yet necessarily Pompey's felicity on this ritual occasion was contingent upon the reaction of the Roman crowd. The games were to celebrate the dedication of his theatre, the first permanent stone theatre in Rome, which would endure as a permanent memorial to himself and his conquests. Located in the southern part of the Campus Martius just to the west of the existent Circus Flaminius, it was a significant addition to the city but nominally an addition to an existing structure, the temple of Venus Victrix, which now it would dwarf. The honour done to the goddess may have been more of a motive than a transparent pretext.[73] Certainly the new structure proclaimed Pompey's achievements. It contained fourteen statues representing nations; and a statue of himself, heroically nude and holding a globe in his left hand, which 'discreetly recalled that he had in principle conquered the

[69] Sall. *Hist*. 3. F 88 (M) = Nonius 239. 3; trans. McGushin 1992. Pompey set up statues of himself in the Pyrenees: ibid., F 89. Other Romans had similar ambitions: most obviously Caesar, who wept at the foot of a statue of Alexander in Spain (Suet. *DJ* 7. 1) but the young P. Crassus (son of the triumvir) wanted to be like Cyrus and Alexander (Cic. *Brut*. 282).

[70] App. *BC* 12. 117.

[71] Plut. *Pomp*. 2; cf. 46.

[72] On the Alexandrine portraiture of Pompey see Corbeill 1996: 178.

[73] Hanson argues that the temple of Venus Victrix was no mere pretext but an important part of the design (Hanson 1959: 47).

world' albeit in the name of the Roman people.[74] The monument would recall Pompey but the thoughts of posterity have focused particularly upon the dedicatory games. Pompey's games were, to put it bluntly, an important political event in the history of the last years of the *res publica*. It occurred just a few years after Pompey's magnificent games earlier, at his third triumph, and only three years after the aedilician *ludi* of M. Aemilius Scaurus in 58 upped the stakes for spectacular showmanship in Rome with his notable animal-killing: others besides and before Pliny remembered Scaurus' leopards, crocodiles, and hippopotamus.[75] Pompey's pre-eminence could shun neither the products of contemporary political competitors nor the judgement of fellow citizens, the ultimate arbiters of his glory. On the whole these games of 55 were a great political success. Velleius Paterculus associated it with the peak of Pompey's prosperity.[76] What is more, the straightforward sensibilities of Velleius Paterculus include a keen appreciation of the physical figure an excellent notable cut.[77] One should try to imagine Pompey basking in the applause of the crowd, since felicity is best recognized in moments of charismatic performance. Sulla's felicity could be thought to lack only the opportunity to dedicate the Capitol,[78] which would have been not only a monument to benefaction but also remembrance of an indisputable ceremonial pre-eminence. Plutarch also has an awareness of *felicitas* as a political phenomenon involving a

[74] Pliny *HN* 7. 98; Nicolet 1991: 38. These items were probably from his triumph of 61.

[75] Ascon. *In Scaur.* p. 23, 27: 'a lavish aedileship'. On the impression: Cic. *Sest.* 116, *Off.* 2. 57. There were 150 African leopards (Pliny *HN* 8. 64), five crocodiles, and a hippopotamus (ibid. 96). He also exhibited the fossilized skeleton of the monster to which Andromeda had been exposed (ibid. 9. 11). On his *ludi scaenici*: Val. Max. 2. 4. 6. He also obtained Prusias' paintings from Sicyon: Pliny *HN* 35. 127. Other 'ornatissimae' aedileships were those of L. Crassus, Q. Scaevola (several lions according to Pliny *HN* 8. 53), C. Claudius (Cic. *Verr.* 2. 4. 133).

[76] 2. 48. 2. Also on the pinnacle of Pompey's life: Luc. 8. 27–31; Prop. 3. 11. 37; Sen. *Marc.* 20. 4; Juv. 10. 283–6; Woodman 1983: 78.

[77] e.g. 2. 27, 29, 41, 75, 94, 97, 100, 107, 108, 117, 118, 127.

[78] Pliny *HN* 7. 138.

popular audience, although he puts the high point of Pompey's career at the time of his third triumph.[79]

A Roman advertisement of pre-eminence in the late Republic had an ancient genealogy and was rooted deep in Hellenistic culture but its validation required popular participations. Roman evidence concerning pomp is generally much more forthcoming about the value put upon the audience's apprehensions, in a city where popular sentiment was brewed of a complex mix of appetites and emotions attendant upon the spectacles of the glorious. It is not mere happenstance that we hear disquiet in reflections upon Pompey's games, for Pompey's competition with precedent and expectations in his appeal to popular favour and national memorability could not succeed without eliciting a potential range of critical reaction. Thus a passage of Seneca underscores the vitality of the example Pompey set through his lavish *ludi*, in both memorability and stimulation of sentimental judgement. Seneca ruminates (*Brev. Vit.* 13. 3–7—self-confessedly a digression) with disciplined grumpiness upon the shortness of life. How much time is frittered away! An inane and wasteful interest for learning useless knowledge had assaulted Romans, and they cared to know who had been the first man to do any number of supposedly significant things? Who was the first to win a naval battle, who the first to lead elephants in his triumph? These examples, he notes, whilst not aiming at real glory, nevertheless are concerned with services to the state. Likewise, indulgence might be granted to those curious about other such matters, such as who persuaded Romans to board a ship, who conquered Messana; perhaps even that L. Sulla was the first to present unchained lions in the Circus at Rome; and Pompey was the first to be the *editor* of a fight in the Circus between eighteen elephants and condemned men. But what is the point ('num . . . ad ullam rem bonam pertinet')? Pompey was a 'princeps civitatis' and, among *principes* of old, reputed to be of especial goodness (*bonitas*) yet he thought it a memorable kind of spectacle to doom men in a novel fashion: 'Fighting to the death—not

[79] *Pomp.* 46; at 68 (cf. *Caes.* 42), however, he tells of Pompey's dream before Pharalus, that he entered the theatre for its dedication and the people were clapping.

enough! Laceration—not enough! They are crushed by the huge bulk of animals. Better that such things be forgotten rather than that a powerful man should learn of them and envy an act that failed to be properly human. O how much blindness does great felicity cast upon our minds!' Pompey, when he cast so much blood before the gaze of the Roman people, believed he was beyond the 'natura rerum'. But ultimately, deceived by Alexandrine treachery, he died, his cognomen nothing but an empty boast of greatness.

Probably Seneca's moral reflections were hardly typical of more closely contemporary reception but all the same a republican environment did not allow the stately monumentality found in the (admittedly more sparse) record of Hellenistic pomp and circumstance.

Great care and expense were invested to elicit such a response but the carping of prominent contemporaries was perhaps inevitable. The theatrical productions were extraordinarily lavish. Yet Cicero sniffed to a friend (*Fam.* 7. 1), whom illness had prevented from attending, that 'apparatus . . . spectatio tollebat omnem hilaritatem' (2); there was a vast quantity of stuff brought into the stagings of drama, which indeed had 'popularem admirationem' even if, Cicero assures Marcus Marius, he would not have enjoyed seeing it. There were athletics and gladiators, and there were animals. Pliny the Elder again provides a record of some of the innovations when it comes to the business of killing animals: Pompey exhibited *cephi* (baboons?) from Ethiopia, which were not seen again through Pliny's lifetime, as well as a rhinoceros and a lynx.[80] But the last day was marked for the climax of the *venationes*, the day when those most impressive objects, the elephants, would be seen and killed.

All must have assumed that this is what would happen. By now the political business of animal-killing, which had long by now been exported to distant cities, had been more routinely extended to elephants at Rome: Fenestella states that the first elephant to fight in the Circus was at the games of Claudius Pulcher as aedile, in 99; twenty years later, elephants were pitted against bulls for the first time.[81] Such violent excitements also had the potential to detract from as well as to

[80] Pliny *HN* 8. 70, 71, 84. [81] Pliny *HN* 8. 19.

confirm historical stature. Not all went happily in Pompey's extravaganza. If the instrumentality of elephants in the history and the streets of Rome had by now become an element in a gloriously reconfigured syntax of spectacular power, they were still bulky things that baulked the forceful imposition of a meaning, particularly through being killed. The crowd that day in 55 was eagerly expectant. But their reactions were complicated:

in quo admiratio magna vulgi atque turbae, delectatio nulla exstitit; quin etiam misericordia quaedam consecuta est atque opinio eius modi, esse quandam illi beluae cum genere humano societatem.

The rabble and throng showed great admiration but no pleasure. There even followed a certain compassion and the feeling that the beasts have some fellowship with humanity.[82]

Pliny has a more elaborate account:

sed Pompeiani missa fugae spe misericordiam vulgi inenarrabili habitu quaerentes supplicavere quadam sese lamentatione conplorantes, tanto populi dolore ut oblitus imperatoris ac munificentiae honori suo exquisitae flens universus consurgeret dirasque Pompeio quas ille mox luit inprecaretur.

But Pompey's elephants, when they had lost all hope of escape, tried to gain the compassion of the crowd by indescribable gestures of entreaty, deploring their fate with a sort of wailing, so much to the distress of the *populus* that they forgot the imperator and his munificence that he had carefully devised for their honour, and bursting into tears rose in a body and called down curses upon Pompey, for which he soon afterwards paid the penalty.[83]

[82] *Fam.* 7. 1. 3 (= Shackleton Bailey 1977: 24).

[83] Pliny *HN* 8. 21 (modified translation of H. Rackham). The embellishment suggests 'that the story had often been retold "with advantages"' (Stockton 1969: 138). Cicero's account is not, however, meant to be exhaustive: this letter to Marius is indeed a carefully composed reflection upon 'the tawdriness and banality of such entertainments when contrasted with the civilized refinement of literary and intellectual pleasures' (Stockton 1969: 28). Moreover, the extra colour of Pliny's account is perhaps indicative of an even greater interest in the reaction of the crowd to the presiding *editor* in the imperial period: on relations between the emperor and the *populus* at the games see esp. Wiedemann 1992: 165–83. Dio (who had seen Commodus dressed as Hercules and decapitating ostriches in the theatre) is also interested in the scenario.

This small part of the proceedings did not mean that the whole did not count in some sense as a success: Velleius had obviously counted the games a success and Dio flatly believed so too.[84] Yet, with much of the brute fear of elephants dissipated by prior experience of elephants and other dangerous beasts exhibited and killed, the crowd knew that Pompey could have spared his elephants,[85] which like all of their kind might know how to behave submissively before a king, but not if they were being harpooned. What is more, the emotions of a crowd are less easy to orchestrate than elephants. Hence Pompey, who craved to be affectively pre-eminent, perhaps did not wholly sate his ambitious desires on this occasion; and perhaps he never really did. The affections aroused in spectacular demonstrations of power did not always afford a sense of felicity.

## THE POLITICAL SENTIMENTS OF THE ROMANS

Not least because of the celebrated unpredictability of popular affections, the late Republic was not wholly welcoming of kingly ambition. Kingliness easily collided with ingrained civil sensibilities. Certainly the most magnificent of the Roman notability was not constrained quite so strictly as were Athenian aristocrats in their polity's democracy. Yet the competition among notables for the brightest light of glorious significance, together with the republican premium placed upon the sentiments of a notionally sovereign voting citizenry, did keep a Pompey from appearing altogether convincingly kingly. In the latter years of the Republic there was as yet nothing like the monopolization of the gaze of the sort upon which Augustus would insist or which, for that matter, had been enjoyed in Antioch or Alexandria—although to be sure in both these cities, at least in the second century, many among the populations clung doggedly to those ideals 'relating to the proper behavior and treatment of royalty'.[86] But there is nothing to be heard

[84] Dio 38. 39: *οὐ σμικρὰ τῷ δήμ ὁ Πομπήιος ἐχαρίσατο.*

[85] As Pliny (*HN* 8. 21) suggests; cf. Beagon 1992: 150.

[86] Barry 1993: 430.

from such places quite like the sad story of citizens upset as well as thrilled to watch elephants made to die.

At Rome the *populus* had long been much more of an integral interlocutor in the community's ritual dialogue that established the success of spectacular advertisers, since obviously there was no point declaring one's national significance and personal magnificence in an empty theatre. And the *populus* did more than to spectate passively. One can, for instance, quickly and emblematically compare a single element of the appurtenances of Hellenistic kingliness, the flowers so lavishly strewn in the Dionysiac bower, with how flowers honoured Pompey. There were flowers for him on his progress through Italy after his recovery from that illness in Naples, a journey of *felicitas*;[87] they were picked (or bought) and then thrown by the humble in a gesture that was familiar in the life of the *res publica*—one can think of flowers for other favourites, such as Curio, cheered through the streets like a victorious athlete after his proposal that both Pompey and Caesar lay down their arms,[88] or flowers for the statue and the memory of Catiline.[89] Or we might register how the wine flowed through the streets from the libating machines of Ptolemy and notice that at Rome we are much more likely to hear of it libated by anonymous folk upon the statues of popular favourites.

If we can hear that humble Romans exercised some inclination to take spectacular politics into their own hands as well as into their own hearts, integral to curiosity about the nature of power relations in the *res publica* must be some examination of the practical habits of the Roman *populus*. The spectacle of Roman politics—and much besides the figure of the orator in the Forum—engaged sensibilities, eliciting reactions as well as shaping tastes to accept and delight in the wonderments which the grandest men in the world could dispose in the city. Yet as valuable as a popular celebrity was, the popularity was evinced in a remarkably unnuanced fashion, both in theatres and

[87] Plut. *Pomp.* 57.

[88] Plut. *Pomp.* 58, *Caes.* 30; App. *BC* 2. 27. In Greece Flamininus had had a wonderful reception: 'What flowers they showered upon the consul!' (Florus 1. 23. 14).

[89] Cic. *Flacc.* 95.

assemblies. In fact, it might even be the case that the rise of grandiose displays by individuals only served to habituate the citizenry to react to prominent political actors as spectacles. The *populus* played a key role in the *res publica* as aesthetic consumers and emotional respondents.

There was a rich variety of venues in the civic life of Rome where demonstrations of popular sentiment could be made and duly registered. Gatherings held for religious festivals and the various attendant shows occurred frequently and, as Nicolet has emphasized, were 'marked by a high degree of religious solemnity, and by bringing together the masses indiscriminately on a vast scale . . . were conducive to the expression of popular feelings and attitudes'.[90] Cicero, in a passage well emphasized by Nicolet, offers important testimony to the attention politicians such as he accorded the direct communication of the sentiment of the people:[91]

Etenim tribus locis significari maxime de re publica <*Baiter*> populi Romani iudicium ac voluntas potest, contione, comitiis, ludorum gladiatorumque consessu.

The verdict and inclination of the Roman *populus* regarding the *res publica* can best be expressed in three places: a *contio*, the Comitia, and the crowd at games and gladiatorial shows.

Cicero, whatever his disdain for *populares*, consistently acknowledges that when popular sentiment was universal, it counted mightily for something:

idemque, cum a summis, mediis, infimis, cum denique ab universis hoc idem fit, cumque ii, qui ante sequi populi consensum solebant, fugiunt, non plausum illum, sed iudicium puto.[92]

And likewise, when it comes too from the highest, the middling, and the lowest—and when from all together, and when those, who previously sought popular consensus, now shun it, I count that not applause but a verdict.

[90] Nicolet 1980: 362. On the republican calendar of festivities: Warde Fowler 1899; Wissowa 1912. On *ludi* in particular: Marquandt 1881–5; Scullard 1981: esp. 38–41. There were eventually over forty types of *ludi* at Rome: *RE Supp.* s.v. *ludi publici* (Habel).

[91] *Sest.* 106; Nicolet 1980: 363. [92] *Phil.* 1. 37.

Here the invocation of unanimity is enough to underscore that the spectrum of support sought by Cicero for his conservative understanding of a healthy political community was largely restricted to men of some property, but nevertheless he looked from his senatorial seat of prominence down the social hierarchy and thus up into the galleries of obscurer citizens. Accordingly Cicero carefully presented to the jury, at the trial of Sestius in 56, his reading of the *sententiae* of the Roman people expressed in the theatre: there was applause for the reading of the decree of the Senate complimentary to Cicero, and for senators as they arrived, one by one so that each could receive his due as an individual.[93] The consul, P. Lentulus Spinther, who was responsible for the games, apparently was welcomed upon taking his seat by a crowd on its feet, hands outstretched and in tears. Cicero takes this behaviour as a manifestation of their 'goodwill and compassion' ('benevolentiam ac misericordiam') toward himself. Clodius' reception, of course, was very different. And the prominent political actors were assimilated to the content of the dramatic performance (L. Afranius' play *Simulans*), and particular passages were read as applying to contemporary events. A *iudicium* was generated too at a gladiatorial show: 'the greatest judgement of the entire *populus Romanus* was made clear by the audience for the gladiators.'[94] This kind of *spectaculum* drew a large crowd ('frequentia') and was popular to 'every kind of person' and to the *multitudo*. Sestius came to show himself to the crowd, proceeding forth from the Maenian column in the Forum: 'from all the rows of spectators, all the way from the Capitol, from the barriers in the Forum, so great was the applause aroused that it was said that never in any cause had the accord of the entire *populus Romanus* been greater or more manifest.'[95] Unanimity again.[96] All such heartening news was conveyed to the exiled,

[93] *Sest.* 117: 'senatoribus singulis spectatum e senatu redeuntibus'.

[94] *Sest.* 124: 'Maximum vero populi Romani iudicium universi consessu gladiatorio declaratum est.'

[95] Ibid.: 'tantus est ex omnibus spectaculis usque a Capitolio, tantus ex fori cancellis plausus excitatus, ut numquam maior consensio aut apertior populi Romani universi fuisse ulla in causa diceretur.'

[96] There are further reminders of unanimity in the *Pro Sestio*'s descriptions of ludic reception at 125.

hopeful Cicero, whose own emotional health and political future were dependent upon the excitation of crowds comprising all social ranks.

We cannot, of course, fail to notice that Cicero is bold in arguing that *contiones*, under the pressure of Clodius' machinery of popular mobilization, gave a distorted view of popular sentiment.[97] We should also note that attention to popular reception is a tricky subject for Cicero to treat: on the one hand, he wants to make use of the reactions to Clodius and others in order to help the case he is making for Sestius, so that the jury can acquit in confidence that their decision is not without popular approval; on the other hand, concern for popularity could be perceived as the mark of a man overly interested in the favour of the people. Cicero seems to have it both ways, his language weaving acknowledgement that the applause of the people is an important recognition of greatness together with insistence that only a 'light' man is truly concerned with his popular standing (*Sest.* 115). Cicero makes his transition to the subject of the popular sentiment at 'theatrales gladiatoriique consessus' by claiming the indulgence of the jurymen at the trial of Sestius. And their readiness for a move to what is signposted as a subject of a lighter vein is adduced from precisely what can be seen in their expressions.[98]

The length of the discussion of the ludic element of political reception (at *Sest.* 115–27) leaves, however, no doubt that the feelings of the 'integra multitudo', rather than the expressions of hired claques (which exert less influence at the games than at *contiones* and Comitia), can and must be duly discerned.[99] For the weight that Cicero put upon demonstrations of feeling at the theatre is corroborated by the secrets of his correspondence. When away from Rome he required news of the behaviour

[97] Millar 1998: 152.

[98] 115: 'Let us come to the ludi. The cast, jurors, of your minds and your eyes upon me' ('Veniamus ad ludos. Facit enim, iudices, vester iste in me animorum oculorumque coniectus').

[99] 115. Cf. *Phil.* 1. 37. Cicero may be remarking upon political practice somewhat baldly here, exaggerating the importance of these demonstrations of popular feeling to the diminution of the validity of the feelings evident in the *contiones* and *comitia*; these had after all swept him into exile. Shackleton Bailey 1965: 389 on exaggeration; also Cameron 1976: 159.

of theatrical audiences: M. Caelius Rufus was happy to oblige with the details of the discomfiture in Curio's theatre of none other than the figure of Hortensius whose practices constantly sought the applause of the crowd.[100] Atticus is urged in April of 44 to send the significant information about the standing of the politically prominent: 'If you have any news of practical consequence, let me have it in our reply; if not, tell me all about the demonstrations in the theatre and the actor's jests.'[101] The sort of demonstration he had in mind is described for us in the letter he sent to Atticus (*Att.* 2. 19. 3) describing popular reception to the triumvirs in July 59. The audience chose to take a portion of the play as an allusion to Pompey:[102] 'It is our misery that you are great.'[103]

[100] *Fam.* 8. 2. 1.

[101] *Att.* 14. 3. 2 (trans. Shackleton Bailey). Atticus had written of a demonstration in favour of Caesar's assassins at a theatre in April 44 (*Att.* 14. 2. 1).

[102] Cf. Bartsch 1994: 69.

[103] The quotation 'Nostra miseria tu es magnus' does not fit the metre of the other verses, trochaic tetrameter catalectic', so Cicero would seem to be quoting carelessly. Valerius Maximus (6. 2. 9) offers 'miseria nostra'. We can compare another occasion, from 61, when popular feeling—this time of a favourable kind—was similarly claimed: 'Itaque et ludis et gladiatoribus mirandas *ἐπισημασίας* sine ulla pastoricia fistula auferebamus' (*Att.* 1. 16. 11). The Greek word *ἐπισημασία* is also used in *Att.* 14. 3. 2. (The reference to 'pastoricia fistula' is intriguing. As How (1926: ad loc.) notes, pipes were used as well as hissing to show disfavour, although Shackleton Bailey is sceptical (1965: ad loc.). How compares Plato, *Leg.* 3. 700c: *οὐ σύριγξ ἦν οὐδέ ἄμουσοι βοαὶ πλήθους*. In *Sest.* 126 Cicero says that Appius Claudius Pulcher crept into a gladiatorial show as inconspicuously as possible to avoid a hostile reception; and in the *In Pisonem* (65) Cicero alleges that Piso will not go to the games held to celebrate the dedication of Pompey's theatre (in 55): 'da te populo, committe ludis. sibilum metuis? . . . ne acclametur times?' Late in 44 Cicero claims that during a performance of another play of Accius at the Ludi Apollinares there were demonstrations in favour of Brutus (*Phil.* 1. 36, 2. 31) but at the time Cicero (*Att.* 16. 2. 3) had little to say on this subject. Cameron 1976: 160 n. 2 succinctly cites modern scholarship on Brutus' games. Appian, *BC* 3. 24, speaks of Brutus' and Cassius' use of hired claques. The choice of plays to be performed was susceptible to political considerations: it seems that the plays performed at the Floralia of 57, which Cicero discusses at *Pro Sestio* 115–26, were particularly suited to the political position of Cicero and his supporters; cf. Nicolet 1980: 370.

From the seats in the theatres came a range of *significationes* that need to be noted, interpreted, and used to map the precise contours of the political environment of Cicero and his correspondents.[104] A good standing before the faces and voices of the crowd was both a tactical asset and a strategic prize. This was because there were as many people at ludic events as there ever were in any other Roman civic space and their physical positioning visibly articulated the state's collective anatomy of status. The seating arrangements represented a political taxonomy and the allocation of prestige within the state, allowing social classes to be discerned individually.[105] Senators were seated in the orchestra (a significant difference from Greek theatres);[106] the seating of the *equites*, and thus the public recognition of their social prestige, was a vexatious political issue in the last century of the Republic.[107] It is notoriously

[104] Other testimony to Cicero's interest in the *significationes*: *Q. Fr.* 2. 15b. 2: Cicero's confidence in his position is supported by what he finds at his house, in the Forum, and in the manifestations of feeling in the theatre ('quod quotidie domus, quod forum, quod theatri significationes declarant'). Writing to Plancus the previous December, Cicero gleefully describes the popular reaction to Antonius: 'incredibile est omnium civium, latronibus exceptis, odium in Antonium' (*Fam.* 10. 5. 3). (The precise identification of the *latrones* can well be left to the imagination.) He tells Decimus Brutus of his standing at home (*Fam.* 11. 8. 1): 'admirabilis enim et quaedam tui nominis, amorque in te singularis omnium civium.' At *Q. Fr.* 3. 1. 24 Gabinius suffers from universal *odium*.

[105] It was an important gesture of egalitarianism and insistence upon the ideological distinction and material value for all Roman citizens when C. Gracchus persisted in taking down the seating for gladiatorial exhibits, which was temporarily erected and intended to be hired out, in the Forum, that sacred space of civic consciousness. Even the poor should be able to watch the show without payment: Plut. *C. Grac.* 12.

[106] Vitruv. 5. 6. 1; Livy 34. 54. 4–8. It is perhaps significant that the plural *spectacula* can be used to mean the seats of the spectators: Plaut. *Curc.* 647; Cic. *Sest.* 124; Ov. *Met.* 10. 668; Livy 1. 35. 8; Tac. *A.* 14. 13; Suet. *Cal.* 35, *Dom.* 10. Note too that Asconius (*In Cic. Cornel.* 61K) has Cicero following Valerius Antias in saying that Scipio Africanus 'passum esse . . . secerni a cetero consessu spectacula senatorum'.

[107] The arrangement of the audience by classes, which continued and was made even more strict under the Empire, made it easier to identify the sentiments of particular political groupings (Nicolet 1980: 365). On the history of concern for seating arrangements see Bollinger 1969: 2–8, Rawson 1991: 508–45, Edwards 1993: 112, and Edmondson 1996.

hard to know the sort of people or proportion of the population who attended the theatre:[108] while some scholars might consider exposure to Roman drama as similar to that of opera nowadays,[109] opera rarely experiences near-riots and readily recognized politicians do not anxiously test their popularity from a box at Lincoln Center or Covent Garden. Repeated performances (*instaurationes*) were opportunities for wider attendance.[110] But, regardless of demographic specifics, the powerful were accorded a physical and/or ideological prominence, becoming the focus of the community's emotional interest as much as the action on the stage. The sentiments of the people were made known either when a political person entered, or when a passage in a play could be interpreted as an allusion to a contemporary figure or political circumstance.[111]

It did not matter that the entire population of citizens obviously could not fit into the Circus or theatre, or, for that matter, into the Forum or the Comitia. The *res publica* might have had elements of a direct, participatory democracy but in practice the sentiments of a multitude were taken to represent something much more; central to Roman politics was the conception that the presence of a small fraction of the Roman people could naturally be read as the whole nation, as a telling passage of Pliny the Elder (*HN* 36. 118–19), describing the games of young Curio to honour his dead father, indicates. Curio, besides reviving 'the traditional public and legislative role of the tribunate in emphatic style', was a masterful impresario of spectacle.[112] Curio, as we might surmise, aimed at winning popular favour but gave new meaning to the swaying voter.[113]

[108] Cèbe 1960 compares the audience of Plautus with that of Aristophanes, which seems both reasonably imprecise.

[109] MacMullen 1991: 421.

[110] Taylor 1937: 291–6.

[111] Abbott 1907: 52. The individual need not actually be present, as Nicolet (1980: 366) seems to assume: in the case of the allusion in *Att.* 2. 19. 3 it is explicit that Pompey is absent at Capua.

[112] Millar 1998: 191.

[113] *HN* 36. 120: 'et per hoc quaeritur tribuniciis contionibus gratia, ut pensiles tribus quatiat.'

Pliny is (rather hysterically) horrified at the precariousness of the seating arrangements of two temporary but revolving wooden theatres, for here is perched the whole nation in all its historic, imperial glory (36. 118–19):

en hic est ille terrarum victor et totius domitor orbis, qui gentes, regna diribet, iura exteris mittit, deorum quaedam immortalium generi humano portio, in machina pendens et ad periculum suum plaudens! quae vilitas animarum ista aut quae querela de Cannis! quantum mali potuit accidere! hauriri urbes terrae hiatibus publicus mortalium dolor est: ecce populus Romanus universus, veluti duobus navigiis impositus, binis cardinibus sustinetur et se ipsum depugnantem spectat, periturus momento aliquo luxatis machinis!

See, here is that conqueror of lands and tamer of the whole world, which sorts out peoples, sorts out kingdoms, and dispatches laws. It is, as it were, the immortal gods' apportionment for humankind and it is hanging on a contraption and applauding its own danger! What worthlessness of lives! Or what was so awful about Cannae?! What a disaster could have happened! Cities are swallowed by chasms in the earth and people suffer sorrow together. Yet look, here is the *populus Romanus universus* suspended by two hinges as though on board two small ships. And it is watching itself fight to the death, doomed at any moment the contraptions should break.

It was not in this case the danger or the blood and pain of the gladiators that conferred value upon the life of his father in this case, but rather the endangerment of *populus Romanus universus*.[114] What is meant by the repeated emphasis upon *universus populus* is nothing more than a synechdochical unanimity. The notion of unanimity was vital but it was never more than an ideological construct of an ideal of civil cohesion—and national community. There could be no other physically expressed unanimity among citizens inhabiting, in the last century of the Republic, wide geographical areas in Italy and even overseas. Nor was attention to universal sentiment confined to the later republican period. We cannot tell how much of Livy's reporting of popular reaction and reception is an anachronistic projection backwards into history, but all the same he confidently relates that Scipio Africanus, in that remarkable assertion of personal

[114] Pliny *HN* 36. 120: 'vere namque confitentibus populus Romanus funebri munere ad tumulum patris eius depugnavit universus.'

power, was escorted to the Capitol in 187 by 'universa contio'.[115] Likewise an anecdote survives to reveal how Cato the Elder was an example of a public figure instantly recognized, known for both his military achievements and his moral rectitude, and obviously the visible centre of some attention when seated before his fellow citizens. He left the *ludi Florales* to save the crowd the embarrassment of watching naked mimes in his presence. Thereupon the crowd escorted him in his exit with loud applause ('ingenti plausu') and admitted that 'it recognized more majesty in Cato alone than it claimed for its universal self'.[116] As long as all the people in an arena cheered, then in a sense it seemed that all had legitimately passed a judgement upon a man. His prominence was thereby ritually glossed with prestige.

Much of the ideological framework of the *res publica*, moreover, can be found in the practical considerations governing the very existence of a central site for popular consumption of spectacle. For a long time the Senate appears to have banned the building of a permanent theatre. The censors of 154, C. Cassius Longinus and M. Valerius Messalla, began the building of one but P. Scipio Nasica spoke against the enterprise and the Senate voted in 151 to demolish the structure.[117] The arguments for the destruction appealed to moral considerations.[118] Insistence that the crowd stand invoked national qualities of *virilitas*.[119] Likewise, a *senatus consultum* also banned sitting down at the *ludi*. In this respect, Rome was to remain self-consciously unlike a Greek *polis*. Appian in fact suggests that Scipio Nasica wanted to prevent *stasis* in the

[115] Livy 38. 51. 12; *supra* Ch. 2. The cries of the crowd ('universorum voces') urge the reconciliation of the feuding censors in 179 BC: 40. 46. 13. In 167, at a *contio* debating (or rather listening to a debate) about the voting of a triumph for L. Aemilius Paulus, M. Servilius points out 'nec L. Paullum minorem aut maiorem imperatorem triumphus faciet—militum magis in hoc, universi populi Romani fama agitur ...' (45. 38. 6).

[116] Val. Max. 2. 10. 8 (trans. Shackleton Bailey): 'plus se maiestatis uni illi tribuere quam sibi universo vindicare.'

[117] On sources and dating see now Gruen 1992: 206 and n. 110.

[118] Livy *Ep*. 48; App. *BC* 1. 28.

[119] Val. Max. 2. 4. 2: 'senatus consulto cantum est ne quis in urbe propriusve passus mille subsellia posuisse sedensve ludos spectare vellet'—to prove the 'virilitas propria Romanae gentis'; cf. Tac. *Ann*. 14. 20.

theatre and to keep the people free from Greek pleasures.[120] The disposition of the human body might indeed affect its reception of all the spectacle of politics. Comfortable seating perhaps encourages more judicious appraisal of proceedings, and Roman political assemblies such as *contiones* certainly did not allow the citizens to sit as they watched and felt and made up their minds.

Possibly the temporary nature of arenas for the liberal expression of sentiment at *ludi* also called attention to the rituals of erecting and dismantling temporary structures, which, as Erich Gruen has observed, 'gave annual notice that the ruling class held decisive authority in the artistic sphere'.[121] But it is hard to imagine that such authority could ever have been seriously doubted. The dismantling certainly prevented the commemoration of any individual in such a key site of the political community. The senatorial order safeguarded its own collective authority and interests yet also acknowledged that the Forum remained a public possession, its space returned to other political business once a festival was over. *Munera* staged in the Forum represented an opportunity to stage oneself as a spectacle in the act of providing, orchestrating, and hosting the people in their own place. In general, the history of the disposition of the space of the Forum was indeed 'in microcosm the history of the Late Republic'.[122]

The business of installing monuments to putatively glorious individuals in this public space was also indicative of republican politics. Romans of every class had something of a passion for statues. There were private collectors who were almost desperate for any magnificent artefacts with which to decorate their

[120] *BC* 1. 28. Taylor (1966: 30–1) suggests that there was fear lest a stone theatre become the site for lengthy popular assemblies at which the people could sit like Greeks to listen and decide. Morgan (1990: 74) insists that the permanent theatre fell victim to fears of loss of *virilitas* in the face of Carthage.

[121] Gruen 1992: 209.

[122] J. R. Patterson 1992: 194, well noting 'the traditional symbolic unity of Senate and people as expressed in the relationship between Curia, Comitium, and the related monuments; the populist reforms of the second half of the 2nd cent. BC, leading to a greater importance for the whole Forum area; the Sullan reaction, and the pre-eminence he gave to the Senate; the aristocratic competition of the final years of the Republic; etc.'

houses and gardens and articulate their taste as the historical coincidence of opportunity and sensibility, as evidenced by Cicero's recurrent appeals to Atticus.[123] When public circumstances demand, Cicero tries to leave a reputation as a connoisseur at home. He projects a naivety to contrast with the rapacious fascination of Verres the collector, particularly in the *Fourth Verrine*.[124] For the benefit of the jury he casts himself as one of the simple folk. Where do they see magnificent statues (which may be characterized as Greek or foreign)? Why, 'if ever he wants to see something of that sort, he goes to the temple of Felicitas, to Catulus' monument, or to the portico of Metellus'.[125] Other alternatives are to apply to the houses of the rich and mighty in Tusculum. These houses are certainly more private than grand houses in Rome which were in themselves monuments representing the *dignitas* of their inhabitants, and they could be viewed as attributes of the *res publica* no less than the Forum itself.[126] And the other option is to look into the Forum.[127]

In the Forum the popular passion for specimens of the *ars statuaria* was indulged to an enormous extent.[128] Cicero often pointed to statues and their inscriptions in the course of his speeches.[129] How did the statues get to occupy positions whence they could command the gaze of congregating citizens?

[123] e.g. *Att.* 1. 8. 2, 10. 3, 4. 3.

[124] Cicero's disingenuousness at *Verr.* 2. 4. 4, 4. 13, 4. 94.

[125] 2. 4. 126: 'si quando aliquid istius modi videre volet, eat ad aedem Felicitatis, ad monumentum Catuli, in porticum Metelli.'

[126] Cn. Octavius' Palatine house, for instance, brought him the *dignitas* of a consulship (Cic. *Off.* 1. 138). Houses as public: Pliny *HN* 34. 17. Note too Sall. *Cat.* 12. 4: 'domos suas gloria decorabant.' Cf. Vitruv. 6. 5. 2; Wiseman 1981.

[127] *Verr.* 2. 4. 126: 'forum ornatum, si quid iste suorum aedilibus commodarit.' The increasingly lavish but temporary spectacles provided by the aediles forms part of an interesting topic in the history of spectacular politics at Rome and is dealt with below. The pieces put on exhibit were often borrowed from private collections and there returned when the show was over. Verres himself provided such loans: *Verr.* 2. 1. 49, 4. 126.

[128] As Pliny the Elder (*HN* 34. 5) commented of the Rome of his own day: 'sed haec ad infinitum effloruit, multorum voluminum opere, si quis plura persequi velit; omnia enim quis possit?'

[129] e.g. *Phil.* 6. 12–15; *Sest.* 83.

And what was the role of the people in attributing worth to them? Cicero espouses a normative value that statues have proper locations: thus Verres' criminality is evinced by the detailed list of statues which he had stolen from their homes in Sicily, such as the statue of the eponymous hero of Tenedos, which would subsequently appear in an exhibition presented by aediles.[130] As Wallace-Hadrill has argued, Greek *poleis* had a clear system for allocation of the honour of a portrait statue, as can be seen in the inscriptions of statue bases. There was apparently not such a clear system at Rome, where both honorific arches and statues were often put up on the sole initiative of the honorand.[131] Statues erected by those who wished themselves to be commemorated—or possibly by friends, clients, or freedmen—had been thrust before the gaze of their contemporaries and of posterity, and were an attempt by those commemorated to embed aesthetically their qualities and achievements into the physical fabric of the *res publica*.[132] Although some constitutionally-minded scholars have assumed that there must have been some 'rule' governing the setting up of statues

[130] *Verr.* 2. 1. 49. In poor recompense Verres littered the island with monuments to his own glorious person, including at Syracuse a *fornix* with a statue of himself on horseback and his son by his side quite naked: 2. 2. 154. Other statues: 2. 2. 145, 2. 4. 138, 2. 2. 160. There was also a festival, the *Verria*, established to perpetuate the memory of the pro-magistrate: 2. 2. 154. At Rome too statues were erected in Verres' honour: 2. 2. 155—inscribed A COMMUNI SICILIAE DATAS. Others: 2. 2. 150 (paid for by farmers), 2. 2. 168 (by *negotiatores*).

[131] Many of course sought to be remembered for their erection of magnificent statues, in the Forum and in temples, that were not of their own selves. Cicero contrasts (*Verr.* 2. 1. 55) Verres' behaviour with that of M. Marcellus, L. Scipio, Flaminius, L. Paullus, and L. Mummius whose houses were empty of statues and pictures.

[132] Pliny the Elder speaks of the desire to be immortalized and of clients' honouring their patrons at *HN* 34. 17: he believed that the first *portrait* statues were those of Harmodius and Aristogeiton. He then remarks: 'excepta deinde res est a toto orbe terrarum humanissima ambitione, et in omnium municipiorum foris statuae ornamentum esse coepere propagarique memoria hominum et honores legendi aevo basibus inscribi, ne in sepulcris tantum legerentur. mox forum et in domibus privatis factum atque in atriis: honos clientium instituit sic colere patronos.' Note the sly inclusion of a portrait of Pompey's mistress included among the paintings and statues with which Caecilius Metellus decorated the temple of Castor and Pollux (Plut. *Pomp.* 2. 4).

in public places, the only evidence is that of Pliny the Elder (*HN* 34. 30) who speaks of an attempt by the censors of 158 to purge the Forum of statues that had no business being there:[133]

L. Piso prodidit M. Aemilio C. Popilio iterum cos. a censoribus P. Cornelio Scipione M. Popilio statuas circa forum eorum, qui magistratum gesserant, sublatas omnes praeter eas, quae populi aut senatus sententia statutae essent... nimirum in ea quoque re ambitionem providebant illi viri.

L. Piso has reported that, in the consulship of M. Aemilius and the second of C. Popilius, statues around the Forum were removed by the censors P. Cornelius Scipio and M. Popilius. They were of men who had held magistracies. They excepted those which had been decreed by the *populus* or Senate... Obviously those men were on the watch against ambition in that matter too.

This is certainly an inadequate basis for the assumption that access to the Forum was for many centuries controlled by the state and so determined by either a decree of the Senate or a vote of the people.[134] Pliny (or more accurately his antiquarian sources) say that for a long time only statues of deities or of men of truly outstanding service to the *res publica* were allowed on public display.[135] Yet the evidence for the Senate's role in granting honorific statues remains 'extraordinarily thin'.[136] It is certainly quite plausible to interpret, as Wallace-Hadrill docs, the censors' action in 158 as an assertion of popular sovereignty and the ideology of *civilitas* over the individualistic aggrandisement of notables. The Senate did take it upon itself to honour deserving men with a statue: Cicero was keen to honour Servius

[133] Wallace-Hadrill 1990: 146, 157, 162–3, 173. He argues that Pliny is retrojecting the practices of his own time, when statues were officially decreed by the state. This has been a particularly helpful article.

[134] As e.g. Weinstock (1971: 40) assumes.

[135] Statues of Pythagoras and Alcibiades were erected in the *cornua comitii* only because Pythian Apollo gave, during the Samnite War, this as his command (34. 26). Those who were wrongfully put to death were customarily granted a public statue (34. 30).

[136] Wallace-Hadrill 1990: 173, *contra* Lahusen 1983. The evidence is conveniently set out in this article at 170–3. There is the notable example of a statue of Africanus that Livy tells us was voted but which was declined by the honorand: 38. 56. 12–13; Val. Max. 4. 1. 6. App. *Iber.* 23, however, reports that the statue was erected despite the protests of Scipio.

Sulpicius, who had died from an illness in trying to reach the camp of Antony as directed by the Senate.[137] His proposal offers a permanent space in the Forum, around the statue to Sulpicius' descendants as a prominent place from which to watch—and presumably to be seen watching—the *ludi* in posterity. The immortalization of a man through a monument is inseparable from some 'privatization' of public space and thus of a small portion of the *res publica* itself. The people persistently regarded the statues that could be seen in public spaces as belonging to those spaces and thus to the community as a whole. Thus Antony is censured for taking the statues and pictures which Caesar willed to the Roman people for himself.[138] The emperor Tiberius will run into similar difficulties when he moves Lysippus' *Apoxyomenos* into his own bedchamber. The people would have none of it and their shouts—in the theatre—prevailed.[139]

In many ways the people traditionally also retained some form of authority in legitimating the prestige of the displayers, either by taking the initiative in erecting statues or by refusing to recognize a statue's right to become part of the fabric of their city. Supposedly the very early statue of L. Minucius was not only an honour paid for by the people but also financed by a tax ('unciaria stipe'). Pliny, as ever interested in the political aspects of artistic display, cites this as possibly the first occasion that such an honour was granted by the people, for formerly it had been granted by the Senate.[140] Cato the Elder received a statue from the people not for military achievements but for the restoration of the state as censor.[141] Thus the later awarding of statues to Marius Gratidianus, neighbourhood by neighbourhood of the city, or of those on the Capitoline and Palatine to honour the aedile M. Seius in 74 for his provision of free grain, was the continuation of a popular tradition.[142] The statues that preserved the memory of the murdered Marius Gratidianus

[137] *Phil.* 9. 16; for the statue cf. Pompon. *Dig.* 1. 2. 2. 43.

[138] Cic. *Phil.* 2. 109.

[139] Pliny *HN* 34. 62.

[140] 434 BC (Pliny *HN* 34. 21).

[141] Plut. *Cato Mai.* 19. 3.

[142] Pliny *HN* 34. 27; Cic. *Off.* 3. 80; Sen. *Dial.* 5. 18. 1; cf. Purcell 1994: 678.

received worshipful honour in the form of libations, incense, and candles.[143]

The power of the people can also be found in the overthrowing of the monuments in public space. Cicero claimed that statues of Verres in Sicily had been violently thrown down by the 'entire multitude'. At Rome the statues of Sulla and Pompey suffered similar treatment.[144] Cicero glosses destruction of statues as 'rituals of conspicuous dishonour'.[145] This is a practice that now seems universally familiar, and especially in an age fortunate enough to have seen toppled Stalins and sundry other tyrants on television and in photo-journalism. There is no more forceful reminder that the affections and the memories of the people remain a repository of a potent form of control over the immortality of an honorand's glorious memory. The gilded equestrian statue of Sulla had, moreover, been very prominently displayed—in the Forum itself and upon the Rostra.[146] This was the most conspicuous location for a statue.[147] Especially given that the statues of Sulla conveyed something of his real physical appearance, the individual took his stand at the heart of the city, the site where the ideology of citizenship was expressed in political practice, with a very personal presence.[148] Appropriately, there too was expressed the judgement of the people upon Sulla himself.

The popular unwillingness to condone the existence of the memorial Sulla left for posterity points to the role of popular

[143] Pliny *HN* 34. 27. They were thrown down upon Sulla's entrance into the city.

[144] Cic. *Verr.* 2. 2. 158; Suet. *DJ* 75. 4. Caesar's restoration of the statue of Pompey was intended to be a monument to himself and his own magnanimity (Plut. *Caes.* 57. 4; cf. *Cic.* 40. 4).

[145] *Verr.* 2. 2. 160. Wallace-Hadrill 1990: 156.

[146] *Phil.* 9. 13; App. *BC* 1. 97; Wallace-Hadrill 1990: 165. The first gilded statue seen in Rome or for that matter in Italy was the equestrian statue of M' Acilius Glabrio's father, placed in the temple of Pietas: Livy 40. 34. 5; Val. Max. 2. 5. 1 supplies the detail that it was equestrian. Cicero's proposal of a statue to commemorate Lepidus in 44 expressly states that the statue is to be 'in rostris aut quo loco in foro vellet' (*Phil.* 5. 41); it is to be 'equestrem inauratam'.

[147] Pliny *HN* 34. 24: 'quam oculatissimo loco, eaque est in rostris.'

[148] Plutarch at least believed that one could get an idea of his physical appearance from them (*Sull.* 2. 1).

sentiment in policing claims to prominence in the community. After the death of Caesar, the crowd would refuse to acquiesce in Antony's suppression of overt reminders of the memory of Caesar in the Forum. Led by Amatius (the fascinating pseudo-Marius), the *plebs* seized control of the Forum and Antony was vociferously denounced. When he ordered troops to drive them from the Forum they pointed to the place where Caesar's statues had been removed from their pedestals and set fire to the place where the statues had been broken up.[149] Humble people would risk their lives to defend those who were perceived as their champions, whether alive or dead. They were fighting for retention of their sovereignty over the fate of those who deserved to keep in death the prominence they had earned or won in life. The foremost exemplar of a man whose merits deserved immortal prominence was Marius. Caesar's restoration of the monuments to Marius' military *virtus* and *gloria* accordingly made him a champion of the people, not merely in the act of acknowledging and rehearsing Marius' popularity, or signalling his own familial participation in that popularity, but also in restoring to the people the Forum and the *res publica* in all its integrity as a physical product and representative accumulation of interwoven individual and collective claims to glory.[150] Caesar was not just providing a temporary show of splendour, as his role as aedile might suggest, but was rather also restoring history to the Forum and to the state. Marius' *tropaea* had every right to remain as much the object of national gaze that they remained after Caesar's restoration of them as did his temple to Honos and Virtus, which could not so easily be displaced.[151] Marius securely belonged to the catalogue of Roman heroes who had successfully waged great military campaigns.[152] Nor had Sulla's obliteration of his memorials

[149] App. *BC* 3. 2–3.

[150] Restoration e.g. Suet. *DJ* 11. Here Caesar does this in a long-running 'feud' with the optimates to damage their *auctoritas* since they had successfully obstructed his designs in the direction of Egypt.

[151] Val. Max. 6. 9. 14: 'cuius bina tropaea in urbe spectantur.' An anecdote at Cic. *De Or.* 2. 266 shows these monuments to be part of the everyday fabric of the Forum.

[152] Cic. *Phil.* 13. 9, cf. 5. 15.

destroyed his place in popular affections. And in due course there would be statues of Caesar everywhere in the city.[153]

Popular remembrance of Marius further illustrates that the popular culture of memory constituted a vital dimension of republican politics, in which there was room for reverence of individuals of extraordinary accomplishment. Marius' popularity was at its greatest height at the time of his triumph in 101: indeed, 'there was nobody who did not pour libations to him at the rituals of his own table as to the immortal gods'.[154] There were certainly few who had enjoyed the exalted position of being regarded as a founder of Rome—that position in which Cicero said *virtus* brought a man closest to the gods and which he himself coveted in regard for his actions in 63.[155] Yet, although his reputation as saviour could have been overshadowed in the years after the awkward involvement with Saturninus, there is no suggestion in Cicero at least that there was any fall in popularity in the following year or decade.[156] For ultimately his fate in the Forum and in posterity was determined by the love shown by the people and his embrace in popular memory—the feelings that responded and drove men so readily to a pseudo-Marius. The resonance of the big names of Roman history as a vital political force over generations shows what a popular audience could give an ambitious man.

Some measure of fame could be given by the *populus* in response to marked liberality. Games were given by various members of a narrow euergetic elite, both magistrates and private individuals. Some have seen the division of responsibility as a reminder that it was the state that supported public entertainment.[157] This view does not shed much light upon the keen competition of the late Republic, however, since clearly

[153] App. *BC* 2. 106.

[154] Val. Max. 8. 15. 7. Plutarch (*Mar.* 27) too notes that the people hailed him as the third founder of Rome and as they made merry at home with their wives and children they would bring ceremonial offerings of food and libations of wine to Marius.

[155] *Rep.* 1. 12: 'neque enim est ulla res, in qua propius ad deorum numen virtus accedat humana, quam civitatis aut condere novas aut conservare iam conditas.' See Weinstock 1971: 180 n. 4 for the Greek antecedents of this doctrine.

[156] Carney 1960: 105.

[157] Gruen 1992: 189 and 197.

some impresarios (*editores*) were well remembered in association with particular entertainments—or, often, previously unseen and remarkable animals. Such competition would also in practice tend to undermine the cohesion of the notability. Pliny thought Curio's games a devastation of *mores*;[158] and this objection, we shall see, is particularly evident in the expression of Cicero's concerns. Ambitious individuals were well able to seek their own prestigious advantage whilst respecting the public domain over the space in which they were spending and showing themselves off so generously.

The principal occasions for *ludi* in the Forum were the anniversaries of gods, particularly the deities whose festivals crowded the month of April; dedications of statues and temples; anniversaries of deaths; and anniversaries of the living.[159] Such a plentiful menu offered opportunities to elicit the ritual approbation of the *populus universus*. Some, the aediles, were actually obligated to show themselves in a glorious light. Their games are really not much of a curiosity in Roman political history.[160] When both money and effective advertising styles—often imported from autocratic environments—were available, there developed the lavish aedilician *munera*, of the sort most famously given in 58 by Scaurus. These afforded a fleeting opportunity for rapt attention on the part of citizen consumers to the spectacle of men providing exciting lessons in imperial history and geography as well as their own embodiment of a capability to command. Although Mommsen was able to detect a marked degree of influence of aedilician games upon elections as early as the last years of the Hannibalic war, Gruen has recently insisted that there is little evidence 'to suggest that conspicuous spending upon such *ludi* was an important factor in aediles' ascent to higher offices of the *cursus*'.[161] Yet aediles—and most conspicuously in the last generation of the Republic—certainly did

[158] *HN* 36. 113.: 'cuius nescio an aedilitas maxime prostraverit mores.'

[159] Piganiol 1923: 144–6.

[160] e.g. as disingenuously found by Veyne (1990: 208) who answers his own question by proceeding to describe festive euergetism as a 'glorious obligation'.

[161] Mommsen 1887: i. 535. Gruen 1992: 188–97, quotation at 189. Gruen's case is stronger for the 2nd cent. BC, whence come our surviving texts of Roman dramas in which he is most interested.

compete against one another and past precedents to make a favourable impression with gladiators, artefacts, and animals against their colleagues in the magistracy in their year of office, and also against the memorable impressions generated by prior holders of the office in recent years. One needed to be rich to stand for the aedileship.[162] Good games indicated not only wealth but also willingness to spend it upon the people.

It is clear that *ludi* were an important factor in ascending to higher offices in the late Republic, although one to be weighed amongst others in assessing the chances of a candidate.[163] At the least, they gave notoriety that could be translated into general persuasiveness with the *populus*, which was ever tactically valuable. So Q. Gallius, finding himself standing for a praetorship without having had decent wild beasts the previous year as aedile, gave a gladiatorial *munus* in the name of his father.[164] Sulla blamed his defeat for a praetorship upon the crowds that expected Bocchus would come through with fine African animals for *venationes* if he had to stand for the aedileship that he had bypassed upon his ascent through the offices of state.[165] There was often no great distinction among candidates' positions of policy. The spending of aediles upon *ludi* and spectacles was as good a standard as any by which they might be judged as deserving of higher office. There were other ways of being memorably generous, including provision of free or subsidized grain, or other material benefits that won over the goodwill of the electorate. Yet even such moves suggested the power of a man to affect ordinary lives in a distinct manner both material and symbolic.[166] Furthermore, those

[162] Plut. *Brut.* 15. Games happen whoever the aediles are (Cic. *Planc.* 13). But of course Cicero is defending *de ambitu*—and *ambitus* in the elections of the aediles.

[163] e.g. Cicero writes to D. Brutus that Lamia who is standing for a praetorship 'magnificentissimo munere aedilicio' (*Fam.* 11. 16. 3). In general see Gelzer (1969: 111 ff.) on aediles and games. Marquardt 1881–5: ii. 86 and ii. 488 document aedilician generosity.

[164] Ascon. *In Tog. Cand.* 88C.

[165] Plut. *Sull.* 5.

[166] Cicero in his aedileship dispensed cheap food from Sicily in the Forum. Plut. *Cic.* 8. In the imperial period Rufus Egnatius organized his fire brigade when an aedile: Vell. 2. 91. 3. Marcellus, who died in 23, we might also note 'magnificentissimo munere aedilitatis edito decessit admodum iuvenis' (Vell. 2. 93. 1).

with loot plundered from barbarians or extracted from slaves and tenant farmers, or borrowed on credit against confident expectations of such expropriations, wanted very seriously to be known for events that people might talk about for years to come and might use to gauge the passage of time in their lifetimes, fixing dates by association with watching elephants, ostriches, crocodiles, and panthers—and their deaths.

At all festivals of controlled violence, individuals could place themselves (and their lineage and family) at the centre of the state. The presence of other Romans of official dignity surely did contribute a sense that the entire state was involved.[167] But the state's dignity was made to reflect upon the significance of the agent temporarily at the centre of it. We notice, for example, Cicero's emphatic and emotional emphasis upon himself in his prosecution of Verres, which he conducted as aedile-elect, as he describes the solemnity of his obligations.[168] At the games the aedile or whoever certainly was ceremonially prominent—even to the point of calling further attention to himself by the clothing he wore.[169] Nobody liked to be upstaged and everybody (even under the Principate) wanted his own fair share of celebrity and time spent waving at a crowd.[170]

The temporary nature of the display, furthermore, surely in itself made the power to transform public space into a world of spectacle, which the more impressively demonstrated suitability for holding still higher office and exercising *imperium*. Famous Scaurus brought 3,000 (according to the text of Pliny)

[167] As Gruen has pointed out (1992: 188), the one festival that did lie in the charge of the aediles, the *ludi Romani*, granted great prominence not to the aediles but to the consul or the urban praetor who acted as starter for the chariot races: e.g. Livy 8. 40. 2.

[168] *Verr.* 2. 5. 36: '*mihi* ludos sanctissimos maxima cum cura et caerimonia Cereri Libero Liberaeque faciundos, *mihi* Floram matrem populo plebique Romanae ludorum celebritate placandum, *mihi* ludos antiquissimos, qui primi Romani appellati sunt, cum dignitate maxima et religione Iovi Iunoni Minervaeque esse faciundos, *mihi* sacrarum aedium procurationem, *mihi* totam urbem tuendam esse commissam.'

[169] P. Lentulus Spinther wore a purple *praetexta* as curule aedile in 63: Pliny *HN* 8. 137.

[170] When the aedile Critonius was giving games, Octavian was ready to display his 'father's' throne. 'Not when I'm paying!' replied the aedile (App. *BC* 3. 28).

statues into the theatre, even though the theatre was only temporary.[171] Others filled the Forum with borrowed objects of beauty.[172] L. Crassus imported six pillars of marble from Mount Hymettus to embellish the *scaena* in his aedileship.[173] For a short time the objects that filled and were destined in time to fill once again the houses of the important were available to the gaze and aesthetic enjoyment of everybody who wished to see them. A community of shared aesthetic response was constructed but, of course, at the will of the *editor*—able too to dispense the patronage of the best positions for viewing[174]—the perfect articulation of the politics of deference within an ideology of *civilitas*. And, it might be added, the ability to control violence is ever the base instrumentality essential to power.

The ritual management of political relations was infinitely preferable to the orchestration of violence, as grotesque as it was carnivalesque, which obtained in the state when there was not that firm monopoly of both spectacle and power, all dressed with exquisite attention to civil *politesse*. Sulla had sent centurions to kill Ofella, whose candidacy for a consulship he did not favour, in the Forum. The tyrant was conspicuous as a spectator of the violence he was ordering, seated upon high, looking down from a temple.[175] The Roman populace was as familiar with the sight of blood in the city as it was with knowledge of pre-eminent responsibility for it. Catiline supposedly killed with his own hands, striking down M. Marius Gratidianus with the people as spectators.[176] Clodius was accused by Cicero of not only having gladiators but of being one.[177] And once Roman

[171] Pliny *HN* 36. 113 mentions various artefacts and (34. 36) the 3,000 statues 'in scaena tantum fuere temporario theatro'.

[172] e.g. Cic. *Verr.* 2. 4. 6. Verres appears a generous lender of artefacts to aediles: ibid. 1. 49, 4. 126. Appius Claudius was accused of carrying off the statue (which Clodius dedicated as Libertas upon Cicero's former property) 'ad ornatum aedilitatis' (Cic. *Dom.* 111).

[173] Afterwards he installed them in his house: Pliny *HN* 17. 6. Murena and Varro obtained murals from Sparta (Pliny *HN* 35. 173: 'propter excellentiam picturae ligneis formis inclusum Romam deportavere . . . ad comitium exornandum').

[174] Wiseman 1987: 79; Livy 34. 44. 4; Cic. *Har. Resp.* 26.

[175] Plut. *Sull.* 33.

[176] *Com. Pet.* 10: 'inspectante populo'.

[177] e.g. *Sest.* 78–80.

armies had been marched upon Rome itself, gladiatorial imagery increasingly became central to the conceptualization of the political life of the late Republic. The commonplaces of historiography commonly described the agency of such commanders as though it was after the fashion of a duel, thereby assimilating discursively the city to the battlefield as well as effacing the ranks of citizen-soldiery. When war becomes the extension of political struggle, generals are glamorous single-combatants as gladiatoriality spilled out beyond the temporary arena.[178] It is usually and rightly understood that there was a close ideological correspondence between the arena and the battlefield.[179] And as battle translated into terror or proscription, a young prince, who probably no more actually killed anybody with his own hands any more than he ever had to take off his own slippers, becomes remembered as an 'adulescentulus carnifex', a 'little boy butcher'.[180]

[178] Velleius' description (2. 21. 3) of Cinna fighting Pompey at the walls of Rome is a good example: 'sed ad ultimum magno atrocique cum Cinna conflixit: cuius commissi patratique sub ipsis moenibus oculisque urbis Romanae pugnantibus spectantibusque quam fuerit eventus exitiabilis, vix verbis exprimi potest.' Florus (2.9) uses gladiatorial combat to discuss the Marian civil war: ' in urbe media ac foro quasi harena cives cum civibus suis gladiatorio more concurrerent', cf. 2. 13. 18: 'prima civilis belli harena Italia fuit', referring to the struggle between Pompey and Caesar. Florus is particularly interesting in his reading of history in terms of gladiatorial combat: he notices a *munus* happening in Rome at the same time as Marius (whom we might repeat did face challenges to single-combat) was winning his victory over the Cimbri (1. 38. 18–21). Cassius is compared to a gladiator at App. *BC* 4. 133. Interestingly Caesar presided as the supreme military spectator over exhibitions of single-combat before crossing the Rubicon (Plut. *Caes.* 32). Suetonius (*DJ* 31. 1) says that he appeared at 'spectaculo publico per dissimulationem' and inspected the design of a new gladiatorial school.

[179] For the correspondences between gladiatorial combats and the Roman military ethos see the fundamental analysis of Hopkins 1983: 1–30, esp. 1 and 2: 'Rome was a warrior state ... Then in memory of their warrior traditions, the Romans set up artificial battlefields in their cities and towns. They re-created battlefield conditions for public amusement.'

[180] Val. Max. 6. 2. 8: in 55 Helvius Mancia accused Pompey's close friend L. Libo before the censors. Pompey attacked Mancia, who thereupon replied with words of vituperation and accuracy.

The business of bloodshed, an obvious understanding of which was shared by all Romans,[181] cast a shadow over all other arenas of power and glory in the late Republic. The scale of gladiatorial spectacle at *munera* perhaps increased as the inhabitants of Rome became more detached from the experience of actual battlefields.[182] Even though violence was for a while, in the heyday of Cicero, kept routinely in its ludic confines, it cast its shadow over those who were both by temperament and for convenience better able to compete for glory in the more politely controlled excitations of oratory than in exercising and advertising possession of a ritual power to have men or animals killed at his own expense and discretion. Spectacular munificence threatened the memorability of oratorical pre-eminence.

Thus we hear of Cicero's worry about lavish spectacle and notice too that he proudly promulgated a law (*lex Tullia de ambitu*) to control the influence of expensive games upon elections.[183] He also wrote (*Fam.* 2. 3. 4) in appeal to Curio, when

[181] References to famous fighters came easily to Cicero: 'cum Aesernino Samnite Pacideianus comparatus viderer.' *Q. Fr.* 3. 4. 2. For Pacideianus cf. Hor. *Sat.* 2. 7. 97—a passage testifying to the commemoration of fighters through portraiture; cf. Pliny *HN* 35. 52. Among Cicero's correspondents, Trebatius for one appears fond of gladiatorial combat, or else his distaste allows a joke: *Fam.* 10. 2. Cicero's freedman Tiro enjoyed such shows too: *Fam.* 16. 20.

[182] Cf. Hopkins 1983: ch. 1; cf. Frézouls 1983*b*: 105. Livy suggests the divergence of militarism from 'gladiatoriality', as it were, when he comments upon the similarity of army manoeuvres to the sights of the arena, in the days when 'mos erat tum, nondum hac effusione inducta bestiis omnium gentium circum complendi, varia spectaculorum conquirere genera' (Livy 44. 9. 4; cf. Val. Max. 2. 3. 2). (A race with four-horsed chariots, bareback riding, and the like.) Livy's own detachment from the battlefield imposed what was familiar to his own eye upon his reading and retelling of events he read about in the past, but nonetheless does testify to a parallel between events on the battlefield and events in the past. Elsewhere he describes Samnite weaponry in a way that is at odds with both the representations of weapons on tombs and the weapons placed with the dead fighter inside (9. 40). Livy has explicitly connected his account with the weaponry of a class of gladiators (Rawson 1991: 593–4).

[183] Cic. *Vat.* 37 and *Sest.* 134. And for all Cicero's concern over expenditures on political spectacle we should remember that his best friend Atticus profited, as surely did many financiers and politicians, in the trade of the stuff of spectacle: he sold *bestiarii* to C. Cato: *Q. Fr.* 2. 5. 3.

(in 53) Curio was planning his games (and his precarious revolving stadium-seating) in honour of his late father. He will obtain 'everything which is most distinguished in the *res publica*' ('omnia, quae sunt amplissima in republica') more easily by his own merits than by *munera*. These are a matter of resources, not *virtus*. This appeal for cohesion of aristocracy went unheeded and the games were duly something special, as Pliny's description has made clear. *Munera* could indeed do things that other rhetorics, more suited to Cicero's own talents and resources as well as to his conception of the *res publica*, could not.

In the *De Officiis* (2. 55–6) Cicero more systematically outlines his sense of the endangerment (of his conception) of the *res publica*. He gives appropriate generosity its due but condemns prodigality, identifying it with the sorts of spectacles with which he and we have been made familiar:

> prodigi, qui epulis et viscerationibus et gladiatorum muneribus, ludorum venationumque apparatu pecunias profundunt in eas res, quarum memoriam aut brevem aut nullam omnino sint relicturi.
>
> The lavish are those who squander their funds on feasts and gifts of meat and gladiatorial displays, on games and animal-hunts. The memory they shall leave will be slight or entirely non-existent.

This perspective is informed by a time-worn, Greek political philosophy: Cicero cites Theophrastus and also Aristotle's assertion that the memory of prodigality was short-lived. Aristotle, though, had lived before elephants were to be seen in the *polis*. And in adducing this authority Cicero's desperation is apparent. He knew full well it was not really so: *munera* could be memorable indeed, as he himself shows in proceeding to offer (57) a telling brief history of memorable aedileships discharged by men whom he admired or of whom he did not seriously disapprove:

> Quamquam intellego in nostra civitate inveterasse iam bonis temporibus, ut splendor aedilitatum ab optimis viris postuletur. Itaque et P. Crassus cum cognomine dives, tum copiis functus est aedilicio maximo munere, et paulo post L. Crassus cum omnium hominum moderatissimo Q. Mucio magnificentissima aedilitate functus est, deinde C. Claudius App. filius, multi post, Luculli, Hortensius, Silanus; omnes autem P. Lentulus me consule vicit superiores; hunc est

Scaurus imitatus; magnificentissima vero nostri Pompei munera secundo consulatu; in quibus omnibus quid mihi placeat, vides.

All the same, I realize that in our state, even in its good times, it has become established that splendid aedileships are demanded of the best men. So P. Crassus, who was not only called Rich but really was, gave the greatest of games when he was aedile. And likewise a little later L. Crassus, along with Q. Mucius, the most unpretentious man of all, had a most magnificent aedileship. Then there was C. Claudius, son of Appius, and after him many others: the Luculli, Hortensius, Silanus. In the year I was consul, P. Lentulus surpassed all before him; and Scaurus copied him. The games of my friend Pompey in his second consulship were most magnificent. You see what my view of all this is.

All the men in this list reached the highest ranks of *dignitas*. The culmination of the list with Pompey's games—and not, of course, any given when he was an aedile—speaks volumes about how Cicero believed that the outward advertisement of the person and power of the provider should coincide with his intrinsic worth. But the realities of grand politics had changed rapidly, as was surely brought home to Cicero when he was badgered at the end of a spectacular decade in Roman politics by M. Caelius Rufus' requests for panthers from Cilicia when Cicero served as pro-consul: 'in almost all my letters I mentioned panthers to you.'[184] And in such petty anxiety for exotica there was much at stake, for if elected aedile, Caelius would have much richer men as colleagues with whom to compete in all the light of the city.[185] Cicero might on principle have resisted such importunement but the value of many commodities of empire was established by the dispositions of popular, political taste. *Urbanitas* demanded that every ambitious man and all his friends perform spectacular duty in what had increasingly become an astonishingly affective political economy.

The significances of panthers, gladiators, or elephants are obviously not the whole story of the *res publica* but nor are they exactly epiphenomena. The narrative of the latter years of its history is obviously one of pervasive mundanities of violence, driven by ambitions that explained themselves through spectacle. While one can only wonder quite what

[184] Caelius in *Fam.* 8. 9. 3; cf. *Fam.* 2. 2. 2, 8. 6. 5, 8. 10.
[185] *Fam.* 8. 3. 1.

apprehension of all such aesthetics of glory did to individuals in the audience, it is certainly clear that in all the intricacies of emotion, attendant upon all the routine wonderments of life in the light of an imperial capital, at once a demarcation and a complicity were fashioned between those who acted and those who consumed. The cohesion of the class of political notables at Rome, or for that matter in Athens, might have been riven by hungers for prestige of heroic, kingly scale but that minority still collectively enjoyed a capability to impress a multitude, who in turn could only make brute noise in their nation's political history, even if that noise was fully and carefully registered. Cicero himself, as I shall be arguing in the following chapter, espoused with eloquence for most of his career the merits of aristocratic solidarity; and in those times when he occupied a position of great prominence within the *res publica* he does appear able to bequeath a realization, *pace* protestations that there be some Roman democracy, of the power of the notability. This was, however, still a constitutional power to impress afforded by traditional spectacles of state, albeit of a style at odds with (and more and more overshadowed by) all that stuff of the advertisements of its most lavishly pompous notables.

# 6
# Ciceronian Consensus

To state the matter shortly, royalty is a government in which the attention of the nation is concentrated on one person doing interesting actions.

Walter Bagehot, *The English Constitution*[1]

Cicero's moments of supreme felicity did not occur when he was the impresario of a gloriously lavish festival. Although as aedile of the plebs (in 69 BC) he had dutifully provided ludic entertainment, its memorability was nothing to compare with that produced in the years after his consulship and ascension to the highest rank of the Republic's notability. Cicero's own political prominence was built upon successes in domestic politics. He was a stirring and beguiling speaker able to sway the hearts and minds of a popular audience. He was not much of a dispenser of wondrous spectacle. He did flourish in a more intimate world of oligarchic intrigue. Cicero never felt much respect for the legislative sovereignty of the *populus Romanus universus*. But he did seek the validity of its judgement upon his own significance in the Republic. Upon occasion he won this through oratorical performance, even as those who gathered to listen to his persuasiveness were also those who more and more were drawn to festive spectacles of glamour and butchery.

Roman crowds, while they might sometimes act upon the desire to insist upon the exercise of sovereignty in all areas of the Republic's decision-making, were also perfectly familiar with the distinction between people like themselves and a noticeably distinct cast of characters who occupied positions of obvious power and prestige. While the citizens of democratic

[1] Bagehot 1963: 86.

Athens were conscious of the value of circumspection in their regard for their leaders yet still succumbed affectionately to charismatic individuals, it is not clear that Roman citizens ever did other than to attend respectfully to the splendour of their commonwealth's *principes*. To be sure, the authority of the Republic's notability was meaningless without confirmation of its effectiveness in popular votes. Many citizens insisted, at times rather violently, upon the prerogatives of their basic liberties and rights of enfranchisement. Appeals to their favour were, however, made all the more persuasive by the style of routine visibility that gave meaning to the very idea of an elite notability. It is instructive that Polybius, who both saw how things worked in an earlier age, that of second-century Rome, and employed a historiography particularly sensitive to the importance of visualization, vividly described not only a constitution but also the spectacle of ritualized elite prominence. All manner of spectacle afforded power to an orator.

Most Romans did not have eloquent or self-important voices, did not ascend the Rostra, and did not enjoy significant individual power to influence their republic's history. Humbler Romans gathered in their Forum not only to hear lofty oratory but also to behold performers whose physical and ideological prominence had the power habitually to impress. In apprehension of the visible, ritualized dialogues which invoked and so defined the *populus* as a political agent lies the simple truth that, as in every historical polity, some citizens obviously were more powerful than others.

While the absence of much specific information about the lives, hopes, and fears of the individuals making up the *populus*, whose presence looms ever larger in recent historical scholarship upon the later Republic, leaves this constituency largely anonymous and demographically ill-defined, the whole business of routine ritualization has much to say about the power of the people at Rome. History's attentions need to be attracted to 'the picture of an orator addressing a crowd in the Forum; a picture of someone using the arts of rhetoric to persuade an anonymous crowd about something'.[2] Such a picture, however, does not readily support the notion that Republican Rome can

[2] Millar 1986: 9 and 1.

be understood as strikingly more democratic in a constitutional sense than has often been assumed. The *populus* and its sentiments were politically significant: we shall find the prominent of the late Republic showing much interest in them. But if the *populus Romanus* had any great power, this does not seem to have been manifested in the exercise of much political authority. Meetings were held and speeches performed. Assemblies balloted and votes were tallied. But only a few were leaders with power to initiate candidacies, legislation, and senatorial approval. Moreover, the personalities speaking out before both Senate and *populus* possessed of ambition and ability (and also money) figure prominently in the principal narratives—both ancient and thus modern too—of the late Republic, its political economy and its effects upon an ever increasing imperial dominion. Democracy's power is surely qualified by the degree of demotic realization, when citizens gaze up at the dignity and hearken to the handsome words of a notable orator, of their sovereign right to refuse to legitimate an 'existing order's uninterrupted discourse about itself, its laudatory monologue'.[3]

There appears to have been no shortage of interruptions for the speeches of Roman orators. But there was no popular revolution. Roman streets in the later Republic became more violent. But the political arenas were squarely monopolized by a few prominent men staging their own personalities, their careers, and their causes as integral to the main narratives of the national history which all Romans in the shared spaces of their city could see unfolding before their eyes. As Yakobson has well said, the 'Roman aristocratic ethos recognized the people as the rightful judge of the relative personal merit of the competing candidates, but it did not regard the magistrates as "people's representatives" carrying out a political mandate'.[4] Big men amassed their *dignitas* in facing and recognizing the *libertas* of the sophisticated consumers of the citizenry. At occasions such as *contiones*, not only was the outcome of legislation at issue but the *populus* could also refuse, by denying its approbation, to validate the worthiness of the *virtus* of a politician—a particularly fraught consideration for a *novus homo* keen to equate himself with the best of the Republic. Humbler Romans

[3] Debord 1983: § 24. [4] Yakobson 1999: 177.

did not, however, call into serious question their very role as spectators in its routine dramas. It should not be forgotten, moreover, that emotions ultimately animated such an intricate ideological dialogue. Political dynamics had their physical expression in a great deal of noise: a crowd consisted of bodies with needs that Cicero seems never to have adequately acknowledged; popularity could be founded upon spectacles and promises more compelling than his *virtus*.

Cicero did not much like noisy crowds nor the liberalities which invited them. Yet in the summer of 44 he excitedly recorded the 'testimony and judgement' of the *populus* delivered upon the assassins of Caesar.[5] He had been impressed by the roar of the crowd at the *ludi Apollinares*. He thought this bespoke a future for his *res publica* and he was wrong. In his own complicated and uncertain fashion Caesar had shown himself willing and more than able to offer easily the better things of civic life. Caesarian autocracy had established itself through food and jobs and cash, monuments and memories in Rome. Augustus too was quite popular and his authority was preeminently spectacular. On his deathbed he joked that his life had been a theatrical, indeed comedic, performance.[6] He hoped the audience had enjoyed the show.

## CICERO'S CROWD

When, on the second day of January 63, Cicero spoke before a *contio*, a public meeting of citizens, he appeared in all the majesty that the trappings of consular office imparted. He spoke in opposition to the agrarian legislation moved by the tribune Rullus and his colleagues; and this oratorical performance can be remembered because of the survival of the text of the speech, the *De Lege Agraria II*. Consul Cicero apparently was persuasive, since the bill was defeated in the subsequent voting of the tribal assembly.[7] Yet while eloquence was Cicero's greatest political asset and the *De Lege Agraria II* can certainly be read as evidence of the power of words, we shall find that he had more at his disposal than merely 'words and the stylistic genius' with which to 'shape men's opinions and move their

[5] *Phil.* 1. 15. [6] Suet. *DA* 99. 1. [7] Pliny *HN* 7. 117.

hearts'.[8] Cicero's argument was predicated upon the physical presence and ideological pre-eminence that the consul brought to the Rostra along with his entourage of lictors bearing the fasces of imperial office.

As an opportunity to establish popular comprehension of Cicero's new, consular dignity in Rome, this first contio was a precious moment for a man devoted to 'living in the light'.[9] For Cicero as for others, to be in Rome meant to have opportunities for his person and activities to be illumined for the attention of fellow citizens, fortunate outsiders and visitors, and even for the edification of posterity. He needed to be seen in the city.[10] Rome indeed was the stage of the world, where no man of worldly ambition could shun the crowds.[11] At the heart of the Republic's civic space, a politician such as Cicero presented in person a basic congruence between his advice and the republican dignity he represented. Cicero could cast himself as a popular champion. And in a political system in which members of the notability provided all political initiative and yet the votes of the people were sovereign, individual actors such as Cicero and the anonymous crowd functioned together, issue after issue, occasion after occasion, in a basic complicity founded upon ideas of dignity. In such was principally constructed a practical sense of aristocratic *dignitas*, that 'most constant ingredient in the active political history of the Republic'.[12]

In Cicero's Rome, the competitive routines of civic visibility were particularly intense, as men strove to occupy positions of prominence before the attentions and judgements of crowds in houses and streets, at the games, or in the Forum. As a primary location at Rome 'for advertising political success' a contio was a crucial element in 'the dense network of communications between political actors and their technically sovereign audiences'.[13] Indeed, the complex denotations of the very word 'contio' suggest its vital communicative role in the life of the

[8] Gotoff 1979: 8. [9] *Fam.* 2. 12. 2.

[10] No eyes were directed upon Cicero when a scrupulous quaestor in Sicily: *Verr.* 2. 5. 35.

[11] Cf. Tac. *Dial.* 36. 6–7. [12] Adcock 1959: 13.

[13] Pina Polo 1995: 216; Nicolet 1980: 388.

Republic. The term could refer to the event of civic assembly, the speeches delivered, and all those attending.[14]

Routinely communicated were the respective standings in importance of all the participating classes of Roman political society. A contio effectively dramatized the seeming naturalness of such distinct political statuses.[15] When Cicero and others spoke at a contio, they were clearly distinct from and elevated above the crowd. 'Contio' could also express the speaker's elevation upon the Rostra.[16] As a ritual a contio articulated the society's signal ideas and assumptions and so also conditioned the relationships of individuals and groups both to one another and to the ideas and assumptions themselves.[17] A contio, by routinely acting upon and through the respective dispositions of the bodies of those participating, helped to normalize the relationships between different participants both doing different things and, of course, being seen to do them. By virtue of his elevated physical station the Roman orator could be understood to belong to an order of political existence superior to that of the multitude constituting his audience.

Before we focus specifically upon Cicero in oratorical performance, it is worth paying some heed to ancient analysis of the allocations of power in the Republic. Polybius' account of the political culture of Rome indicates that important aspects of political power are located in the ritualized aesthetics of the Roman 'ceremonial script', which imposed an obvious distinction between acting and watching. This vivisection of a political culture is thus particularly valuable in directing attention to fall squarely upon men conspicuously presenting themselves to an audience with eyes, ears, bodies, emotional dispositions, and habitual expectations. Likewise consideration of the *Commentariolum Petitionis*, which describes the challenges facing Cicero when he was a candidate running for consular office, shows the importance at Rome of the aesthetic dimension of republican politics.

[14] Pina Polo 1995: 204. [15] Cf. Gleason 1995: xxiii.

[16] Cic. *Q. Fr.* 1. 2. 5; Gell. 18. 7. 6–8 (quoting Cic. *Contra Contionem Q. Metelli* = Frag. 2 (Crawford)).

[17] Lukes 1975.

Polybius does offer empirical testimony, based upon standard Greek political theory, for the existence of a democratic element in a mixed constitution in second-century Rome. In perceiving democracy, Polybius was, according to Millar, 'right and modern critics are wrong'.[18] Yet Millar, because he is interested chiefly in Polybius as a political scientist rather than a guide to the visualization of the political culture of Rome, does not appear to be fully sensitive to the implications of his own focus upon the picture of an orator.[19] Polybius does point in Book Six to the important constitutional role of the people, as the only legitimate bestower of honour and penalty within the polity:[20] the people elected and the people served as jurors. But, by calling attention to specific visible practices in the life of the city that now ruled his world, Polybius is also providing a phenomenology of political roles able to supplement any assessment of a simple predominance of either notables or people which is derived primarily from constitutional roles.

Polybius was acutely aware of the powerful impression made on both historical observers and Roman spectators by the visibility of significant political actors who deserved the attention. His historiography itself operates self-consciously as an act of spectatorship, in presenting the historian himself as a spectator of events described in his text and then in turn encouraging the reader's mind to gaze upon what his narrative reveals.[21] Ancient historiography had long placed an authoritative premium upon a writer's empirical visualization; and from the outset Polybius presents his narrative as founded upon the axiom that truth is to history as eyesight is to a living creature.[22]

[18] Millar 1984: 2 and 1998 *passim*. Cf. the most important essays on republican history written in the twentieth-century, by P. A. Brunt (conveniently gathered in 1988).

[19] The prefatory footnote of Millar 1986 speaks a suggestive metaphorical language of vision: 'As will be equally obvious, [this article] pretends to be no more than an essay or sketch, recommending one way of seeing the politics of this period . . .'

[20] 6. 14. 4. The focus upon the election of officers and the law-courts is found in Plato *Laws* 3. 697a–b: Walbank 1957–79: i. 682.

[21] Cf. Davidson 1991: 10–24.

[22] 1. 14. 6; quoted again at 12. 12. 3; cf. 34. 4 if correctly ascribed to Polybius; Walbank 1957–79: i. 10. Note too the importance of *enargeia*, in particular at 15. 36. 2.

Although at times his description must speak only of hearing events, for the most part it expressly employs an idiom of visual perception to explain its presentation of information.[23] Hence a comment such as 'next bringing into view' serves to orient the reader's engagement with the narrative.[24] Furthermore, in regard to war, the reader is in the position of spectator, as at a sporting event, in order to see and to learn from the sight.[25] A battlefield is a strange and marvellous spectacle not only for those actually present but also 'for all who could take the event into view afterwards'.[26] Such an historiographical trope makes an implicit commentary upon 'the processes of reading

[23] The person actually present at events described is contrasted with the hearer of the narrated event (e.g. 1. 26. 8–9 and 15. 36. 4), although the activities contrasted do not seem meant to be entirely exclusive of each other. His grand purpose as a historian is to mimic the work of Tyche, who steers the affairs of the world in one direction: the historian must *διὰ τῆϲ ἱϲτορίαϲ ὑπὸ μίαν ϲύνοψιν ἀγαγεῖν τοῖϲ ἐντυγχάνουϲι* ('through history bring into comprehensive view for his readers') (1. 4. 1). The idea of a specific and single point of view also occurs at 14. 1a. 1. Rome is a 'fine spectacle' in history (*θέαμα καλόν*): 1. 64. 3; cf. 32. 6. 4.

[24] 3. 3. 6: *μετὰ δὲ ταῦτα θέντεϲ ὑπὸ τὴν ὄψιν*. Events and individuals are obviously presented didactically as worthy of both attention and emulation: esp. 9. 9. 10, re war-leaders. (Note that in the following chapter (9. 10. 6–8) the narrative posits a spectator whose identity slips from one actually present to a hypothetical observer who, for all Polybius' strictures on avoidance of emotion in historiography, is merely gazing upon a vivid representation of events; cf. 16. 8. 8.) On a vivid yet relatively trivial level the plight of the man who went mad when held in chains, refusing to eat or take care of his own person, provides a *θέαμα θαυμάσιον* (32. 3. 7—a certain Isocrates, a particularly hapless grammarian).

[25] War can be compared to a boxing match in which generals gain an idea of respective strengths and weaknesses: 1. 57. 1. (Other comparisons with athletics: 2. 65. 11, 16. 28. 9, 27. 9. 2, 29. 8. 5, 29. 8. 9, 17. 4, 39. 18. 8, 39. 1. 8; with fighting cocks: 1. 58. 7–8.) There is a lesson in Philopoemen's behaviour as a cavalry commander (10. 24. 3): he did not ride out in front of his troops; it might be more important to see than to be seen. A plain of battle (the Campanian) is turned into a theatre where the Carthaginians could stage an object lesson in their superiority (3. 91. 10). The reader can be presumed to learn from the events of history staged by Tyche (29. 19; cf. Livy 45. 3. 3). Tyche is elsewhere dramatic: as a producer of plays (11. 5. 8 and 29. 19. 2), as an umpire (1. 58. 1), and as a stager of contests (2. 66. 4); on the image see Walbank 1957–79: i. 21. n. 6. My examples are meant to be only casually illustrative.

[26] 2. 28. 11.

and representation' but it is not merely fanciful. People did (and, thanks to television, nowadays still do) watch battles just as they did boxing matches.[27] The ancient historian might put spectators in his texts not just because they reflect his own activity but because he is also replicating the very real business of watching and comprehending that shaped sensibilities in ancient polities.

Political matters are also historiographically visible. Polybius suggests the desirability of perceiving how in the living, breathing Roman constitution individual distinction impressed itself upon spectators.[28] Moreover, in explaining how various constituencies fitted together within the constitution as a whole, Polybius is also demonstrating (6. 11. 2) how respective roles are articulated for all to see. He is accordingly a well-placed witness of the advertisement of sociopolitical distinction to a popular audience at Rome. Just as the historian's knowledge is sensibly brought before the view of the reader, so too is the physical distinction of successful generals articulated before the gaze of the Roman people in triumphs, 'through which the generals bring the vividness of their accomplishments into the view of the citizens'.[29] Funerals too make prestigious achievement sensible. They are represented in Polybius as a regular (and thoroughly ritualized) set of practices at the heart of the republican community. Individuals can become immortal through recognition of their glory that will live on into posterity, because 'the many' are gathered to recollect and take the deeds of the dead 'into view'. Both the eulogized and eulogizer are conspicuous—the cadaver is manifest at the Rostra and the speaker is positioned above (6. 53. 1–2); the whole people stands about as the audience (ibid. 2). The display of funeral masks, *imagines*, which

[27] Walker 1993: 353–77, at 354. Obviously there is little that is modern about post-modernism.

[28] Polybius refuses comparison (6. 47. 7) between the Roman mixed constitution and the constitution of Plato's *Republic*, on the grounds that comparison of something not tested in action with actual constitutions would be like comparing a statue with living and breathing men (ibid. 10). Polybius may not have been particularly well-acquainted with Plato (cf. Cole 1964: 484 n. 113) but his analogy of a statue is a pertinent critique of the mimetic nature of the *Republic* itself.

[29] 6. 15. 8.

were undoubtedly very important reminders of aristocratic accomplishment, is recounted in detail (ibid. 4–9). In sum, the institution is a highly attractive spectacle (ibid. 9–10) of aristocratic distinction.

The religious life of Rome also appears predicated upon a practical distinction between actors and audience. Fear of the gods (*deisidaemonia*) famously exerts power in the state. In Polybius' strikingly objectifying approach (6. 56. 8–11), the appetitive and emotional multitude is kept in its proper constitutional place. Religiosity was 'staged' (ἐκτετραγῴδηται) at Rome: as Polybius stands proudly aloof from any Phylarchan project of drawing a universal truth from events invested with emotion, the recurrence of τραγ-cognates points rather to an awareness of the importance of political theatricality. This could either be routinely familiar or somewhat melodramatically exceptional but was clearly in any event a manifestation of power.[30]

Although there is no Polybius to admire the drama of a contio in the later Republic, there is a political actor quite willing to signal, and able to exploit, his conspicuousness as consular protagonist. Cicero took great pride in the spectacle he made of himself and how thereby he gloriously played his part in maintaining the authority of the senatorial order. It was no routine matter for Cicero to address a contio: waiting until sure of both his oratorical ability and his authority, he did not speak from the Rostra before he was a praetor (in 66).[31] Such assets were essential to the glorious business of winning over the sympathies of the starveling rabble.

In 60, Cicero was determined that his political prestige lose no lustre in the face of chronic turbulence in the politics of Rome. In a letter of June (*Att.* 2. 1) he detailed to Atticus the problems he faced in 'Romulus' cesspool':[32] not only was his

[30] Apelles enters Corinth 'in pomp' (Walbank 1957–79: i. 559) at 5. 26. 9; 'melodramatic' (ibid. 579 ad 5. 48. 9).

[31] *De Imp. Pomp.* 2. Caesar perhaps addressed the same *contio*: Dio 36. 43. 2.

[32] Cato meanwhile, opposing concessions to *equites*, spoke in the Senate as though he was living in Plato's Republic, jeopardizing Cicero's policies: in January of 60 it seemed (*Att.* 1. 18. 3) as though the two foundations of the *res publica* he alone had established, the *auctoritas* of the Senate and the *concordia* of the Senate and *equites*, had been overturned.

enemy Clodius intent on becoming a tribune, but Flavius' agrarian bill (2. 6), which seems to have made provision for not only Pompey's veterans but all needy citizens,[33] was (although fading) still very much a pressing issue: the consul Metellus Celer had been imprisoned by Flavius for his opposition; and there was rioting (2. 8). Cicero was still seeking to protect the 'army of men of wealth' upon whom the state rested from 'that contional leech upon the treasury, the wretched and starving mob'.[34] In such a context he understood praise for himself, which reflected his achievements in his consulship, to be in the best interests of the *res publica*.[35] While leading optimates ('nostri principes') thought they touched heaven if their mullets ate from their hands, he was a pragmatic optimate capable of exerting beneficent influence even upon Caesar.[36] His political effectiveness demonstrated by his steadfastness as consul, Cicero now wished to maintain his authority by ensuring that the significance of his achievements was not forgotten. Hence he sought validation through comparison with eternal models of good statesmanship. The letter in which he describes to Atticus the increasingly hostile environment at Rome begins with animated consideration of the aggrandisement of his consular reputation: he has written an account in Greek, which he would like circulated in Athens and other towns: 'I think it may shed some light upon my achievements.'[37] He compared,

[33] Dio 37. 50. 1; Shackleton Bailey 1965: 333. In March, Cicero had told Atticus (*Att.* 1. 19. 4) that he was trying to satisfy the *populus* and Pompey but was insisting upon purchase rather than expropriation of land for 'draining the dregs of the city and repopulating Italy'; the rich after all were his army. 'Dregs': cf. *Leg. Agr.* 2. 70, supposedly Rullus' term of contempt (and of course duly criticized by Cicero).

[34] *Att.* 1. 19. 4; ibid. 16. 11; cf. Brunt 1971: 124–6.

[35] He justified (*Att.* 2. 1. 6) his friendly relations with Pompey by noting that Pompey had become less inclined to court the *populus* and had taken to eulogizing Cicero's achievements in saving the state; he did not know how much this praise helped his own cause but was certain it helped the *res publica*.

[36] *Att.* 2. 1. 7, asking 'Don't you think I do service enough if I succeed in removing the desire to do harm from those who have the power?' ('nonne tibi satis prodesse videor si perficio ut ii nolint obesse qui possunt?') (trans. Shackleton Bailey).

[37] *Att.* 2. 1. 2: 'videtur enim posse aliquid nostris rebus lucis adferre'. 'Achievements': Shackleton Bailey ad loc. This concern was uppermost in his mind after his receipt of his friend's own, less ornamented monograph

moreover, his political stature with that of Demosthenes; and also sent to Atticus a selection of speeches that 'might be called consular'.[38]

This selection highlighted Cicero's oratorical effectiveness in dominating a contio. He included among the ten speeches (plus two *apospasmatia* on the Rullan legislation) a preponderance of speeches that evinced his ability to sway the *populus*, including the defence of Rabirius, two speeches delivered in the Senate, and no less than seven speeches that had been delivered directly to the *populus*.[39] With the possible exception of his declining a province, none of the positions he advocated in these speeches would seem inherently popular. In advertising his ability to prevail on unpopular issues, Cicero was establishing himself as a worthy successor to the roll-call of exemplary orators of the past.[40] The challenges facing such orators had ever increased: long gone were the days when Scipio Nasica (as consul in 138) could simply tell a restive audience that he knew best

(2. 1. 1). In March, Cicero recollected the 'immortal glory' he had won in the last month of his consulship and which Pompey had acknowledged in the Senate and announced to Atticus that he was sending him a memoir in Greek of his consulship: *Att.* 1. 19. 6–7 and 10.

[38] *Att.* 2. 1. 3. Since the speeches were intended to show Cicero's oratorical prowess, the published texts are hence likely to testify accurately to the persuasive tactics he adopted: cf. Brunt 1978: 160–1. Although Cicero does sometimes impart to a text the illusion of being a real speech actually being delivered (Kennedy 1972: 164, with the example of *Verr.* 2. 3. 167 and an allusion to Verres' countenance), the text of *De Lege Agraria II* is unlikely to offer a verbatim transcript of Cicero's oratorical performance. Cicero was not one to deliver his words with eyes downcast upon a script, unlike (a less compellingly eloquent) Pompey: *Sest.* 129. It is possible that texts of consular speeches were already in some sort of public circulation: so McDermott 1972.

[39] Besides the *De Lege Agraria II*, there was the speech opposing repeal of Sulla's law that deprived the sons of the proscribed of their full citizen rights, the (sadly now lost) speech he had delivered to the people in a (surely tricky) defence of Otho, calming their anger (Pliny *HN* 7. 116) that had long festered at his bill (of 67) governing seating in the theatre; there were also two Catilinarian speeches delivered to the *populus*, and the speech he delivered to a *contio* in which he renounced his claim to a province.

[40] With these speeches Cicero satisfied the keen interest of younger contemporaries (*Att.* 2. 1. 3), offering presumably useful lessons.

what was in the best interests of the *res publica* and they should keep quiet.[41]

The *De Lege Agraria II* certainly provided an exemplary lesson in how to appear popular upon the Rostra when a land bill, a traditional staple of *populares*, might appeal as an idea to some in the Forum, even if actual soil would not.[42] Little is known for certain about the contents of the bill or those secretly supporting it: Cicero claims in Senate and contio that powerful figures lurk in the background; but nothing in his account of the bill is wholly trustworthy.[43] What is clear is that, even if the urban plebs had relatively little direct material interest in agrarian reform, this bill threatened to expose the incompatibility between optimate pilotage of the *res publica* and traditional popular concerns. The measure was, therefore, also a significant challenge to Cicero himself, who certainly hated the very idea of agrarian legislation and whose status as a *popularis* extended little beyond the public support of Pompey that had helped ensure his ascent of the *cursus*.[44] Consequently, in his first contio Cicero had to show that a consul could be as much a popular champion as any tribune.[45]

[41] Val. Max. 3. 7. 3.

[42] *Leg. Agr.* 2. 71; cf. Brunt 1988: 245 and 250–1. Rullus presumably had made himself vulnerable to Cicero's charge that he planned 'to drain off' city dwellers: *supra*, n. 29.

[43] Modern scholarship has followed Cicero's lead (*Leg. Agr.* 1. 11, 16, 22; 2. 20, 23, 63, 98) in looking behind Rullus for ulterior powers. Sumner (1966) provides a useful summary of various theories, whilst arguing for Pompey's ultimate support of the bill. This is unconvincing: few senators in that case could have been expected to be influenced by Cicero's insistence that the bill attacked Pompey (*Leg. Agr.* 1. 13), since such a grand secret was unlikely to be kept in Roman political society. Tribunes, moreover, surely consulted their own political interests as well as powerful friends. Cicero's discussion of the bill's contents seems especially fanciful at *Leg. Agr.* 2. 37 and 53.

[44] Besides the Rullan and Flavian schemes, Cicero opposed Caesar's legislation: *Att.* 2. 16. 1–2. Naturally Cicero publicly claims (*Leg. Agr.* 2. 10) to support agrarian reform and to be sympathetic to the Gracchi and the tradition they and their popularly prized memory generated. Pompey: esp. *Comn. Pet.* 5, 14, and 51.

[45] *Leg. Agr.* 2. 14; he will further insist towards the close of the oration (ibid. 101–2) that he is not frightened of a contio and is indeed *popularis*. He so established the nature of his contest with Rullus in the Senate: ibid. 1. 23.

At this point it should be admitted that the exact nature of Cicero's contribution to the demise of tribunal legislation can only be surmised: it is known only that Rullus' bill did not become law and so Cicero would face further battles against land-distribution proposals.[46] But it can be assumed that, if Cicero particularly wished the world to remember this contional speech in 60, when provision had still not been made for Pompey's veterans (let alone the urban mob), the bill's failure was an achievement in which he had reason to take great pride. Through publication of this contional speech Cicero commemorated a glorious triumph for himself and his conception of a healthy *res publica* in his handling of the sympathies of a contio. His success in defeating the Rullan bill indeed was built upon his presentation of himself as a *popularis*.

Cicero bases his credentials as a popular champion upon respect for his audience: he begins his speech with a customary expression of gratitude for his election (*Leg. Agr.* 2. 1); he also stresses (2. 1–4) that he is a *novus homo*. Then he solemnly declares (2. 6) his willingness to make appearances at the Rostra, in marked contrast with the habits of his predecessors:

> Mihi autem, Quirites, omnia potius perpetienda esse duco quam non ita gerendum consulatum, ut in omnibus meis factis atque consiliis vestrum de me factum consiliumque laudetur. Accedit etiam ille mihi summus labor ac difficillima ratio consulatus gerendi, quod non eadem mihi qua superioribus consulibus lege et condicione utendum esse decrevi, qui aditum huius loci conspectumque vestrum partim magnopere fugerunt, partim non vehementer secuti sunt.

> It is my belief, Quirites, that in my consulship endless endurance is preferable to failure to ensure that in my case your considered action finds praise in all my actions and counsels. In addition I am faced with a considerable challenge and a very difficult business in the conduct of the consulship: I have made it my policy not to employ the same law and provisions as previous consuls, who either hurried to shun or else only half-heartedly pursued the approach to this place and the view of you.

In his majestically wheedling play with legalistic vocabulary evoking constitutional *gravitas*, Cicero made his very visibility constitute a formal acknowledgement of the Quirites' entitle-

[46] Millar 1995: 104.

ment to expect respect from those it elevated in dignity. Clearly there were protocols—as important as any constitutional rubrics—that informed political communication: Cicero knew well how to make a ritual show of deference in order to prevail. Nor did he find his visibility unwelcome. A dignified Cicero now had no hesitation about mounting the Rostra: there was no shortage of other men seeking the limelight and in a true republic no citizen monopolized the popular gaze.[47] Hitherto Cicero had worked hard to appear *popularis* in winning election. Once elected, he used his skills in speciousness to illuminate an optimate's credentials—those of one who could late in life claim (somewhat heroically) never to have respected the applause won by *populares*.[48]

It was necessary to gesture respectfully towards popular sensibilities. Cicero's career was built upon successful advertisement of qualities appealing to Romans of every social rank. Lowly citizens surely cherished the spectacle of notables deigning to recognize the existence of men whom they would rather disdain. 'Blessed state which brings all so nearly on a level... I wish it were election time always!' wrote an eighteenth-century American artisan, who frankly savoured 'a shake of the hand, a pleasing smile and a little familiar chat with gentlemen; who have not for these seven years past condescended to look at them'.[49] In the absence of a lowly Roman's perspective, such comparative information helps to inform our picture of Roman sociopolitics at election-time, when the *populus* determined political destinies.

Although the votes of wealthier citizens counted for more in the Comitia Centuriata, elections involved more than a simple assaying of votes according to property-class. By analysis of electoral bribery in the late Republic, the recent work of Yakobson has shown that even in the Comitia Centuriata the urban plebs enjoyed influence greater than has often been supposed;

[47] That would be indicative of autocracy—the time of Sulla, for instance, was a time 'when all gaze upon one' (Cic. *Rosc. Am.* 22). On this occasion Cicero remarks (*Leg. Agr.* 2. 56) that Sulla acted outrageously but at least did not avoid the *conspectus* of those he outraged.

[48] *Phil.* 1. 37.

[49] From a letter submitted by an artisan reader to *The Pennsylvania Evening Post* on 27 April 1776 (quoted in Fliegelman 1993: 110–11).

and, furthermore, that the divide between rich and poor in Rome has too readily been overestimated.[50] The votes of the citizens of the lower centuries could be decisive in some elections; and there were men living far from poverty who would nevertheless welcome a material consideration for their vote.[51] Bribery need not be a simple purchasing of a constitutionalist's commodity.[52] Expenditure upon the *tenues* aimed to win their favour;[53] and their favour, when advertised, created a trend.

In no way was favour better advertised than by the sight of crowds attending a man of consequence, and making the occasion of their presence in his company a notable and memorable event. Escorts and entourages had always been an important part of the life of the *res publica* in signalling political consequence.[54] According to Sempronius Asellio, Tiberius Gracchus never left his house without the attendance of three or four thousand well-wishers.[55] Drusus (in 91) returned from the Forum 'surrounded by the huge and uncouth crowd that always accompanied him'.[56] Such popular demonstrations indicated

[50] Yakobson 1992, remarking (at 43) that 'the social gap between the lower strata and many of those registered in the first class was less dramatic than is often assumed'; cf. 1999: *passim*. Sallust speaks (*BJ* 73. 6) of the unusual presence of *opifices* and *agrestes* at the consular elections of 108.

[51] While details of this sociopolitical class are hard to reconstruct, the generosity of Caesar (though not in an electoral context), in giving rent relief of up to 2,000 sesterces, is suggestive: Suet. *DJ* 38.

[52] Yakobson acknowledges (1992: 32–3) that 'a Roman politician could have many reasons, personal as well as political, to practise and display generosity; not all of them had to do with elections'.

[53] Lintott 1990: 11.

[54] As Nicolet has emphasized (1980: 356–61). Of course, escorts marked the fame and celebrity of some who are not obviously politically powerful or greatly consequential—at least in imperial times: Thessalus, a doctor in the time of Nero, had bigger escorts than any actor or any driver of three-horse chariots: Pliny *HN* 29. 9.

[55] Gell. 2. 13. 4. Also, 'the many' saw C. Gracchus surrounded by contractors, artisans, ambassadors, magistrates, soldiers, and *philologoi*: Plut. *C. Grac.* 6.

[56] Vell. 2. 14. 1 ('immensa illa et incondita, quae eum semper comitabatur, cinctus multitudine'). The crowd had to be dismissed when the assassins struck: App. *BC* 1. 36. Even the infamous pseudo-Marius was a serious political force, for he drew a large crowd: e.g. Nic. Dam. F 128. 32.

support for a man and his course of action.[57] Thus an ambitious candidate tried to seem popular according to the terms of a communal script that placed a premium upon conspicuous popular approval. Escorts in public were, according to the evidence of the *Commentariolum Petitionis* (36–7), simply indispensable to the candidate.

The *Commentariolum*'s systematic and rational discourse perhaps diminishes distaste for truckling and ingratiating, flattering and falsely promising, by making these techniques of candidacy seem quite natural.[58] In any event, the account makes explicit that impression-management must be orchestrated.

[57] e.g. for Caesar in 62: Suet. *DJ* 16. 2. A passage of Nicolaos (F 130. 127) also gives some idea of the audience attending a great notable at a crucial political moment: when Octavius was accused by Antonius of trying to have him murdered, Octavius made his protests to those who came to greet him at his *salutatio*. Senators, however, might have different favourites. Cato was escorted by senators when led off to prison on Caesar's orders in 59: Gell. 4. 10. 8. Cato again acted unexpectedly and thus memorably in remaining silent: Plut. *Caes.* 14. Cato had, it seems, a habit of being oblivious to grand receptions: e.g. Vell. 2. 45. 5. His extraordinary behaviour was nonetheless spectacular.

[58] A summary of views on its authorship is provided by Richardson 1971. Arguments for composition in the early Empire depend upon the silence over the supposed 'first Catilinarian conspiracy' of 65, parallels to speeches of M. Cicero, and puzzlement over the function of the work. It declares its aim (1) 'ut ea quae in re dispersa atque infinita viderentur esse ratione et distributione sub uno aspectu ponerentur' ('so that things which in practice seem scattered and limitless can be brought by rational classification into a single focus'). It is also tempting to believe that this is a conscious innovation: the epistolary form is often the medium for discourses that have as yet no appropriate generic home. *Ratio* lies, in the letters of M. Cicero himself, at the heart of a *petitio*, conveying a sense of system: *Att.* 1. 1. 1. The last *sententia* of the *Commentariolum* is an expression of a desire that 'hoc commentariolum petitionis haberi omni ratione perfectum' (that 'this handbook of candidacy be considered complete in every *ratio*'). The work's claim (58) to pertain to M. Cicero himself and not to all who seek honours does not preclude others from profiting from it. The solicitation of desired changes in the final paragraph need not prevent some circulation of the text in this form, although the absence of comment by ancient authors about this text would suggest 'non-publication' (Richardson 1971: 439 n. 34). It can nevertheless be used as a guide to the practicalities of politics in the late Republic, since at worst an imperial writer still knew more about, or at least could better visualize, politics than any modern historian, while Quintus' authorship cannot certainly be disproved.

Success is presented as dependent upon two 'partes': not just the need for friends but also a concern with popular strategy (16 and 41). It is important that Cicero advertise the number and variety of his friends (3). There are certainly some friends who can exert influence: if the *principes* in the *collegia*, the suburbs, the *pagi*, and the *vicinitates* and throughout Italy can be secured as friends, they can easily ensure the support of the 'rest of the multitude' (30); friends too can somehow confirm the support of the centuries (29). Yet the category of 'friends' is also to be widened to include 'whoever shows some goodwill, cultivates you, or visits your house regularly' (16). Friends of different distinction can perform tasks appropriate to their status: at one extreme are *illustres* (18); at the other, freedmen or even slaves who have the power to affect the *fama* of the candidate (17). Some citizen friends can provide *adsectatio* (34) for the candidate at home, in moving from home to public spaces, and everywhere.

Those who are only potentially friends are, of course, the especial object of the *popularis ratio*, which 'needs knowledge of names, charm, constant attendance, generosity, publicity, show in the res publica'.[59] These aspects of the electoral environment shape the public behaviour of a consular candidate (41–53); and all depend upon a rhetoric of appearances rather than mechanisms of clientage. Cicero must show that he knows people's names; possession of what is missing in his nature must be simulated (42). *Blanditia* is necessary to solicit friendship; it is thus indispensable for a candidate whose 'countenance, expression, and conversation' ('et frons et vultus et sermo') must be made to suit those he meets (ibid.). *Adsuitas* means leaving no voter able to say that he has not been canvassed. *Benignitas* means generosity to one's friends which will win praise pleasing to the *multitudo*; as well as wider expenditure on banquets organized by tribe (44); it also demands a general air of approachability day or night (44): *vultus* and *frons* (which is the 'gate of the mind') are of crucial importance. Likewise promises are to be made in an obviously easy way (46), since men are charmed more 'by looks and rhetoric than by any actual

[59] *Comm. Pet.* 41: 'desiderat nomenclationem, blanditiam, adsiduitatem, benignitatem, rumorem, speciem in re publica.'

benefit'.[60] Since appearances determine how the candidate is interpreted, *fama* is ever at stake (49). *Rumor* is to be constructed upon Cicero's strong points as a candidate, from fame as an orator and as champion of the interests of the *equites* to the evidence of the crowds of supporters from the *municipia* (50); the *urbana multitudo* knew at first hand of Cicero's efforts on behalf of Pompey and the tribunes Manilius and Cornelius (51). The last item in the list of essentials is *species*, which emphatically caps the list and implicitly subsumes many of the earlier points: 'finally, make sure that the whole candidacy is full of pomp, that it is brilliant, splendid, *popularis*, that it has supreme attractiveness and dignity . . .'[61] Obviously, electoral success depended upon a candidate's skills of showmanship as he busied himself about town and hid his true feelings about inferiors respectfully beneath his smile.

Cicero understood well that the logic behind such rituals of egalitarianism was that ultimately it preserved civic harmony.[62] So, like other ambitious men, he was to be seen looking disingenuously into the faces of the crowd, committed at election-time to satisfying emotional needs rather than studiously considered criteria.[63] The reciprocal relationship was unavoidable and hallowed by tradition. It also had its advantages for a man whose political prestige depended upon his ability to preserve the bulwark of the *res publica* through his own popularity in the Forum.[64] Cicero triumphed at his first contio of 63 because he presented a *conspectus* that was as awesome as it was pleasing.

[60] 'sic homines fronte et oratione magis quam ipso beneficio reque capiuntur.'

[61] *Comm. Pet.* 52: 'postremo tota petitio cura ut pompae plena sit, ut inlustris, ut splendida, ut popularis sit, ut habeat summam speciem ac dignitatem . . .' The passage continues with the exhortation that the flaws of competitors be publicized.

[62] *Leg.* 3. 24, so defending the tribunate's contribution to a sense of equality with senators. Such egalitarianism was still an important theme in the Principate. Wallace-Hadrill (1982) argues that for an emperor 'to be honored in the same coin as his subjects ensured that the currency retained its value' (at 47).

[63] e.g. Cic. *Planc.* 9.

[64] Two thousand men of substance: Cic. *Off.* 2. 73.

When Cicero, after all the hard work of the campaign, finally ascended the Rostra and issued with consular authority dire warnings of the threats contained in the tribunician proposals, his speech drew great persuasive power from its vignettes, which seemed to offer 'objective proof for the stated and unstated contentions' of his words.[65] On this occasion his vignettes were particularly effective, because Cicero was now projecting the *maiestas* of his rank. If he knew how to intimate his deference to the *populus*, he also certainly knew how to command the *populus*' deference at a contio by virtue of the aesthetic impressiveness of his office. Polybius would have found nothing amiss in this aspect of Cicero's power. His person was embellished by the appurtenances of power—the fasces, lictors, and everything else that signified the distinction between holders of *imperium* and citizens who might be expected to obey orders—and respectful heed to admonishments about the welfare of the *res publica*.[66]

The Roman ceremonies of state are, as Marshall has remarked, not 'neutral clues in an investigation of constitutional theory which has as its aim precision of technicalities and recovery of the archaic origins of state-ceremonial rather than its significance in the life of the developed Republic and Principate'.[67] The significance here is that there was no mistaking the man who moved at the head of a small crowd of official lictors as merely one citizen among many, since such an escort immediately proclaimed his distinction.[68] Such dignity must have made a great impression on all who saw it, just as

[65] Vasaly 1993: xi.

[66] As Plutarch (*Rom. Quaest.* 81) observes, pomp and circumstance befit magistracies with *imperium* but not the tribunate. Cicero had been elected consul *prior* or *maior* so he held the fasces in the first month of the year. For alternation of the *fasces* see Cic. *Rep.* 2. 55; Livy 2. 1. 8; Dion. *Ant. Rom.* 5. 2. 1; Festus *Gloss. Lat.* p. 154 Lindsay; A. J. Marshall 1984: 131. On the Etruscan origin of lictors see Dion. *Ant. Rom.* 3. 61; the consuls retained all the regalia except the crown and the embroidered robe (ibid. 62. 2; cf. 4. 74).

[67] A. J. Marshall 1984: 120. On the awe-inspiring aura surrounding higher magistracies throughout the Republic cf. Hölkeskamp 1993: 20.

[68] It is suggestive that in desperate times an official-looking escort might work well as a disguise for the proscribed: Val. Max. 7. 3. 9.

it did upon an alien observer such as Nicolaos.[69] Hence the realization of *dignitas* in the form of lictors was invariably prized highly by those who could claim them: Julius Caesar, perhaps more concerned with physical displays of prominence than most, actually drew up legislation to make his consular retinue more impressive in the months when his colleague Bibulus held the fasces;[70] dictators traditionally were able to indicate their exceptional authority by keeping extra-large escorts;[71] even senators travelling in the provinces coveted the signs of their importance.[72]

This prize of office was valued for its own sake; it also made its possessor attractively emblematic of the *res publica* itself.[73] Lictors and fasces had the power to evoke two powerful emotions in those who beheld them: pride and fear.[74] Both of these were active in Cicero's contio. National pride was central to his persuasive strategy that day; so too was his insistence that his very presence bespoke his close relationship to the *populus*. These affections were not over-awed by the sight of the consul: because the source of a magistrate's power was the *populus*, protocol dictated that lictors dipped the fasces to pay respect to the consul's audience, just as they did to Vestals or to a

[69] F 130. 78, describing the procession of lictors 'restraining the crowd on both sides' (ἔνθεν καὶ ἔνθεν τόν ὄχλον ἀνείργοντες).

[70] Suet. *DJ* 20. 1; cf. Taylor and Broughton 1949.

[71] e.g. Q. Fabius had two dozen to show the μέγεθος καὶ ὄγκος of the office: Plut. *Fab.* 4. Sulla had twenty-four axes and a big bodyguard: App. *BC* 100; Livy (*Ep.* 89) also found the display of Sulla's power worth attention great enough for the wretched epitomator to mention. The early dictator Larcius wished thus to show the might of his office: Dion. *Ant. Rom.* 5. 75. 2. In 47 Antonius as *magister equitum* was accompanied by six lictors: Dio 42. 27. 2.

[72] On this practice see esp. Cic. *Fam.* 12. 21, commending the *dignitas* of C. Anicius (who was on a *legatio libera* to Africa). Verres as *legatus* had lictors; one was killed in Lampsacus, which caused quite an uproar: *Verr.* 2. 1. 67–8.

[73] Cicero reels off the prizes of office (*Cluent.* 154) as 'locus, auctoritas, domi splendor, apud exteras nationes nomen et gratia, toga praetexta, sella curulis, insignia, fasces, exercitus, imperia, provinciae' ('place, authority, splendour at home, name and influence abroad, trim on the toga, an official chair, decorations, fasces, armies, commands, provinces').

[74] A. J. Marshall 1984: 130, although perhaps with too much emphasis on fear—Dionysius describes (*Ant. Rom.* 7. 35. 5)—with some consideration of what his own eyes told him—the power of the fasces to evoke rather αἰδώς.

magistrate of higher station than the man they escorted.[75] This gesture 'was a pleasing spectacle to the multitude'.[76] Moreover, the magistrate could take personal credit for such ingratiation. Besides the requirements of etiquette, the official entourage was also the personal instrument, and almost an appendage, of the man they followed, going wherever he went and allowing nobody to step between them.[77] Because his power was symbolically understood as emblematic of the *res publica*, Cicero's assertion that there was tribunician contempt for his consular dignity gained great emotional force.[78] The other emotions aroused by the fasces also helped to increase Cicero's authority as spokesman for the whole community.[79]

Cicero's persuasiveness was also increased by the consul's pre-eminent role in the religious life of Rome which Polybius perceived as powerful. Before his contio, Cicero had already been seen charismatically involved in maintaining Rome's links to the gods. The ceremony in which consuls were installed in office seems to have started with the taking of the auspices and then, in a procession with lictors and an escort of friends, the new consul made his stately way to the Capitoline. There he sat upon his official chair, the *sella curulis*. Then he sacrificed.[80] Consuls, and lesser magistrates too, sacrificed on behalf of the entire state. It is one thing to sacrifice as a priest or even as a

[75] The gesture was made to the people when gathered in either comitial or contional assembly. Cic. *Rep.* 1. 62, 2. 53; Plut. *Public.* 10; Quint. *Inst.* 3. 7. 18; Florus 3. 9. 4; Dio 3. 13. 2.

[76] Livy 2. 7. 7; cf. A. J. Marshall 1984: 132.

[77] Val. Max. 2. 2. 4. There is evidence to suggest that magistrates actively order the *fasces* to be lowered before a superior; e.g. Coriolanus even orders this to be done before his mother: Dion. *Ant. Rom.* 8. 44. 4. Lictors were very conscious of protocol: Quadrigarius (F 59 Peter = Gell. 2. 2. 13) relates that lictors told Q. Fabius Maximus to dismount from his horse when he encountered his son, the consul: the consular *imperium* came directly from the *populus*.

[78] Esp. *Leg. Agr.* 2. 55.

[79] Cf. the observation of Catherine Bell (1992: 221–2) that 'in terms of its scope, dependence, and legitimation, the type of authority formulated by ritualization tends to make ritual activities effective in grounding and displaying a sense of community without overriding the autonomy of individuals or subgroups'.

[80] Details of all such at Versnel 1970: 302.

private citizen,[81] but quite another degree of spectacular prestige to do so as a consul. Magistrates setting out from the city sacrificed to carry the favour of the gods with them to their provinces and to advertise their splendour to the crowd; Antonius' neglect of this ritual, for instance, was cited as evidence of thorough unsuitability to hold *imperium*.[82] On the other hand, a splendid sacrifice made a man seem ideally suited to high office: when Octavius entered Rome as consul for the first time he promptly sacrificed.[83] Twelve ominous vultures were not the only spectators.

The practical ingredients of a sacrificial ceremony made it a striking civic spectacle. In Appian, a writer perennially interested in memorable sacrifices and religious outrages, there is a description of the terrible death of a praetor which strikingly conveys the aesthetic impression made by the ritual of magisterial sacrifice. Asellio was set upon and lynched (in 89 BC) by moneylenders whilst engaged in the preliminaries of sacrifice (to Castor and Pollux) in the Forum, with a crowd standing around him 'as was usual at a sacrifice'.[84] Then,

*οὕτω μὲν καὶ Ἀσελλίων στρατηγῶν τε καὶ σπένδων καὶ ἱερὰν καὶ ἐπίχρυσον ἐσθῆτα ὡς ἐν θυσίᾳ περικείμενος ἀμφὶ δευτέραν ὥραν ἐσφάζετο ἐν ἀγορᾷ μέσῃ παρὰ ἱεροῖς.*

Thus Asellio, whilst a praetor and pouring the libation, clad in the sacred and gilded vestment for sacrifice, was slaughtered about the second hour in the middle of the Forum amidst the rites.

The horror of the scene was all the greater because of the distinction afforded by the special clothing, the ceremony, and by the presence of an audience in the Forum. The legitimate sense of pre-eminence bestowed by a sacrificial occasion is

[81] Caesarian 'charismatic' politics is an instructive example: when C. Iulius Caesar was sacrificing, his great-nephew stood close by him. Others too who wished to be seen close to the most powerful man in the western world. But these Caesar ordered to yield to the young man (Nic. Dam. F 127. 17–18: Octavius was everywhere to be seen with Caesar).

[82] Cic. *Phil* 3. 11; cf. 5. 24.

[83] App. *BC* 3. 94.

[84] *BC* 1. 54. Regarding the distinctiveness of the clothing it is worth noticing how C. Iulius Caesar combined the associations of different roles in one ceremony when he obtained the right to sacrifice in triumphal dress: e.g. App. *BC* 2. 106.

conveyed in artistic monuments, in which the focal point for the observer is always the sacrificant: thus upon a third-century *cista* a triumphant general is the centre of interest; in the last years of the Republic the same prominence is to be found in L. Domitius Ahenobarbus' relief commemorating a ceremony of ritual purification he conducted.[85] This centrality might be understood as a form of power, if control of religious ceremonial was as 'fundamental to political power in Republican Rome' as really seems to be the case.[86] As Purcell has stressed, 'the amount of time devoted to public cult by the *primores* at Rome was considerable, and . . . this provided the centre of the visibility of these people to the population of the city at large'.[87] Moreover, 'Romans were well aware of the resemblances between the orator's address in the Forum, the priest's sacred activity in the sanctuary, and the actor's performance on the stage—all witnessed and shared in by thousands of observers.'[88]

Magistrates had charismatic power. In their religious prominence men such as Domitius, or for that matter Cicero, were maintaining the community's link to its gods and upholding its place in the grand, cosmic scheme of things. To be perceived as a charismatic leader is to be such, regardless of whether the perception was generated by an individual's unprecedented status in the society or upon opportunities afforded by traditional routines and ritualized roles.[89] Roman magistrates were able to elicit awe as individuals even if their charisma originated in offices bestowed by the *populus*.

Visual messages clearly had an important place in republican politics and in *contiones*.[90] To understand the full context of oratorical performance it is necessary to remember that the messages were constructed around specific vivid sights. So it should be assumed that a great deal of persuasion had taken place before Cicero began his speech in the first days of his

[85] Ryberg 1955: 20–2, 27–34, esp. 29: 'the composition is managed in such a way as to throw the emphasis upon the sacrificant . . .' The Ahenobarbus scene seems to have generic similarities to representations of sacrifice on official Roman monuments: Brendel 1979: 133. Gordon stresses (1990: 206) how the visual representation of Roman sacrifice 'summarily reproduces key aspects of the social and political system' in the Empire.

[86] North 1990: 17.

[87] Purcell 1996: 800.

[88] Ibid. 804.

[89] Cf. Tucker 1968.

[90] Cf. Millar 1995: 103 and 111.

consulship, when the crowd had beheld a consul charismatically embellished by ritual drama. As Cicero unfolded his arguments about the dangers lurking in Rullus' legislation, no one who listened could fail to be reminded of why the national leader was entitled to a respectful hearing, since Cicero's speech persistently alluded to emblematic national ceremony. The charismatic aspects of Cicero's visibility thus brought to bear a power beyond that of simple eloquence, beguiling cadences, or reasoned arguments about material interest.

When Cicero wishes to explain the danger Rome will face from Capua if the Rullan bill is passed into law, he characterizes the threat primarily by reference to the central ceremonial practices of the state—and of course to the presently pre-eminent ritual actor in the state. He stresses that Capua can be seen (*Leg. Agr.* 2. 90). He makes himself a direct witness of what was to be seen in Capua, at least when he was a young man, and offers a description (2. 92) so that the Roman citizens may 'perceive and understand' the *superbia* inherent in the very place.[91] The Capuan magistrates, L. Considius and S. Saltius, who founded the colony, are brought dramatically to life so that the constitution can be grasped through reference to the rituals performed there by the officials. Sinister ambitions are imputed to the titles of the magistrates, who call themselves *praetores*, not *duumviri* as in other colonies: perhaps in a few years they will be eager for the name of *consules*. This point is reinforced by emphasis upon the similarity of Capuan and Roman lictors and sacrifice, which also implicitly invokes Cicero's personal impressiveness. The leading Capuans will obviously be a threat to Rome's security (2. 93–4):

Deinde anteibant lictores non cum bacillis, sed, ut hic praetoribus urbanis anteeunt, cum fascibus. Erant hostiae maiores in foro constitutae, quae ab his praetoribus de tribunali sicut a nobis consulibus de

[91] Although he treads carefully, he does this at some risk of reminding his audience that the M. Brutus (mentioned at 89 and 92), who proposed as tribune in 83 establishing a colony at Capua, had been a supporter of the popularly beloved young C. Marius killed by Sulla: Cic. *Quinct.* 65; Plut. *Sul.* 9; App. *BC* 1. 88 and 95; Livy *Ep.* 89. This event was perhaps too remote for popular memory or else inserted into the circulated text for optimate consumption.

consilii sententia probatae ad praeconem et ad tibicinem immolabantur. Deinde patres conscripti vocabantur. Iam vero vultum Considi videre ferundum vix erat. Quem hominem 'vegrandem ac retorridum' Romae contemptum, abiectum videbamus, hunc Capuae Campano supercilio ac regio spiritu cum videremus, Blossios mihi videbar illos videre ac Vibellios.

Then lictors went before carrying not staffs but fasces, just as here they go before urban praetors. The full-grown sacrificial victims stood in the Forum; they were approved by the praetors on the tribunal in consultation with their panel, just as is done by us consuls, before being slaughtered to the accompaniment of herald and flute-player. Then the conscript fathers were summoned. The look of Considius was now scarcely bearable. We saw the 'stunted and wizened' man despised and abject at Rome; at Capua we saw him with Campanian haughtiness and regal airs—I seemed to be seeing those Blossii or Vibellii!

Imagine the ferocity that will come from Capuan soil if the bill strengthens the vernacular arrogance with Roman-ness in the form of five hundred colonists, a hundred *decuriones*, ten augurs, and six *pontifices*! Rome will be ridiculed and scorned (2. 96). Capua is being painted luridly as dangerously and inappropriately potentially too much like Rome.[92] After representing the fundamental nature of both communities in aesthetic terms, Cicero, presumed to be the visible embodiment of Roman qualities, proceeds to guide his audience's reading of the person of Considius, who had visited Rome. In Cicero's verbal vignette the figure this man cut at Rome is limned as a grotesque figure from the ludic stage, a far cry from the regal air he possessed at Capua. Cicero could count on those who are watching him to supply, in their own minds' eyes, details and connotations supplementary to his reading.[93]

Capua had lingered, moreover, safely and loyally in the depths of inertia and sloth ('inertissimum ac desidiosissimum otium') by virtue of the foresight of a wiser generation of Romans—precisely because there could be none of the lust for glory which by implication characterizes the powerful Rome (2. 91): 'there can be no desire for glory where honour has no

[92] Jonkers (1963: 128–31) seems genuinely outraged at Cicero's claims.
[93] Cf. Quint. *Inst.* 8. 3. 64.

public existence; neither rivalry nor ambition breaks their harmony.'[94] This harmlessness was a result of the lack of power of the Capuan people: 'nobody had the power of holding a contio nor of taking public counsel.'[95] Strength lies in the practices and institutions of the *res publica* allied to its moral supremacy. The casting of Capua as an 'anti-Rome' attacks the content of the bill whilst also celebrating the people's consul. Rome's *otium* is also linked by Cicero to the cohesive fabric of political practice.[96] The consul, 'armed with your arms, and adorned with most honourable *insignia*, with *imperium*, with authority . . .' (2. 101), is a spectacular emblem of the power and meaning of the *res publica*, and so is able to discredit a tribune's pretence of safeguarding the popular interest.

Rullus' own looks, demeanour, and behaviour had already been critiqued by the consul. Earlier in the oration (2. 12–13), Cicero, already the self-proclaimed, visible *popularis*, told of his eagerness to learn of the tribunes' plans: he was shut out from their counsels, his offer to help in passing legislation useful to the people spurned. The tribunes met in secret at night.[97] Then they entered office:

> Ineunt tandem magistratus tribuni plebis; contio valde expectatur P. Rulli, quod et princeps erat agrariae legis et truculentius se gerebat quam ceteri. Iam designatus alio vultu, alio vocis sono, alio incessu esse meditabatur, vestitu obsoletiore, corpore inculto et horrido, capillatior quam ante barbaque maiore, ut oculis et adspectu denuntiare omnibus vim tribuniciam et minitari rei publicae videretur.

Finally the tribunes of the plebs enter the magistracies; the contio of P. Rullus is particularly awaited, both because he was the principal man behind the agrarian bill and because he carried himself more

[94] 'ubi honos publice non est, ibi gloriae cupiditas esse non potest; non contentione, non ambitione discordes.'

[95] *Leg. Agr.* 2. 91: 'contionandi potestas erat cuiquam nec consilii capiundi publici.'

[96] *Otium* is indeed a 'catch-word' of the oration, treated with 'astonishing variation' in 102–3 (Vasaly 1993: 237).

[97] Secretiveness is a topos for suggesting malevolent deliberation. Livy (3. 38) casts Appius and the 5th-cent. decemvirs acting as supposedly does Rullus; the similarity is perhaps suggestive, especially given the proposed decemvirate, of the persistence of such themes in both oral and historiographical tradition.

churlishly than the others. Once elected he studiously had a different expression, a different tone of voice, a different walk; more old-fashioned clothing, unfussy and shaggy grooming, with more hair and a bigger beard than before, so that with his eyes and his stare he seemed to all to announce tribunician violence and threaten the *res publica*.

Rullus was probably aiming at a guise replete with archaic and mournful associations to make him seem a graver proponent of public policy. Cicero urges his audience 'to put before their eyes' ('ponite ante oculos vobis') Rullus acting contemptibly, just as he imagines men of evil design themselves doing (2. 53 and 59). These fancies are feasible because Rullus has been before the popular gaze (and presumably had tried to advertise a sense of distinctiveness). Cicero calls attention to Rullus' self-fashioning and dooms it to ridicule as the deviant mark of a man who was seditiously *levis*.

Laughter could be understood as an element of republican liberty.[98] Consequently it was the business of an orator to make mirth.[99] Individuals corporally distinctive, be it through deformity or a more common departure from the ideals of attractiveness such as baldness, were ready targets for orators who sought to effect a sense of complicity with their audience in a gale of laughter.[100] But if laughter was readily stirred by appearances that could be perceived as deviant in some way, orators also needed to attune their jibes to the sensibilities of the crowd, which might be prompted to notice and find oddities funny but yet, besides being quite able to see and interpret for

[98] Cic. *Planc.* 33. While it was remarkable and abnormal never to laugh, laughter had its proper time and place: the grandfather of M. Licinius Crassus was known for never laughing (Pliny *HN* 7. 79); a man was reduced to the status of a member of the *aerarii* by the censors for jocular levity (Gell. 4. 20. 3–6).

[99] Cic. *De Or.* 2. 236: 'it is plainly the orator's business to stir laughter.' On the politics of laughter in oratory see Corbeill 1996.

[100] A physical deformity might prevent a man from winning office: Shackleton Bailey, ad *Att.* 1. 16. 3. The Twelve Tables adjured that deformed infants were to be killed: Cic. *Leg.* 3. 19. As for more mundane bodily issues, C. Iulius Caesar was particularly happy to wear wreaths because it saved elaborate combing to cover his baldness, which attracted jibes (Suet. *DJ* 45. 2).

itself, had definite affections.[101] A distinctive rhetoric of self was only effective if supported by other merits; without such a man was vulnerable to ridicule. Thus L. Quinctius found his character, as manifested by his *vultus* and his mode of wearing his *amictus*, the object of jurymen's scornful gaze, because Cicero, who was always deft in pointing such things out, knew that such a look was a liability in the absence of supporting claims to distinction.[102] Cicero noticed how a certain hapless Tuditanus' flamboyantly theatrical dress and comportment in the Forum made him memorable only as an object of ridicule.[103] On the other hand, the dress of Caesar notably failed to conform to prevailing norms at Rome but this seems never to have diminished his popularity. Successful orators whom Cicero emulated had elicited mirth to memorable effect.[104] Cicero himself, a witty man after all, would have learned from experience how ridicule could best be conjured forth in the Forum. If he succeeded in making a mockery of Rullus, he had prevailed in a contest of political affections; and the victory could be cited as a popular verdict upon both the individual and the political positions with which he was associated.[105]

Rullus perhaps played ill his own chosen part as hoary, hairy statesman. But because the benefits of consular prestige allowed

[101] *De Or.* 2. 237. [102] *Cluent.* 111.

[103] It was his habit to scatter money to the *populus* from the Rostra while dressed in tragic garb: *Phil.* 3. 16; cf. Val. Max. 7. 8. 1.

[104] As can be imagined from the example of Crassus' comparison of an individual to a picture of a Gaul: Cic. *De Or.* 2. 266. Physical, gestural mimicry might effectively accompany witty words in a contio (ibid. 242).

[105] Cicero claims (*Har.* 8) that when Clodius spoke about religious protocols, 'even his own contio laughed at the man'; the occurrence is cited to show that the whole *res publica* knew the hypocrisy of Clodius' show of religiosity and, by extension from the person, that Clodius' accusations were without foundation. Note too Cicero's citation of the laughter ('homines inridentes') at Numerius Quintius Rufus (tribune in 57?) (*Sest.* 72). *Odium* too could be invoked as a stamp of deserved humiliation bestowed by the *populus* upon individuals: Scipio Nasica was called accursed and a tyrant; over a century later Titius, the murderer of Sextus Pompey, was driven out of Pompey's theatre 'from the spectacle which he was providing, by the execrations of the *populus*' (Vell. 2. 79. 6). Cicero reported (*Q. Fr.* 3. 1. 24), upon Gabinius' reception before a large crowd the day after his sneaky return from his province at night, when he suffered the *odium* of the *universus populus*. Ridicule could also have consequences in military operations (Livy 41. 10. 10).

Cicero to present himself as a stately model of the qualities the *populus* should expect to see in a pre-eminently respectable person, the sight of Rullus was made a metonym for the legislation. Cicero's reading of Rullus seems to have prevailed in the Forum and in history. In the Forum, once the laughter subsided, the sinister intent of the legislation was exposed: nobody, Cicero claimed, could understand Rullus' first contional speech and its fancy language; nobody could say if its obscurity was duc to insidious intent or to his delight in such eloquence.[106] Rullus' ultimate aim was as obscure as his use of language, his designs as unattractive to the popular standards as his physical appearance. Cicero made it impossible to disentangle the merits of Rullus' legislation from the political hermeneutics of his hairstyling.

The employment of such visual representations indeed constituted, as Vasaly has observed, an important part of the ensemble of techniques and presumptions underlying oratorical performance.[107] Capua, too much like Rome, and a tribune who was no true *popularis* might be perceived as perilous because they were described by a consul of majestic dignity. Yet persuasive techniques drew strength from the great practical and ideological gulf, maintained by the rituals of religious and civic ceremony, separating Cicero from most other citizens. Yet although belonging to an order stationed at great remove, the conspicuous orator had no choice but to expend great care and effort in making himself and the political programmes he favoured attractive, because the *populus* elected, legislated, and had interests and affections of its own for which it expected respect. The various responses of the contional crowd, whether cheers, chortles, or even a stony silence or worse, naturally do not leave traces in the surviving script. Yet Cicero's power to doom a piece of (possibly worthy) legislation clearly speaks volumes on the question of where power lay in the late Republic. In political practice, 'democratic' constitutional prerogatives notwithstanding, it would seem that the notable big men had the capability to activate habits of deference in a free citizenry, even if Cicero had to impersonate a man of the people

[106] *Leg. Agr.* 2. 13–14. [107] Vasaly 1993.

in order for his arguments and eloquence to accomplish their business.

Citizens could not be ignored and it was 'a normal political necessity' to flatter and persuade them.[108] But this necessity should not be understood exclusively in terms of popular sovereignty in the assemblies, however vital that may be to any understanding of the history of the late Republic. The *populus* was also an important audience for senatorial orators eager to live in the light and there win everlasting glory. Cicero was determined that history remember his contional triumph because he knew that great men were especially notable in national history if their prestigious prominence was remembered as having been soundly validated in popular reception.

After the heyday of triumphantly posturing Scipiones, a crowd was less likely to be told, as they had been by Scipio Nasica, to keep quiet and mind their own business. As the population of Rome grew, political participation became the business of more citizens. Particularly after the Gracchi, it was advantageous to the ambitious and the avaricious to claim a plausible affective allegiance with those who had sovereignty over their fates, including their memory. C. Marius, for instance, might be thought a clumsy man in domestic politics but he was ever to be commemorated as a *popularis* hero. His glory, although at its height after his Gallic triumph, easily survived Sulla's destruction of his monuments.[109] It is quite possible that such a potent and deathless status as popular and national hero was all that men such as Scipio, Marius, or, indeed, Pompey and Caesar, really craved. History can judge but cannot explain megalomania, except for the suspicion that the applause of a crowd might often really be all that much ambition sought.[110]

[108] North 1990: 13 n. 35.

[109] Val. Max. 8. 15. 7, Plut. *Mar.* 27. Survival: esp. Cic. *Acad.* 2. 13; in general Carney 1960. Caesar's restoration of the monuments (e.g. Suet. *DJ* 11) made them conspicuous in the fabric of the Forum: Cic. *De Or.* 2. 266, Val. Max. 6. 9. 14.

[110] Imagine, urged Velleius Paterculus (2. 48. 2), if Pompey Magnus had died in his theatre at the height of *felicitas* when his dedicatory celebrations were taking place. Plutarch thinks much the same (*Pomp.* 46) had he died after his third triumph and also tells (ibid. 68; cf. *Caes.* 42) of Pompey's dream

Occasions when prominence was validated by the verdict of the *populus Romanus universus* were treasured. Cicero explicated the legitimacy of Pompey's pre-eminence by citing popular demonstrations of 'universal' sentiment of which the whole world must have heard.[111] Indeed, Cicero is always notable for his proud assertions, even before the prosperous occupants of judicial benches, that he had been elected consul 'by both the complete approval of the *universus populus Romanus* and the remarkable enthusiasm of all the best men—the most magnificent election in memory'.[112] Taking his stand upon the Rostra at that first consular contio, he proudly and repeatedly struck the same note, that his dignity was based upon a manifest unanimity of sentiment: 'the single voice of the entire Roman people announced me consul.'[113]

Audible acclaim was clearly counted as valuable all round; and men naturally liked to be able to claim that they had not merely been elected but were to be remembered for being elected well.[114] The ability to invoke unanimity was, furthermore, an asset in meeting various political challenges. It added strength to Cicero's demolition of pernicious agrarian reform, hope in the face of impending exile, and a sense of triumph on the day of joy for all when the entire people welcomed him home.[115] Likewise, in 63, Cicero stressed to the Senate the commonality of sentiment of 'all orders, all men, the entire Roman *populus*' in the face of a threat to the *res publica*; twenty years later he pointed, rather more hopefully this time, to a

before Pharsalus that he entered the theatre for its dedication and the people were clapping; cf. Millar 1995: 106. Caesar famously desired simply to be first in his community, e.g. Suet. *DJ* 29. 1.

[111] *De Imp. Pomp.* 44.

[112] *Vat.* 6. The crowd of spectators for forensic proceedings might be much the same as at *contiones*: e.g. *Flacc.* 66, *Cluent.* 93. There were some in the crowd who had the means to attend trials frequently and so escape historical anonymity, e.g. L. Valerius Heptachordo who positively loved trials: Val. Max. 7. 8. 7.

[113] *Leg. Agr.* 2. 4; also 7 and 17 (twice).

[114] Lesser magistrates too: e.g. Cic. *Planc.* 49 (an aedileship).

[115] *Dom.* 15. His return from exile was of course an event willed by the entire state, even though the bill for his recall was able to risk a vote only in the Comitia Centuriata (*Red. Sen.* 29): Pompey's support for his recall was supposedly given in person before 'the entire people'.

similar consensus.[116] Approbation was, both tactically and strategically, valuable.[117]

In the affections of an imagined community the *res publica* had much of its meaning—and not least for its prominent men whose eyes fed hungrily on crowds of faces that could be known only to the best *nomenclatores*. It would be simple (if nevertheless ideologically revealing) pomposity to sniff at the *clamor* of the 'ignorant crowd', but we all well know that nobody active in politics ever seems to have relished finding, in the emotions of his audience, his own unpopularity staring him in the face.[118] Cicero, of course, was not fully comfortable in his concern for popular sentiment: on one occasion he managed cannily to combine acknowledgement that the applause of the people is significant with an insistence that only a *levis* would really be concerned with his popular standing.[119]

But Cicero's interest in the validating power of popular judgement is always present. Great orators of steadfast and patriotic purpose had been able to win a nation's verdict upon their statesmanship from a contio. Cicero's discussion of hypocritical flattery in the *De Amicitia* (91–5) offers a train of thought that, after quotation of a passage of ludic drama (Terence), proceeds to assume the existence of the same phenomenon in a more directly political context, namely, a contio: it is the contio 'which, though composed of very ignorant men, habitually discriminates between a *popularis*, namely a flatterer and an inconstant citizen, and one who is resolute, sincere, and weighty'.[120] Cicero had speciously played the *popularis* on the political stage, although he did not care to be thought a truckler

[116] *Cat.* 4. 19; *Fam.* 10. 12. 4, 12. 5. 3.

[117] Cf. Vanderbroeck 1987: 163.

[118] This pomposity ('imperita multitudo') is that of Valerius Maximus (3. 8. 6), describing the reception of Equitius, the attractive pseudo-Marius.

[119] *Sest.* 115.

[120] *Amic.* 95: 'contio, quae ex imperitissimis constat, tamen iudicare solet, quid intersit popularem, id est assentatorem et levem civem, et inter constantem et verum et gravem.' Laelius had spoken against C. Papirius' bill to make tribunes eligible for re-election but now stresses instead, as the generous friend he is, Scipio's contribution to the downfall of the legislation (96): it was certainly as though he were their leader rather than their comrade! ('Quanta illi, di immortales, fuit gravitas, quanta in oratione maiestas! ut facile ducem populi Romani, non comitem diceres'). The train of thought continues

fickle in his principles. After all, he could not avoid addressing the people in a polity with some formally democratic elements. Nor did he want to, since he took pride in his consular performances and confidence that their commemoration would give him profound historical signification.[121] There was another issue too. Neither his sincerity nor his glory rested securely upon the personal qualities so apparent in national heroes such as Scipio or Marius.

Cicero lacked the most obvious claims to *virtus*. There were certainly few Romans who enjoyed the exalted condition of being regarded as a founder or preserver of their state—the achievement through which, Cicero said, a man's *virtus* brought him closest to the gods.[122] Cicero encouraged such regard for his actions in 63. In general, *virtus* had no easily articulated essential meaning except that it made Roman men distinctive.[123] It signified the ideal of manliness.[124] And it made men deserving of reward, particularly in dignity of office.[125] Scipio or Marius commanded popular adulation for enormous military accomplishments rather than just wearing a breastplate about the city. Although battlefields might be thought to be its best proving grounds, Cicero used the term to denote general

into a directly stated and important correspondence between the political and the dramatic stage (97): 'Now if on the stage, I mean in a contio, where there is more than ample opportunity for deceptions and deceits' ('Quod si in scaena, id est in contione, in qua rebus fictis et adumbratis loci plurimum est'). Here too falls (96) mention of Crassus as the first man to begin the practice of facing towards the Forum in addressing the people (which Plutarch (*C. Grac.* 5) interestingly associates with C. Gracchus).

[121] Cicero was always greatly concerned for posterity's estimation of his service to the *res publica* in 63: e.g. *Att.* 2. 5. 1, fearing far more what history will say a thousand years hence than the 'rumusculi' of his contemporaries; there is particularly pointed contrast with the ambition of the men of the fishponds at 2. 1. 7. Throughout the rest of his life, Cicero believed he had established the *res publica* at its best in 63, in the *potestas* of the best men: the praise comes from 'Atticus' at *Leg.* 3. 37.

[122] *Rep.* 1. 12.

[123] Cic. *Phil.* 4. 13. Likewise Milo suffers no exile wherever there is a place for *virtus*: *Mil.* 101.

[124] Cicero acknowledges the derivation at *Tusc.* 2. 43; cf. Varro *LL* 5. 75. The inherent virility in *virtus* can, however, also be 'feminized': *Tusc.* 1. 95, 2. 21. As far as I know, Cicero finds it in three women: a Caecilia (*S. Rosc.* 147), Terentia (*Fam.* 14. 1; cf. 14. 3), and Tullia (*Fam.* 14. 11, *Att.* 10. 8. 9, 11. 17. 1 and 14. 11).

[125] *Cat.* 3. 26, *Mil.* 97, *Brut.* 281, *Fam.* 10. 10. 2.

excellence in other areas of activity, such as oratory or administration, all with the overarching notion that it was something that existed only in action.[126] *Virtus* was a key ideological quality and, because his career was short of military indications that he possessed it, Cicero had no recourse but to contional performance in order to record the popular approbation that warranted his claim. The *populus*, therefore, had the power to make Cicero the sort of man he could never be on solely his own merits.

It could be thought that *virtus* was whatever it was that Romans liked when they saw it, since Cicero depicted it as embodied and in terms of physical illumination.[127] *Virtus* was eminently perceptible.[128] It had, moreover, the possibility of having *ornamenta*, *signa* or *insignia*.[129] But these marks of *virtus*, Cicero warns, may be empty of genuine content or susceptible to hollow imitation and simulation;[130] many considered *virtus* to take the form of mere 'vaunting and display'.[131] Clearly *virtus* depended for much of its meaning in a highly rhetorical

[126] *Rep.* 1. 2; *Off.* 1. 19, re praise for *virtus*; cf. *Part.* 76, re *virtus* manifest in oratory. The problem of a divergence in meanings between technical and popular usages is acknowledged at *Off.* 2. 35.

[127] The *virtus* of the exemplary Cato 'shone forth as outstanding' (*Mur.* 32; cf. ibid. 54, *Dom.* 23). Lucullus easily appears before Cicero's eyes as an example of general excellence (*Fin.* 3. 8. 18). Sestius' *virtus* 'shines in the darkness' (*Sest.* 60). Plancius' 'memorable and divine *virtus* brings light to the *res publica*' (*Phil.* 13. 44). Milo's (*Sest.* 92). 'The light of *virtus* shines out' (*Fam.* 12. 5. 3; cf. *Amic.* 28 and 48, *Fin.* 3. 10).

[128] *Balb.* 16; cf. *Pis.* 2, *Verr.* 2. 2. 4. *Virtus* may also be 'spectata' (*Flacc.* 63, *Ad Brut.* 24.10). Piso, claims Cicero, would not know by sight the remarkable *virtus* of a C. Caesar (*Pis.* 81). That of Lucullus possessed *vis*: 'his vast power of *virtus* and talent was absent abroad, invisible to Forum and Senate, for longer than I might have wanted' ('diutius quam vellem tanta vis virtutis atque ingenii peregrinata afuit ab oculis et fori et curiae', *Acad.* 2. 3). *Virtus* can also have beauty (*Fam.* 9. 14. 4). The phrase is also found at *Att.* 14. 17a. 5; cf. *Fin.* 4. 42. *Virtus* can also have *splendor* (*Off.* 1. 20, *Fin.* 3. 45 and 4. 37, *Hort.* 46). *Virtus* can also be represented in an *effigies*, or a *monumentum* (*Arch.* 30, *Tusc.* 3. 3, *Phil.* 9. 12, *Dom.* 100).

[129] *Phil.* 13. 24, *Fam.* 15. 2. 8, *Amic.* 48; *Pis.* 63.

[130] *Fam.* 3. 13. 1. Imitation and simulation: *Acad.* 2. 140, *Inv.* 1. 3. *Off.* 1. 46. Note too that *imitatio virtutis* is labelled aphoristically as *aemulatio* at *Tusc.* 4. 17.

[131] *Amic.* 86. Cicero was well aware (*Off.* 2. 43) of the dictum attributed to Socrates (Xen. *Mem.* 2. 6. 39) that the quickest way to glory was through careful counterfeiting. Note too the 'species virtutis adsimulatae' of Catilina, at *Cael.* 14.

political culture upon its phenomenology. Marius, the most famous *novus homo* to advertise his *virtus* to the *populus*, made his own self a political spectacle: 'I understand that the faces of all have been turned upon me.'[132] His *virtus* was assured because, rather than being identified by noble pedigree reflected in *imagines*, or a record of forefathers' triumphs and consulships, his scars of battle were his nobility.[133]

Cicero had no such scars: the only bodily disfigurements he shared with the other new man from Arpinum were varicose veins.[134] Yet at the very beginning of the *De Lege Agraria II* Cicero echoes the theme of *novitas* that was the emotional premise of Marius' contio at the beginning of 107. Cicero has no *imagines*, his ancestors 'lacked the praise of the *populus* and the light of the honour you bestow'.[135] But with himself as leader, he declares (2. 3), the *populus* has broken down the fortified position of privilege that the *nobilitas* guarded: 'you wanted it to be open to *virtus* for the future.'[136] The evocation of *virtus* thus conforms to a popular tradition yet all the while Cicero is soliciting a popular seal of approval for *virtus* unproven by scars or triumphs.

In this he was continuing a campaign dating from when he had proclaimed the merits of Pompey to the *populus* in 66. Cicero stressed then the range of an *imperator*'s virtues which were possessed by Pompey and esteemed by the common people; thus perhaps he tried to shift emphasis away from

[132] Sall. *BJ* 85. 5.

[133] Ibid. 85. 31: '*Virtus* shows itself well enough' ('ipsa se virtus satis ostendit'). Scars: ibid. 29–30; cf. Plut. *Mar.* 9.

[134] Marius' veins: Plut. *Mar.* 6. Cicero's: Macrob. *Sat.* 2. 3. 5; Quint. *Inst.* 11. 3. 143; Sidon. *Epist.* 5. 5.

[135] 'laude populari atque honoris vestri luce caruerunt.' Regrettably, little is known about the *novi homines* who held consulships between Marius and Cicero. T. Didius (in 98 BC) was responsible for a bill that required a period of three *nundinae* between promulgation and voting upon legislation (see Cic. *Dom.* 41, *Sest.* 135, *Phil.* 5. 3, *Schol. Bob.* 140 (Stangl)). He too prided himself upon his scars and an empty eye-socket as well (Sall. *Hist.* 1. 88 (M) = Gell. 2. 72. 2). Though not a consul, Q. Sertorius had similar disfigurements which he advertised in the Marian tradition (Plut. *Sert.* 4).

[136] 'virtutique in posterum patere voluistis.' The expression also occurs at *Mur.* 17 and *Sest.* 137.

preoccupation with *virtus* testified by military conquest.[137] In his first speech against the bill before the Senate, there are references to *virtus* that make its meaning dependent upon personal capability in military service but there is no reference to the intrinsic *virtus* of Cicero himself.[138] It was in his second speech to the *populus* that Cicero showed a particular need to be accepted as virtuous. He associated his individual possession of it with its general existence in the *res publica*, both his at the start of the speech and the people's at the close together resting upon a presupposed consensus.[139] For the Republic at least, the idea of Horace of a pure *virtus* laying claim to *fasces* independently of the judgement of fickle populace and vulgar crowds was happy poetic fancy.[140] Only the people made Cicero what he wanted to be: a man whose election to a consulship not only gave him further authority to direct popular sentiment wheresoever his interests and ambitious inclinations pointed but also a valid entitlement to be deemed praiseworthy.[141]

An oratorical text of Cicero thus reveals the *populus Romanus* to be the repository of most of the ideological spoils of a Roman political career. Hence the *populus* fully enjoys historical significance when attention turns, as it should, toward the sight of an orator with the power to persuade those who have little personal dignity and perhaps few prospects for material happiness. For notables humble citizens probably had names only at election-time: political actors probably only ever saw the faces of lesser Romans as a single, mass entity quite distinct from their own class.[142] In the collective rituals of the Roman citizenry, senators (and often *equites* too) occupied elevated orders of socio-political existence, whether sitting remote in the theatre or talking tall upon the Rostra. A contio authorized the elevation of the orator but provided the *populus* no power of political

[137] *Man.* 29 and 36; cf. Eisenhut 1973: 63.

[138] Rullus is proposing to sell assets acquired 'by arms and *virtus*' (1. 4), including the royal territory in Macedonia conquered by T. Flamininus and L. Paullus and the Carthaginian lands in Spain acquired by the Scipiones—or rather by the *virtus* of these famous commanders (1. 5).

[139] *Leg. Agr.* 2. 103.

[140] Hor. *Odes* 3. 2. 17–24; cf. 3. 5. 29.

[141] *Honores*, one might say (Cic. *Amic.* 22), existed 'ut laudere'.

[142] For the *voltus* of a crowd see Sall. *BJ* 34. 1.

participation commensurate with his words and posturing. Most Romans had no ritual opportunities to voice an eloquence other than that of a collective crush of bodies in public space. When the crowd shouted, its noise was usually read without nuance as a single unanimous force, albeit able to club a bird down from the city's skies.[143]

Shouting, not taking one's turn to orate or even ask careful questions, was a liberty fundamental to the meaning of the *res publica*.[144] Even when a greater precision was lent to the crowd's voice (particularly to register its hostility) the initiative came from above: Clodius took the organization of the popular voice to a new level of sophistication: the 'racy paragraphs' (through which Cicero gives Quintus 'and us a ringside seat from which to watch the show' of February 56) reveal that the questions were thrown down to the crowd.[145] Even the new styles of probably rhythmical applause, such as those that greeted the Senate's passing of Cicero's motion that Pompey be placed in charge of the corn supply, were probably orchestrated.[146] Emotional expression had considerable power in its own right yet all too often it was directed by wilful actors who needed the crowd more than it needed them. Triumphantly noisy judgements were remembered, whether upon Cicero or upon past figures remembered in exemplary fashion, that Scipio, say, processing in popular majesty up to the Capitoline, or upon L. Licinius Crassus whose contio was notable for being unmatched in *clamores*.[147] Naturally Cicero craved such remembrance.

But despite a consulship which was in some respects quite glorious, Cicero's popularity was only temporarily embellished

[143] Livy 29. 25. 3–4; Plut. *Flam.* 10, *Pomp.* 25; Val. Max. 4. 8. 5; Dio 36. 30. 3.

[144] Marcellinus told the people at a contio (on the subject of Pompey): 'shout, citizens, while you may' ('adclamate Quirites dum licet'): Val. Max. 6. 2. 6.

[145] Stockton 1969: 22 provides the spectacular characterization; *Q. Fr.* 2. 3. 2; cf. Plut. *Pomp.* 48; Dio 39. 19. On the leadership and orchestration of gangs see Vanderbroeck 1987.

[146] Cicero remarked upon the new style, in September of 57: *Att.* 4. 1. 7.

[147] Crassus memorably defeated Cn. Domitius Ahenobarbus in 92: Cic. *Brut.* 162, *De Or.* 2. 227.

by the *fasces*. His success as consul had only 'seduced him into entertaining ideas above his real station'.[148] There were few other opportunities to stand charismatically in the full light of immortalizing Rome.[149] Cicero never owned the persistent and practical allegiance of the plebs but from time to time cosseted his sense of his own virtuousness with the more abstract legitimation of a *populus*. His relations with those who worried as much as he about liberty but far more about the price of bread were unlikely to endure in chronic happiness.

Others fared better, in constructing a personal popularity without dependence upon the formal ceremonies upon which Cicero's glorious legitimation was founded. Cicero never effected pre-eminence beyond that expected to be shared amongst the notability he had joined. In the latter years of the Republic other sites for the solicitation of the citizen body's emotion competed with the Rostra. To be a prominent star of the Rostra was no longer proof of 'summa amplitudo'.[150] Cicero could not point to *virtus* confirmed in triumphant deeds, nor had he the funds to cut a wondrous and magnificent figure as ludic *editor*.

The inflation in the impression made by ludic spectacle that Rome experienced in the years immediately after Cicero's consulship fundamentally changed the polity forever. Not only did possession of kingly wealth become essential for popular preferment and memorability but its expenditure also dissolved cohesion among the class of the prominent. Individuals could aspire to a grand popularity in visible rituals of Roman civic life away from the Forum and the rhetorical spaces favoured by Cicero. Primacy in spectacular impression-management supplemented—and increasingly would supersede—the prominence derived from the charisma of magistracy. Let us be honest: champion gladiators or exotic animals were more entertaining to many more folk than even the most accomplished oration. An awesomely big man could hope to lay perennial claim to charismatic pre-eminence.

[148] Stockton 1971: 334.

[149] An augurship was coveted, perhaps as both an honour and as a means to be seen at a solemn remove from other men: *Att.* 2. 5. 2, 8. 3. 1, *Phil.* 2. 4.

[150] Cic. *Brut.* 281.

The presence of Pompey bulked big throughout the 50s without dependence upon the crass instrumentality of violence which was the buttress for Sulla's autocratic place in the state. Pompey had returned from the East with veteran legionaries as loyal as they were skilled with blade or could be with cudgel in urban operation. He came with treasure too; and also with a regal self-assuredness, which had probably been evident in his comportment in his youth, when he was the 'young boy butcher' commanding the killing of men whose kin he would later be best served with as friends. In the East, where he boasted the allegiance of kings and nations, Pompey was a cosmic force.[151] Yet as we know, Pompey's grandiose authority, even when presented in his theatre at Rome, did not automatically produce reliable and consistent political homage. Three years later, however, amid rampant corruption and general disorder in the streets of the city, Pompey the Great became consul without a colleague. Such political predominance was supported by the conservative aristocrats, such as Bibulus and Cato.[152] They feared Caesar and all that eventually would accompany him back from Gaul. They preferred an unprecedented consulship to a dictatorship already known and always anticipated. Moreover, nothing like their ideal *res publica* could function with organized gangs shouting and spitting, terrorizing and lynching at large in the city. Milo's men killed Clodius in 52.

Pompey's desire to effect kingly pre-eminence without a Sullan sort of revolution against the tradition of peaceable domestic competition strained oligarchy severely. In addition, Pompey's failure to stand securely and perennially first in popular affections was but an encouragement to spectacular demagoguery. As ludic events became key occasions for the solicitation of that popular favour which ambitious and rich notables sought all the more earnestly and frequently, they also became opportunities for populist politicians to advance their programmes. Brilliantly chief among them was P. Clodius Pulcher. Starting in 57, Clodius 'resorted to rituals of popular justice' against Cicero and Pompey, who could be blamed for

[151] Cic. *Fam.* 9. 9. 2; Syme 1939: 30; *ILS* 9459.
[152] Syme 1939: 39.

the high prices of grain and consequent hunger.[153] *Libertas*, furthermore, had been established in the ruins of Cicero's townhouse.[154] Its destruction was highly visible political theatre.[155] Rome was indeed the stage of a global drama. For Cicero—and for all that his career and his rhetorics represented—the spectacular politics of the 50s became a tragedy.

Long gone was the applause for the new man's virtuous virtuosity. Gone too, therefore, was the potential of continued complicitous concord among citizens of different fortune. Some scented the chance for glory upon every political wind. Many were habitually hungry and happy for excitation of the more munificent sort. Suffering (fancifully republican) nostalgia, men of later generations could look back to the days when men of the Republic 'had persuaded themselves that without eloquence nobody was able either to reach or to maintain a conspicuous or prominent position in the state'.[156] The importance of eloquence did not die entirely when Caesar and his army crossed the Rubicon in 49. Caesar not only commanded soldiers, who were bound by oath and bought by barbarian booty to maintain allegiance to their *imperator*, but in contional performance he had also eloquently persuaded them as citizens to destroy *otium* in the cause of his *dignitas*.[157] As we already know, Caesar knew, or at least always desired to know, his audiences. And among his successors, one emerged preeminently capable of showing himself to Roman citizens as a republican prince.

## THE END OF REPUBLICAN AFFECTIONS

Octavian (or Augustus as he would become after 27) did not find the fanciful cosmopolitanism displayed by Antony to be particularly appealing. When in Greece, Antony looked to Greek populist taste in order to affirm and enjoy a significance

[153] Nippel 1995: 76. [154] Cic. *Dom.* 108–11; Brunt 1988: 334.

[155] Beacham 1999: 57.

[156] Tac. *Dial.* 37. 6: 'quin immo sibi ipsi persuaserant neminem sine eloquentia aut adsequi posse in civitate aut tueri conspicuum et eminentem locum.'

[157] Caes. *BC* 1. 7.

reaching far beyond the city—we have seen that general, like Sulla before him, ensconced amid the festive affections of the Athenians. Antony could also be remembered for remarkably extravagant comportment and costume. Whereas Pompey had postured with the cloak of Alexander the Great, Antony was believed to have looked greedily at Dionysiac allusiveness and ordered that he be called Liber Pater. In procession his head was bound with a wreath of ivy and he wore a saffron robe, along with a thyrsus wand and buskin boots.[158] His consort queen Cleopatra was surely able to look very fetching herself, styled as Aphrodite or as Isis.[159] In the years after Caesar's experiments in self-definition others too had clad themselves in the striking idioms of divinity. Sextus Pompey may well have changed the colour of his robe from purple to a dusky blue, to mark a special relationship with Poseidon.[160] Antony, like Caesar, looked upon an urban populace, seated aloft (in 34) upon a gilded throne set upon a silver platform (*bēma*).[161] But while that ceremony did have elements of Roman triumph blended with processional festivity associated with Dionysus,[162] it took place in the last of the great Hellenistic cities to rule over a kingdom free of direct Roman rule. Its power was small. Alexandrians, although they knew well pomp and circumstance, did not produce especially effective soldiers. Their cheers too, if it can be assumed that there was such, left little impression upon posterity. Octavian did not need the legitimacy that evocation of Alexander, the greatest king of all time, had once brought.[163]

Octavian's pre-eminence was founded upon ceremonial visibility in Rome itself. There, while Antony's memory and monuments suffered formal *damnatio*,[164] a great many honours

[158] Vell. 2. 82. 4. Others were even more radical in fancy dress. Antony's flatterer of a friend, Plancus, dressed at a banquet as Glaucus the Nereid—naked, his body painted blue and his head girt with reeds, as he crawled upon his knees wearing a fish's tail: Vell. 2. 83. 2.

[159] Plut. *Ant.* 26 and 54.

[160] App. *BC* 5. 100; further references at Beacham 1999: 96–7.

[161] Dio 49. 40. 4.

[162] Reinhold 1988: 76.

[163] In Alexandria he had the sarcophagus of Alexander the Great brought out for him to see and he placed a crown and flowers upon it: Suet. *DA* 8. 1. For a time he used an image of Alexander as his seal: Suet. *DA* 50.

[164] Dio 51. 19. 3–4; Reinhold 1988: 146–7.

were voted to Octavian by Senate and *populus*.[165] Among them were prayers, statues, an arch, a festival every fourth year, thanksgivings on the anniversaries of his birthday and his great victory, and front-row seating in the theatres. The gates of Janus were closed. When priests and priestesses prayed on behalf of Senate and people, they also prayed for Octavian; at all public and private feasts, everybody poured a libation to him as well.[166] His name became incorporated in song; he would wear a triumphal crown at all festivals. It was planned that the day on which he entered the city would be honoured and forever after commemorated by sacrifices in which the whole populace participated.

Ritual pre-eminence was in fact Octavian's due as soon as he actually did return to the capital from the East in the summer of 29. The consul Potitus Valerius Messalla publicly offered sacrifices on behalf of Senate and *populus*—which had never been done for any man previously.[167] Soon was staged a splendid three-day parading of triumphs. There was royalty in the display of captives: 'in my triumphs there were led before my chariot nine kings and kings' children.'[168] But as the grand finale, there was the sight of Octavian riding into the city followed (and not preceded) by the senators who had campaigned under his command. Again, such ceremonial deference was unprecedented.[169] Future returns to Rome were also marked by great ceremony. The occasion of his coming home from the East in 19 elicited great ceremonial and also a permanent observance in the state calendar. Clearly the past few years, when Augustus had been bringing by his presence the blessings of his peace for Asia and the Orient, had been times of uncertain fortune in Rome.[170] The only consul elected for 19 had felt obliged to suppress the populist conspirator, fire-brigadier, and veritably 'cheap victim' Egnatius Rufus.[171] There was an

[165] Conveniently listed if imprecisely dated at Dio 51. 19. 1–20. 6; Octavian did not accept all of them (20. 4).

[166] Dio 51. 19. 7.

[167] Dio 51. 21. 1–2.

[168] *Res Gestae* 4. 3: 'in triumphis meis ducti sunt ante currum meum reges et regum liberi novem.' Among the captives were Alexander Helios and Cleopatra Selene (the children of Antony and Cleopatra), and Alexander of Emesa (Dio 51. 21. 8–9; Reinhold 1988: 156–8).

[169] Dio 51. 21. 9.

[170] Vell. 2. 92. 1–2.

[171] Syme 1939: 372.

official entourage to accompany him once he had reached Campania. This consisted of some praetors and tribunes of the plebs along with the consul and *principes viri*. Such an honour too was unprecedented, so Augustus himself proudly observes.[172] A new altar, to Fortuna Redux, was consecrated in front of the temples of Honos and Virtus and the Senate ordered the pontiffs and Vestals to make an annual sacrifice there upon the anniversary of his return to the city.[173] Augustus infiltrated the calendar.

Grand spectacle articulated Augustus' pre-eminence upon his return from his conquests in the wake of Actium. To celebrate the dedication of a temple to Divus Julius there were ludic spectacles.[174] The equestrian exhibition of the *lusus Troiae* was performed. There were gladiators. And there were animals, both wild and tamed, killed in great numbers. Chief among them were a rhinoceros and a hippopotamus, which Dio claims were now seen for the first time in Rome.[175] He is not quite right in this: M. Aemilius Scaurus had been the first to show a hippopotamus in Rome, in his 'spectacular aedileship of 58' and Pompey had had a rhinoceros at his disposal.[176] Although a kind of kingly spectacle had arrived in the latter years of the Republic, it was natural for Dio perhaps to identify the beginnings of a great new age of emperor-sponsored display with magnificently spectacular novelties. Certainly Rome now had its first permanent amphitheatre of stone, paid for by Statilius Taurus out of the spoils of war.[177] A new age of spectacle was being opened and it was one in which 'none could compete with Augustus in material resources, skill of organization and sense of the dramatic'.[178] Republican

[172] *Res Gestae* 12. 1. In future his returns to Rome from abroad were generally welcomed with song as well as prayer and sacrifice (Suet. *DA* 57. 2).

[173] *Res Gestae* 11. In commemoration of his return from Spain and Gaul (in 13) it was decreed by the Senate that there should be another altar, this time of Pax Augusta. It stood by the Campus Martius and annual sacrifices were performed by the pontiffs, magistrates, and Vestals (*Res Gestae* 12. 2).

[174] Dio 51. 22. 4–9.

[175] Dio 51. 22. 5, with a brief vague description of the rhinoceros. By his own day the hippopotamus was both much described and frequently seen.

[176] Reinhold 1988: 159; Pliny *HN* 8. 71.

[177] Suet. *Aug.* 29; Tac. *Ann.* 3. 72. 1.

[178] Syme 1939: 468.

competition in solicitation of 'the favour of the sovran people by lavish display at games, shows and triumphs' was at an end.[179] Henceforward Augustus would be able to surpass all his predecessors in the number, variety, and splendour of his games.[180] Aediles lost (in 22) the opportunity to advertise themselves expensively in production of the grand ludic festivals.[181] These became instead the responsibility of the praetors who were forbidden also from spending more from private resources than a colleague. Gladiatorial shows, moreover, required an authorizing decree of the Senate. Augustus' own nephew Marcellus was the last aedile to give truly memorable games.

And Augustus gave a good show. He was extraordinarily attentive to the duties of both giving and presiding over spectacles, acting also as though he had competitors.[182] He gave *ludi* in his own name four times but also paid deference to oligarchy, twenty-three times helping magistrates lacking sufficient funds on their own. All manner of games, including *venationes*, were staged in the Circus and the Saepta (the large enclosed space in the Campus Martius) besides the Forum. He gave hunts of African animals twenty-six times in his own name or in that of his sons or grandsons; three and a half thousand animals were slain.[183] Furthermore, if anything not seen before or worthy of attention was brought to Rome, he gave special exhibitions of it: a rhinoceros was shown in the Saepta, a tiger in the *scaena*, and a snake fifty cubits in length in front of the Comitium. He appears particularly proud of his staging of a great naval battle (in 2 BC) in which three thousand men fought in his fleets.[184] Great set-piece festivities focused attention upon him and in all likelihood elicited affection. Augustus 'had filled the hearts and eyes of the Roman people with unforgettable images'.[185]

[179] Syme 1939: 468. [180] Suet. *DA* 52. [181] Dio 54. 2. 4.

[182] Suet. *DA* 43–4: 'spectaculorum et assiduitate et varietate et magnificentia omnes antecessit.' All the following details are from this passage.

[183] *Res Gestae* 22. 3.

[184] *Res Gestae* 23. Caesar had given such a show. The emperor Claudius paid for an even more lavish mock naumachia: Tac. *Ann.* 12. 56–7; Suet. *Claud.* 21.

[185] Vell. 2. 100. 2: 'magnificentissimis . . . spectaculis . . . animos oculosque populi Romani repleverat.'

This impresario of spectacle, *editor* supreme, also made sure that he was seen performing properly his ceremonial duties in such matters.[186] In addition to dividing the seating at shows appropriately among the (male) body politic, he made sure either to be present in person in a prominent place, or to explain absences and appointing presidents in his stead. Thus once 'it happened that at the circus games he had vowed he was struck by illness and led the cavalcade lying in a sedan-chair'.[187] When he was present upon the *pulvinar*, the 'royal-box', he scrupulously gave, unlike his adoptive father, his undivided attention to the proceedings. Augustus did not betray any disdain of ennui as had great-uncle Julius. His successors performed these spectacular duties with varying degrees of success, ideally managing to balance a presiding elevation with adherence to the ideology of the collectivity.[188]

All eyes were presumed to be upon Augustus—and quite probably they were much of the time, at least when there were not gladiators and tigers to behold. In ritualized spectacle his popularity was made manifest. In religious rites and theatrical performance his pre-eminence and its legitimacy were appreciable as they were not in the Forum. Memories of his grandly generous festivities must have massively informed all their participating spectators' sense of the significance of the first man of Rome. In any case his image was pervasively present and seemingly consumed gladly; his spectacular monumentalism was 'internalized and absorbed until it becomes an integral part of Roman self-awareness'.[189] He was a new national hero.

[186] The construction of permanent theatres creates a formal notion of audience and in addition the mass audience is able to watch the monarch who 'must not merely see the play, he must be seen to see it' (Orgel 1975: 16, speaking of the English Renaissance theatre).

[187] *DA* 43. 5, detailing too how at the games for his grandsons it seemed that the theatre might collapse, and Augustus instilled calm by actions rather than words and went to take his place that appeared most at risk.

[188] Thus from on high Claudius hailed the audience as 'domini' (Suet. *Claud.* 21. 5). *Comitas* was a prevalent ideology at the games: Tac. *Ann.* 1. 76; Suet. *Tit.* 8. 2; Wallace-Hadrill 1982.

[189] Wallace-Hadrill's (1989: 159) précis of the vital contribution of Zanker 1988.

Augustus was, however, certainly not to be remembered for his oratory.[190] He had delivered as a boy a public ('pro contione') eulogy for his grandmother Julia;[191] but his subsequent youth was most likely to be associated with snappy expressions of cruelty directed towards vanquished and grovelling peers.[192] As a triumvir he may perhaps have delivered effective exhortations towards his troops but no such speeches are recorded.[193] To both *populus* and Senate he spoke from a carefully prepared text, even if he did have the ability to orate extemporaneously.[194] But, again, both his temper and his authority were more likely to produce curtness rather than eloquence. He rebuked the crowd 'severissima voce' when there was complaint about the high price of wine.[195] And when the *populus Romanus* lobbied him to restore Julia from exile, he prayed *pro contione* that they suffer the same sort of womenfolk.[196] He knew well too how to communicate as much with a theatrical gesture as with words. When a riotous populace offered him a dictatorship, it was with a theatrical gesture that he begged to refuse, kneeling and baring his shoulders.[197] The title of Pater Patriae was offered by popular demand on more than one occasion, including in the theatre.[198] The public refusals were significant and memorable as events in themselves; he had no need to circulate texts of his speeches nor pamphlets of his reasoning. He said (in the Senate) that he hoped only to enjoy the consensus of the senators through to the end of his life.

In the mundanely impressive rituals which must have evoked much of the meaning of a republic for the majority of Romans, Augustus was scrupulous in his recognition of popular, aristocratic, and provincial sensibilities. He was something to everybody, in 'a web of interactions, mutualities, and

[190] Contrast the eloquence of Julius Caesar: Suet. *DJ* 55.

[191] Suet. *DA* 8. 1. [192] Ibid. 13. 1–2.

[193] When as a triumvir he was addressing soldiers whom not only a crowd of bystanders but also an *eques* who was making notes had joined, he had the note-taker stabbed on the spot as a spy (Suet. *DA* 27. 3).

[194] Ibid. 84. Sometimes he suffered from weakness of voice and then employed a herald to speak his words for him.

[195] Ibid. 52. 1. [196] Ibid. 65. 3. [197] Ibid. 53. 1.

[198] Ibid. 58. 1.

reciprocities'.[199] With regard to anonymous citizenry, even if suffrage was now being buried deeper among the advantages of being a Roman citizen, he accompanied candidates at election-time, soliciting votes in person.[200] And when he held a consulship he was to be seen walking through the city, whereas when he was not consul he usually travelled in a sedan-chair.[201] Generally he was available to petitioners—even if sometimes he seemed as intimidating as an elephant.[202] Likewise, in his dealings with his notional peers in the notability Augustus was also respectful. He addressed the Senate frequently and was scrupulously polite in his behaviour towards senators, greeting them as equals whom he did not expect to offer *salutatio* at his own house. Nor did he want senators to rise in respect when he entered or quit the Senate-house.[203] His authority needed no emphasis. Exquisite, highly visible and ritualized demotic and oligarchic tact addressed and affected every audience. Augustus was something to everybody. Of course there was awareness of legions loyal in provinces far away and memories of innate and sometimes ruthless self-assertion, as well as of fiscal indispensability and all the paperwork efficiently processed and decisions made in meetings of suave and sensible minds. Above all there was peace and prosperity; and there was a popularity consecrated in a grand pre-eminence surpassing that of previous *principes*. Not for nothing was Augustus—much like an excited Cicero—proud until the end of his life of signal demonstrations of his popularity.[204] Maintenance of the traditional institutions of the *res publica* had brought Augustus prestige of the most valuable currency; authority was fuelled by the massive earnings of charismatic pre-eminence.

Obviously Octavian had never intended to be subsumed within the aristocratic ranks of a traditional *res publica*. But Augustus did not overplay his hand by constantly seeking opportunities to dominate the ritual environment in what turned

[199] Galinsky 1996: 288. [200] Suet. *DA* 56. 1. [201] Ibid. 53. 2.
[202] Ibid. [203] Ibid. 53. 3.
[204] As is clear in his determination for remembrance that 'a multitude of a size never before reported flowed together from all Italy' for his election to the office of *pontifex maximus* in 12 (*Res Gestae* 10. 2). Lepidus, its previous incumbent, is not named.

out to be a long life of imperial power and dominating authority in the city. Assuredly he expected credit for restraint and self-effacement.[205] There were not many triumphal processions.[206] He knew the advantages of sharing attention. At the most singular festival of his career, for example, he did not stand as a solitary intermediary between Rome and the gods. The Secular Games (of 17) were a most unusual if wholly memorable performance. Augustus sacrificed (nine ewes and nine goats in holocaust) in the Campus Martius to the Fates and prayed that they be propitious to the Roman people, the board of fifteen, and to himself, his house and his household.[207] But the next day both he and M. Agrippa each sacrificed (a perfect bull) to Jupiter Optimus Maximus and together prayed for every good fortune for the Roman people. The next day they offered the same prayer (and a cow each) to Juno. Agrippa led 110 matrons in further prayer. At night he sacrificed (a pregnant sow) to Mother Earth and made the same prayer. The next day Augustus and Agrippa sacrificed to Apollo and Diana. Their performance was followed by a choir singing Horace's hymn, theatrical presentations, and then chariot-racing and fancy horse-riding (arranged by Messalla). Augustus' style would have impressed a kingly Greek. But if royalty 'is a government in which the attention of the nation is concentrated on one person doing interesting actions',[208] this was a more complex—and more impressively idiosyncratic—political phenomenon.

Others had offices to perform and others were at his side. In spectacle the prosopography of a regime and a dynasty was advertised. Members of his immediate family sometimes shared

[205] Thus he did not remove Pompey's name from his theatre—and tells the world of his magnanimity (*Res Gestae* 20. 1).

[206] He did celebrate three curule triumphs yet, although he was hailed as *imperator* twenty-one times, he did not accept further triumphs decreed by the Senate (*Res Gestae* 4. 1). He enjoyed two ovations, jointly with Antony in 40 and one after victory over the Pompeian pirates and their slave manpower after 36 (Brunt and Moore 1967: 66–7). Fifty-five times the Senate voted that there should be thanksgiving for military or naval successes won by Augustus or legates operating under his auspices; 890 days were given to the thanksgiving (*Res Gestae* 4. 2).

[207] This and the following details from *CIL* VI 32, 323. 90–168.

[208] Bagehot [1867] 1963: 86.

the limelight.[209] He was, moreover, a collegial man, becoming 'pontifex maximus, augur, quindecimvir sacris faciundis, septemvir epulonum, frater arvalis, sodalis Titius, fetialis'.[210] He was certainly very keen on reviving religious tradition and his membership of these colleges gave them prestige. He was one priest among many.

But he was everywhere, a priest for every occasion. The role was a habit, and the habit made the emperor the embodiment of the state in the eyes of every constituency. People do indeed learn from what they see.[211] One can only imagine the feelings of those watching Augustus as an old man performing the sacrifice of the *suovetaurilia* in the Campus Martius. There were a lot of people to see an ominous eagle fly about him in the centre of the city he had made largely his own.[212] It is not an easy business to establish a monarchy. But how many could imagine somebody else so in charge of a knife and a crowd? Indeed, 'quotus quisque reliquus qui rem publicam vidisset?'[213]

[209] The hapless and graceless prince Claudius was not to be allowed by Augustus to be seen at the Circus—'we do not approve of him watching the circus games from the *pulvinar*; for he will be exposed in full view in front of the audience' ('spectare eum circenses ex pulvinari non placet nobis; expositus enim in fronte prima spectaculorum conspicietur', Suet. *Claud.* 4. 3). He sat at a public show with the children of Germanicus to make a point about the desirability of marriage and children (Suet. *DA* 34. 2).

[210] *Res Gestae* 7. 3.

[211] e.g. Pliny *Ep.* 14. 4.

[212] Suet. *DA* 97. 1: 'cum lustrum in campo Martio magna populi frequentia conderet . . .'

[213] Tac. *Ann.* 1. 3: 'how many were there left who had seen the *res publica*?' For consideration of the place of the crowd in the future Principate see Yavetz 1988.

# Afterword

P really on edge, anticipating Romanian reception. Bucharest welcome exceeded all expectations. Was really unbelievable. People massed along entire route except where prohibited. Very enthusiastic, clapped as whole motorcade went by, threw flowers into P's car, shouted, 'Hurrah' and 'Nixon,' really spectacular. P elated and really cranked up. Stood up in car with President Ceauşescu almost all the way...

P went by car to State Building for talks, and returned in driving rain. Huge crowds along the streets both ways still clapping and cheering... Really great...

P feels Ceauşescu is extremely shrewd and bright, and was very much impressed by him.

Diary entry of H. R. Haldeman for 2 August 1969[1]

There is a great deal of truth in Machiavelli's proposition that 'people in general judge more with their eyes than with their minds. Everyone can see; few have understanding.... In the world the crowd is everything.'[2] This is perhaps as true for the political actors as for the spectators. However cynical and knowing they may be in the rhetorics, leaders cannot but be affected themselves by ritualized aesthetics. In the flow of the motorcade, animated by the spectacle and sounds of the cheering crowds, Richard Nixon noticed little about the nature of the ruler of Romania and his regime beyond the geopolitical utility of his deviancy from the constellation of communist states. Mr Ceauşescu of course had little to offer his subjects. There was no empire, no money, and precious little festivity or joy. He did remake the city in which he ruled, with horrendous

[1] Haldeman 1994: 77–8.

[2] *The Prince* §18 (translation by K. F. Thompson).

results.[3] He ruined a nation. His history is instructive but far less than are the politicians who in competitive polities draw crowds without compulsion.

The behaviour of Mr. Nixon prompts curiosity about the politics of free republics. For all his shyness and secretiveness, for all his comfort in wielding the mighty resources and instruments of power which a president of a great and imperial republic has at his constitutionally limited disposal, Mr. Nixon liked to look good before a crowd.[4] He had learned well to make the most of the majesty that the modern American presidency provides. Quite possibly, '[i]f asked to draw a freehand sketch of their president, most modern Americans would begin with a podium'.[5] Many American presidents have enjoyed the ceremonial power of their office. So, for example, 'under Kennedy's tutelage, Johnson learned that people behave especially well during ceremonies, that they quickly defer to the individual conducting the ritual . . . [K]nowing these things, Johnson ceremonialized constantly.'[6] This habit is now all the more firmly entrenched, with elaborate and emblazoned slogans the backdrop to the man offering sound-bites at his podium. In coverage of politicians and political events, the majority of American televised news reports have close-ups of politicians' faces.[7] Citizens have the opportunity to enter into some sort of aesthetic and emotional relationship with political principals. Ultimately the sentiments so generated greatly affect voting.

It may often be a refrain of contemporary political critique that style seems to overshadow substance in republics or democracies. But perhaps it has always been like that. If to be a Greek or Roman citizen was in some measure to have dignity in

[3] He commanded bulldozers to destroy forty thousand buildings in Bucharest, to make space for the five hundred foot-wide boulevard of Victory of Socialism leading to an enormous personal palace 'so big (its reception area is the size of a soccer field), so ugly, so heavy and cruel and tasteless, that its only possible value is metaphorical' (Judt 2001: 44).

[4] Haldeman 1994: *passim*. [5] Hart 1987: 1. [6] Ibid. 26.

[7] Hart 1994: 38. The issues stressed in electoral campaigns, and reported upon the most popular television news programmes, are usually few. According to Kahn and Kenney (1999: 238), US Senatorial candidates on average make issues the fundamental focus of their advertisements only 36 per cent of the time; they typically only discuss two issues during a campaign.

being a political consumer entitled to expect a good spectacle, study of classical politics has the power to offer insight into habits of consumption and affection, scrutiny and judgement. If rhetorics of visibility fix the models and memories of individual power, then we may all wonder at the capacity of even the humble to realize power in their cheers or jeers; and so enjoy liberal dignity.

# REFERENCES


Abbott, F. F. (1907), 'The Theatre as a Factor in Roman Politics', *Transactions of the American Philological Association* 38: 49–56.

Adcock, F. E. (1953), 'Greek and Macedonian Kingship', *Proceedings of the British Academy* 39: 163–80.

——(1959), *Roman Political Ideas and Practice*. Ann Arbor, Mich.

Adkins, W. (1960), *Merit and Responsibility*. Oxford.

Ahl, F. (1976), *Lucan: An Introduction*. Ithaca, NY.

Allen, W. Jr. (1938), 'On the Importance of Young Men in Ciceronian Politics', *Classical Journal* 33: 357–9.

Althusser, L. (1971), 'Ideology and Ideological State Apparatuses', in *Lenin and Philosophy and other Essays*. London: 127–86.

Anderson, J. K. (1985), *Hunting in the Ancient World*. Berkeley, Calif.

Andrewes, A. (1956), *The Greek Tyrants*. London.

——(1962), 'The Mytilene Debate: Thucydides 3.36–49', *Phoenix* 16: 64–85.

Arendt, Hannah (1958), *The Human Condition*. Chicago.

Asad, Talal (1983), 'Anthropological Conceptions of Religion: Reflections on Geertz', *Man* 18: 237–59.

——(1993), *Genealogies of Religion: Discipline and Reasons of Power in Christianity and Islam*. Baltimore.

Astin, A. E. (1967), *Scipio Aemilianus*. Oxford.

——(1988), '*Regimen Morum*', *Journal of Roman Studies* 78: 14–34.

——(1989), 'Roman Government and Politics 200–134 BC', *Cambridge Ancient History* (2nd edn.). Cambridge: viii. 8.

Atkinson, Max (1984), *Our Masters' Voices: The Language and Body Language of Politics*. London.

Austin, M. M. (1986), 'Hellenistic Kings, War and the Economy', *Classical Quarterly* 36: 451–8.

Aymard, Jacques (1951), *Essai sur les chasses romaines des origines à la fin du siècle des Antonins*. Paris.

Bagehot, Walter (1963) [1867], *The English Constitution*. Ithaca, NY.

Balsdon, J. P. V. D. (1969), *Life and Leisure in Ancient Rome*. New York.

BARRY, WILLIAM D. (1993), 'The Crowd of Ptolemaic Alexandria and the Riot of 203 B.C.', *Echos du Monde Classique/Classical Views* 37: 415–31.

BARTON, CARLIN A. (1993), *The Sorrows of the Ancient Romans: The Gladiator and the Monster*. Princeton.

BARTSCH, SHADI (1994), *Actors in the Audience: Theatricality and Doublespeak from Nero to Hadrian*. Cambridge, Mass.

BASSI, KAREN (1998), *Acting Like Men: Gender, Drama, and Nostalgia in Ancient Greece*. Ann Arbor.

BAYER, ERICH (1969), *Demetrios Phalereus der Athener*. Darmstadt.

BEACHAM, RICHARD C. (1999), *Spectacle Entertainments of Early Imperial Rome*. New Haven.

BEAGON, MARY (1992), *Roman Nature: The Thought of Pliny the Elder*. Oxford.

BEARD, MARY, and NORTH, JOHN (eds.) (1990), *Pagan Priests*. London.

BEARD, MARY, NORTH, JOHN, and PRICE, SIMON (1998), *Religions of Rome*, i. *A History*. Cambridge.

BELL, ANDREW J. E. (1999), 'The Popular Poetics and Politics of the *Aeneid*', *Transactions of the American Philological Association* 129: 263–79.

BELL, CATHERINE (1992), *Ritual Theory, Ritual Practice*. New York.

BENEVISTE, E. (1973), *Indo-European Language and Society*. Miami.

BERS, V. (1985), '*Thorubos*', in Cartledge and Harvey 1985: 1–15.

BERTRANDY, FRANÇOIS (1987), 'Remarques sur le commerce des bêtes sauvages entre l'Afrique du Nord et l'Italie', *Mélanges d'archéologie et d'histoire de l'École française de Rome* 99: 211–41.

BEST, STEVEN (1994), 'The Commodification of Reality and the Reality of Commodification: Baudrillard, Debord, and Postmodern Theory', in Douglas Kellner (ed.), *Baudrillard: A Critical Reader*. Oxford: 41–67.

BIERSACK, ALETTA (1989), 'Local Knowledge, Local History: Geertz and Beyond', in Hunt 1989: 72–96.

BIKERMAN, ELIE (1938), *Institutions des Séleucides*. Paris.

BILLOWS, RICHARD A. (1990), *Antigonos the One-Eyed and the Creation of the Hellenistic State*. Berkeley.

BLASS, F. (1962), *Die Attische Beredsamkeit*, ii (reprint). Hildesheim.

BLEICKEN, JOCHEN (1981), 'Die Nobilität der römischen Republik', *Gymnasium* 88: 236–53.

BLOEDOW, EDMUND F. (1990), '*Not the Son of Achilles, but Achilles himself:* Alcibiades' Entry on the Political Stage at Athens II', *Historia* 39: 1–19.

BLOEDOW, EDMUND F. (1992), 'Alcibiades "brilliant" or "intelligent"?', *Historia* 41: 139–57.

BOLLINGER, TRAUGOTT (1969), *Theatralis Licentia. Die Publikumsdemonstrationem an den öffentlichen Spielen im Rom der früheren Kaiserzeit und ihre Bedeutung im politischen Leben*. Winterthur.

BONNEFOND, MARIANNE (1983), 'Espace, Temps et Idéologie: le sénat dans la cité Romaine républicaine', *Dialoghi di Archeologia* 3: 37–44.

BOORSTIN, DANIEL J. (1962), *The Image*. New York.

BORZA, EUGENE N. (1983), 'The Symposium at Alexander's Court', *Ancient Macedonia* 3: 45–55.

——(1990), *In The Shadow Of Olympus: The Emergence of Macedon*. Princeton.

BOSWORTH, A. B. (1988), *Conquest and Empire: The Reign of Alexander the Great*. Cambridge.

BOURDIEU, PIERRE (1975), 'Note sur les conditions sociales de l'efficacité du discours rituel', *Actes de la Recherche en Science Sociales* 5–6: 183–90.

——(1977), *Outline of a Theory of Practice*. Cambridge.

——(1984), *Distinction: A Social Critique of the Judgement of Taste*. London.

——(1990), *The Logic of Practice*. Stanford, Calif.

——(1992), 'Doxa and Common Life', *New Left Review* 191: 111–21.

BOWRA, C. M. (1960), 'Euripides' Epinician for Alcibiades', *Historia* 9: 68–79.

——(1964), *Pindar*. Oxford.

BRAUDEL, F. (1973), *Capitalism and Material Life 1400–1800*. New York.

BRAUDY, LEO (1986), *The Frenzy of Renown: Fame and its History*. New York.

BREMMER, JAN, and ROODENBURG, HERMAN (eds.) (1991), *A Cultural History of Gesture*. Cambridge.

BRENDEL, O. (1979), *Prolegomena to the Study of Roman Art*. New Haven.

BRILLIANT, R. (1963), *Gesture and Rank in Roman Art*. New Haven.

BRISCOE, JOHN (1982), Review of Greenhalgh (1980) and Seager (1979), *Journal of Roman Studies* 72: 184–5.

BROOKHISER, RICHARD (1996), *Founding Father: Rediscovering George Washington*. New York.

BROUGHTON, T. R. S. (1972), 'Senate and Senators of the Roman Republic: The Prosopographical Tradition', *Aufstieg und Niedergang der römischen Welt* I 1. 250–65.

BRUNT, P. A. (1952), 'Thucydides and Alcibiades', *Revue des études grecques* 65: 59–96.

——(1961), Review of V. Ehrenberg, *The Greek State. Classical Review* 11: 143–4.

——(1966), 'The Roman Mob', *Past & Present* 35: 3–27.

——(1968), Review of Meier 1966, *Journal of Roman Studies* 58: 229–32.

——(1971), *Social Conflicts in the Roman Republic*. New York.

——(1978), '*Laus imperii*', in P. D. A. Garnsey and C. R. Whittaker (eds.), *Imperialism in the Ancient World*. Cambridge: 159–91.

——(1988), *The Fall of the Roman Republic*. Oxford.

——and MOORE, J. M. (1967), *Res Gestae Divi Augusti*. Oxford.

BULL, PETER E. (1987), *Posture and Gesture*. Oxford.

BULLOCH, ANTHONY, GRUEN, ERICH S., LONG, A. A., and STEWART, ANDREW (eds.) (1993), *Images and Ideologies: Self-Definition in the Hellenistic World*. Berkeley, Calif.

BULLOCK, ALAN (1992), *Hitler and Stalin: Parallel Lives*. New York.

BURCKHARDT, L. A. (1988), *Politische Strategien der Optimaten in der späten römischen Republik*. Stuttgart.

——(1990), 'The Political Elite of the Roman Republic: Comments on Recent Discussion of the Concepts *Nobilitas* and *Homo Novus*', *Historia* 39: 77–99.

BURKERT, WALTER (1983), *Homo Necans*. Berkeley, Calif.

——(1985), *Greek Religion*. Cambridge, Mass.

BUSH, BARBARA (1994), *Barbara Bush: A Memoir*. New York.

BUXTON, RICHARD (1994), *Imaginary Greece: The Contexts of Mythology*. Cambridge.

CAIRNS, FRANCIS (1982), 'Cleon and Pericles: A Suggestion', *Journal of Hellenic Studies* 102: 203–4.

——(1989), *Virgil's Augustan Epic*. Cambridge.

CALHOUN, GEORGE MILLER (1913), *Athenian Clubs in Politics and Litigation*. Austin, Tex.

CALINESCU, MATEI, and TISMANEANU, VLADIMIR (1992), 'The 1989 Revolution and Romania's Future', in Daniel N. Nelson (ed.), *Romania After Tyranny*. Boulder, Colo.: 11–44.

CAMPBELL, DAVID A. (1992), *Greek Lyric*, iv. Cambridge, Mass.

CAMERON, ALAN (1976), *Circus Factions*. Oxford.

CANNADINE, DAVID (1987*a*), 'Introduction' to Cannadine and Price 1987*b*: 1–19.

——and PRICE, S. R. F. (eds.) (1987*b*), *Rituals of Royalty*. Cambridge.

CAREY, CHRISTOPHER (1994), 'Comic Ridicule and Democracy', in Osborne and Hornblower 1994: 69–83.

CARNEY, T. F. (1955), 'Once Again Marius' Speech after Election in 108 B.C.', *Symbolae Osloenses* 35: 63–70.

——(1960), 'Cicero's Picture of Marius', *Wiener Studien* 73: 83–122.

——(1975), *The Shape of the Past: Models and Antiquity*. Lawrence, Kan.

CARTER, L. B. (1986), *The Quiet Athenian*. Oxford.

CARTLEDGE, P. A. (1987), *Agesilaos*. London.

——and HARVEY, F. D. (eds.) (1985), *Crux: Essays Presented to G.E.M. de Ste. Croix on his 75th Birthday*. Exeter.

——MILLETT, PAUL, and VON REDEN, SITTA (eds.) (1998), *Kosmos: Essays in Order, Conflict and Community in Classical Athens*. Cambridge.

CEAUSESCU, NICOLAE (1987), *An Independent Foreign Policy for Peace and Cooperation*. Washington, DC.

CÈBE, J.-P. (1960), 'Le niveau culturel du public Plautinien', *Revue des études latines* 38: 101–6.

CHARTIER, ROGER (1997), *On the Edge of the Cliff: History, Language, and Practices* (trans. L. G. Cochrane). Baltimore.

CLAUSEN, W. (1964), 'An Interpretation of the *Aeneid*', *Harvard Studies in Classical Philology* 48: 139–47.

CLAVEL-LÉVÊQUE, M. (1984), *L'Empire en jeux: espace symbolique et pratique sociale dans le monde Romain*. Paris.

CLINTON, KEVIN (1974), *The Sacred Officials of the Eleusinian Mysteries*. Transactions of the American Philosophical Society 64, part 3. Philadelphia.

CODRESCU, ANDREI (1991), *The Hole in the Flag: a Romanian Exile's Story of Return and Revolution*. New York.

COHEN, ABNER (1969), 'Political Anthropology: The Analysis of the Symbolism of Power Relations', *Man* 4: 215–35.

——(1981), *The Politics of Elite Culture: Explorations in the Dramaturgy of Power in a Modern African Society*. Berkeley, Calif.

COLE, THOMAS (1964), 'The Sources and Composition of Polybius VI', *Historia* 13: 440–86.

COLEMAN, K. M. (1996), 'Ptolemy Philadelphus and the Roman Amphitheater', in Slater 1996: 49–68.

CONNOR, W. R. (1968), *Theopompus and Fifth-Century Athens*. Washington, DC.

——(1971), *The New Politicians of Fifth-Century Athens*. Princeton.

Connor, W. R. (1984), *Thucydides*. Princeton.
——(1986), 'The New Classical Humanities and the Old', *Classical Journal* 81: 337–47.
——(1987), 'Tribes, Festivals, and Processions: Civic Ceremonial and Political Manipulation in Archaic Greece', *Journal of Hellenic Studies* 107: 40–50.
——(1996), 'Civil Society, Dionysiac Festival, and the Athenian Democracy', in Ober and Hedrick 1996: 217–26.
Corbeill, Anthony (1996), *Controlling Laughter: Political Humor in the Late Roman Republic*. Princeton.
Cornell, Timothy J. (1991), 'Rome: The History of an Anachronism', in Molho, Raaflaub, and Emlen 1991: 53–69.
Cornford, F. M. (1907), *Thucydides Mythistoricus*. London.
Crawford, M. (1974), *RRC* = *Roman Republican Coinage* (2 vols.). Cambridge.
Crossley, Nick (1995), 'Merleau-Ponty, the Elusive Body and Carnal Sociology', *Body & Society* 1: 43–63.
Crotty, K. (1982), *Song and Action: The Victory Odes of Pindar*. Baltimore.
Crowther, N. B. (1985), 'Male "Beauty" Contests in Greece: The Euandria and Euexia', *L'Antiquité classique* 54: 285–91.
Cullen, Robert (1990), 'Report from Romania: down with the tyrant', *New Yorker* (April 2): 94–112.
D'Arms, J. D. (1984), 'Control, Companionship, and Clientela: Some Functions of the Roman Communal Meal', *Echos du Monde Classique/Classical Views* 3: 327–48.
Davidson, James (1991), 'The Gaze in Polybius' *Histories*', *Journal of Roman Studies* 81: 10–24.
——(1993), 'Fish, Sex and Revolution in Athens', *CQ* 43: 53–66.
——(1997), *Courtesans and Fishcakes: The Consuming Passions of Classical Athens*. London.
Davies, J. K. (1971), *Athenian Propertied Families 606–300 B.C.* Oxford.
——(1981), *Wealth and the Power of Wealth in Classical Athens*. Salem, NH.
——(1984), 'Cultural, Social and Economic Features of the Hellenistic World', in *The Cambridge Ancient History* (2nd edn.), 7.1. Cambridge.
——(1992), 'Greece After The Persian Wars', in *The Cambridge Ancient History* (2nd edn.), 5.2. Cambridge.
Davison, J. A. (1958), 'Notes on the Panathenaea', *Journal of Hellenic Studies* 78: 23–41.
Debord, G. (1983), *Society of the Spectacle*. Detroit.

De Lacy, Phillip (1952), 'Biography and Tragedy in Plutarch', *American Journal of Philology* 73: 159–71.

Detienne, M. (1989), 'Culinary Practices and the Spirit of Sacrifice', in M. Detienne and J.-P. Vernant (eds.), *The Cuisine of Sacrifice among the Greeks*. Chicago: 1–20.

Deubner, L. (1932), *Attische Feste*. Berlin.

Deutsch, Monroe E. (1924), 'The Apparatus of Caesar's Triumphs', *Philological Quarterly* 3: 257–66.

Develin, R. (1985), *The Practice of Politics at Rome 366–167 B.C.* Brussels.

Dihle, Albrecht (1993), 'Response' to Part IV of Bulloch *et al.* 1993.

Donlan, Walter (1979), 'The Structure of Authority in the Iliad', *Arethusa* 12: 51–70.

——(1980), *The Aristocratic Ideal in Ancient Greece: Attitudes of Superiority from Homer to the End of the Fifth Century B.C.* Lawrence, Kan.

Dougherty, Carol, and Kurke, Leslie (eds.) (1993), *Cultural Poetics in Archaic Greece: Cult, Performance, Politics*. Cambridge.

Dover, K. J. (1972), *Aristophanic Comedy*. Berkeley, Calif.

——(1974), *Greek Popular Morality in the Time of Plato and Aristotle*. Oxford.

——(1993), Aristophanes *Frogs*. Oxford.

——(1994), *Marginal Comment: A Memoir*. London.

Drews, Robert (1983), *Basileus: The Evidence for Kingship in Geometric Greece*. New Haven.

Dreyfus, Hubert L., and Rabinow, Paul (1982), *Michel Foucault: Beyond Structuralism and Hermeneutics*. Chicago.

Dupont, F. (1985), *L'Acteur-roi, ou le théâtre dans la Rome antique*. Paris.

Durand, Jean-Louis (1989), 'Greek Animals: Towards a Topology of Edible Bodies', in Detienne and Vernant 1989: 87–118.

Durkheim, Emile (1995) [1912], *The Elementary Forms of Religious Life* (trans. Karen E. Fields). New York.

Dyson, Stephen L. (1991), *Society in Roman Italy*. Baltimore.

Eagleton, Terry (1990), *The Ideology of the Aesthetic*. Oxford.

Earl, Donald (1961), *The Political Thought of Sallust*. Cambridge.

——(1967), *The Moral and Political Tradition of Rome*. Ithaca, NY.

Eck, W. (1984), 'Senatorial Self-representation: Developments in the Augustan Period', in F. Millar and E. Segal (eds.), *Caesar Augustus*. Oxford: 129–67.

Edelman, Murray (1988), *Constructing the Political Spectacle*. Chicago.

EDMONDSON, J. C. (1996), 'Dynamic Arenas: Gladiatorial Presentations in the City of Rome and the Construction of Roman Society during the Early Empire', in Slater 1996: 113–28.

EDMUNDS, LOWELL (1971), 'The Religiosity of Alexander', *Greek, Roman and Byzantine Studies* 12: 363–91.

EDWARDS, CATHERINE (1993), *The Politics of Immorality in Ancient Rome*. Cambridge.

EDWARDS, MARK W. (1987), *Homer: Poet of the Iliad*. Baltimore.

EISENHUT, W. (1973), *Virtus romana: ihre Stellung im romischen Wertsystem*. Munich.

ELIAS, NORBERT (1978), *The Civilizing Process*, i. *The History of Manners* (trans. E. Jephcott). New York.

ELLIS, WALTER M. (1989), *Alcibiades*. London.

ELLUL, JACQUES (1965), *Propaganda* (trans. K. Kellen and J. Lerner). New York.

——(1973), *Propaganda*. New York.

ELSTER, JON (1991), 'The Possibility of Rational Politics', in David Held (ed.), *Political Theory Today*. Stanford: 115–42.

ERRINGTON, R. MALCOLM (1990), *A History of Macedonia*. Berkeley, Calif.

ÉTIENNE, R. (1965), 'La naissance de l'amphithéâtre: le mot et la chose', *Revue des Études Latines* 43: 213–22.

FAVRO, DIANE (1996), *The Urban Image of Augustan Rome*. Cambridge.

FEARS, J. RUFUS (1981*a*), 'The Theology of Victory at Rome', *Aufstieg und Niedergang der römischen Welt* II 17.2: 736–826.

——(1981*b*), 'The Cult of Virtues and Roman Imperial Ideology', *Aufstieg und Niedergang der römischen Welt* II 17.2: 827–948.

FEAVER, DOUGLAS D. (1957), 'Historical Development in the Priesthoods of Athens', *Yale Classical Studies* 15: 123–58.

FERGUSON, WILLIAM SCOTT (1911), *Hellenistic Athens: an Historical Essay*. London.

FINLEY, M. I. (1962), 'Athenian Demagogues', *Past and Present* 21: 3–24.

——(1973), *Democracy Ancient and Modern*. New Brunswick.

——(1977), 'The Ancient City: from Fustel de Coulanges to Max Weber and Beyond', *Comparative Studies in the Study of Society and History* 19: 305–27.

——(1978), *The World of Odysseus* (rev. edn.). Harmondsworth and New York.

——(1979), *The World of Odysseus* (rev. edn.). Harmondsworth.

——(1982), *Authority and Legitimacy in the Classical City-State*. Copenhagen.

FINLEY, M. I. (1983), *Politics in the Ancient World*. Cambridge.
——(1987), *Ancient History: Evidence and Models*. Harmondsworth.
FIRTH, RAYMOND (1973), *Symbols Public and Private*. Ithaca, NY.
FISCHER, MARY ELLEN (1989), *Nicolae Ceausescu. A Study in Political Leadership*. Boulder, Colo.
FISHWICK, DUNCAN (1987), *The Imperial Cult in the Latin West*, i.1. Leiden.
FLIEGELMAN, JAY (1993), *Declaring Independence: Jefferson, Natural Language, and the Culture of Performance*. Stanford, Calif.
FLOWER, HARRIET I. (1996), *Ancestor Masks and Aristocratic Power in Roman Culture*. Oxford.
FOERTMEYER, VICTORIA (1988), 'The Dating of the Pompe of Ptolemy II Philadelphus', *Historia* 37: 90–104.
FONTENROSE, J. (1968), 'The Hero as Athlete', *California Studies in Classical Antiquity* 1: 73–104.
FORDE, STEVEN (1989), *The Ambition to Rule: Alcibiades and the Politics of Imperialism in Thucydides*. Ithaca, NY.
FORNARA, CHARLES W. (1971), *The Athenian Board of Generals from 501–404*. Stuttgart.
——(1983), *The Nature of History in Ancient Greece and Rome*. Berkeley, Calif.
FOUCAULT, M. (1978), *History of Sexuality*, i (trans. R. Huxley). New York.
——(1980), *Power/Knowledge*. New York.
——(1986), *The Care of the Self*. New York.
FRASER, P. M. (1972), *Ptolemaic Alexandria* (3 vols.). Oxford.
FRÉZOULS, E. (1983*a*), 'La construction du *theatrum lapideum* et son contexte politique', in *Théâtre et Spectacles dans L'Antiquité: Actes du Colloque de Strasbourg, 5–7 November 1981*. Strasbourg.
——(1983*b*), 'Le Théâtre Romain et la culture urbaine', in *La città antica come fatto di cultura*. Como: 105–30.
FRIEDRICH, CARL J. (1961), 'Political Leadership and the Problem of Charismatic Power', *Journal of Politics* 23: 3–24.
FROST, F. J. (1981), 'Politics in Early Athens', in *Classical Contributions: Studies in Honour of Malcolm Francis McGregor*. Locust Valley: 33–40.
GALINSKY, KARL (1996), *Augustan Culture: An Interpretive Introduction*. Princeton.
GARGOLA, DANIEL J. (1995), *Lands, Laws, and Gods: Magistrates and Ceremony in the Regulation of Public Lands in Republican Rome*. Chapel Hill, NC.

GARLAND, R. S. J. (1984), 'Religious Authority in Archaic and Classical Athens', *Annual of the British School at Athens* 79: 75–123.

GARTON, CHARLES (1972), *Personal Aspects of the Roman Theatre*. Toronto.

GEDDES, A. G. (1984), 'Who's Who in Homeric Society', *Classical Quarterly* 34: 17–36.

——(1987), 'Rags and Riches: The Costume of Athenian Men in the Fifth Century', *Classical Quarterly* 37: 307–31.

GEERTZ, CLIFFORD (1965), *The Social History of an Indonesian Town*. Cambridge, Mass.

——(1973), *The Interpretation of Cultures*. New York.

——(1977), 'Centers, Kings and Charisma: Reflections on the Symbolics of Power', in J. Ben-David and T. Nichols Clark (eds.), *Culture and its Creators*. Chicago: 150–71.

——(1980), *Negara: The Theatre State in Nineteenth Century Bali*. Princeton.

GELZER, MATTHIAS (1968), *Caesar: Politician and Statesman* (trans. P. Needham). Cambridge, Mass.

——(1969), *The Roman Nobility* (trans. R. Seager). Oxford.

GEORGES, PERICLES (1993), 'Review Article: Athenian Democracy and Athenian Empire', *The International History Review* 15: 84–105.

GERGEN, KENNETH J. (1996), 'Technology and the Self: From the Essential to the Sublime', in D. Grodin and T. R. Lindlof (eds.), *Constructing the Self in a Mediated World*. Thousand Oaks, Calif: 127–40.

GIGANTE, M. (1979), *Civiltà delle forme letterarie nell'antica Pompei*. Naples.

GILL, CHRISTOPHER, POSTLETHWAITE, NORMAN, and SEAFORD, RICHARD (eds.) (1998), *Reciprocity in Ancient Greece*. Oxford.

GLEASON, M. W. (1995), *Making Men: Sophists and self-presentation in ancient Rome*. Princeton.

GOFFMAN, E. (1959), *The Presentation of the Self in Everyday Life*. New York.

——(1963), *Behaviour in Public Places: Notes on the Social Organization of Gatherings*. New York.

GOLDBERG, SANDER M. (1995), *Epic in Republican Rome*. New York.

GOLDHILL, S. (1987), 'The City Dionysia and Civic Ideology', *Journal of Hellenic Studies* 107: 58–76.

——(1998), 'The Seductions of the Gaze: Socrates and his Girlfriends', in P. Cartledge *et al.* 1998: 105–24.

——(1999), 'Programme Notes', in Goldhill and Osborne 1999: 1–29.

GOLDHILL, S., and OSBORNE, ROBIN (eds.) (1999), *Performance Culture and Athenian Democracy*. Cambridge.

GOMME, A. W. *HCT = A Historical Commentary on Thucydides*. i (1945); ii (1956). Oxford.

—— ANDREWES, A., and DOVER, K. J. (1970), *HCT = A Historical Commentary on Thucydides*, iv. Oxford.

GOODE, WILLIAM J. (1978), *The Celebration of Heroes: Prestige as a Social Control System*. Berkeley, Calif.

GOODY, J. (1961), 'Religion and Ritual: the Definitional Problem', *British Journal of Sociology* 12: 142–64.

GORDON, R. L. (1979), 'The Real and the Imaginary: Production and Religion in the Graeco-Roman World', *Art History* 2: 5–34.

—— (1990), 'The Veil of Power', in M. Beard and J. North (eds.), *Pagan Priests*. London: 199–234.

GOTOFF, H. C. (1979), *Cicero's Elegant Style: An Analysis of the* Pro Archia. Chapel Hill, NC.

GOW, A. S. F. (1965), *Theocritus* (2 vols.). Cambridge.

GRAF, FRITZ (1991), 'Gestures and Conventions: The Gestures of Roman Actors and Orators', in Bremmer and Roodenburg 1991: 36–58.

GRANT, MICHAEL (1982), *From Alexander to Cleopatra*. London.

GREEN, PETER (1978), 'Caesar and Alexander: *Aemulatio, Imitatio, Comparatio*', *American Journal of Ancient History* 3: 1–26.

—— (1990), *Alexander to Actium: The Historical Evolution of the Hellenistic Age*. Berkeley, Calif.

GREENFIELD, L. (1985), 'Reflections on the Two Charismas', *British Journal of Sociology* 36: 117–32.

GREENHALGH, PETER (1980), *Pompey: The Roman Alexander*. London.

GREENIDGE, A. H. J., and CLAY, A. M. (1960), *Sources for Roman History 133–70 B.C.* (2nd edn.). Oxford.

GREENWALT, WILLIAM (1986), 'Macedonia's Kings and the Political Usefulness of the Medical Arts', *Ancient Macedonia* 4: 213–22.

GRIBBLE, DAVID (1999), *Alcibiades and Athens: A Study in Literary Presentation*. Oxford.

GRIFFIN, JASPER (1980), *Homer on Life and Death*. Oxford.

—— (1985), *Latin Poets and Roman Life*. London.

—— (1998), Review of Meier 1998. *New York Times Review of Books*, 11 October: 33.

GRIFFITH, MARK (1985), 'What Does Aeneas Look Like?', *Classical Philology* 80: 309–19.

—— (1995), 'Brilliant Dynasts: Power and Politics in the *Oresteia*', *Classical Antiquity* 14: 62–129.

GRIMAL, M. P. (1975), 'Le Théâtre à Rome', in *Actes du IXe Congrès Budé 9(1): April 1973*. Paris: 249–305.

GRUEN, ERICH S. (1990), *Studies in Greek Culture and Roman Policy*. Leiden.

——(1991), 'The Exercise of Power in the Roman Republic', in Molho, Raaflaub, and Emlen 1991: 251–67.

——(1992), *Culture and National Identity in Republican Rome*. Ithaca, NY.

——(1995), 'The "Fall" of the Scipios', in Malkin and Rubinsohn 1995: 59–90.

——(1996), 'The Roman Oligarchy: Image and Perception', in J. Linderski (ed.), *Imperium Sine Fine*. Stuttgart: 215–34.

HABICHT, CHRISTIAN (1970), *Gottmenschentum und Griechische Stadte* (2nd edn.). Munich.

——(1989), 'The Seleucids and their rivals', in *Cambridge Ancient History* (2nd edn.). Cambridge: viii: 324–87.

——(1997), *Athens from Alexander to Antony* (trans. D. L. Schneider). Cambridge, Mass.

HADLEY, ROBERT A. (1964), *Deified Kingship and Propaganda Coinage in the Early Hellenistic Age: 323–280 B.C.* Dissertation, University of Pennsylvania.

HALDEMAN, H. R. (1994), *The Haldeman Diaries: Inside the Nixon White House*. New York.

HAMEL, DEBRA (1995), '*Stategoi* on the *Bema*: The Separation of Political and Military Authority in Fourth-Century Athens', *Ancient History Bulletin* 9: 25–39.

HAMMOND, N. G. L. (1985), 'Some Macedonian Offices c.336–309BC', *Journal of Hellenic Studies* 105: 156–60.

——(1989), *The Macedonian State*. Oxford.

——and GRIFFITH, G. T. (1979), *A History of Macedonia*. Oxford.

HANDELMAN, DON (1990), *Models and Mirrors: Towards an Anthropology of Public Events*. Cambridge.

HANSEN, MOGENS H. (1987), *The Athenian Assembly in the Age of Demosthenes*. Oxford.

——(1989), 'On the Importance of Institutions in an Analysis of Athenian Democracy', *C&M* 40: 101–13.

——(1991), *The Athenian Democracy in the Age of Demosthenes*. Oxford.

——(1994), 'The 2500th Anniversary of Cleisthenes' Reforms and the Tradition of Athenian Democracy', in Osborne and Hornblower 1994: 25–37.

HANSON, J. A. (1959), *Roman Theater-Temples*. Princeton.

HARDING, PHILLIP (1994), *Androtion and the Atthis*. Oxford.

HARIMAN, ROBERT (1995), *Political Style: The Artistry of Power*. Chicago.

HARRIS, W. V. (1979), *War and Imperialism in Republican Rome 327–70 B.C.* Oxford.

——(1989), *Ancient Literacy*. Cambridge, Mass.

——(1990), 'On Defining the Political Culture of the Roman Republic: Some Comments on Rosenstein, Williamson, and North', *Classical Philology* 85: 288–94.

HARRISON, MARK (1988), *Crowds and History: Mass Phenomena in English Towns, 1790–1835*. Cambridge.

HART, RODERICK P. (1987), *The Sound of Leadership: Presidential Communication in the Modern Age*. Chicago.

——(1994), *Seducing America: How Television Charms the Modern Voter*. New York.

HATCH, ELVIN (1989), 'Theories of Social Honor', *American Anthropologist* 91: 341–53.

HATZFELD, JEAN (1940), *Alcibiade: Étude sur l'histoire d'Athènes à la fin du Ve siècle*. Paris.

HELLEGOUARCH, J. (1963), *Le Vocabulaire Latin des relations et des partis politiques sous la République*. Paris.

HERZOG, R. (1928), *Heilige Gesetze von Kos = Abandlungen der preussischen Akademie der Wissenschaften* 6. Berlin.

HOLDEN, H. A. (1895), *Commentary on Xenophon's* Oeconomicus. London.

HÖLKESKAMP, KARL-J. (1993), 'Conquest, Competition and Consensus: Roman Expansion in Italy and the Rise of the *Nobilitas*', *Historia* 42: 12–39.

HÖLSCHER, TONIO (1991), 'The City of Athens: Space, Symbol, Structure', in Molho, Raaflaub, and Emlen 1991.

HOPKINS, KEITH (ed.) (1983), *Death and Renewal*. Cambridge.

——(1991), 'From Violence to Blessing: Symbols and Rituals in Ancient Rome', in Molho, Raaflaub, and Emlen 1991: 479–97.

——and BURTON, GRAHAM (1983), 'Political Succession in the Late Republic (249–50 B.C.)', in Hopkins 1983: 31–119.

HORNBLOWER, JANE (1981), *Hieronymus of Cardia*. Oxford.

HORNBLOWER, SIMON (1987), *Thucydides*. Baltimore.

——(1991), *A Commentary on Thucydides*, vol 1. Oxford.

HOW, W. W. (1926), *Cicero: Select Letters*. Oxford.

HUBBELL, HARRY M. (1935), 'Ptolemy's Zoo', *Classical Journal* 31: 68–76.

HUIZINGA, J. (1950), *Homo Ludens*. Boston.

HUMPHREYS, S. C. (1993), *The Family, Women and Death: Comparative Studies* (2nd edn.). Ann Arbor, Mich.

Hunt, Lynn (ed.) (1989), *The New Cultural History*. Berkeley, Calif.

Jacoby, F. (1944*a*), '*Patrios Nomos*', *Journal of Hellenic Studies* 64: 37–67.

——(1944*b*), '*ΓΕΝΕΣΙΑ*, A Forgotten Festival of the Dead', *Classical Quarterly* 38: 65–75.

——(1949), *Atthis*. Oxford.

——(1954), *FGrHist = Die Fragmente der griechischen historiker*. Leiden.

Jameson, M. H. (1965), 'Notes on the Sacrificial Calendar from Erchia', *Bulletin de Correspondance Hellénique* 89: 154–72.

——(1999), 'The Spectacular and the Obscure in Athenian Religion', in Goldhill and Osborne 1999: 321–40.

Jamieson, Kathleen Hall (1992), *Packaging the Presidency: A History and Criticism of Presidential Campaign Advertising*. 2nd edn. New York.

Jebb, R. C. (1973), 'The Speeches of Thucydides', in *The Speeches of Thucydides* ed. H. F. Harding. Lawrence.

Jennison, George (1937), *Animals for Show and Pleasure in Ancient Rome*. Manchester.

Johnson, W. R. (1987), *Momentary Monsters: Lucan and his Heroes*. Ithaca, NY.

Johnstone, Steven (1994), 'Virtuous Toil, Vicious Work: Xenophon on Aristocratic Style', *CP* 89: 219–40.

Jones, C. P. (1971), *Plutarch and Rome*. Oxford.

Jonkers, E. J. (1963), *Social and Economic Commentary on Cicero's* De Lege Agraria Orationes Tres. Leiden.

Judt, Tony (2001), 'Romania: Bottom of the Heap', *The New York Review of Books*, 1 November: 41–5.

Kagan, Donald (1981), *The Peace of Nicias and the Sicilian Expedition*. Ithaca, NY.

Kahn, Kim Fridkin, and Kenney, Patrick J. (1999), *The Spectacle of U.S. Senate Campaigns*. Princeton.

Kallet-Marx, Lisa (1994), 'Institutions, Ideology, and Political Consciousness in Ancient Greece: Some Recent Books on Athenian Democracy', *Journal of the History of Ideas* 55: 307–35.

Kaplan, Alice, and Ross, Kristin (1987), Introduction to *Yale French Studies* 73: 1–4.

Kaufmann, Walter (ed.) (1967), *Friedrich Nietzsche: On The Genealogy of Morals and Ecce Homo*. New York.

Kearns, Emily (1985), 'Change and Continuity in Religious Structures after Cleisthenes', in Cartledge and Harvey 1985: 189–207.

——(1989), *The Heroes of Attica*. London.

Kennedy, G. (1963), *The Art of Persuasion in Greece*. Princeton.

——(1972), *The Art of Rhetoric in the Roman World 300 B.C.–A.D. 300*. Princeton.

Kershaw, Ian (1987), *The 'Hitler Myth': Image and Reality in the Third Reich*. Oxford.

Kertzer, David I. (1988), *Ritual, Politics and Power*. New Haven.

Kirk, G. S. (1985), The Iliad: *A Commentary on Books 1–4*. Cambridge.

Knoche, Ulrich (1934), 'Der römische Ruhmesgedanke', *Philologus* 43: 104–24.

Knox, Bernard M. W. (1964), *The Heroic Temper: Studies in Sophoclean Tragedy*. Berkeley.

Koenen, Ludwig (1993), 'The Ptolemaic King as a Religious Figure', in Bulloch *et al.* 1993.

Kurke, Leslie (1991), *The Traffic in Praise: Pindar and the Poetics of Social Economy*. Ithaca: 94.

——(1993), 'The Economy of *Kudos*', in Dougherty and Kurke 1993: 131–63.

——(1999), *Coins, Bodies, Games, and Gold: The Politics of Meaning in Archaic Greece*. Princeton.

Kyle, Donald G. (1993), *Athletics in Ancient Athens* (2nd rev. edn.). Leiden.

Lahusen, G. (1983), *Untersuchungen zur Ehrenstatue in Rom*. Bretschneide.

Lane, Christel (1981), *The Rites of Rulers: Ritual in Industrial Society—The Soviet Case*. Cambridge.

Lane Fox, Robin (1974), *Alexander the Great*. London.

——(1989), *Pagans and Christians*. New York.

——(1996), 'Ancient Hunting: from Homer to Polybios', in Graham Shipley and John Salmon (eds.), *Human Landscapes in Classical Antiquity: Environment and Culture*. London: 119–53.

Lateiner, Donald (1995), *Sardonic Smile: Nonverbal Behavior in Homeric Epic*. Ann Arbor.

Lendon, J. E. (1996), *Empire of Honour: The Art of Government in the Roman World*. Oxford.

Lewis, Sian (1996), *News and Society in the Greek Polis*. Chapel Hill, NC.

Lindholm, Charles (1990), *Charisma*. Oxford.

Lindstrom, L. (1984), 'Doctors, Lawyers, Wise-man, Priest: Big-man and Knowledge in Melanesia', *Man* 19: 291–309.

Lintott, A. W. (1968), *Violence in Republican Rome*. Oxford.

——(1990), 'Electoral Bribery in the Roman Republic', *Journal of Roman Studies* 80: 1–16.

LIPOVETSKY, GILLES (1994), *The Empire of Fashion: Dressing Modern Democracy* (trans. Catherine Porter). Princeton.

LLOYD, CHRISTOPHER (1986), *Explanation in Social History*. Oxford.

LONG, A. A. (1986), *Hellenistic Philosophy* (2nd edn.). Berkeley.

L'ORANGE, H. P. (1953), *The Iconography of Cosmic Kingship*. Oslo.

LORAUX, N. (1986), *The Invention of Athens*. Cambridge, Mass.

LUKES, S. (1975), 'Political Ritual and Social Integration', *Sociology* 9: 289–308.

LUND, HELEN S. (1992), *Lysimachus: A Study in Early Hellenistic Kingship*. London.

MACCORMACK, S. (1981), *Art and Ceremony in Late Antiquity*. Berkeley, Calif.

MCDERMOTT, W. C. (1972), 'Cicero's Publication of his Consular Orations', *Philologus* 116: 277–84.

MCGLEW, JAMES F. (1993), *Tyranny and Political Culture in Ancient Greece*. Ithaca and London.

MCGUSHIN, PATRICK (1992), *Sallust: The Histories*, i. Oxford.

MACKAY, K. L. (1964), 'Animals in War and *Isonomia*', *American Journal of Philology* 85: 124–35.

MACLEOD, COLIN (1983), *Collected Essays*. Oxford.

MACMULLEN, R. (1980*a*), 'How Many Romans Voted?', *Athenaeum* 68: 454–7.

——(1980*b*), 'Roman Elite Motivations: Three Questions', *Past and Present* 88: 3–16.

——(1991, 'Hellenizing the Romans (2nd Century B.C.)', *Historia* 40: 419–38.

MALKIN, I., and RUBINSOHN, Z. W. (eds.) (1995), *Leaders and Masses in the Roman World: Studies in Honor of Zvi Yavetz*. Leiden.

MANVILLE, PHILIP BROOK (1990), *The Origins of Citizenship in Ancient Athens*. Princeton.

MARIN, LOUIS (1988), *Portrait of the King* (trans. M. Houle). Minneapolis.

MARINATOS, N. (1988), 'The Imagery of Sacrifice', in R. Hägg, N. Marinatos, and G. Nordquist (eds.), *Early Greek Cult Practice*. Stockholm: 9–20.

MARQUARDT, J. *et al.* (1881–5), *Römische Staatsverwaltung* (3 vols.). Leipzig.

MARSHALL, ANTHONY J. (1984), 'Symbols and Showmanship in Roman Public Life: the Fasces', *Phoenix* 38: 120–41.

MARSHALL, B. A. (1972), 'Crassus' Ovation in 71BC', *Historia* 21: 669–73.

MEIER, CHRISTIAN (1966), *Res Publica Amissa*. Wiesbaden.

——(1990), *The Greek Discovery of Politics*. Cambridge, Mass.

MEIER, CHRISTIAN (1995), *Caesar* (trans. D. McClintock). London.
——(1996), *Caesar*. New York.
——(1998), *Athens: A Portrait of the City in Its Golden Age* (trans. R. and R. Kimber). New York.
MEIGGS, RUSSELL, and LEWIS, DAVID (1980), *A Selection of Greek Historical Inscriptions to the End of the Fifth Century B.C.* Oxford.
MIKALSON, JON D. (1982), 'The *Heorte* of Heortology', *Greek, Roman and Byzantine Studies* 23: 213–22.
MILLAR, FERGUS (1977), *The Emperor in the Roman World*. Ithaca, NY.
——(1984), 'The Political Character of the Classical Roman Republic, 200–151 B.C.', *Journal of Roman Studies* 74: 1–18.
——(1986), 'Politics, Persuasion and the People before the Social War (150–90 B.C.)', *Journal of Roman Studies* 76: 1–11.
——(1989), 'Political Power in Mid-Republican Rome: Curia or Comitium?', *Journal of Roman Studies* 79: 138–50.
——(1995), 'Popular Politics in the Late Republic', in Malkin and Rubinsohn 1995: 91–113.
——(1998), *The Crowd in Rome in the Late Republic*. Ann Arbor, Mich.
MILLER, MARGARET C. (1997), *Athens and Persia in the Fifth Century BC: A Study in Cultural Receptivity*. Cambridge.
MILLETT, PAUL (1989), 'Patronage and Its Avoidance in Classical Athens', in A. Wallace-Hadrill (ed.), *Patronage in Ancient Society*. London: 15–48.
——(1998), 'Encounters in the Agora', in Cartledge, Millett, and von Reden 1998: 203–28.
MOLHO, A., RAAFLAUB, K., and EMLEN, J. (eds.) (1991), *City-States in Classical and Medieval Italy*. Ann Arbor, Mich.
MOMIGLIANO, ARNALDO (1971), *The Development of Greek Biography*. Cambridge, Mass.
——(1984), 'The Theological Efforts of the Roman Upper Classes in the First Century B.C.', *Classical Philology* 79: 199–211.
MOMMSEN, Th. (1887), *Römisches Staatstrecht* (3 vols.; 3rd edn.). Leipzig.
MOORE, S. F., and MYERHOFF, B. G. (eds.) (1977), *Secular Ritual*. Amsterdam.
MORGAN, M. GWYN (1990), 'Polybius, Antiochus Epiphanes and the "Day of Eleusis"', *Historia* 39: 37–76.
MORRIS, IAN (1993), 'Poetics of Power: The Interpretation of Ritual Action in Archaic Greece', in Dougherty and Kurke 1993: 15–45.

——(1994), 'Everyman's Grave', in Alan L. Boegehold and Adele C. Scafuro (eds.), *Athenian Identity and Civic Ideology*. Princeton: 67–101.

——(1996), 'The Strong Principle of Equality and the Archaic Origins of Greek Democracy', in Ober and Hedrick 1996: 19–48.

MOXON, I. S., SMART, J. D., and WOODMAN, A. J. (eds.) (1986), *Past Perspectives: Studies in Greek and Roman Historical Writing*. Cambridge.

MUIR, E. (1981), *Civic Ritual in Renaissance Venice*. Princeton.

MÜLLER, OSWYN (1973), *Antigonos Monopthalmos und das 'Jahr der Könige'*. Bonn.

MURRAY, OSWYN (1965), 'Philodemus on the Good King according to Homer', *Journal of Roman Studies* 55: 161–82.

——(1967), 'Aristeas and Ptolemaic kingship', *Journal of Theological Studies* 18: 337–71.

——(1983), *Early Greece*. Stanford, Calif.

——(ed.) (1990*a*), *Sympotica*. Oxford.

——(1990*b*), 'The Affair of the Mysteries: Democracy and the Drinking Group', in Murray 1990*a*: 149–60.

——(1990*c*), 'Cities of Reason', in Murray and Price 1990: 1–25.

——and PRICE, S. R. F. (eds.) (1990), *The Greek City*. Oxford.

NAGY, B. (1994), 'Alcibiades' Second "Profanation"', *Historia* 43: 275–85.

NAGY, G. (1979), *The Best of the Achaeans: Concepts of the Hero in Archaic Greek Poetry*. Baltimore.

——(1990), *Pindar's Homer*. Baltimore.

——(1996), *Poetry as Performance*. Cambridge.

NEWBY, HOWARD (1975), 'The Deferential Dialectic', *Comparative Studies in Society and History* 17: 139–64.

NG, SIK HUNG (1980), *The Social Psychology of Power*. London.

NICOLET, CLAUDE (1980), *The World of the Citizen in Republican Rome*. Berkeley, Calif.

——(1991), *Space, Geography, and Politics in the Early Roman Empire*. Ann Arbor, Mich.

NIPPEL, WILFRIED (1991), 'Introductory Remarks: Max Weber's "The City" Revisited', in Molho, Raaflaub, and Emlen 1991.

——(1995), *Public Order in Ancient Rome*. Cambridge.

NOCK, ARTHUR D. (1972), *Essays on Religion and the Ancient World* (2 vols.). Cambridge, Mass.

NORTH, J. A. (1989), 'The Roman Counter-Revolution', *Journal of Roman Studies* 79: 151–6.

——(1990), 'Democratic Politics in Republican Rome', *Past and Present* 126: 3–21.

OAKLEY, S. P. (1985), 'Single Combat in the Roman Republic', *Classical Quarterly* 35: 392–410.

OBER, JOSIAH (1989*a*), *Mass and Elite in Democratic Athens*. Princeton.

——(1989*b*), 'The Nature of Athenian Democracy' (Review Article). *Classical Philology* 84: 322–34.

——(1996), *The Athenian Revolution: Essays on Ancient Greek Democracy and Political Theory*. Princeton.

——(1998), *Political Dissent in Democratic Athens: Intellectual Critics of Popular Rule*. Princeton.

——and HEDRICK, CHARLES (eds.) (1996), *Demokratia: A Conversation on Democracies, Ancient and Modern*. Princeton.

——and STRAUSS, BARRY (1990), 'Drama, Political Rhetoric, and the Discourse of Athenian Democracy', in J. J. Winkler and F. Zeitlin (eds.), *Nothing to Do with Dionysos? Athenian Drama in Its Social Context*. Princeton.

O'BRIEN, JOHN M. (1992), *Alexander the Great: The Invisible Enemy*. London and New York.

ORGEL, STEPHEN (1975), *The Illusion of Power: Political Theater in the English Renaissance*. Berkeley, Calif.

OSBORNE, ROBIN (1987), 'The Viewing and Obscuring of the Parthenon Frieze', *Journal of Hellenic Studies* 107: 98–105.

——and HORNBLOWER, SIMON (eds.) (1994), *Ritual, Finance, Politics: Athenian Democratic Accounts Presented To David Lewis*. Oxford.

PARKER, ROBERT (1996), *Athenian Religion: A History*. Oxford.

——(1997), 'Gods Cruel and Kind: Tragic and Civic Theology', in Pelling 1997: 143–60.

PATTERSON, CYNTHIA (1992), Review of Ober 1989. *American Journal of Philology* 113: 110–15.

PATTERSON, JOHN R. (1992), 'The City of Rome: From Republic to Empire', *Journal of Roman Studies* 82: 186–215.

PELLING, C. B. R. (1986), 'Plutarch and Roman Politics', in Moxon, Smart, and Woodman 1986: 159–87.

——(1988), *A Commentary on Plutarch's* Life of Antony. Cambridge.

——(1992), 'Plutarch and Thucydides', in Stadter 1992: 10–40.

——(ed.) (1997), *Greek Tragedy and the Historian*. Oxford.

PIGANIOL, A. (1923), *Recherches sur les jeux romains*. Strasbourg.

PINA POLO, F. (1995), 'Procedures and Functions of Civil and Military *contiones* in Rome', *Klio* 77: 203–16.

PINKER, STEVEN (1997), *How the Mind Works*. New York.

POLLITT, J. J. (1986), *Art in the Hellenistic Age*. Cambridge.

POPE, MAURICE (1988), 'Thucydides and Democracy', *Historia* 37: 276–96.

POWELL, ANTON (1989), 'Mendacity and Sparta's Use of the Visual', in A. Powell (ed.), *Classical Sparta: Techniques Behind Her Success*. Norman, Okla.

PRICE, S. R. F. (1984), *Rituals and Power: The Roman Imperial Cult in Asia Minor*. Cambridge.

PRITCHARD, J. B. (1955), *Ancient Near Eastern Texts* (2nd edn.). Princeton.

PURCELL, NICHOLAS (1984), 'Town in Country and Country in Town', in W. F. Jashemski (ed.), *Ancient Roman Villa Gardens*. Washington, DC: 185–204.

——(1994), 'Rome and the *Plebs Urbana* in the late Republic', *Cambridge Ancient History* (2nd edn.). Cambridge: ix. 644–88.

——(1996), 'Rome and its Development under Augustus and his Successors', *Cambridge Ancient History* (2nd edn.). Cambridge: x. 782–811.

QUILLER, B. (1981), 'The Dynamics of the Homeric Society', *Symbolae Osloenses* 56: 109–55.

RAAFLAUB, KURT A. (1996), 'Equalities and Inequalities in Athenian Democracy', in Ober and Hedrick 1996: 139–74.

RAUBITSCHEK, A. E. (1951), 'Sylleia', in *Studies in Roman Economic and Social History in Honor of Allan Chester Johnson*. Princeton: 49–57.

RAWSON, ELIZABETH (1975), 'Caesar's Heritage: Hellenistic Kings and their Roman Equals', *Journal of Roman Studies* 65: 148–59.

——(1985), *Intellectual Life in the Late Roman Republic*. Baltimore.

——(1991), *Roman Culture and Society*. Oxford.

REDFIELD, JAMES (1984), 'Warfare and the Hero in the Classical World', *Laetaberis* 3: 1–16.

REHM, R. (1937), 'Antike "Automobile"', *Philologus* 46: 317–30.

REINHOLD, MEYER (1969), 'On Status Symbols in the Ancient World', *Classical Journal* 64: 300–4.

——(1970), *History of Purple as a Status Symbol*. Brussels.

——(1988), *From Republic to Principate: An Historical Commentary on Cassius Dio's* Roman History *Books 49–52 (36–29 B.C.)*. Atlanta.

RHODES, P. A. (1982), *A Commentary on the Aristotelian* Athenaion Politeia. Oxford.

——(1986), 'Political Activity in Classical Athens', *Journal of Hellenic Studies* 106: 132–44.

RICE, E. E. (1983), *The Grand Procession of Ptolemy Philadelphus*. Oxford.

RICHARDSON, J. S. (1971), 'The *Commentariolum Petitionis*', *Historia* 20: 436–42.

——(1975), 'The Triumph, the Praetors and the Senate in the Early Second Century BC', *Journal of Roman Studies* 65: 50–63.

RITVO, HARRIET (1987), *The Animal Estate: The English and Other Creatures in the Victorian Age*. Cambridge, Mass.

ROBERT, L. (1940), *Les Gladiateurs dans l'Orient grec*. Limoges.

ROBINSON, ERIC W. (1997), *The First Democracies: Early Popular Government Outside Athens*. Stuttgart.

ROSENBERG, SHAWN W. (with Bohan, L., McCafferty, P., and Harris, K.) (1986), 'The Image and the Vote: The Effect of Candidate Presentation on Voter Preference', *American Journal of Political Science* 30: 108–27.

——and MCCAFFERTY, PATRICK (1987), 'The Image and the Vote: Manipulating Voters' Preferences', *Public Opinion Quarterly* 51: 31–47.

ROSENMEYER, THOMAS (1992), 'Beginnings in Plutarch's Lives', *Yale Classical Studies* 29: 205–30.

ROSENSTEIN, N. (1993), 'Competition and Crisis in Mid-Republican Rome', *Phoenix* 47: 313–38.

ROSTOVTZEFF, M. (1941), *Social and Economic History of the Hellenistic World* (3 vols.). Oxford.

RUDÉ, G. (1981), *The Crowd in History 1730–1848* (rev. edn.). London.

RUNCIMAN, W. G. (1983), 'Capitalism without Classes: The Case of Classical Rome', *British Journal of Sociology* 34: 157–81.

RUSSELL, BERTRAND (1938), *Power: A New Social Analysis*. London.

RUSSELL, D. A. (1973), *Plutarch*. London.

——(1995), 'On Reading Plutarch's *Lives*', in B. Scardigli (ed.), *Essays on Plutarch's* Lives. Oxford: 75–94.

RYBERG, INEZ SCOTT (1955), *Rites of the State Religion in Roman Art*. Memoirs of the American Academy in Rome 22.

SAHLINS, MARSHALL (1963), 'Poor Man, Rich Man, Big-man, Chief: Political Types in Melanesia and Polynesia', *Comparative Studies in Society and History* 5: 285 ff.

——(1972), *Stone Age Economics*. Chicago.

STE. CROIX, G. E. M. DE (1954/5), 'The Character of the Athenian Empire', *Historia* 3: 1–41.

——(1972), *The Origins of the Peloponnesian War*. Ithaca, NY.

——(1981), *The Class Struggle in the Ancient Greek World*. Ithaca, NY.

SAMUEL, A. E. (1983), 'From Athens to Alexandria: Hellenism and Social Goals in Ptolemaic Egypt', *Studia Hellenistica* 26.

——(1988), 'Philip and Alexander as Kings: Macedonian Monarchy and Merovingian Parallels', *American Historical Review* 93: 1270–86.

SAUVAGE, A. (1979), 'Les éléments du prestige: le fonctionnement et la nature du pouvoir d'*Énée', Revue des Études Latines* 57: 204–30.

SCHMITT-PANTEL, P. (1990), 'Collective Activities and the Political', in Murray and Price 1990.

SCOTT, JAMES C. (1989), 'Prestige as the Public Discourse of Domination', *Cultural Critique* 12: 145–66.

——(1990), *Domination and the Arts of Resistance: Hidden Transcripts*. New Haven.

SCOTT, KENNETH (1928), 'The Deification of Demetrius Poliorcetes', *American Journal of Philology* 49: 137–66 and 217–39.

——(1929), 'Octavian's Propaganda and Antony's *De Sua Ebrietate*', *Classical Philology* 24: 133–41.

SCULLARD, H. H. (1970), *Scipio Africanus: Soldier and Politician*. Ithaca, NY.

——(1974), *The Elephant in the Greek and Roman World*. Ithaca, NY.

——(1981), *Festivals and Ceremonies of the Roman Republic*. Ithaca, NY.

SEAFORD, RICHARD (1994), *Reciprocity and Ritual: Homer and Tragedy in the Developing City-State*. Oxford.

SEAGER, ROBIN (1967), 'Alcibiades and the Charge of Aiming at Tyranny', *Historia* 16: 6–18.

——(1979), *Pompey: A Political Biography*. Oxford.

SEGAL, CHARLES (1995), 'Spectator and Listener', in Jean-Pierre Vernant (ed.), *The Greeks*. Chicago and London: 184–217.

SENNETT, RICHARD (1994), *Flesh and Stone: The Body and the City in Western Civilization*. New York.

SHACKLETON BAILEY, D. R. (1965–70), *Cicero's* Letters to Atticus (7 vols.). Cambridge.

——(1977), *Cicero: Epistulae ad Familiares* (2 vols.). Cambridge.

SHAW, BRENT D. (1991), 'The Paradoxes of People Power', *Helios* 18: 194–214.

SHERWIN-WHITE, A. N. (1956), 'Violence in Roman Politics', *Journal of Roman Studies* 46: 1–9.

——(1973), *The Roman Citizenship* (2nd edn.). Oxford.

——(1982), 'The *Lex Repetundarum* and the Political Ideas of C. Gracchus', *Journal of Roman Studies* 72: 18–31.

SHERWIN-WHITE, SUSAN, and KUHRT, AMÉLIE (1993), *From Samarkhand to Sardis: A New Approach to the Seleucid Empire*. London.

SHILLING, CHRIS (1993), *The Body and Social Theory*. London.

SHILS, E. (1965), 'Charisma, Order and Status', *American Sociological Review* 30: 199–213.

SINCLAIR, R. K. (1988), *Democracy and Participation in Athens*. Cambridge.

SINOS, REBECCA H. (1993), 'Divine Selection: Epiphany and Politics in Archaic Greece', in Dougherty and Kurke 1993: 73–91.

SKUTSCH, OTTO (1968), *Studia Enniana*. London.

SLATER, W. J. (ed.) (1996), *Roman Theater and Society*. Ann Arbor, Mich.

SMITH, BRUCE JAMES (1985), *Politics and Remembrance: Republican Themes in Macchiavelli, Burke, and Tocqueville*. Princeton.

SMITH, JONATHAN Z. (1987), 'The Domestication of Sacrifice', in R. G. Hamerton-Kelly (ed.), *Violent Origins*. Stanford: 191–205.

SMITH, R. R. R. (1985), 'Roman Portraits: Honours, Empresses, and Late Emperors', *Journal of Roman Studies* 75: 209–21.

——(1988), *Hellenistic Royal Portraits*. Oxford.

——(1993), 'Kings and Philosophers', in Bulloch *et al.* 1993: 202–11.

SNODGRASS, ANTHONY (1971), *The Dark Age of Greece*. Edinburgh.

——(1974), 'An Historical Homeric Society?', *Journal of Hellenic Studies* 94: 114 ff.

SOKOLOWSKI, F. (1962), *Lois sacrées des cités Grecques: supplement*. Paris.

SOLZHENITSYN, ALEKSANDR I. (1973), *The Gulag Archipelago*. New York.

SOMMERSTEIN, ALAN H. (1997), 'Audience, *Demos*, and Aeschylus' *Suppliants*', in Pelling 1997: 63–79.

STADTER, PHILIP A. (1989), *A Commentary on Plutarch's* Pericles. Chapel Hill, NC.

——(ed.) (1992), *Plutarch and the Historical Tradition*. London.

STEVENS, C. E. (1959), 'Julius Caesar's Elephant', *History Today*: 626–7.

STEWART, ANDREW (1993), *Faces of Power: Alexander's Image and Hellenistic Politics*. Berkeley, Calif.

——(1997), *Art, Desire, and the Body in Ancient Greece*. Cambridge.

STOCKTON, DAVID (1969), *Thirty-Five Letters of Cicero*. Oxford.

——(1971), *Cicero: A Political Biography*. Oxford.

STRASBURGER, H. (1956), *Concordia Ordinum* (repr.). Amsterdam.

STRAUSS, BARRY (1985), 'Ritual, Social Drama and Politics in Classical Athens', *American Journal of Ancient History* 10: 67–83.

——(1993), *Fathers and Sons in Athens. Ideology and Society in the Era of the Peloponnesian War*. Princeton.

SULLIVAN, F. A. (1941), 'Cicero and *Gloria*', *Transactions of the American Philological Association* 72: 382–91.

SUMNER, G. V. (1966), 'Cicero, Pompeius, and Rullus', *Transactions of the American Philological Association* 97: 569–82.

SWEENEY, JOHN (1991), *The Life and Evil Times of Nicolae Ceauşescu*. London.

SYME, RONALD (1939), *The Roman Revolution*. Oxford.

TAEGER, FRITZ (1957), *Charisma. Studien zur Geschichte des antiken Herrscherkultes* (2 vols.). Stuttgart.

TAYLOR, LILY ROSS (1937), 'The Opportunities for Dramatic Performances in the Time of Plautus and Terence', *Transactions of the American Philological Association* 68: 284–304.

——(1941), 'Caesar's Early Career', *Classical Philology* 36: 113–32.

——(1949), *Party Politics in the Age of Caesar*. Berkeley, Calif.

——(1966), *Roman Voting Assemblies from the Hannibalic War to the Dictatorship of Caesar*. Ann Arbor, Mich.

——and BROUGHTON, T. R. S. (1949), 'The Order of the Two Consuls' Names in the Yearly Lists', *Memoirs of the American Academy in Rome* 19: 1–14.

TAYLOR, MICHAEL W. (1981), *The Tyrant Slayers*. New York.

THALMANN, W. G. (1988), 'Thersites: Comedy, Scapegoats, and Heroic Ideology in the Iliad', *TAPA* 118: 1–28.

THOMAS, CAROL G. (1965), *Early Greek Kingship*. Northwestern University Dissertation, Evanston, Ill.

THOMPSON, DOROTHY J. (1997), 'Philadelphus' *Pompe*: Ptolemaic Wealth and Power'. Paper presented at the University of Chicago-Stanford University Symposium on 'Innovation and Adaptation in the Hellenistic World'.

THOMPSON, E. P. (1971), 'The Moral Economy of the English Crowd in the Eighteenth Century', *Past & Present* 50: 76–136.

——(1973/4), 'Patrician Society, Plebeian Culture', *Journal of Social History* 7: 382–405.

THOMPSON, W. E. (1981), 'Athenian Leadership: Expertise or Charisma?' in *Classical Contributions ... M. F. McGregor*. Locust Valley: 153–9.

——(1987), 'Athenian Ideologies', *Prudentia* 19: 22–33.

TOMLINSON, R. A. (1970), 'Ancient Macedonian Symposia', *Ancient Macedonia* 1: 308–15.

TONDRIAU, J. L. (1948), 'Comparisons and Identifications of Rulers with Deities in the Hellenistic Period', *The Review of Religion* 13: 24–47.

——(1949), 'Romains de la République assimilés à des divinités', *Symbolae Osloenses* 27: 128–40.

TOYNBEE, J. M. C. (1973), *Animals in Roman Life and Art*. London.

TOYNBEE, ARNOLD (1969), *Some Problems in Greek History*. Oxford.

TREGGIARI, SUSAN M. (1980), 'Urban Labour in Rome: *Mercennarii* and *Tabernarii*', in P. Garnsey (ed.), *Non-Slave Labour in the Greco-Roman World* (Cambridge Philological Society Supplement 6). Cambridge: 48–64.

——(1998), 'Home and Forum: Cicero between "Public" and "Private" ', *Transactions of the American Philological Association* 128: 1–23.

TREPTOW, KURT W. (1996), *A History of Romania*. New York.

TUCKER, ROBERT C. (1968), 'The Theory of Charismatic Leadership', *Daedalus* 97: 731–56.

——(1978), *The Marx–Engels Reader*. New York.

TULIS, JEFFREY K. (1987), *The Rhetorical Presidency*. Princeton.

TURNER, V. (1986), *The Anthropology of Performance*. New York.

VANDERBROECK, P. J. J. (1987), *Popular Leadership and Collective Behavior in the Late Roman Republic (ca.80–50 BC)*. Amsterdam.

VAN STRATEN, FOLKERT (1993), 'Images of Gods and Men in a Changing Society: Self-identity in Hellenistic Religion', in Bulloch *et al.* 1993: 248–64.

VAN WEES, HANS (1992), *Status Warriors: War, Violence and Society in Homer and History*. Amsterdam.

VASALY, ANN (1993), *Representations: Images of the World in Ciceronian Oratory*. Berkeley, Calif.

VEESER, H. ARAM (1989), *The New Historicism*. New York.

VERDERY, KATHERINE (1991), *National Ideology Under Socialism: Identity and Cultural Politics in Ceausescu's Romania*. Berkeley, Calif.

VERSNEL, H. S. (1970), *Triumphus*. Leiden.

VEYNE, PAUL (1976), *Le Pain et le cirque*. Paris.

——(1979), 'The Hellenization of Rome and the Question of Acculturations', *Diogenes* 106: 1–27.

——(1988), 'Conduct without Belief and Works of Art without Viewers', *Diogenes* 143: 1–22.

——(1990), *Bread and Circuses* (abridged version of *Le Pain et le cirque*). Harmondsworth.

VICKERS, MICHAEL (1987), 'Alcibiades on stage: *Philoctetes* and *Cyclops*', *Historia* 36: 171–97.

——(1989*a*), 'Alcibiades on Stage: *Thesmophoriazusae* and *Helen*', *Historia* 38: 41–65.

——(1989*b*), 'Alcibiades on Stage: Aristophanes' *Birds*', *Historia* 38: 267–99.

VILLE, G. (1981), *La Gladiature en Occident des origines à la mort de Domitien*. Rome.

WADE-GERY, H. T. (1958), *Essays in Greek History*. Oxford.

WALBANK, F. W. (1955), 'Tragic History: a Reconsideration', *Bulletin of the Institute of Classical Studies* 2: 4–14.

——(1957–79), *A Historical Commentary on Polybius* (3 vols.). Oxford.

——(1967), 'The Scipionic Legend', *Proceedings of the Cambridge Philological Society* 13: 54–69.

——(1972), *Polybius*. Berkeley, Calif.

——(1984*a*), 'Monarchies and Monarchic Ideas', *Cambridge Ancient History* (2nd edn.). Cambridge: vii. 1.

——(1984*b*), Review of Rice (1983). *Liverpool Classical Monthly* 9.4: 52–4.

——(1996), 'Two Hellenistic Processions: A Matter of Self-Definition', *Scripta Classica Israelica* 15: 119–30.

WALKER, ANDREW D. (1993), '*Enargeia* and the Spectator in Greek Historiography', *Transactions of the American Philological Association* 123: 353–77.

WALLACE-HADRILL, ANDREW (1982), '*Civilis Princeps*: Between Citizen and King', *Journal of Roman Studies* 72: 32–48.

——(1988*a*), 'The Social Structure of the Roman House', *Papers of the British School at Rome* 43: 43–97.

——(1988*b*), 'Greek Knowledge, Roman Power', *Classical Philology* 83: 224–33.

——(1989), 'Rome's Cultural Revolution', *Journal of Roman Studies* 79: 157–64.

——(1990), 'Roman Arches and Greek Honours: The Language of Power at Rome', *Proceedings of the Cambridge Philological Society* 36: 143–81.

WARD FOWLER, W. (1899), *The Roman Festivals of the Period of the Republic*. London.

WARDMAN, A. E. (1967), 'The Description of Personal Appearance in Plutarch and Suetonius: The Use of Statues as Evidence', *Classical Quarterly* 17: 415–20.

——(1974), *Plutarch's Lives*. London.

WARREN, LARISSA B. (1970), 'Roman Triumphs and Etruscan Kings', *Journal of Roman Studies* 60: 49–66.

WEBER, MAX (1947), *The Theory of Social and Economic Organization* (ed. T. Parsons). New York.

WEINSTOCK, S. (1971), *Divus Julius*. Oxford.

WEST, S. R. (1975), 'Problems with Lions: Lucretius and Plutarch', *Philologus* 119: 150–1.

WESTLAKE, H. (1968), *Individuals in Thucydides*. Cambridge.

WHITEHEAD, DAVID (1983), 'Competitive Outlay and Community Profit', *Classica et Mediaevalia* 34: 55–74.

——(1986), *The Demes of Attica*. Princeton.

——(1993), 'Cardinal Virtues: The Language of Public Approbation in Democratic Athens', *Classica et Mediaevalia* 44: 37–75.

WIEDEMANN, THOMAS (1992), *Emperors and Gladiators*. London.

WILSON, PETER J. (1991), 'Demosthenes 21 (*Against Meidias*): Democratic Abuse', *Proceedings of the Cambridge Philological Society* 37: 164–95.

——(1997), 'Leading the Tragic *Khoros*: Tragic Prestige in the Democratic City', in Pelling 1997: 81–108.

——(1999), 'The *aulos* in Athens', in Goldhill and Osborne 1999: 58–95.

WINKLER, JOHN J. (1990), *The Constraints of Desire*. New York.

WISEMAN, T. P. (1981), '*Conspicui postes tectaque digna deo*: The Public Image of Aristocratic and Imperial Houses in the Late Republic and Early Empire', *Mélanges d'archéologie et d'histoire de l'École française de Rome* 98: 393–413.

——(1985), 'Competition and Co-operation', in T. P. Wiseman, (ed.), *Roman Political Life 90 B.C.–A.D.69*. Exeter: 3–20.

——(1986), 'Monuments and the Roman Annalists', in Moxon, Smart, and Woodman 1986: 87–100.

——(1987), *Roman Studies Literary and Historical*. Liverpool.

——(1989), 'Roman Legend and Oral Tradition', *Journal of Roman Studies* 79: 129–37.

WISSOWA, G. (1912), *Religion und Kultus der Romer* (2nd edn.). Munich.

WISTRAND, ERIK (1978), *Caesar and Contemporary Society*. Göteborg.

WOHL, V. J. (1993), 'εὐσεβείας ἕνεκα καὶ φιλτιμίας: Hegemony and Democracy at the Panathenaia', *Classica et Mediaevalia* 47: 25–88.

WOLIN, SHELDON (1988), 'On the Theory and Practice of Power', in J. Arac (ed.), *After Foucault*. New Brunswick: 179–202.

WOODHEAD, A. G. (1970), *Thucydides on the Nature of Power*. Cambridge, Mass.

WOODMAN, A. J. (1983), *Velleius Paterculus: The Caesarian and Augustan Narrative (2.41–93) Edited with a Commentary*. Cambridge.

YAKOBSON, ALEXANDER (1992), '*Petitio* et *Largitio*: Popular Participation in the Centuriate Assembly of the Late Republic', *Journal of Roman Studies* 82: 32–52.

——(1999), *Elections and Electioneering in Rome: A Study in the Political System of the Late Republic*. Stuttgart.

YAVETZ, ZWI (1983), *Julius Caesar and his Public Image*. Ithaca, NY.

——(1988), *Plebs and Princeps* (rev. edn.). New Brunswick.

ZANKER, PAUL (1988), *The Power of Images in the Age of Augustus*. Ann Arbor, Mich.

ZIOLKOWSKI, J. E. (1981), *Thucydides and the Tradition of Funeral Speeches at Athens*. New York.

# INDEX